EUROSECURITIES AND THEIR RELATED DERIVATIVES

Frederick G. Fisher, III

Published by Euromoney Books

Published by
Euromoney Publications PLC
Nestor House, Playhouse Yard
EC4V 5EX

Copyright © Euromoney Publications 1997
ISBN 1 85564 596 3

All rights reserved. This publication is not included in the CLA Licence. No part of this book may be reproduced or used in any form (graphic, electronic or mechanical, including photocopying, recording, taping or information storage and retrieval systems) without permission by the publisher

Frederick G. Fisher, III asserts and gives notice of his right under Section 77 of the Copyright, Designs and Patents Act 1988 to be identified as the author of this book.

Euromoney Publications PLC believes that the sources of information upon which the book is based are reliable and has made every effort to ensure the complete accuracy of the text. However, neither Euromoney, the author, nor any contributor can accept any legal responsibility whatsoever for consequences that may arise from errors or omissions or any opinions or advice given.
It is not a substitute for detailed local advice on a specific transaction.

Typeset by PW Graphics
Printed in Great Britain by Stability Press Limited

Contents

Acknowledgements v

Preface vii

Introduction xi

CHAPTER 1 **Background and development of the international bond market** 1

CHAPTER 2 **Issuers and investors** 41

CHAPTER 3 **New issue procedures and syndication** 65

CHAPTER 4 **Documentation, Eurobond listing and rating** 87

CHAPTER 5 **Bond trading and portfolio management** 129

CHAPTER 6 **Forwards, futures, options and swaps** 157

CHAPTER 7 **Regulations and back office** 221

Chapter 8	**Eurobonds and their currency sectors**	239
Chapter 9	**Equity linked and FRN issues**	257
Chapter 10	**Euro-MTNs and Euro-CP & CDs**	277
Chapter 11	**Asset securitisation**	297

Glossary 313

Bibliography 337

Index 341

ACKNOWLEDGEMENTS

This book is dedicated to my wife Ann E. Fisher whose editing skills were rivalled only by the patience and forgiveness necessary to bring this book into existence. A good friend Edward McDonald also assisted in the production of the manuscript. Frederick and Charles were patient helpers, too.

I wish to give a special thanks to Ian Jackson and Claude Brown of the London law firm, Clifford Chance, for having reviewed and revised approximately half of this book. The commentary on the ISDA Master Swap Agreement belongs entirely to them. The valuable contribution of Clifford Chance is difficult to overstate. I am deeply indebted as well to Professor Samuel L. Hayes, III whose fine preface is a credit to this work.

There have been a number of individuals in the financial community who have also made significant contributions to this book. Foremost amongst these was Clifford Dammers, Secretary General of IPMA, who cheerfully set me back in the right direction on a number of occasions. Other people who provided outstanding assistance were Brian Woolley of Bank of China International, Bim Hundal of Goldman Sachs, Mark Ames of Lehman Brothers, Jonathan Keighley of Barclays Bank, Thomas Jans of the BIS, Anthony Raikes of SPV Management, Katrina Madsen of Standard and Poor's, Ann Holtwick of Moody's Investors Service, Genon Jensen of Euroclear, Susanne Jaenicke of Cedel Bank, Mathew Elderfield of ISDA, Joanna Eede of LIFFE, John Sandner of the Chicago Mercantile Exchange, Susan Harris of the Chicago Board of Trade, Sarah Small of the London Stock Exchange, William Peto of Webster Capital Markets and several assistants (particularly Tim Long) from Capital Net and Capital Data.

Responsibility for any errors remains of course my own.

Frederick G. Fisher, III

PREFACE

It is fitting that Frederick Fisher should bring forth a new version of his classic book on Euromarket securities as we head into the next millennium. Global diversification of both debt and equity portfolios has become the rule rather than the exception, thereby creating an appetite for a wide array of sovereign and private investment instruments with features tailored to particular portfolio objectives. Barriers to financial service competition within the European Union are finally beginning to crumble, thus creating an environment in which financial innovation is likely to accelerate further.

True, there have been well-publicised instances of portfolio strategies involving derivatives that have gone badly awry. Barings lost its independence as a result of a rogue trader's miscalculations and Bankers Trust was publicly embarrassed when financial contracts sold to customers resulted in legal actions aimed at recovering funds from Bankers Trust for large losses sustained.

While Freddie describes the regulatory adjustments made in response to these missteps, they have not blunted the momentum of financial innovation. Sophisticated financial structuring for the benefit of both investors and borrowers continues to be compelling, not just a 'fad' as some commentators have suggested.

The Euromarkets epitomise this transformed international financial marketplace. Here, as Freddie points out, a minimum of the regulatory superstructure which encumbers most national markets has permitted a free-wheeling auction between capital suppliers and users that has drawn important interest and participation in huge volumes from all over the world.

It is notable just how much the capital markets have changed over time. One can trace back over many years, as Freddie does, the record of financing activity across national boundaries. Although the international banking and financing arrangements of previous generations look primitive compared to the elaborate mosaic in evidence today, some of the players in those earlier times were actually the direct forebears of participants engaged in present day finance. In the 1700s, for instance, there were European loan contractors who intermediated the financing needs of selected credits and a few private sector companies. These early prototypes of the modern merchant banks operated out of commercial centres such as London and Berlin, where they acted as early loan syndicators. At that time there were few of the capital-rich institutions which Freddie discusses in the context of the modern 20th century markets; funds were drawn in large part from wealthy individuals. These investors naturally had either to know and respect the name of the foreign borrower or had to rely on the banker's assurance that as a result of careful investigation he was prepared to vouchsafe for the borrower's creditworthiness. Thus the 18th century loan contractor assumed the role of merchant banker and underwriter, a role which by the late 1990s had become a key element in the growth of the international capital markets.

The pattern of international financing accommodations grew and evolved through the years in concert with important political and economic developments, as the book points out. Much of the growth in international finance during the 19th and early 20th centuries followed closely the pattern of economic development in the colonial empires of the major European powers. Thus, one can note the development of a series of bilateral capital markets between the capital-surplus European powers and their colonial possessions, many of which are counted among today's more vibrant economies. Typically, the colonial power maintained tight control over all aspects of its far-flung possessions, including an effective monopoly of its banking institutions and foreign capital imports.

These European-sponsored banks, positioned in various commercial outposts around the world, became so well entrenched that even after the dismantling of the colonial systems many of them survived and flourished either under the control of banks located in Europe or as independent financial institutions with a western banking tradition. Over time a number of these colonial banks broadened the scope of their financing activities and became active in accommodating foreign credits. They thus grew to assume an important role in the modern day international capital market community.

Another group of participants in international finance described by Freddie have been the US banks. After the World War II the US, as the dominant economic power, moved into a commanding position in international trade. And, in parallel with the pattern established during the earlier colonial period, some of the large US banking institutions followed US multinational companies into many of the foreign markets previously dominated by the European powers. Aided by the adoption of the US dollar as the free world's official reserve currency, these banks had become well-established in a number of foreign financial markets by the 1960s when the post-war resurgence of the European and Japanese economies began to fuel a renewed foreign push by their own banks.

Interrelated financing trends such as these serve as background for Freddie's description and analysis of the beginnings of the Eurodollar market. Many of the necessary institutional arrangements were already in place when several currency defence moves by the US government initiated the build-up of foreign dollar balances outside the regulatory control of the US or any other national government.

Freddie correctly perceives the supranational character of the Euromarket as a key to its enormous growth during the last 30-odd years. It was to impose fundamental changes on the patterns of international finance and, in the process, force organisational and strategic changes in the financial institutions servicing the international sector.

The system of bilateral markets which had prevailed up to that point had severely limited the types and credit qualities of borrowers who could seek public financing outside their home country. Only sovereign governments and a few well-regarded private companies could sell bonds in the foreign capital market centres. While there had, as a rule, been some international selling activity when a foreign bond offering was made in one of these money centres, various institutional and regulatory factors tended to limit its scope. After the launching of the Eurodollar market, however, the possibilities for organising a truly international selling programme were realised.

Freddie focuses on bonds and other hybrid debt instruments because these have been the financing form most acceptable to this market. He also gives attention to equity-linked securities, which have been popular at various times. Similarly, he notes the standard use of bearer certificates as a reflection of the penchant for secrecy among the important investor groups (particularly on the part of those investors whose anonymous savings have thus far gone undetected and untaxed by their own countries' treasury officials!).

The role of advanced communications technology and rapid transportation is also implicit in Freddie's narration of the development of the international capital markets. Bankers have come a long way in information gathering since the Battle of Waterloo when Rothschild was said to have used a series of semaphore stations stretching from the battlefield to London to signal him advance word of the winner so that he could get ahead of the crowd in buying massive amounts of British corporate and government securities.

Worldwide communications networks allow banks as well as borrowers and investors to scour the globe for those markets offering the most favourable financing terms. In the process, this arbitraging operation has effectively linked a variety of formerly isolated national markets into a grid which has rationalised and made more uniform the terms that are available in various geographical locations. This development has also strengthened the Euromarkets.

One watershed in the growth of the Eurobond market was the four-fold oil price rise in 1973-74. While this was indeed a bleak period for the bond market, it was also to have a profound effect on the future development of international finance. It marked a turning point in the direction of international capital flows and presaged a massive jump in the volume of financings in the international marketplace.

The price rise transferred large amounts of incremental spending power from consuming nations to a few countries with small populations and a limited ability to plough capital back into their economic infrastructures. Thus, in the immediate aftermath of the first oil price increases, the annual surpluses of Saudi Arabia, the UAE and Qatar ballooned from $4 billion in 1973 to $38 billion in 1974 and then doubled again after the second round of price increases in 1979. These low-absorbing oil producers moved substantial amounts of this money through the international financing community into a variety of western investment vehicles, including Euro-securities. After the US government forced its banks to freeze Iranian accounts in retaliation for their hostage-taking in late 1979, more of this excess capital was reported diverted from US banks and channelled through European (particularly Swiss) banks. It is likely that this influx of new money added to the investor demand for Euro-securities.

On the user side, the oil price rise drained spending power out of both industrialised and developing countries and created national deficits which in many cases had to be financed by external borrowing. The strongest among these sovereign credits either tapped the Euromarkets, financed in selected foreign bond markets or else arranged direct loans with the OPEC surplus countries, particularly Saudi Arabia.

As the supply-side balance for oil shifted in the early 1980s, the OPEC countries receded in importance as capital suppliers to the international financial markets, and in recent years these national governments have actually become net borrowers in the international markets (although certain funds and private individuals in the Gulf area continue to provide a net contribution to the pool of international capital). For a time, their place was taken by the Japanese. Estimates of the annual capital exports vary but there is agreement that in the late 1980s their impact was at least as great as that of the OPEC countries at their peak. Like others before them, the Japanese sought to use their capital exports as a means of building a leading position in international commercial and investment banking. When their 'bubble economy' collapsed in the late 1980s, however, their financial institutions suffered severe reversals from which they had not recovered a decade later. Fisher points out that the Japanese banks have been succeeded by the efforts of large European universal banks to dominate the financial marketplace via acquisitions of merchant banks and aggressive recruitment from other vendors.

Freddie gives attention in the book to the financial instruments in the Euromarkets that are now being tailored to appeal to yen, DM and other currency-denominated investors, including swaps, forwards and futures. This gives emphasis to the point that while US dollars remain the most important sector of the marketplace which Freddie examines, he gives ample recognition to the other hard currencies.

Freddie has targeted this book for laymen with a need to understand the dimensions of this market as investors, as capital users or as observers of the organisation and workings of a fast-growing segment of world finance. In this new edition he succeeds admirably in the mandate. The book is laid out in a logical, straightforward way and is lucidly written, with a helpful glossary of terms at the end. The author brings clarity and understanding to arcane financing arrangements that have long intimidated or confused many.

The successful production of this book is not surprising, since Freddie approached the task with exceptional qualifications. He has spent his entire career as a practitioner and commentator/writer in the arena of international finance. After earning degrees from both Oxford and Harvard Universities, he set up his base of operations in London where he has served successively with several distinguished banking houses. He has also been a columnist and contributor to *Euromoney* magazine, the principal journal read throughout the international financial community, and has been a frequently-invited participant in academic and professional colloquiums on the financial markets in both the US and Europe.

Samuel L. Hayes, III

INTRODUCTION

This book provides issuers and investors with background and current information on a wide variety of financing and investment opportunities in the international markets.

The book is practical and non-academic. Its chief objective is to outline the way business is carried on in the market. The book begins with a brief review of the history and background of the international securities market. It then identifies key groups of investors, their particular investment criteria and general approaches to portfolio strategy. Borrowers are in turn analysed and a detailed outline given as to how a new bond issue is syndicated and offered to the public.

The discussion then moves to the secondary market, with primary emphasis on securities trading and portfolio management. Complimenting this discussion is a chapter on hedging which explores the use of the forward markets, futures, options and swaps.

The growing use of derivatives (like forwards, futures, options and swaps) has attracted increasing attention by regulatory authorities, especially since the virtual collapse of Barings. Whilst the markets are enjoying a general trend towards de-regulation (permitting greater access to domestic capital markets) there is countervailing pressure to place new controls on the individual and institutional participants in the markets. It is, therefore, appropriate to turn the discussion towards the new regulatory framework in which participants must now operate.

With this new framework in mind, attention then turns to the traditional markets for international bonds: both Eurobonds and their domestic counterpart, foreign bonds. The US dollar sector has been a mainstay of the international markets since their re-opening in the early 1960s. However, major alternative currency sectors such as Deutschmark, Swiss franc and Japanese yen bonds also merit discussion.

Following the discussion of traditional bonds in the international markets is a chapter on convertibles and other equity-linked securities. Attention is then drawn to Floating Rate Notes (FRNs) and other hybrid bonds. The massive growth in Euro-Medium Term Notes (Euro-MTNs) is discussed together with Euro-Commercial Paper and Euro-Certificates of Deposit. The final section of the book concentrates on asset securitisations and one of the world's largest markets, that for US mortgage-backed securities. A glossary of terms is included at the end of the book.

The market

Confusion exists as to what is meant by the international bond market. The cause of this confusion lies in part with the market itself. Extending around the world, and sub-divided into numerous national and regional sectors, the market is both vast and complex. Special care must therefore be taken when defining the various elements which make up the market.

To begin with first principles, there is the definition of the term bond. For the purposes of this book, all fixed and floating securities over one year in maturity will be referred to as bonds. Such fixed and floating rate securities are variously referred to in practice as bonds, debentures or notes; but these terms do not indicate any internationally acknowledged distinctions of meaning (except that notes have historically been associated with short or medium-term maturity instruments) and, therefore, the term bonds will here be applied to all such securities.

Bonds are evidence of indebtedness. A bond is a contractual obligation of the borrower to make payments of interest and repayments of principal on borrowed funds at certain fixed times. Bonds typically enjoy considerable liquidity as they can be freely bought and sold in an active over-the-counter secondary market. Where a stock exchange listing has been obtained, bonds can also be traded through the mechanisms of the relevant stock exchange.

Bond issues can themselves be classified as either public issues or private placements. Public issues are normally distributed widely through a syndicate of co-managers (or group of banks) which underwrite and sell bonds. They are also usually listed on one or more of the leading stock exchanges. Private placements are not widely syndicated or distributed. In many cases, they are not publicly announced and are not listed on a recognised stock exchange, at least initially.

International bond issues are typically public securities offerings which are sold largely outside the country of residence of the borrower. They may be sub-divided into two categories: Eurobonds and foreign bonds.

As defined in the EU Prospectus Directive (89/298/EEC) 'Euro-securities' shall mean transferable securities which:

- are to be underwritten and distributed by a syndicate at least two of the members of which have their registered offices in different states, and

- are offered on a significant scale in one or more states other than that of the issuer's registered office, and

- may be subscribed for or initially acquired only through a credit institution or other financial institution.

Foreign bonds are international bond issues underwritten by a syndicate of banks composed primarily of institutions from one country, distributed in that country in the same way as domestic issues, and denominated in the currency of that country. In the case of both Eurobonds and foreign bonds, they are usually in bearer form, preserving anonymity of ownership, and interest is normally paid free of withholding tax to investors not resident in the country of issue. It should be noted that most foreign bond markets are being integrated into the over-arching Euro-securities market and, indeed, the EC Prospectus Directive accommodates this trend by the generality of its definition of "Euro-securities". A recurrent theme running through this book is the integration of specific domestic markets, such as that in the United States which has been drawn closer to its offshore counterpart by virtue of new securities regulations such as Rule 144A and Regulation S.

In the title of this book, "Euro-securities", refers to all international bond and short-term instruments. As Europe is the birthplace of the present international market, the term "Euro-" is mostly of generic relevance. From time to time in this book, reference is also made to floating rate securities. These are debt instruments with a rate of interest which changes at set intervals according to current rates of return in a recognised money market (ie, short-term rates) for the currency in which the security is denominated.

Since the Euromarket provides a wide range of opportunities for borrowing and investment in bonds of different qualities, maturities and currencies, a major part of this book is devoted to the variety of such securities. Historically, both borrowers and investors, provided they were free from domestic exchange controls, were able to participate in the Euromarket independent of any regulation by a national authority. Certain national and international (ie European Union) laws and stock exchange regulations have, however, been promulgated to govern the contents and distribution of new issue prospectuses and sometimes restrict the initial distribution of Eurobond offerings.

Importance of the market

Why is the international securities market so important? The obvious answer is that the market plays a major role in the worldwide flow of capital, a role which gives the market political as well as economic significance. Eurobonds themselves account for over $500 billion equivalent each year in new financings. This compares with approximately $250 billion each year in the US public corporate bond market (excluding Yankee issues). A proper understanding of the international securities market is, therefore, important not only for market participants and investors but also for anyone concerned with world financial developments and trends.

The market is an important source of money for borrowers. In the five years 1992-1996, new international bond issues were completed for a total of approximately $2.5 trillion principal amount. The borrowers making these issues came from all parts of the world, including both industrialised and developing nations and representing both public and private sector entities. For them the attraction of the international market was the ready availability of funds for a maturity, amount and cost which compared favourably with alternative sources of capital.

The market's relative freedom from regulation (particularly in the Eurobond sector) has also produced another benefit: enormous flexibility. Hybrid financing instruments such as bond swaps and other derivative-linked issues, debt warrant issues, bonds convertible into common shares of the borrower or into a currency other than that used to denominate an issue, and modifications of more traditional types of securities, are developed each year and provide an array of financing opportunities which assist borrowers in tapping particular segments of international capital resources. A major objective of most borrowers is to widen their potential financing market and thus broaden the areas from which they may raise future funds. The international bond market's size and flexibility ensure one of the widest distributions of securities available in the world. It is probably this flexibility and depth of distribution, more than any other advantage, which prompts borrowers to come to the market year after year. It is also, therefore, one of the main claims the market has to permanence.

The international securities market is also of growing importance and interest to investors. A major attraction is the wide range of financial instruments providing the combination of yield, maturity and safety best suited to their requirements. Derivatives have also given an enormous boost to the market, allowing investors to reduce risk through hedging or to achieve other specific portfolio objectives such as yield enhancement. The international securities market also typically provides anonymity of beneficial ownership. This advantage is enhanced by the fact that, as a rule, international securities pay interest free of all tax at source. The continuation of these attractions has generated a growing number of willing investors. This powerful constituency of supporters lends substantial weight to the continued expansion of the market.

Trends in the market

Over recent years the international securities market has undergone substantial changes which has altered it virtually beyond the point of recognition. It was, for instance, once fashionable to talk of different national and regional markets for capital. The so-called Asian dollar market was one such example. Issuers found, however, that bonds placed in such apparent investment pockets often turned up or flowed back to somewhere else, usually Europe. A major evolutionary trend over recent years has thus been the gradual breakdown of national or regional boundaries to capital flows. The bond market of today conducts its business on a global basis and is correspondingly subject to a far greater range of influences than has ever previously been the case.

Financing techniques utilising derivatives have also been developed which allow both issuers and investors to compare sectors of the international bond market which were once wholly separate. An example of this is the bond swap, one variety of which involves the use of the foreign exchange market to hedge an issue's principal and interest payments in one currency against another specific currency, typically the national currency of the borrower. This process, referred to as creating dollars or Deutschmarks or Swiss francs or whichever, allows the borrower to, for example, issue a Sfr-denominated bond and convert it through hedging into an effective US dollar liability. Using this mechanism of financial engineering, the issuer is able to straddle two seemingly independent markets. Such novel financing techniques also open up valuable arbitrage possibilities. Borrowers can seek low cost funds in sectors which had previously remained closed and investors can locate new opportunities to enhance their returns. In the process, different sectors of the international market are effectively bridged and a convergence of all markets is forced. One currency sector can be hedged into another. Floating rate interest securities can be swapped for liabilities similar in every respect except that they carry a fixed rate of interest. Bonds can be issued which have most of the characteristics of equity, and commercial banking finance may be replaced with bond-like, long-term securities.

The trend towards the convergence of different markets is itself a product of other structural changes in the financial world. One such change is the increase in competition amongst financial intermediaries which has promoted product innovation at a quickening pace. Another factor has been the global recession of the early 1990s which created large national deficits and encouraged governments to liberalise market access with a view to attracting investment flows. A third factor is the growth in derivatives. This latter trend has given birth to a whole family of new financial instruments designed to meet the complementary needs of both borrowers and investors as they deploy their financial strategies.

A major new category of instruments are frequently referred to by the general name of Medium Term or Euro Notes. Similar instruments have carried colourful labels such as NIFs, RUFs, SNIFs and TRUFs, all denoting the latest innovation in this rapidly evolving hybrid security. These financings can involve the issuance of notes which mature in under a year, say, 30 days and closely resemble Euro-commercial paper. If an investor no longer wishes to hold a note to maturity, then it is purchased by the underwriting syndicate supporting the facility and placed with another willing buyer. Underwritten facilities can have maturities which extend out to 30 years into the future and are easily tradable in a highly liquid secondary market. Indeed, Medium Term Note (MTN) programmes can be used as launch pads for Eurobonds. The growing popularity of this instrument is evident by its rapid increase in volume. In 1984 only $15 billion of Euro-notes were placed on offer. During 1996, however, the amount of these securities brought to market topped $ 257 billion.

Other securitised products such as asset-based issues have acted to replace traditional commercial bank lending. These new instruments have also caught the attention of would-be regulators with their speed of evolution and the fact that their creators, the relatively free-wheeling investment banks, are assuming an increasingly prominent role in world financial intermediation. The quickening pace of financial innovation and the convergence of different markets gives a competitive advantage to those bondhouses and other intermediaries which are prepared to operate with a range of instruments simultaneously in different market sectors.

The freedom and growing integration of the international marketplace demands that its participants adopt a global approach to financing. Several mergers of merchant banks in the City of London with larger universal banks, confirm this trend. The institutions that will dominate the market in the coming decades will be the ones that do their business as the markets develop – on a global basis.

Frederick G. Fisher, III

1

BACKGROUND AND DEVELOPMENT OF THE INTERNATIONAL BOND MARKET

Early international bonds

The international bond market is not a new phenomenon. Examples of cross-frontier financings may be traced back at least to the late Middle Ages when a burgeoning European wool trade and other transnational enterprises provided the economic underpinning for financial intermediation. Efficient resource mobilisation, as well as existing threats to established routes encouraged the Crusades. Later, the wealth of Florentine merchants and bankers assisted in financing the Renaissance.

One of the first examples of international branch banking activities was the establishment of operations by Italian banks in the City of London in the late 13th century. The name Lombard Street recalls the origins of banking in the City. Following the expulsion of the Jews under the English King, Edward I, Italian funds and financial expertise were required to pay for his wars. Two groups, Bardi and Peruzzi, volunteered this support and looked to a tax on wool exports as a source of repayment. The intermediation of the Italians continued with the reign of Edward III who felt that his domestic merchant class might also be mobilised to provide needed finance. With this alternative in hand, the new monarch exercised his right as sovereign and promptly repudiated the Italian debt precipitating the collapse of each of the banks of Bardi and Peruzzi. In all this there seems to be some forewarning to cross-border lenders of a more recent era. Few banks appear to have avoided this pitfall. The historian of the Medici Bank, Raymond de Roover, observed that "Rather than refuse deposits, the Medicis succumbed to the temptation of seeking an outlet for surplus cash in making dangerous loans to princes".

During the period when European powers colonised the New World, international lending was directed towards development finance. Such capital transfers were bilateral in nature and linked individual European countries to their respective colonies and trading outposts. Investment funds for these development loans were raised essentially from wealthy individuals. The unequal distribution of wealth at the time produced a high domestic savings rate. A relatively stable economic and social environment also encouraged people to invest. Early intermediaries tapped these resources of surplus capital and organised direct loans for foreign borrowers, typically sovereign states or top-quality private undertakings. The chief financial centres during this period were London, Paris and Berlin. New York joined the market, too, but at a later stage. There were also smaller financial centres in Italy, the Netherlands, Switzerland, Belgium and Sweden.

The work of the early financial intermediaries was formalised in the rise of the 19th century merchant banks, and their experience in originating loans was soon transferred to the issue of securities or bonds. As a parallel development, markets for short-term debt or money markets began to emerge. Capital-poor merchant houses took advantage of this and raised funds for short periods of time to finance holdings of newly issued bonds which were temporarily difficult to sell. The practice was the forerunner of underwriting and proved critical to the development of the market as it provided a mechanism for assuring a borrower that his agreed financial requirements would be met irrespective of the then current market conditions. Underwriting also reduced the total cost of raising finance. Previously, new issues of securities had to be priced on extremely generous terms to investors to attract full subscription. The practice of underwriting allowed for more precise pricing on terms which balanced the interests of the borrower with those of the investor. To minimise the risk which underwriting clearly involved, merchant houses began to share amongst themselves the contingent liability to purchase a fixed amount of securities at a set price. This process has come to be known today as syndicating.

European merchant banks, which have evolved into the bond houses and other financial intermediaries, currently a mainstay of the international markets, benefited as well from their location in capital-rich countries that enjoyed virtually uninterrupted balance of trade surpluses. The early institutions were thus able to perform a recycling function moving capital investment from the established economies of Europe to finance growth in what were then the developing countries of the world. Among other achievements, the railways of Russia, South America and China were built largely by virtue of bond financings subscribed for by European investors. The rapid industrial expansion of the United States towards the end of the 19th century also owes much to this transnational financing.

After a quiescent period in the international bond market during World War I, which saw defaults on the Imperial Russian bonds, the flow of capital was thrown out of equilibrium. The 1920s industrial boom in the US attracted substantial foreign capital at the same time that the country was enjoying high export surpluses. Such massive flows of investment challenged the international payments system, but as long as the boom continued, capital finance poured in. It was during this period that foreign exchange or currency values were first called into question. The so-called gold clause was included in borrowings, chiefly dollar denominated, to assure the value of the obligation to the investor. Prior to World War I, foreign exchange instability was slight, and economic nationalism and exchange controls unheard of. Most borrowers honoured their commitments, as they prized their ability to raise funds internationally on a regular basis.

This was to change. Certain Latin American borrowers defaulted on issues in the late 1920s, but it was the Great Depression, precipitated by the 1929 Wall Street crash, which brought with it a wave of bankruptcies and defaults. Investors lost heavily in a financial crisis which was reminiscent of the debt repudiations and capital losses sustained as a result of World War I. The 1930s saw new international bond issues reduced to a trickle. With minor exceptions, this situation persisted until after World War II.

Post-World War II recovery

Following the war, the financial markets of Europe were left in disarray. A modest number of bond issues were completed for international borrowers, but the vast portion of finance capital was directed towards the crucial task of domestic reconstruction. Those foreign bonds which were issued were offered primarily in the UK, Switzerland, Belgium, the Netherlands and West Germany. The World Bank was the largest borrower and its issues in the domestic capital markets of Europe played an invaluable role in re-establishing investor confidence in foreign securities.

Just as the US dollar replaced the UK pound sterling as the principal international currency, New York asserted its primacy over London as the centre for international bonds. Foreign issues in New York were organised like domestic US securities offerings, with a US bond house or investment bank acting as lead manager and other US investment banks acting as co-managers and underwriters. Often, however, a very major portion of these new issues, particularly those offered by European borrowers, were sold abroad. In brief, European issuers were coming to New York to sell bonds, most of which ended up back in Europe – a form of turntable financing. As participants in the selling group for these New York-organised issues, European banks, however, soon learned US techniques of offering bonds, and were able to modify them later to suit the particular circumstances of the growing Euromarket.

Era of the Eurodollar

The chief building block of the newly emerging international market was the Eurodollar. A Eurodollar is a dollar held by a non-resident of the US, usually in the form of a bank deposit. Dollars only exist within the US banking system but they can be held and exchanged by foreigners. Following World War II, most western nations were on the dollar standard: they held dollars much like gold as a reserve asset to establish and maintain the external value of their own domestic currencies. This created a natural demand for offshore or Eurodollars.

Dollars were particularly sought after because the countries of Europe had agreed at the Bretton Woods Conference in 1944 to maintain fixed values for their currencies and to sell their international reserves, if necessary, to defend their currencies. The fixing of exchange values, or parities, at Bretton Woods allowed only 1% appreciation or depreciation from the exchange value agreed. Later, some countries narrowed this limitation further. The problem which most countries faced was depreciation. If there was severe downward pressure on a country's currency, it might decide on extreme measures, such as devaluation or reducing the exchange parity from that originally agreed at Bretton Woods. For some countries, however, devaluation carried a stigma. It could also become an emotional political issue and was often implemented only as a last resort. To stave off that decision, many countries built up large reserves of dollars which could be sold to support the external value of their currencies. In the late 1940s and early 1950s demand for dollars was strong, creating the so-called dollar shortage. This was exacerbated by US balance of payment surpluses, causing an outflow of dollars from Europe immediately after World War II.

The strong demand for dollars caused the currency to be maintained at an unrealistically high level in foreign exchange markets. US goods grew less competitive, and as trade increased, the US began paying out more money, almost entirely in dollars, than it was receiving back. The US had balance of payment deficits throughout the 1950s. By the end of the decade, these became a matter of public concern, especially as gold reserves dwindled. During the early 1960s, the earlier dollar shortage in Europe had become a dollar glut.

The surplus dollars were mostly kept on deposit in European banks, which in turn held this currency in their New York branches, subsidiaries or correspondent banks. The dollars rarely came to Europe in a physical sense, but were owned by Europeans through financial institutions. There were enough of these dollars for the banks receiving them as deposits to have some available for lending on to, or re-depositing with, other financial institutions. The business of re-depositing dollars flourished before the late 1950s, but the large extra supply of the currency, from the balance of payments deficits of the US, gave it a new impetus. Soon, a vigorous market developed, with banks lending money to other banks in the form of dollar deposits at competitive rates of interest. This came to be known as the interbank deposit market. Because London was initially and is to this day, the centre for this type of activity, it is often called the London interbank deposit market.

The market grew rapidly as US banks were quick to follow their corporate clients in expanding overseas. The international aspects of the market had definite advantages. The pool of Eurodollars was not under the control of any national authority, allowing the banks relative freedom from exchange control and other regulations. There was no requirement, for instance, for US banks to set aside a certain percentage of the Euro-deposits they took, in reserves. Reserves on deposit were obligatory in the US and reduced the amount of money available for loans, while increasing the cost of funds.

On top of this, interest rates paid on Eurodollar deposits were generally higher than those available in the US capital market. The Euro-deposit market thrived. Much of the huge monetary surpluses amassed by the oil-producing OPEC states (and more recently, the Japanese) has been invested in the form of Euro-deposits, stimulating the further rapid expansion of the market and raising the level of offshore dollar liquidity (free money supply) to historically high levels.

The figures in Exhibit 1.1 give a clear indication of the growth of Eurocurrency deposits, including those in Eurodollars. The figures are shown on a net as well as a gross basis, to eliminate the double counting which is a natural by-product of a re-depositing market. The totals include, with US dollars, a number of other freely exchangeable, or convertible, currencies, chiefly the Deutschmark, Swiss franc, UK pound sterling and, more recently, Japanese yen. International banks are quite free to take deposits and deal in any convertible and widely accepted currency. The banks canvassed to produce the figures below were not only those in European financial centres, but also in the most recent figures approximately 100 other countries including such centres as the Bahamas, Bahrain, Canada, Cayman Islands, Hong Kong, Japan, Panama, Singapore and the US. The growth of the market has been geographical as well as in size. The term Euromarket is now generic only.

Two important observations emerge from a study of the Eurocurrency deposit market. The first is the importance of the US dollar, which has accounted for between 41%-84% of this pool of offshore money. European currencies only returned to full external convertibility in 1958. Before that time, international transactions had to be carried out using something other than domestic money. Dollars were often used for this purpose, and consequently dollars began as a very high percentage of total Eurocurrencies. Second, the position of the dollar has tended to be eroded over time. Major slippages in 1971 and 1973 corresponded with the first and second dollar devaluations. A steady decline which began in 1976 accelerated through the 1980s. By 1983, Eurodollars represented only 60% of all Eurocurrencies. This reflected not only a weakening of the dollar on foreign exchange markets but also the growing desire of investors, particularly central banks, to diversify their currency holdings. Liberalisation of certain national capital markets encouraged the further use of their currencies in international financial intermediation. Furthermore, the basis on which the statistics have been compiled has changed over time. Initially there were only some 13 reporting countries, but the most recent figures record over 100 reporting countries. Their respective currency deposits (as included in the overall market) have had the effect of reducing the proportionate importance of the US dollar. The absolute amount of dollars has in fact risen somewhat in recent years.

The great growth in Eurocurrency deposits has, however, been in non-dollar moneys which have doubled in volume terms between 1987 and March 1996. Major gains were made by these currencies in the late 1980s. There then followed a period of near quiescence during the global recession years of 1990-1993. Activity has subsequently picked up through the mid-1990s as investor sentiment together with global liquidity were both on improving trends.

Exhibit 1.1
Eurocurrency deposit market, 1964-96 (March) ($ billion equivalent)

	1964 Dec.	1965 Dec.	1966 Dec.	1967 Dec.	1968 Dec.	1969 Dec.	1970 Dec.	1971 Dec.
Estimated size								
Gross*	20	24	29	36	50	85	110	150
Net**	14	17	21	25	34	50	65	85
Eurodollars as % of all Eurocurrencies – gross	83	84	83	84	82	84	81	76

	1972 Dec.	1973 Dec.	1974 Dec.	1975 Dec.	1976 Dec.	1977 Dec.	1978 Dec.	1979 Dec.
Estimated size								
Gross*	205	310	390	480	590	725	925	1,185
Net**	110	160	215	250	310	380	485	600
Eurodollars as % of all Eurocurrencies – gross	78	73	77	78	79	76	74	72

	1980 Dec.	1981 Dec.	1982 Dec.	1983 Dec.	1984 Dec.	1985 Dec.	1986 Dec.
Estimated size							
Gross*	1,581	1,862	2,047	2,396	2,496	3,018	3,858
Net**	810	945	1,020	1,085	1,285	1,485	1,775
Eurodollars as % of all Eurocurrencies – gross	62	63	61	60	61	55	52

Exhibit 1.1 *continued*

	1987 Dec.	1988 Dec.	1989 Dec.	1990 Dec.	1991 Dec.	1992 Dec.	1993 Dec.	1994 Dec.
Estimated size								
Gross*	4,157	4,485	5,031	5,907	6,240	6,196	6,465	7,103
Net**	2,220	2,390	2,640	3,350	3,610	3,660	3,780	4,240
Eurodollars as % of all Eurocurrencies – gross	52	52	51	46	45	46	44	43

Estimated size		
Gross*	7,926	8,010
Net**	4,645	4,800
Eurodollars as % of all Eurocurrencies – gross	41	41

*Definition of Gross includes gross external assets for banks in the target geographic area and other selected banks. Target area includes a changing number of reporting countries.

**Definition of net figures: claims on non-banks, banks outside market area, unallocated claims and use of Euro-funds for domestic lendings by banks in the BIS reporting area. European market area includes: major European countries and the Bahamas, Bahrain, Canada, Caymen Islands, Hong Kong, Japan, Panama, Singapore and the US. Figures net of re-deposited funds among reporting banks.

Source: Bank for International Settlements.

Emergence of syndicated loans

Eurodollar funds, later Eurocurrency funds, were soon used for short-term loans between banks to finance, for example, foreign trade invoiced in dollars. As the Eurocurrency pool grew, the deposits were lent out for longer periods. At first these funds were lent as bank loans to government entities and multinational corporations to finance their investments. This was the first phase of what is now called the floating rate or syndicated loan market.

After the oil crisis of 1973-74, and again after the more than doubling of oil prices in 1979, an increasing number of developing and developed nations borrowed from groups or syndicates of banks (hence syndicated loans) to finance their balance of payments deficits. Thus, the international banks which attracted funds from OPEC nations also performed the vital task of recycling these moneys to countries which were paying for higher-priced oil. More recently, exporting economies like that of

Japan have amassed substantial surplus capital which their own banking systems assisted in recycling. Borrowing countries welcome the syndicated loan market as a source of substantial funds: individual financings of well over $1 billion can be arranged. The market also offers the advantage of imposing relatively few restrictions on the borrower nations in contrast, for instance, to the International Monetary Fund (IMF).

The syndicated loan market grew massively during the 1970s and early 1980s. In the five years leading up to 1981, lending averaged over twice the size of the entire international bond market. Total loans arranged in US dollars and other currencies in 1981 reached a then record of $181.0 billion (equivalent) and exceeded by 3.4 times the volume of all international bonds.

During 1982, volume growth of syndicated lending remained strong through the first half of the year. By August 1982, however, the edifice of international financing was shaken to its foundation with the burgeoning Third World debt crisis. As may be noted in the table above, total developing country lending during 1983 dropped to less than half that recorded in 1981. From 1983 through 1986, there was a further significant decline in developing country lending. Indeed, even these poor figures paint too rosy a picture of the actual situation. If one excludes managed lending (ie involuntary loans sponsored by official bodies and groups of major creditor banks) and loan amounts used simply to refund maturing facilities, then this sector of the syndicated loan market showed actual contraction. More funds were repaid than raised through new financings.

It may be argued that during the Third World debt crisis, syndicated lending was re-directed towards the industrialised countries. From 1983 to 1984 this form of financing nearly tripled. Furthermore, total bank loans for 1984 topped the volume recorded during 1981. Once again, however, it pays to look behind the figures. The statistics compiled for the table above combine true syndicated loans with intermediate forms of financings, such as RUFs (revolving underwriting facilities) and other exotically named fundings. Although these novel instruments are purchased largely by commercial banks, they are frequently organised by their investment banking counterparts. Furthermore, their negotiability provides them with characteristics perhaps more reminiscent of Eurobonds than of pure syndicated loans. This process of securitising syndicated loans has proven to be one of the most significant trends in financial intermediation during the 1980s.

By comparison, the bond market strengthened its position up through the mid-1980s. Following the crisis of August 1982, interest rates dropped dramatically to assist those developing countries with a crushing debt burden. This sharp decline in rates also encouraged a wave of new bond issues and during 1983, the volume of these financings nearly caught up with total recorded bank loans. During 1984, the situation reversed with loans rising to two times the volume of bond issues.

Another major jump came in 1987, when (despite the loss of confidence created by the Stock Exchange crash) syndicated loans increased to 1.6 times total international bonds. Of greater significance still was the level of financing to non-oil producing developing nations. This exceeded the volumes reached prior to the debt crisis. Third World lending remained strong through 1995, with 1992 representing the only real down year. It would appear then that banks were successful in reserving against earlier difficult loans and regained an appetite for higher margin emerging market lending.

Syndicated loans to oil-producing nations remained fairly stable through 1990. As a consequence of the Gulf War, however, nations such as Kuwait were obliged to raise finance to pay for the damage inflicted. Lending activity remained fairly strong

Exhibit 1.2
Syndicated bank loans, 1970-96 ($ billion equivalent)

Borrowers	1970	1971	1972	1973	1974	1975	1976	1977	1978
Industrial countries	4.2	2.6	4.1	13.8	20.7	7.2	11.3	17.2	28.9
Developing countries									
Non-OPEC countries	0.3	0.9	1.5	4.5	6.2	8.2	11.0	13.5	26.7
OPEC countries	0.2	0.4	0.9	2.8	1.1	2.9	4.0	7.5	10.6
Total developing countries	0.5	1.3	2.4	7.3	7.3	11.1	15.0	21.0	37.3
CIS, Eastern Europe & China	–	0.1	0.3	0.8	1.2	2.6	2.5	3.4	3.8
International institutions	–	–	–	–	–	0.1	0.1	0.2	0.2
Total	4.7	4.0	6.8	21.9	29.2	21.0	28.9	41.8	70.2
As a multiple of the international bond market	1.1x	0.7x	0.7x	3.0x	4.3x	1.1x	0.9x	1.3x	2.1x

Borrowers	1979	1980	1981	1982	1983	1984	1985	1986	1987
Industrial countries	34.2	42.8	111.6	79.5	64.1	176.2	198.0	174.1	264.8
Developing countries									
Non-OPEC countries	43.9	28.4	49.3	42.7	25.5	29.3	21.4	18.4	45.1
OPEC countries	13.7	11.2	14.5	16.5	6.0	3.1	3.9	3.2	6.6
Total developing countries	57.6	39.7	63.8	59.2	31.5	32.4	25.3	21.6	51.7
CIS, Eastern Europe & China	8.3	5.0	4.3	8.0	1.4	3.6	5.6	5.9	8.0
International institutions	1.5	1.0	1.3	1.9	3.0	2.8	2.9	1.2	2.9
Total	101.6	88.4	181.0	148.5	99.9	215.1	231.6	202.6	327.4
As a multiple of the international bond market	2.6x	2.4x	3.4x	1.9x	1.3x	2.0x	1.4x	0.9x	1.6x

Borrowers	1988	1989	1990	1991	1992	1993	1994	1995	1996
Industrial countries	391.9	407.7	430.2	393.0	528.6	607.9	958.5	1,356.2	1,440.7
Developing countries									
Non-OPEC countries	74.0	80.2	89.3	115.6	89.7	118.3	113.5	151.3	105.5
OPEC countries	5.8	9.7	6.3	24.0	20.6	13.7	13.2	22.8	13.8
Total developing countries	79.8	89.9	95.6	139.6	110.3	132.0	126.7	174.1	119.3
CIS, Eastern Euurope & China	11.9	6.8	16.1	12.6	8.5	10.1	17.2	24.7	23.3
International institutions	4.5	3.4	2.6	9.9	12.3	7.2	8.3	4.4	0.4
Total	487.9	507.8	544.5	555.1	659.7	757.2	1,110.7	1,559.4	1,583.7
As a multiple of the international bond market	2.1x	1.9x	2.4x	1.8x	2.0x	1.5x	2.2x	3.1x	2.3x

Source: Capital Data.

through 1996, although representing only a relatively small portion of the total developing country borrowings. Similarly, supranational institutions also evidenced a spike in their borrowings in 1991 and 1992.

Compared to the international bond market, syndicated loans reasserted their old pre-eminence in the mid-1990s. This reflected the generous liquidity in the banking system following the recession of the early 1990s. Despite growth in developing country borrowing, the great percentage of new finance was still concentrated on the industrialised countries which accounted for 91% of all new credits in 1996.

Imposition of the Interest Equalization Tax

The outflow of currency from the US which created the Eurodollar pool, and in the process a major new capital market, reached alarming proportions by the early 1960s. On top of this outflow, there was a big surge in foreign investment by US companies endeavouring to avoid import restrictions by setting up operations overseas. Although these investments ultimately paid dividends, which were repatriated in dollars back to the US, such amounts were small in comparison to the continuing outward flow of investment funds. Furthermore, many companies decided to reinvest part or all or their dividends overseas because of profitable opportunities available there. Finally, as mentioned earlier, European borrowers looking for capital began to go to the U. S. market for their money. These borrowers were attracted by the openness of the US market, the availability of capital and the universal acceptability of the dollar. Thus, they also contributed to the steady flow of dollars out of the US. By 1962, this amount had reached $1.2 billion, and in the first half of 1963 it increased to over $1.5 billion. By mid-1963 the US government was ready to take measures designed to halt such outflows.

On July 18, 1963, President Kennedy made a speech to Congress about the worsening US balance of payments. One of the measures he proposed was the imposition of an Interest Equalization Tax (IET). The tax was later approved by Congress but applied retrospectively to take effect from the date of the president's speech.

The proposed tax was meant to stem the flow of capital from the US, which had been encouraged by foreign borrowings in the US domestic capital market. The tax was levied on the purchase price of the foreign bond or equity investments made by a US citizen. The rate of IET varied with maturity, and was graduated from 2.75% for bonds of at least three years of remaining maturity, but less than three and a half years, to 15% for bonds of more than 28½ years remaining maturity. The 15% rate was applied to investments in common stock of foreign companies. In theory, the percentages of tax applied to foreign bonds put the low interest rates prevailing in the US on an equal footing with the higher rates in Europe. It was estimated at the time that the tax raised the effective annual rate to foreign borrowers in the US market by 1%, bringing the rate into line with borrowing costs overseas. Hence the name Interest Equalization Tax.

With some exceptions, the tax acted to discourage the foreign bond market in the US. One such exception was the issue of bonds by international institutions, such as the World Bank, of which the US was a member. Others were issues by Canadian, Mexican and less developed country borrowers. Bank loans were also exempted because of their traditional short maturities. However, it later turned out that they served as substitutes for bond issues, and their use was soon restricted under new legislation. Although the IET was initially intended to be a temporary measure, it was extended in 1965, 1967, 1969 and finally in 1971. In the 1967 extension, the tax was raised to add 1½% to annual borrowing costs. In 1969, the president was given the authority to vary the effective annual rate from zero to 1½%. It should be remembered that while the effective annual adjustments were relatively modest, the full amount of the tax, with all its yearly adjustments, had to be paid at the time a foreign security was acquired by a US person. This was an effective disincentive to investment in such securities. After January 1974, however, the tax was reduced to zero and finally eliminated in June 1974.

The tax was criticised for failing to help the US balance of payments problem. It did, however, discourage US investors from buying certain foreign securities and thus forced the reopening of capital markets in Europe. Indeed, it is paradoxical that a law which was intentionally prejudicial to the interests of foreign borrowers, had the effect of creating the largest international capital market the world has known.

Appendix A to this chapter details the growth of the international bond market; Appendix B provides a time-line showing the major events, such as the IET, which helped to shape the market.

The period from 1963-74 was vital for European investment institutions because it gave impetus to their own development by removing direct competition from New York. During this relatively sheltered period, European institutions and offshore subsidiaries of US investment banks had an opportunity to develop professional relationships among themselves, and client relationships with borrowers, as well as the issuing techniques suitable to the new market.

Development of the market

1963-68

The beginning of the Eurobond market is commonly associated with the imposition of the IET. This did, in fact, mark the time when European borrowers were turned back to their home markets and a stateless pool of Eurocurrency funds, primarily Eurodollars, was transformed into an issuing market for international bonds. Just as the accumulating Eurodollars could be employed to make loans, so they could be used as the investment base for bonds.

The first Eurodollar bond issue made in 1963 was for Autostrade, the concessionaire and operator of toll motorways in Italy. This $15 million financing of 15-year bonds was guaranteed by IRI, the principal industrial and financial holding corporation owned by the Italian state. A unique feature of the issue was that its lead manager was a London-based bank, while its co-management group was comprised of banks in Belgium, West Germany, the Netherlands and Luxembourg. The issue was also underwritten and sold throughout Europe. There had been earlier experiments with this form of distribution, the first in 1961 being for SACOR, the Portuguese oil company. The SACOR bonds were denominated in a composite currency, European Units of Account (EUA), and were both underwritten and sold internationally. These two qualities are taken today to be key characteristics of a Eurobond.

The Eurobond market enjoyed enormous growth following the early attempts at international syndication. Dollar bonds, in particular, made impressive gains. The IET had reduced competition from New York, but another factor was at work as well. The war in Vietnam worsened US balance of payments deficits, with most of these funds pouring into Europe. Rather than revaluing their currencies to counteract this problem, many European countries made no foreign exchange adjustments and chose instead to accumulate the excess dollars in their reserve holdings. As dollar liquidity expanded in Europe so did the base for dollar-denominated bonds.

Other currency markets opened up and added new dimensions to the Eurobond market. The authorities in Europe had paved the way for this advance. When, in 1958, most European countries moved to full convertibility, this allowed non-residents to deal freely in these currencies. Other controls were also lifted, such as those restricting ownership of foreign bonds. Soon it was possible to contemplate dealing in external or Euro-Deutschmarks, Euro-French francs, Euro-Dutch guilders and Euro-Luxembourg francs, just as Eurodollars had become actively traded assets outside their home nation.

The first important non-dollar Eurobond sector to open up was that for Deutschmarks. In March 1964, the German government announced a 25% coupon tax (essentially a withholding tax) on domestic DM bonds held by non-residents. Issues for foreign borrowers denominated in DM were exempted from this tax, so non-residents were attracted to DM securities issued by non-German entities. These non-German securities formed the foundation for what is now called the Euro-DM bond market. The goal of the coupon tax was to reduce the flow of speculative funds into Germany, which threatened to overstimulate its economy. This worked and, in the process, the second most important sector of the Eurobond market was spawned. The year 1965 saw the first flotation of Euro-Dutch guilder bonds and 1967, the first Euro-French franc bonds. Numerous other currency sectors have been opened since.

These non-dollar currency sectors were important additions to the Eurobond market. They provided new capital resources and gave issuers a choice of currencies in which to borrow. A corporation wishing to invest in France, for example, might prefer to borrow French francs rather than US dollars. They also provided an important element of diversification. When one sector had difficulties, new issue activity could be switched to alternative sectors. If, for instance, a depreciating dollar brought the dollar sector to a halt, the overall Eurobond market would not stop. Borrowers could raise their money elsewhere: in DM, Dfl, Ffr, or in some other Eurocurrency. One innovative financing for the Italian Electric Company, ENEL, in 1965 took the form of six simultaneous issues denominated in the then six EEC currencies and offered in the same countries. An earlier issue for the City of Turin was denominated in sterling but provided the investor with the choice of receiving interest and principal in DM.

The dollar sector has, however, retained its pre-eminence in the Eurobond market. This is chiefly because there have been so many dollars available and because the dollar has been the most widely accepted of international currencies. Many of the non-dollar sectors have, historically, also been subject to some measure of control by national governments, as authorities were wary of how non-residents used their currency. During more recent years, however, most OECD nations have liberalised the rules restricting access to their domestic capital markets. For example, in 1995 the Japanese authorities removed the 'lock-up' requirement for Euro-yen issues. This step merged the domestic (or Samurai) with the international (or Euro) market for non-Japanese borrowers issuing in yen. Today, both public and private foreign issuers can place their bonds directly with investors in Japan.

The Eurobond market has broadened with the addition of new currency sectors. Commercial and merchant/investment banks have become active underwriters and distributors of securities as new issue volume has increased. The large universal European banks, which entered the market at its inception, have been quick to adapt many of the issuing techniques introduced by New York investment banks in combination with those used by UK merchant banks. More recently, Japanese securities houses and commercial banking institutions have emerged as substantial participants in the market. Their ability to mobilise vast quantities of capital have underpinned their strong position.

Another factor which contributed to the international market's growth was the continuous effort of the US government to reduce the outflow of its currency. In February 1965, President Johnson announced a Voluntary Restraint Program for US corporations making direct investments in subsidiaries and affiliates overseas. The internationalisation of large companies in the US had contributed to the country's payments deficits. The new programme set voluntary limits on the amount of direct investment overseas, but allowed companies to offset balance of payments savings against investment above these limits. For instance, if a company could show increased exports, then additional overseas investment could be justified. The programme encouraged corporations to export more and to repatriate dividends and short term liquid balances. Further, it provided an incentive to finance foreign operations through foreign capital sources. One of the most important of these sources was the Eurobond market, particularly its dollar sector.

In a very similar programme, US commercial banks were discouraged from making loans of one year or more to foreign borrowers, including subsidiaries owned by US companies. This had the effect of further shifting the burden of supplying overseas capital needs to markets outside the US.

Persistent US payments deficits and the devaluation of sterling in November 1967, prompted President Johnson to seek mandatory restrictions on overseas direct investment. Under the revised controls imposed in 1968 and administered by the newly created Office of Foreign Direct Investments (OFDI), US corporations were prohibited from making investments above set quotas. These quotas varied according to the type of country in which the investment was to be made (developing countries, for example, had the highest quotas), and the quotas were also geared to an individual company's past record of investment in the period 1965-66. Dividends and liquid balances had to be repatriated in an amount commensurate with historical experience. Commercial banks were not subjected to these mandatory restraints: their limitations remained voluntary.

This Mandatory Restraint Program forced numerous US corporations to finance their foreign operations in foreign markets. The volume of Eurobonds by these companies increased from $527 million in 1967 to $1,963 million in 1968. During the years 1968-73, when the programme was in force, US corporations floated a total of 271 Eurobond issues aggregating $6,978 million, or nearly 33% of the entire new issue market over the period.

One type of bond which US corporate issuers found particularly attractive was a bond convertible into their own common shares. These convertible bonds (discussed in a later chapter) typically paid a lower rate of interest than a standard Eurobond, and gave the issuer the prospect of converting debt into equity in its or another company. The securities were also popular with investors when US stockmarkets were strong, because the value of the bonds rose in line with the value of the shares into which they were convertible. The stockmarkets in 1968 were particularly bullish. Nearly $1.5 billion of convertible bonds were issued by US corporations in that year.

As the Eurobond market flourished, the foreign or Yankee market in New York made some progress. Participation was restricted to certain nationalities of borrowers, with the vast majority of new issues introduced by Canadian entities. The Sfr market too, was active from 1963. Only one Euro-Sfr bond, however, was ever floated, and that in 1963. Subsequently, the authorities prohibited Euro-offerings and encouraged, instead, the development of a foreign bond market which was more susceptible to control. The stability of the Sfr and low interest rate levels acted to stimulate new issue activity, and the volume of foreign bond offerings more than doubled between 1963-68.

1969-72

With the dollar under pressure on foreign exchange markets during 1969, holders of dollars took refuge in the more stable DM. Bond activity followed this general trend, and in the Euro-DM market, for instance, new issue volume jumped by over 56%. In the same year, Eurodollar bond volume was down 27%. This illustrated one of the fundamental forces which dominates the international bond market: currency value.

It is particularly interesting to follow the behaviour of the DM sector during this period. The upward pressure on the currency during 1969 was so great that the DM was temporarily freed from its Bretton Woods parity and allowed to float to whatever level market forces determined. Two months later, in October 1969, the DM was revalued for the second time since Bretton Woods (the first time was 1961) by 9.3%. As pressure built on the foreign exchange markets, so too did heavy demand for DM-denominated Eurobonds. This speculative interest, however, was short-lived. Market statistics suggest that once the DM was revalued and returned again to a fixed parity, foreign investors sold their DM bonds to realise their profits. Movement out of the Euro-DM sector caused this market to close from January to March 1970. New issue volume for 1970 as a whole was down by nearly half, lower even than that recorded in 1968.

One of the virtues of bond markets is their stability. Speculation, while it can produce short-term gains, often impedes the longer-term development of a market.

The year 1969 also marked the beginning of the long decline of the US stockmarkets and the volume of convertible issues for American borrowers dropped by 66%. In 1970, US convertibles were down by a further 82% and remained at a relatively low level through 1971. The 1972 stockmarket recovery breathed new life into this area and issuing volume for the year totalled $920 million.

One of the depressing factors for share prices, and thus for convertible bonds, was the rapid rise in short term interest rates. As rates increased, investors tended to take their money out of the stockmarket and place it in short-term investments such as bank deposits. A spurt in short term interest rates did occur at the end of the first half of 1969. One indicator of this increase, the London Inter-bank Offered Rate (Libor) for six-month dollar deposits, jumped from approximately 8½% to 10¼% between April and May 1969.

Rising short-term interest rates also damaged the bond markets. With short rates increasing rapidly and exceeding interest levels offered on longer-term bonds, investors sold their bond holdings, just as they did their shares, to invest their funds short-term. Standard bonds, or straight bonds, were hurt in much the same way as convertible issues. In 1969, the issuing volume of the overall Eurobond market recorded a decline: the first decline since the market began.

The period 1969-72 were unsettled years for the Eurobond market. In part this was due to interest rate volatility, but another factor was at work too: foreign exchange uncertainty. In May 1971, the DM was floated together with its frequent follower, the Dfl. The Austrian schilling and Sfr (whose foreign bond volume nearly tripled from the level of 1970) were revalued immediately. In December 1971, new parities for the floating currencies were agreed in meetings held at the Smithsonian Institute. The DM and Dfl were revalued by 13.6% and 11.5% respectively, and the dollar was devalued by 7.9%. This was the first dollar devaluation. Under the new Smithsonian parities, each currency was given greater room to fluctuate in value as the intervention limits to either side of parity level were widened to 2¼%, compared with ¾%-1% under the Bretton Woods definition.

Against this difficult economic backdrop, a new sector for foreign bonds opened up. In December 1970 a ¥6 billion issue for the Asian Development Bank was offered in the Japanese domestic capital market. This was the first of the so-called Samurai bonds. Supporting this issue was the decision of the Japanese authorities to internationalise their capital markets. Over time, Tokyo has gradually joined London and New York as one of the three most important centres for international financings. The Euro-Ffr sector reopened after the establishment of a two-tier foreign exchange market (commercial and financial) for the Ffr. The first Ffr Eurobonds were completed in 1967-68 but various problems, including the student protests of May 1968, brought new issue activity to a halt. Finally, in the early 1970s the first floating rate note issue was offered, for the Italian electric power utility, ENEL. It was destined to take six years and a change in the type of borrower, before this instrument increased in usage. However, over time the floating rate note has gained in popularity and is now one of the most significant instruments in the international markets.

The 1969-72 period also witnessed important progress in the physical handling and exchange of securities. Bond transfers were tricky because of the international nature of the market and risky because bearer bonds required no proof of ownership. If they were stolen, they were virtually as good as money. What the market needed was a central agent, a clearing house, which could store the securities owned by market participants and record transfers among them, while the bonds remained in safekeeping in the clearing house. The first such agent to set up business was Euroclear in Brussels in December 1968, joined later by a competitor, Cedel Bank, which started operations in Luxembourg in January 1971.

Although Euroclear and Cedel Bank are different firms, the services they offer have grown increasingly similar, largely due to market pressure, and now are fully compatible with each other. Bonds owned by a member of the Cedel Bank system can be easily transferred to a member of Euroclear. Efficient transfers have been vital to the smooth operation and development of the Eurobond secondary market.

In April 1969, the Association of International Bond Dealers (AIBD) was established as the self-regulatory body of the Eurobond market. This organisation changed its name in 1992 to the International Securities Market Association (ISMA). ISMA's most notable achievements to date have been in the area of standardising secondary market practices, and it has been instrumental in harmonising the efforts of Euroclear and Cedel Bank. ISMA also acts as a representative for the market in its relationships with national authorities and major domestic capital markets. In 1988, ISMA was itself authorised as a Designated Investment Exchange (DIE) by the UK Securities and Investments Board. That same year, the UK Secretary of State for Trade and Industry approved ISMA as an International Securities Self-Regulating Organisation (ISSRO) for the purposes of the UK Financial Services Act 1986.

During the 1980s, the primary (or new issue) market's counterpart was founded. This association, called IPMA (the International Primary Market Association), has set out to set new standards of new issue disclosure and syndicate practices. Euroclear, Cedel Bank, ISMA and IPMA will be discussed more fully in later chapters of this book.

1973-74

The years 1973-74 were probably the bleakest in the history of the Eurobond market, with even the Sfr and Japanese yen foreign bond markets giving up ground. The period began with another dollar devaluation and ended in the energy crisis, record high short-term interest rates and fears of a breakdown in the international banking system. By 1974, new issue volume in the Eurobond market was only 35% of that recorded in 1972, and was at the lowest level seen since 1967.

Despite the Smithsonian realignment, the US continued to experience payments deficits through 1972, which forced the second dollar devaluation by the beginning of 1973. On February 12, 1973, the dollar's official value was reduced by 10% and then the currency was floated. Two days later, the DM and Dfl were revalued by 11.1% and 11.0%, respectively. On March 11, 1973, the first European monetary snake was formed with its value independent of the dollar, and a few days later the DM was raised by 3.0% against the international composite currency, Special Drawing Right (SDR), which had the effect of further strengthening its position relative to the dollar.

The dollar made up some lost ground in late 1973 and the beginning of 1974, but the removal of capital controls in January-February 1974 reversed this trend. After being detached from its Smithsonian parity, the dollar was free to float in accordance with market pressures. The US and other governments were able to smooth out volatile swings in its value by direct intervention, but this was typically a short-run measure and did not halt the currency's intermediate-term decline. Another measure employed to attract support for the dollar was the use of high interest rates to encourage dollar investment. In 1974 short-term dollar interest rates were pushed up to the region of 13%, prompting a flight of investment funds into money market instruments.

Bonds suffered and new issue activity in the Eurodollar sector was down almost 48% in 1974. The difficulty was not only finding buyers for new bonds but also the investment community's problem of financing its own bond inventories. In order to issue securities, investment houses had to carry a large supply or inventory of bonds. These bonds were (and still are) mostly financed through short-term borrowings.

The problem arose when short-term interest costs began to exceed the return offered by the bonds financed, which they did by 2%-3%. This is called 'negative carry'. As a result, many issuing houses ran into difficulties during 1973-74 and some closed down their new issue businesses altogether. Borrowers were understandably hesitant to issue new securities during a time of such high interest rates, and the majority delayed their financing plans as long as possible.

In the final months of 1973, the Yom Kippur War was fought in the Middle East and the oil embargo was imposed. US prestige declined overseas, but the major question was how the world would adjust to the four-fold increase in the price of oil. This uncertainty touched off a flight of capital into safer havens, such as US Treasury bills. A further problem which grew out of the energy crisis was the need to recycle funds from the oil exporters to the oil importers, allowing them to purchase new supplies of this commodity to fuel their economies. There was not then, and there is not to this day, an international body capable of performing the task. It was left primarily to the international commercial banks. As was noted earlier, they accomplished this job chiefly by taking deposits from the oil-rich nations and re-lending the funds to the oil importers. There was concern, however, about how well the banking system would stand up under these new pressures. Equally, there were rumours of massive foreign exchange losses incurred by certain banks due to the severe instability of currency values. In May 1974, huge losses were announced at the New York-based Franklin National Bank, which resulted chiefly from their currency trading activities. A month later, the German Herstatt Bank collapsed. Bank failures such as those were reminiscent of the Great Depression of the 1930s, and the resulting atmosphere of market uncertainty caused the flow of new bond issues to slow to a trickle. New issues offered record high coupons to attract investor interest. Furthermore, average issue size was cut back and maturities shortened. Not until 1975-77 did the Eurobond market recover sufficiently to offer borrowers the type of attractive terms which had been available in 1972.

When US capital controls, such as the IET, were removed early in 1974, many bankers predicted that the Eurodollar bond market would be reintegrated into the New York capital market. The New York market was larger than that in Europe, and its investment institutions were highly sophisticated, producing a continuing structured flow of funds into the market. The number of Yankee issues did increase after the removal of the IET in 1974. According to statistics compiled by Morgan Guaranty Trust Company of New York and Inter-bond Services Ltd, new issue volume increased by 3.2 times from 1973 to 1974, totalling $3,291 million. In 1975 and 1976, the amounts were $6,462 million and $10,604 million respectively. The volume of Yankee issues declined year by year, however, through the end of the 1970s. By 1981, the Yankee market staged a modest recovery, but from that time through the remainder of the 1980s up to the mid-1990s, it resumed its weakening trend. By 1996, US foreign bonds (registered with the SEC) sank to an all time low of 0.2% of the international bond market. The past weaknesses of the Yankee issues contrasted sharply with the competitive advantages offered by Eurobonds which were quicker and easier to float (ie with no requirement to register with the Securities and Exchange Commission or SEC) and frequently less expensive for the borrower. The development of fixed price 'bought deals' (which removed the borrower's risk of market movements during the offering period) also proved to be another positive attraction of Eurobonds.

1975-78

Despite the gloom of 1973-74, the first Euro-Canadian dollar and Kuwaiti dinar bond issues were completed during that time. In the following three years, two other significant currency sectors were opened up: the Euro-yen and the composite currency SDR. Years 1975-77 were characterised by consistent growth in the Eurobond market, supported by generally low short-term interest rates. For much of this boom period, six-month Libor was in the region of 6% and sometimes lower: a healthy margin below the interest rate level offered by bonds. The Yankee market achieved its highest ever volume of financings with $10.6 billion of new issues in 1976. A similar three-year peak was achieved by the Sfr sector in 1976 with $5.4 billion worth of new issues, while yen foreign bonds showed a substantial net gain over the period as a whole.

Beginning in 1975, new issue procedures were modified in certain financings to direct securities to specific pockets of surplus capital (particularly in the OPEC countries). These financings came to be known as targeted issues, the best example of which today are those whose terms and management groups are specially designed to attract Japanese investors.

The authorities in the US responded to the weakness of their currency on the foreign exchange markets and in November 1978 introduced a package of intervention measures. Two large domestic issues in DM and Sfr (DM3 billion and Sfr2 billion Carter bonds) were undertaken in Germany and Switzerland to strengthen the dollar. These two events were viewed by many market participants as the first official recognition of the need to manage the foreign exchange value of the dollar.

1979-81

One of the major characteristics of the market during 1979-81 was the boom/bust cycle of issuing windows opening, only to be slammed shut later on. A major new underwriting technique was developed which provided the quick reaction timing needed to take advantage of issuing windows. This form of placement has come to be known as the bought deal (mentioned earlier). It was first used extensively in the first quarter rally of 1979. In a bought deal, final issue terms are agreed between the lead manager and the borrower prior to announcement rather than waiting until the formal offering day, about a week later, when such terms are adjusted (only modestly) in the light of investor demand and then prevailing market conditions. The bought deal introduced new risks for underwriters. However, it did have the advantage of being quick to arrange on guaranteed terms acceptable to the issuer.

The advent of the bought deal was indicative of the innovative character of the market. This has been the key to its longevity in the face of highly uncertain conditions. The year 1979 saw the introduction of the first quarterly (instead of semi-annual) payment FRN, the FRN convertible into fixed rate bonds, the rolling rate FRN, and the so-called drop-lock FRN with different conversion formulas, one of which was tied to the weekly 10-year US Treasury rate. Innovation was not just for innovation's sake. The new instruments were designed to meet the changing needs of borrowers and investors in a rapidly moving market. FRNs accounted for about 35% of total Eurodollar bond volume in 1979.

Perhaps the single most important innovation during the year was the first bond swap. This financing involved Roylease Ltd, a subsidiary of the Royal Bank of Canada, which raised five-year funds in the German market and then hedged this liability through the forward foreign exchange market. The effect was that a Canadian dollar borrowing was created out of the DM bond initially offered. The use of swaps (both currency and interest rate) linked to Eurobonds has been a major factor shaping the markets in the 1980s and 1990s. So pervasive has this influence been that at peak times swap-linked transactions account for some 80%-90% of total new issue volume.

There was also further experimentation with other new types of underwriting procedures. In the summer of 1979, the Kingdom of Sweden introduced New York-style pricing to the Euromarkets in a $100 million five-year note issue. Contrary to standard Eurobond procedure, this placement gave no indication of coupon, price or even yield in its underwriting invitation telexes. The terms were only fixed during the offering period after consultation with potential investors (called price discovery). These discussions took note of the yield levels being offered by comparable issues in the secondary market to assure the relative attractiveness of the new issue. Commissions were also cut to discourage discounting, and when finally offered, the securities traded very close to their initial pricing level. The European Investment Bank (EIB) introduced another innovation during the same month which had a similar objective. This was an auction issue for which numerous managers were invited to tender competitively on a yield basis. The auction produced bids totalling $675 million, and EIB accepted a principal amount of $100 million from three banks with a coupon of 9.7% and a bid price of 98.06%. As with the Kingdom of Sweden issue, these bonds finally traded close to their original price.

A significant development occurred in March 1979 with the introduction of the European Monetary System (EMS) as a successor to the older monetary snake. The EMS linked the currencies of Germany, France, Italy, the Netherlands, Belgium, Denmark and Ireland, and limited their volatility with reference to cross exchange rates and the central rate of the European Currency Unit (Ecu), defined as a basket of European currencies.

In the second half of 1979, the dollar encountered new difficulties on foreign exchange markets and the DM was revalued within the EMS in September. Strong currencies were very much in demand, and the Sfr market enjoyed its best year to date with nearly $9.5 billion of new offerings. The yen market was cautious due to rising interest rates and concern over the impact of OPEC price increases in June. The authorities in the US reacted to the weakening dollar by introducing the October Volker package, which included a 1% hike in the discount rate to 17% and an 8% marginal reserve requirement on certain categories of bank-managed liabilities. The dollar sector took the worst plunge most people could remember, with price declines of 10% and more, producing total losses from new issues during the year of about $360 million. New issues activity was quite low for the remainder of the year, although a modest recovery was experienced in December.

If 1979 was volatile, 1980 produced even greater movements. The US Prime rate ranged from 20% in March, following the second Volker package to 10¾% in the summer, before again climbing to 21½% by year end. A bond market which began 1980 in the shadow of Afghanistan and had seen the price of gold climb from $500 per ounce to over $850, was about to encounter some of the greatest strains in its history. Before the end of the first quarter, market losses were estimated to be running into the hundreds of millions. Rapidly rising interest rates which produced these losses also had the effect of boosting the dollar on foreign exchange markets, where it appreciated by 8% against the Sfr and 9% against the DM. The hard currency sectors experienced losses similar to the dollar bonds. During the year as a whole, the DM and Sfr foreign bond markets declined by 10% and 21% respectively, and the yen by 41%.

Interestingly, the volume of Eurobond offerings overall increased, despite the tough issuing conditions. The year's totals were 15% above those recorded in 1979, and the dollar sector retained its ascendancy, accounting for 67% of all new offerings. Once again, a major factor in this strong performance was the ability of the market to innovate, to devise new instruments to meet the needs of borrowers and investors at a particular point in time.

Following Easter 1980, the market experienced one of the sharpest rallies in its history. The dramatic improvement was initiated by a fall-off in short-term interest rates, and lead managers raced each other to the market with bought deals whose terms often anticipated further interest rate declines. Easter's rally came to an end in June as short-term rates again began to firm. Several of the new issues then on offer fell to deep discounts. This was particularly true if their terms were fixed and could not be altered to suit the changed market environment. The market had also become inundated with new issues. A total of 42 offerings were launched during June totalling $3.9 million, the highest monthly underwriting volume then ever recorded.

The year was also marked by the large amount and variety of equity convertible bonds. Notwithstanding the rising interest rate levels, numerous convertibles, particularly for oil and energy-related companies, were warmly welcomed. By year end, a total of approximately $2.5 billion of convertible bonds had been brought to market, up from $1.2 billion in 1979. December saw another important innovation: bonds carrying warrants to buy additional bonds. The first of these issues was the $50 million 13¾% five-year notes for Crédit National which carried six-month warrants to purchase the same principal amount of 13¾% 10-year bonds. During later years, debt warrant bonds were incorporated into a number of Eurobonds. The primary advantage such instruments offered investors was the potential for capital gains on the warrants if interest rates declined. Such attractions stimulated significant innovation with debt warrants and prompted their use in numerous Eurobond financings.

The period 1980-81 was also characterised by experimentation with asset-backed bonds. Inflationary pressure during the 1970s and the rapid rise in certain commodities (most visibly: oil and gold) encouraged investment in so-called 'real' assets which were viewed as lasting reservoirs of value. Two issues for Sunshine Mining's silver-backed bonds were followed in February 1981 by the first Eurobond linked to the price of gold. This issue by Refinement International had no set principal amount but the individual bonds had a face value of 10 ounces of gold. In the immediate secondary markets, the bonds were traded as though they were the metal itself and their price was quoted on a per ounce basis. The Refinement and other asset-backed issues were reasonably successful when they were first issued but suffered from the high interest rate environment which persisted through 1981 and the first half of 1982. Such high interest rates had the desired effect of dampening down inflation, but this also meant that commodity prices fell in real terms as well.

High dollar interest rates did not, however, deter the Eurodollar bond sector of the market. In 1981 this sector advanced in volume terms by 65.8% and represented 82.2% of total Eurobonds. Yankee bonds also had a good year increasing in amount by 2.2 times. This strength of dollar-denominated bonds was largely at the expense of certain strong currency sectors. Euro-DM bonds, for instance, recorded a volume decline of 60%.

The high interest rate environment also placed liquidity strains on both private and public sector borrowers. Corporations came back into the market as a matter of necessity more than of choice. Financial innovation was called upon and produced the zero coupon or streaker bond. The first example of this innovation was the $75 million (nominal) three-year note issue for PepsiCo. The bond was priced at 67¼%, thus raising some $50 million for the borrower. There was no coupon or interest payment but the investor did receive a significant capital gain when the notes reached maturity and were redeemed at par or 100%. This gain represented the equivalent return of 14.14% per annum over the life of the securities.

The zero coupon bond had favourable cashflow consequences for the corporate issuers and tax advantages as well for both borrower and investor in certain national jurisdictions. Some time after the PepsiCo issue, GMAC advanced this concept by issuing 10-year zero coupon bonds which were priced at 25¼% to provide an equivalent yield return of 14.76% a year. In the GMAC issue, investors were told they could quadruple their money in 10 years without concern that interest rates might decline. Of course, creditworthiness was a consideration because the borrower had to be sufficiently sound to redeem his bonds at par in 10 years time. The market was, therefore, largely restricted to the highest quality issuers.

The early 1980s also witnessed the introduction of interest-rate swaps where, typically, a fixed rate interest payment (like the coupon on a bond issue) was swapped for interest paid on a floating rate basis (like that on a syndicated loan or a floating rate note). These exchanges provided borrowers with access to forms of financing which otherwise would have been unavailable or available only at a higher price than that achieved through the swap. The emergence of swaps has helped to unify what had previously been separate pools of investment capital, to form a truly global financial market. Swaps themselves were subject to a great deal of innovative development. In 1981, for example, the World Bank and IBM entered into a series of transactions in which DM and Sfr financings were swapped for US dollar bonds. This technique was dubbed an exchange of borrowings and the reputation of the parties involved underpinned the respectability of bond swaps as a financing technique.

Japanese issuers were also quite active during 1981. Many of their bonds were equity-linked and gained support from the buoyant Tokyo Stock Exchange. The rising popularity of such securities has been a prominent feature of the bond market through the years. Issuing activity has sometimes displayed a stop-go performance – just as the 1981 boom in Japanese convertibles led to a setback in this sector in 1982. However, the overall trend in Japanese borrowings has been very strong, reflecting the dynamism of that nation's economy.

1982-84

The three years from 1982 through 1984 brought with them some of the most fundamental changes to affect the Euromarkets. During this period major nations in developing regions of the world were caught up in a debt crisis which threatened not only their own future prospects for growth but also the very viability of the international banking system. In contrast to this trend, at the end of the period, significant moves were made by major industrialised countries to liberalise access to their domestic capital markets and to encourage greater freedom of transnational investment.

1982 began with interest rates at a high level in real as well as nominal terms. Refuge was sought from volatile conditions and the stable Ecu-denominated bonds became a major attraction amongst investors, gaining 6.4 times in volume terms. High interest rates also reduced inflation which in turn acted to depress commodity prices. Timing could not have been worse for developing countries which depended on strong commodity linked export earnings in order to meet record high debt service payments. The strain was overwhelming and the conclusion inevitable. In August 1982, Mexico signalled to its international creditors that it was on the brink of bankruptcy.

This country's problems turned out to be the tip of the iceberg. As word spread about the possible impairment of developing country credits, many banks chose to reduce abruptly their lending to these nations. Such actions turned out to be self-fulfilling because the denial of additional credit itself precipitated a crisis of liquidity. Latin America was one area of major difficulty but eastern Europe had its mounting problems as well as Africa.

So great were the sums involved that it was in everyone's interest to find a solution. The US Federal Reserve Bank took the first step by reducing interest rates dramatically in order to ease the pressure of debt charges. Commercial bankers generally held their breath as they were forced to lend on a mandatory basis to allow their sovereign state clients to keep interest payments current.

The lower interest rates were very good news for the bond houses, many of whom remained unscathed by the Third World debt crisis. New issue activity also boomed. Eurobonds gained 87.2% over 1981 largely on the strength of Euro-dollar financings which increased by an almost identical 87.4%. During the year dollar bonds reached a record 82.2% of the total Eurobond market. Foreign bonds also strengthened by 19.1% over the previous year but did not display the dynamism of the Euromarket. The upsurge in new issue volume was also boosted by refunding operations where borrowers chose to issue new lower coupon bonds in order to pre-pay older, more expensive financings.

During 1983 the floating rate note sector began to replace bank lending and increased in strength, representing some 30% of all Eurobonds. The debt crisis had become a permanent feature of the landscape of international finance. Indeed similar pressures led to the overthrow of the Nigerian government by the end of the year.

Commercial bank creditors were virtually powerless to influence events and innovation of new product ideas moved away from these intermediaries towards the more fleet-footed investment banks. Financial experimentation, thus, tended towards 'securitisation' of lending. Traditional syndicated loans were substituted by other debt instruments which enjoyed the benefit of a liquid secondary market where they could be easily bought and (more importantly) sold. The commercial banks were active, though less than enthusiastic supporters of these developments. The huge amount of illiquid Third World debt on their books forced them to place a new priority on debt instruments which were tradable.

During 1983 the US dollar continued its relentless appreciation despite a mounting domestic fiscal deficit and widening trade gap. US dollar bonds remained at 75% of all Eurobonds and 53% of the total international bond market. Sfr and yen foreign bond sectors were both reasonably strong but the DM sector suffered from domestic recessionary pressures which prompted a restriction to be placed on new issue activity at the end of the year to allow time for recovery.

The next year, 1984, represented a watershed in the history of the international bond market. The transition was not smooth and its course was erratic at times. The outcome was, however, predictable.

The year 1984 marked a milestone in the Eurobond market in a number of different ways. Euro-commercial paper became popularised and its growth furthered the trend towards the securitisation of bank credit. There was also experimentation with debt issues which shared common characteristics with equity financings, thus forging a convergence between these once quite separate markets. Also, towards the end of the year, IPMA (International Primary Markets Association) was incorporated. As its name implies, this organisation is chiefly interested in the new or primary market for securities. So far its major contributions have included improving and standardising the information disclosed about new issues and reforming syndicate practices.

What made 1984 a year of historical importance was, however, something different. A milestone in the Eurobond market was reached on Wednesday morning, July 18, 1984, when President Reagan signed the tax bill which removed the existing 30% withholding tax on interest and dividend payments to non-residents of the US. Previously this tax had to be paid by nearly all foreign investors in US securities (although there was frequently a measure of relief under relevant double taxation treaties), and it had forced many US corporations to set up either domestic '80/20' or Netherlands Antilles finance subsidiaries to avoid imposition of this tax on their Eurobond issues. The repeal of the withholding tax allowed these corporations to issue their debt directly from the United States to Europe, or what was more likely to be the case, in the United States and Europe simultaneously. The repeal of the withholding tax thus opened the door to a reunification of the two largest capital markets in the world and introduced a new era of the global integrated market.

There were precedents for global bonds: Texaco, in March 1984, floated a record-sized $1 billion convertible issue in New York while at the same time offering a virtually identical tranche of this placement in the Euromarkets. All the same, it was Citicorp, followed swiftly by Household Finance, that was the first US corporation to issue withholding tax-free securities on both sides of the Atlantic simultaneously.

The repeal of the US withholding tax was not greeted by all parties with unalloyed joy. Fears spread of the suspected disruptive changes which could ensue. Of particular concern was the possibility that the Euromarket might be reabsorbed into New York, thus giving a significant competitive advantage to Wall Street investment banks at the expense of European institutions. As it has turned out, the Wall Street investment banks showed greater assertiveness but this might be explained too as a function of the strength of dollar-based financings or the continuation of a trend evident in the preceding years.

Somewhat surprising was the debate which also ensued between the US Treasury and the US Internal Revenue Service (IRS) concerning the issuance of government securities in the Euromarket. With a huge domestic deficit to finance, the Treasury was eager to raise funds in the relatively cheap Euromarkets. Because of this market's preference for anonymity, it was initially suggested that the Government securities should be issued in bearer form (which would not expose the identity of the ultimate investor). The IRS, fearing that US citizens would seize upon this as an attractive way to evade domestic taxes, moved to block the bearer option and insisted that all government bonds had to be placed with European investors on a registered (or named) basis only. Furthermore, there was the threat of penalties for non-compliance. Many Europeans, and particularly those institutions which had to abide by strict bank secrecy laws, looked askance at this extra-territorial extension of the US legal system. The attitude displayed by the IRS also raised doubts that a new US administration might possibly act in an arbitrary manner by enforcing existing or new laws to the detriment of Euro-investors who had acquired US securities. So real were these fears that a form of new 'disaster language' was incorporated in the bond offerings of certain US private sector issuers. Provision was made either to allow the borrower to gross up in the event that a penalty tax was imposed or to call the entire issue at par.

It was generally thought untenable that the US government should have to adopt this same language to indemnify investors against its own laws. However, this made investors uneasy and helped to sour the market attitude towards the first public auction issue of US government securities in Europe. During this period of uncertainty, in the early autumn, a host of US corporate issuers ($4.4 billion in September alone) took the opportunity once again to float new bonds on advantageous terms. As it happened, IBM Credit was one of the leaders in this surge and scored a highly successful saving of some 50 basis points, ie ½% in yield less than the equivalent maturity US Treasury bonds.

Given the desire for a successful introduction of government debt to the European market, a form of compromise was reached whereby targeted US government securities were issued with annual coupons standard for Europe and specially registered. This meant that they were held in the name of the institutions which bought them on behalf of clients. Upon purchase and on each coupon date, that institution had to give the negative certification that the ultimate beneficial owners of such securities were not otherwise liable for the payment of US income tax. The US authorities were presumably to accept the word of the reporting institutions. This somewhat imperfect solution was sufficient to permit the first $1 billion auction of four-year notes which took place towards the end of October. In the event the issue turned out to be reasonably successful, recording bids which totalled $4 billion on an average yield level 31 basis points below very similar notes offered in the domestic market. On the basis of this reception, further auctions of $1 billion of five-year, two-month Treasury bonds and $300 million of three-year, 11-month FNMA (a US government agency) notes, took place prior to the end of 1984.

Another yardstick of the success of the US withholding tax repeal was the number of imitators which quickly introduced a similar measure. By the beginning of October, both West Germany and France joined in a competitive repeal of their own withholding taxes.

1985-87

The natural incentive to open up domestic capital markets which began in 1984 continued to gather pace through the mid-1980s and achieved much in the internationalisation of such markets. These developments took place in concert with a trend towards deregulation which had the same effect of creating an unfettered global market for capital. Sustaining this was the progressive lifting of restrictions on the nationality of banks which could lead manage certain currencies of issues. During this period it became possible for non-Japanese bond houses to lead manage Euro-yen issues. Both the German and Dutch authorities dropped similar restrictions and permitted foreign-owned affiliates located in the respective countries to act as managers in new issues. During the 1987 IMF meeting, the French finance minister made a similar announcement with respect to his domestic capital market. As with the sterling market though, foreign affiliates had to be able to demonstrate competence in managing new Ffr issues and there needed to be some form of reciprocity with the nations involved allowing French institutions to conduct similar securities business within their own territories.

Restrictions on new issue terms and procedures were also loosened in order to improve access to the market and encourage greater financing activity. The DM market had, for example, made important strides in this direction. After removing the 25% coupon tax in 1984 (though replacing it with a similar 10% investment tax in 1987), the foreign bond market became largely absorbed by the DM-Eurobond sector. Thereafter, nearly all major foreign affiliates located in Germany could lead manage these issues. From 1985 the Central Capital Market Committee was abolished together with its Sub-Committee for Foreign Issues. These bodies had acted to regulate market access and new issue terms for foreign borrowers. They had also operated a queuing system which rationed the number of new issues during each forthcoming month (which limited the responsiveness of issuing activity to short-term movements in the market). Similar forms of deregulation were carried out in both the Dfl and Sfr markets.

Liberalisation measures were also introduced in the Euro- and domestic yen markets which showed dynamic growth during the period. Much of this increase in activity was attributable to the strength of the domestic Japanese economy and its mounting current account surplus. Such surpluses were being recycled just as the petro-dollars were in the 1970s. During 1986, it was estimated that some $95 billion (net) of foreign securities were purchased by Japanese investors alone. Due to the sheer weight of this money the international bond market understandably shifted its focus towards the Far East. Particularly visible were the specially targeted issues (the so-called Sushi bonds) whose terms were tailored to meet the criteria of different categories of Japanese investment institutions.

The process of capital market liberalisation has not been wholly unrestricted. Following the City of London's Big Bang in late 1985, the Financial Services Act 1986 (the 'Act') was made law and established the SIB (Securities and Investment Board) with senior authority to govern the securities and investments business in the UK. As the majority of Eurobond activity is conducted through London, such regulatory measures represented a significant challenge to a market which was known for its free-wheeling operations. Concern was expressed at the outset that over-regulation would stifle the creative energy of the Eurobond market which was chiefly responsible for prompting its growth and providing its versatility. As mentioned previously, however, ISMA (International Securities Market Association) became a designated exchange for the purposes of the Act which meant that its membership of approximately 890 institutions could continue to conduct their business in accordance with established ISMA rules. Such rules are not subject to the approval of the British authorities nor can changes be required to be made. In short, the bond market succeeded in preserving its fundamental self regulation.

Seen from another point of view, re-regulation is a natural consequence of the growth and expansion of the Eurobond market into different areas of financial intermediation. Institutions active in the debt market have also proved instrumental in creating an international market in common shares, the so-called Euro-equities. Large privatisation issues in the UK and other countries also played a role in popularising this sector. So important was this development that it was a factor in prompting the regulatory side of the London Stock Exchange to merge with the International Securities Regulatory Organisation (ISRO, which ISMA itself helped to establish) . During this period the two bond clearers, Euroclear and Cedel Bank, expanded their services to cope with the international equities business. So extensive is the influence of the international market that a degree of regulation must be viewed as a practical necessity and probably in the longer term, a benefit as well.

During the period 1985-87 of sweeping change, the Eurobond market went from strength to strength. Total international bonds advanced in 1985 by 58.1% over the preceding year, while 1986 recorded a further advance of 35%. Due to the depreciation of the US dollar much new growth derived from other currency sectors. The DM sector advanced by 42.8% over the period 1985-87, compared with an 381.2% increase in Dfl bonds. As noted previously, the yen sector was also highly dynamic. Sfr foreign bonds grew in importance during this period and featured a shift in investor preference away from private note placements in favour of public bond issues.

Perhaps one of the most spectacular developments during this period was the rise and fall of perpetual floating rate notes. The first such issue was completed for National Westminster Bank in April 1984 and totalled $500 million, providing a 3/8% margin over Libor. As the name implied this perpetual FRN had no fixed maturity. It was also structured so that failure to make timely interest payments would not be considered an event of default, as long as the bank decided to halt dividend payments on its common shares at the same time. Because of these characteristics, NatWest's FRN had many similarities with preference shares. Indeed, its subordination to the claims of depositors (together with the other equity-like characteristics mentioned previously) allowed the bank to account for the financing as though it were primary capital for Bank of England ratio purposes.

Such was the demand by banks to augment their capital bases, that perpetual FRNs became very popular during 1985. The volume of new issues gathered pace during 1986, with the second half total of $6.4 billion of such financings representing a three times increase over the first half. This rush of new issues created a glut on the market. Investors also began to question the fundamental value of these instruments, particularly when they were subordinated to bank deposits. Liquidity had always been taken for granted because of the secondary market which initially existed for such FRNs. However, when selling pressure increased many market makers restricted or curtailed their activity altogether. Investors holding the perpetuals were then truly stuck with them forever. The situation became so extreme in certain instances that whole issues became untradeable.

The demise of the perpetual FRNs occurred in December 1986 and in time the crisis spread to the normal FRN market where progressive tightening of terms in the borrowers' favour had begun to discourage investors. During the first half of 1987, FRN new issue activity dropped to 7% of the total Eurobond market, well down from the high point of approximately 40% recorded over the 1984-85 period. Only after mid-year 1987 did FRN prices and activity begin to recover.

A certain degree of liquidity was also introduced to the perpetual sector by repackaging these financings with complex interest rate swaps. Among other things such repackagings proved the flexibility and value of bond swaps. Swapping has become a permanent feature of the bond market, improving terms for both borrowers and investors by exploiting anomalies which exist in different sectors of the international capital market. The utility of this form of financial engineering is exemplified by the use made of otherwise unwanted securities. The popularity of swapping is also reflected in the volume of such transactions which have been concluded. By mid 1996 there were approximately $15.6 trillion (notional) of interest rate swaps outstanding together with a further $1.3 trillion (notional) of currency swaps.

Crash of 1987

1987 may be remembered as the year of the crashes, beginning with the plight of the FRNs (particularly the perpetuals) and concluding with the melt-down of the world's equity exchanges and effective devaluation of the US dollar. Particularly surprising was the timing of the latter two crashes. Together with the predictable correction of the stockmarkets, the other fundamental problem – the US economy and its twin fiscal and current account deficits – had been identified and commented upon for some time. Ironically, just before Black Monday, October 19, 1987, when Wall Street fell by 508 points, both deficits had begun to show signs of improvement, however modest. If the crash was late in arrival, it compensated for this in the speed with which it occurred. In a matter of a few days, trillions of dollars of investment value was lost as securities prices around the globe experienced something akin to free-fall.

Large computer-driven 'sell' programs no doubt contributed to the early stages of the fall but later the financial panic began to acquire a life of its own. Each market appeared to take its cue from every other market, seemingly oblivious to the fundamental strengths of different regional and national economies. No doubt the globalisation of the securities market supported by the technological revolution in worldwide communications, helped to spread the panic. However, globalisation and technology were not themselves to blame. Herd mentality, immaturity, fear and frenzy are all very human qualities. What made this crash different was that the process of globalisation had cleared away many of the earlier barriers between markets which might have helped contain, or at least slow down, the panic.

1988-1989

The crash of 1987 was relatively short-lived. Within months equity markets recovered their footing and were poised to make up lost ground. Naturally, memories lingered about the aftermath of the earlier Great Crash of 1929. However, what made that crash so horrid was the ensuing decade of the Depression. Was the Depression a necessary consequence of the 1929 Crash? Probably not. Following the earlier crash, authorities tightened money supply. The theory was that the 1929 Crash had been caused by financial excess (a correct diagnosis) and the damage would only be put right by constricting credit expansion (the wrong cure). Indeed, this cure turned out to be worse than the disease itself. The 1929 Crash was essentially deflationary: the dramatic fall in stockmarket values had a knock-on effect throughout the economy. Prices of all assets were affected. When the government decided to tighten further still by restricting the money supply, that converted an economic cold into double pneumonia.

Nearly 60 years later, government authorities had a better grasp of economic theory. They were absolutely determined not to make the same mistake twice. The solution was simple – reflate. If anything the authorities went overboard in loosening money control. Soon credit expansion, fuelled in part by consumer credit card purchases (increasingly a feature of everyday life in countries like the United Kingdom), began an amazing upward spiral. The resurgence of asset values took many people by surprise, but in a short time, inflationary exceptions had a firm grip on society. Rises in the values of real assets, like houses, created the illusion of wealth and encouraged home-owners to spend more on other asset purchases. Pre-emptive buying also went on. In the UK, for instance, there was the widely-accepted concept of the 'housing ladder'. The rungs of this ladder represented different house sizes, which increased as one ascended the ladder. In theory, the different groups of houses all appreciated at approximately the same rate. Hence, it became necessary to join the ladder, say, by acquiring a 'starter' home, at an early stage to preserve the option of trading up later on. Missing the first rung meant possibly losing out on home ownership altogether. In any event, a fair amount of assets were purchased simply because people were afraid of being left behind. Psychology such as this led to one inevitable consequence: inflation.

In the bond markets, the low interest rates which resulted from government-sponsored monetary loosening, sparked a boom across a broad front. Indeed, it should be borne in mind that the crash of 1987 did not really hurt the bond market that much. Total international bond volume slumped by 11.6% compared with the preceding year, but there was good news as well. After the crash, a total of 19 jumbo bonds were floated and faired reasonably well. A ¥300 billion ($ 2.1 billion) issue for the Republic of Italy was floated on October 26, 1987 and soon sold out. Naturally, there was a flight to quality in the aftermath of the crash but this meant that sovereign issues enjoyed a reasonable boost.

As equity markets recovered, the warrant market reopened. Issues by Japanese corporate borrowers were especially sought after. By the end of 1988 there were some $18 billion of such issues outstanding. Emerging markets also showed signs of new life as commercial banks experimented with debt for equity swaps and other institutional investors increased their exposure to these countries due to the abundant returns available. By the end of 1988, total international bonds exceeded the $227 billion level, just above the previous record-breaking year of 1986. Significant gains were scored in Euro-dollars and Euro-DM bonds which advanced over 1987 by 20% and 51.8% respectively. Swiss franc foreign bonds also recorded a respectable showing with a year-on-year gain of 11.8%. 1989 showed a continuation of this upward trend by the markets with total international bonds advancing 17.4% in volume terms to set a further underwriting record of $267 billion. The star performer during 1989 was the Euro-dollar sector which accounted for 53.6% of all Eurobonds (up from 42% in 1988). A total of over $125 billion of new financings were organised in this currency sector alone.

Economic overheating and inflationary pressure characterised the end of the 1980s. Governmental authorities were left with little alternative but to apply the brakes again. Interest rates were hiked and kept high (at the 15% level for three years in the UK) until even the most conservative central banker conceded that inflation had been dampened.

1990-1993

Authorities though that economic collapse had been avoided following the 1987 stockmarket crash. Actually, it was merely deferred. The early 1990s represented one of the worst periods of financial decline in living memory. There may not have been soup kitchens like the 1930s but unemployment rates soared into double digits. The long-term unemployed became so discouraged that many simply gave up looking for jobs. New expressions were added to the everyday lexicon. Negative equity (the surplus of mortgage debt above the deflated value of homes) was soon part of the vernacular.

Once interest rates subsided, however, the equity and bond markets started to boom. This occurred precisely when the early 1990s were beginning to look more like a depression than a recession. It is said that Main Street distrusts Wall Street. Perhaps, Main Street could have been forgiven on this occasion for having such doubts. Stock exchange profits and huge personal bonuses paid to market professionals, simply looked bad when millions were out of work and feared the loss of their homes.

Following a slowdown in issuing activity for international bonds in 1990, a rapid rebound occurred in the period 1991-1993. By the end of this period new issues totalled an amazing $489 billion, a full 83.4% ahead of 1989's record underwriting. Compared with 1989, the Eurodollar sector showed respectable strength gaining 24.7% in volume terms. The real winners, though, were the so-called strong currency sectors. Swiss franc foreign bonds jumped by 63.6% and yen Eurobonds leapt by 125.7% over this same period. DM Eurobonds scored an absolutely staggering gain of 332.7% in issuing volume. As will be discussed later, this particular sector acted as a safe harbour when other European currencies experienced turbulence on foreign exchange markets.

The beginning of this eventful period was focused not on Europe, but thousands of miles away in the US where changes were to occur which would reshape the international markets for years to come. 1990 marked the historic enactment of two new US securities regulations: the so-called Reg. S and Rule 144A. Both sets of regulations will be discussed in detail in Chapter Three of this book. It is sufficient now to point out that the new rules greatly eased the marketing of US securities in the Euromarkets (Reg. S) and increased the accessibility of the domestic US capital markets for foreign issuers (Rule 144A). The two new regulations were complementary in their impact and taken together, were instrumental in bridging the gap between the Euromarkets and the US domestic market. The impact has been enormous. For example, US issuing practices like spread pricing (fixing new issue terms on the basis of yield spread over the identical maturity US Treasury bond), have become the norm of the Euromarkets. Maturities have also lengthened out in harmony with the very long-dated (out to 100 years) securities which can be floated in the US. This sea change also extended to the various currency sectors of the international market. Consequently, today domestic French franc issues are issued in a manner similar to Eurobonds, which themselves increasingly resemble US domestic issues.

Though sweeping, such changes must be viewed as inevitable. The US dollar is, after all, the major monetary unit of exchange in the world. Likewise, the US capital market is not only huge (benefiting particularly from ample institutional liquidity) but highly sophisticated as well. What is curious is that market integration had not happened earlier. However, what had held the US separate before was a raft of laws and regulations which may have provided jobs for lawyers but was also effective in discouraging many foreign borrowers unfamiliar with such disciplines. Reg. S and

Rule 144A helped enormously in removing the barriers to entry. They assisted in clarifying ways in which securities could be distributed without running foul of the US's tough securities laws. As a result, there is now a much steadier stream of issuers making their way across the Atlantic in both directions. This fundamental shift will continue to re-shape the Euro-markets.

What matters over the long term is the impact of changes like Reg. S and Rule 144A. Markets, however, are more short-sighted. They have no alternative. New issues are either floated or not due to then prevailing investor sentiment. As it happened, by 1991 the earlier monetary tightening had achieved its objective of cooling the economy and interest rates began to tumble. Renewed optimism in the markets led to sharp rallies. Eurobonds had a record year with some $277 billion floated. Convertible bonds were also boosted by recovering stock exchanges.

The year itself began in a threatening manner. War seemed inevitable. Following Saddam Hussein's invasion of Kuwait on August 2, 1990, several initiatives had been made to find a peaceful solution to the debacle. None proved successful. Gathering allied military might around Kuwait also failed to deter the invaders. When Desert Storm (the Gulf War) started in February 1991, there was a sense that a definitive resolution needed to be achieved, at least with respect to the sovereignty of Kuwait. That objective was achieved but only at the cost of many lost lives, particularly among the one-time conquering Iraqis.

The outcome of wars is never certain. The Gulf War was no exception. Financial markets understandably held their breath as the conflict was resolved, in a mercifully short time. Still, during this period of uncertainty, bond houses began to take a close look at the wording of their own underwriting agreements. What was of particular concern was a specific clause: force majeure (literally acts of God). This clause supposedly gave new issue managers the right to suspend an offering in the event of major disruptions in the markets caused by external circumstances. There was debate, though, about what this actually meant. To begin, there is no concept of force majeure in English law (under which most bonds are floated). Also there was the need to balance the legitimate interests of the issuer with those of the financial institutions contracted to raise money – the managers. The crisis in the Gulf sparked hot debate among market professionals. IPMA helped as a focal point, co-ordinating much of the discussions and mediating a solution. As a consequence, today there are two specifically worded force majeure clauses approved by IPMA. It is a requirement that every new issue invitation telex specifies which version is to be employed.

The collapse of BCCI and a coup (ultimately unsuccessful) in Russia in August 1991 also served to unsettle the markets. However, 1991 will be remembered as a year of surprising optimism. This sanguine attitude was fostered by the Maastricht Treaty which, at least at the outset, promised a new era of currency stability within the Exchange Rate Mechanism (ERM) leading to a single European currency in 1999. Sterling had joined the ERM in October 1990. So, despite the UK's opt-out clause regarding the single currency, there was a new found sense of confidence. This in turn inspired a re-opening of the Ecu sector which proved to be a star performance during 1991. New issue activity surged from $17 billion in 1990 to exceed $30 billion in 1991. With successes like this, talk soon spread not only of a single currency but also of a single market for capital.

Meaningful developments took place in other areas of the market. For example, the Deutschmark sector warmed to the idea of structured securities. Issues of so-called inverse floaters and bonds with embedded options linked to equity indices, were welcomed by the investment community. Asset securitisation also took a firm hold.

The first UK transaction securitising car leases (Cars I) had been concluded in July 1990. Soon other categories of assets like home loans and credit card receivables were assembled as collateral to back new path finding securities offerings.

The optimism of 1991 spilled over into 1992, at least for the first few months. The seeming promise of stability and prosperity under the aegis of the EMU beguiled the markets. By early June, however, people were jolted out of their reverie. This rude awakening took the form of the Danish vote rejecting Maastricht. Other fault lines also showed up between economies which supposedly were on the path towards convergence. The high cost of integrating East Germany into West Germany produced huge capital requirements and DM interest rates were kept high to attract the necessary funding. Unfortunately, other currencies were also linked to the Deutschmark through the ERM. Hence, interest rates across Europe had to be maintained artificially high simply to keep up with the mighty German currency. Something was bound to give. Economies just emerging from a terrible recession had no need for tight monetary policy as embodied in high interest rates. For some economies there really was not much of a choice. The crunch came on September 16, 1992, Black Wednesday.

In the beginning it had all seemed so wonderful. By Black Wednesday, the real truth had hit the streets. Forced convergence had claimed it first victims: both the UK pound sterling and the Italian lira dropped out of the ERM and the Spanish peseta devalued by 6%. Not surprisingly, the Ecu bond sector saw a blood bath. Prices plummeted. At the beginning of 1992 there were 42 reported market-makers in this sector, but by the end of the year, this number had fallen to only 10. Subsequently, Ecu issues struggled to compete in an incredulous marketplace.

Not all currency sectors suffered during 1992. Paradoxically, DM bonds found new favour with investors looking for safety from the turbulence elsewhere. French franc bonds also proved their sophistication by adapting highly structured techniques and offering long maturities. Floating rate notes also revived. After the debacle created in 1986-1987 by perpetual FRNs, some commentators virtually wrote off this sector. But, in 1992 the rebound occurred in the form of new issues totalling some $48.0 billion (up from a total of $17.5 billion in 1991).

During 1993, the ERM suffered another humiliation as currency trading bands were widened to 15%, to provide extra room for volatility which was supposedly a thing of the past. Ironically, those currencies which had exited the ERM seemed to thrive. In the UK, departure from the ERM allowed interest rates to come down. The economy benefited from export-led growth and certain politicians began to refer to it as White, not Black Wednesday. By September 1993, Italy managed to float an amazing $5.5 billion global bond divided in two tranches of 10 and 30-year securities. This government had never before been able to launch a 30-year bond, even in its own domestic capital market.

Around the world a general consensus emerged that inflation had been beaten for the time being and that a number of factors, such as residual high unemployment, would help block its return. Interest rates continued to trend downwards. Domestic capital markets were also incentivised to reform themselves. The deep recession of the early 1990s had produced staggering national deficits, which all required financing. Hence, there was an impetus to liberalise capital market access to attract investors who would fund the record amount of government IOUs. Gone were controls on capital movement and withholding taxes were either reduced or abolished altogether. Significantly, in Japan the distinction between Euro-yen and Samurai bonds was eroded.

Understandably, the markets had a sensational bull run. Everything boomed. Issuing volume of new Eurobonds reached $447 billion, up nearly 47% on the 1992 record amount of $304 billion. The bonuses of many market professionals reached levels unthinkable in earlier periods. Everything was bigger and better. Globals and jumbo deals crowded the new issue calendar. Hundred-year bonds were floated in the US and the Eurobond market similarly extended its outreach to 30 years.

Floating rate notes continued their renaissance. Of course, with lower short-term interest rates, something had to be done to provide a yield enhancement. Enter the so-called collared FRN. This instrument featured both an imbedded cap and a floor and boosted interest return to the investor. Another derivative-based product was the Step-Up Recovery Floater (SURF) with its coupons linked to the 10-year constant maturity US Treasury index. Little wonder with this level of innovation that FRNs leapt 50% in issuing volume over the previous year and registered some $72.3 billion of new offerings.

Bonds in the Asian markets flourished. The Deutschmark sector drew strength from de-regulatory moves and declining interest rates. Only the strong showing of Russian nationalist Vladimir Zhirinovsky at the end of the year, gave the markets cause for pause.

1994-1995

The euphoria of 1993 lasted less than two months into the new year. In February 1994, the US Federal Reserve raised interest rates by 25 basis points (¼%). The modest scale of this increase totally belied the market's response. There were shock waves throughout the global financial community. It was felt that the four-year bond rally had now ended. New bond issue activity dried up, and this hiatus lasted through to May. Substantial losses were experienced by bond houses as the value of their securities inventories plummeted. Highly geared institutions and hedge funds dumped bonds to meet margin calls. Both repo (ie repurchase agreements) and derivative positions were unwound, nearly all at a significant loss.

As a consequence of this trauma, the market re-evaluated its views on risk. Significant dis-investments occurred away from derivative linked products. Later that year, it emerged that Orange County had lost some $2 billion in its derivative-based investment fund. In the Euromarkets collared FRNs fell in price and the innovative SURF FRNs slipped to below 90% of their initial purchase price (assuming that there was a market maker who would bid for these securities). Money was also withdrawn from high yielding currencies and emerging markets. The pinch was soon felt. In December 1994, the Mexican peso was devalued. This financial crisis had been exacerbated by the revival of the Chiapas revolt which had first begun at the start of the year.

There was a further flight to quality in the markets. US agency issuers responded to this trend by increasing their placing activity in the Euromarket. Plain vanilla-type products also faired well. For example, standard (non-structured) FRNs had a banner year with total new issue volume rising 41.4% over 1993 to reach a level of some $102.3 billion. The appeal of these FRNs was that they answered investors' concerns about the future course of interest rates. If rates rose, so did the return offered by the FRNs. Other market sectors also did well. The most shining example was the sector for yen-denominated Eurobonds. Here, substantial liquidity had built up as Japanese investors returned to their domestic currency following sometimes costly experiences with other investments, notably the US dollar. Targeted issues to Japan grew in popularity. Over the year, this sub-sector doubled in size.

Despite the bursting of the global financial bubble, the markets still did a creditable job. Issuing volume of international bonds was some $496 billion 1.4% ahead of the boom year 1993. There were changes, too, in market practices as cost saving initiatives boosted the use of MTN programmes as launch pads for new bond issues. During the year, nearly 40% of new issues were initiated from such programmes. Market participants, too, decided to make a change. Pressure grew for institutions to globalise, and a merger was proposed between Morgan Stanley and Warburg. This engagement was finally broken off but the move towards finding marriage partners throughout the markets was only just beginning.

The venerable Barings Bank virtually collapsed in February 1995 as a consequence of uncontrolled derivative trading by Nick Leeson in Singapore. A hitherto low-profile Dutch financial group, ING, was prepared to stump up for the then unquantified losses and acquired the blue-blooded Barings for only a nominal consideration. Subsequently, other British merchant banks found new owners. For instance, Kleinwort Benson was sold to Dresdner Bank and Warburgs finally found a home with Swiss Bank Corporation. Smith New Court was also merged into Merrill Lynch, as the process of consolidation in the securities industry gathered momentum.

The markets began 1995 on a sour note. Not only were the difficulties of 1994 still fresh in people's minds, but there were also the spill-over problems of Mexico which soon seemed to engulf all of Latin America and much of the developing world. Indeed, the year will be remembered for its accident-prone nature. First there was the earthquake in Kobe which cast doubts on economic conditions in Japan. Then there were the often-repeated sceptical remarks about monetary union in Europe. A $1 billion trading loss was discovered belatedly in Daiwa Bank in New York during the summer. And by autumn, there was even talk of a possible default by the United States government itself as a Republican Congress clashed with Democratic President Clinton on a succession of budget issues.

Markets, though, are cyclical and if things go bad for a while, they usually correct themselves and improve. Mexico, for one, returned to the markets only seven months after its peso debacle. A number of other emerging markets rebounded. US agencies managed to float some $13 billion of their own securities in the Euro-markets.

Institutional investors may have remained somewhat timid. However, investment interest from retail customers, chiefly out of the Swiss private banking network, compensated for much of the lost demand. With this revised customer profile came a new appetite for corporate debt investment. Hence, new issue calendars were adjusted to suit this appetite. General Electric Credit Corporation (GECC) completed no less than 69 issues during the year for a total of $9.4 billion. Certain of these issues were priced to yield less than comparable maturity US Treasuries and as a bull market developed in the fourth quarter, ended up a full 35 basis points below Treasuries. The rally in fixed rate securities dampened demand for floating rate notes. However, the Euro-yen sector was especially strong, advancing 13.4% during the year. Both retail and institutional buyers sought out foreign issuers in order to gain yield enhancement. The Japanese finance ministry encouraged greater access to its domestic markets by removing the few remaining distinctions between Euro-yen and the foreign bonds (called Samurais). Investment interest originally from the Asia was sufficiently strong to bolster other currency sectors. Deutschmark Eurobonds benefited and consequently increased issuing volume from $60 billion in 1994 to $99 billion in 1995. For the year overall, the international bond market was ahead by 2.7%. More significantly, underwriting volume broke the half trillion mark and aggregated a full US$509 billion.

A new realism emerged in the primary market for securities. After the losses of

1994, bond houses were particularly mindful of their bottom lines. Consequently, 1995 saw a serious attempt to curb the overcompetitive excesses of the market. There was, for instance, a return to negotiated deals where the issue price was set in consultation with the issuer instead of being submitted to auction-like bidding. Negotiated deals had been the norm in the Euro-markets until this practice was overtaken by the bought deal approach. Other techniques were also tested during the year. One of these was called 'price discovery' and involved the sampling of investor interest at varying yield returns. An indication of pricing was only publicly announced once the lead manager had received expression of strong investment interest at a specific pricing level. There were examples too of issuers who rejected pricing proposals if their terms appeared so aggressive as to discourage end investors.

1996

Compared to the cautious approach of 1995, the following year 1996 saw a return to boom times in the market. Relatively stable and low short-term interest rates helped to unleash a flood of new bond issues. The Eurobond market hosted flotations which exceeded $584 billion in principal amount, representing a mammoth 34.4% increase over the preceding year. The main contributor to this surge in activity was the US dollar sector which accounted for 47.3% of all Eurobonds. During 1995, dollar bonds had represented only 29.6% of Euromarket underwriting volume. The dollar sector powered ahead in 1996 partly because of the strong performance of so-called global bonds. These flotations, nearly all dollar-denominated, accounted for nearly 20% of all new issues activity during 1996.

The foreign bond market also saw an increase in issuing amounts from $74 billion in 1995 to $92 billion in 1996, an advance of 24.3%. Relatively speaking, however, the foreign bond market tended to underperform the Eurobond sector, which itself comprised 86.4% of the overall international market. This was probably a reflection of the progressive merging of the one-time foreign bonds into the Eurobond arena. One of the strongest performing foreign bond sectors was that for DM placements. However, DM Eurobonds actually experienced a decrease in issuing activity. Hence, it may be possible to conclude that there was a counter cyclical shift amongst DM borrowers away from Eurobonds toward the calmer waters of the foreign bond market. It is fair, however, to note that other 'strong currency' sectors also performed in a lacklustre manner. For instance, in 1996 Sfr. bonds sank in issuing volume to $26.4 billion (equivalent) and represented only 3.9% of the international market. Yen-denominated bonds also lost market share, declining from 14.4% of all new issues in 1995 to 8.2% in 1996.

1996 will also be remembered as the year of close-calls and the survival of incumbents. By mid-year uncertainty ran high prior to the Russian election. Markets feared that a major shift in political focus would prejudice the gains made in liberalising the Russian economy and would sow the seeds of political upheaval in other neighbouring parts of the world. The ongoing war in Chechnya did not tend to inspire confidence. By the time the votes were counted, however, it became evident that Boris Yeltsin had retained his presidency. Despite Yeltsin's subsequent need for a serious operation, it was clear that business would continue as usual. Over in the US, the status quo was also being upheld. The Republican 'Revolution' of two years prior failed to unseat the incumbent President Clinton. However, for good measure, the American electorate retained Republican majorities in both houses of Congress. Clearly, few people were in the mood for much change.

Steady-as-she-goes seemed to suit the markets as well. Stock exchanges around the world were a particular beneficiary, as most major markets (except Tokyo) exceeded all-time highs. Equity-linked bonds surged and recorded total issuing volume in excess of $28 billion, over twice that recorded during the previous year. Convertible bonds were an especially hot commodity in 1996, gaining nearly 150% over 1995. Straight bonds also surged ahead. Paradoxically, FRNs leapt in performance as well. During 1996, FRN issues (for both public and private sector issuers) recorded a total underwriting volume of $160 billion, over two-thirds ahead of the previous year. The attractions of the FRN structure appeared particularly remarkable given the low absolute level of international interest rates.

Future outlook

Looking forward, it may be that the enthusiastic FRN investors in 1996 had a premonition that short-term interest rates could not stay at their then current low levels forever. The early to mid-1990s were, of course, blessed with low interest rates. Some market participants came to feel that such levels could be sustained. Certainly the booming stockmarket performance, say in the United States, seemed to suggest that inflation had been beaten for all time. There were other observers who had seen one or two market cycles during their careers and remained to be convinced that governments had totally overcome the temptation to print money. In their view, stock exchanges could not go on breaking one record after another. Surely, that would violate the Newtonian equivalent of market dynamics. One could only hope that when the inevitable correction occurs, people will react to it with greater maturity than, say, in October 1987.

Another great question mark is the issue of monetary union in Europe which is scheduled to start in 1999. There are major uncertainties ahead, such as which currencies will join EMU and when. Indeed, there are still lingering doubts as to whether the scheme can be launched on the current schedule. Certainly, there is significant political pressure pushing Europe towards the 1999 starting line. However, weak economic performance in those countries which are key proponents of the single European currency, does introduce a degree of uncertainty – both with respect to the timing and the ultimate strength of the euro once it is launched.

The markets have been and will continue to be profoundly influenced by the introduction of a single currency in Europe. Already long-term interest rates have begun to converge in different European currency sectors. The market, therefore, seems to be betting on a smooth transition. What would happen, however, if certain countries were left behind due to their inability to meet the Maastricht convergence criteria? What would happen to the euro itself if political will overcame economic common sense and the Maastricht criteria were relaxed or disregarded? How keen would holders of solid DM-denominated bonds be to see them converted into relatively weak euro-denominated securities? When the conversion takes place, what will be the exchange ratio? What will happen to swaps involving currencies which are going to disappear? Might disadvantaged counterparties be tempted to question the validity of their transactions?

Questions such as the above have the nasty habit of unsettling normal investment behaviour. Together with the economic uncertainty, there could be political uncertainty as well. This might occur if retaliatory steps were taken against those countries which wilfully remained outside the common currency. It would not take much in the way of capital flow or regulatory directives to begin to undermine the position of London as the centre of the international market. Perhaps such uncertainties will give a further boost to non-European markets, particularly the US domestic market. Tokyo and the upcoming emerging markets could also be other beneficiaries. In any event, the coming two to three years will be anything but dull. There will be much to analyse and discuss, as well as (hopefully) to make money on.

Appendix A
International bond issues 1963-96 ($ million equivalent)

Eurobond market	1963	1964	1965	1966	1967	1968	1969	1970	1971
US dollars	90.5	565.5	607.5	858.5	1,577.3	2,251.0	1,649.5	1,703.0	1,898.0
Deutschmarks	–	91.3	105.0	391.3	145.0	726.3	1,133.3	569.2	827.2
Dutch guilders	–	–	7.0	–	–	–	33.2	385.7	269.3
Other European currencies	14.0	–	25.6	–	12.2	22.3	–	–	6.7
Canadian dollars	–	–	–	–	–	–	–	–	–
Composite and dual currencies	43.0	24.0	64.4	93.6	39.2	85.8	60.0	104.0	287.5
Middle East currencies	–	–	–	–	–	–	–	–	–
Far East currencies	–	–	–	–	–	–	–	–	–
Total Eurobonds	147.5	680.8	809.5	1,343.4	1,773.7	3,085.4	2,876.0	2,761.9	3,288.7

Foreign bonds	1963	1964	1965	1966	1967	1968	1969	1970	1971
Yankee bonds	1,374.0	1,149.0	1,317.0	1,312.0	1,719.0	1,803.0	1,767.0	1,216.0	1,104.0
Swiss francs	164.4	94.5	87.6	121.0	173.4	356.8	305.2	312.5	867.1
Deutschmarks	40.0	58.0	123.0	–	10.0	674.0	531.0	89.0	308.0
Yen	–	–	–	–	–	–	–	15.0	92.0
Luxembourg francs	–	3.0	0.6	–	–	–	–	–	16.5
Dutch guilders	3.3	26.3	18.0	–	13.8	30.3	–	17.0	17.0
Others	202.7	91.7	156.4	284.0	226.2	192.7	100.0	64.0	435.5
Total foreign bonds	1,784.4	1,422.5	1,702.6	1,726.0	2,142.4	3,056.8	2,703.2	1,713.5	2,840.1
Total international bonds	1,931.9	2,103.3	2,512.1	3,069.4	3,916.1	6,142.2	5,579.2	4,475.4	6,128.8

Appendix A *continued*

Eurobond market	1972	1973	1974	1975	1976	1977	1978	1979	1980
US dollars	3,153.0	1,910.0	1,036.0	3,365.5	8,652.6	10,215.0	5,538.5	11,607.9	12,757.9
Deutschmarks	1,167.1	902.4	213.7	1,723.1	2,018.7	3,833.4	4,922.1	2,597.7	3,069.5
Dutch guilders	392.9	198.6	342.4	500.5	418.3	402.6	384.5	338.0	497.4
Other European currencies	629.5	256.1	13.1	350.3	38.0	216.0	421.7	632.3	1,878.6
Canadian dollars	–	–	58.0	575.0	1,387.0	641.0	–	424.2	279.6
Composite and dual currencies	165.7	189.7	222.2	585.8	102.2	33.0	198.7	371.0	96.3
Middle East currencies	–	252.0	51.3	181.4	288.5	137.0	464.3	372.8	26.5
Far East currencies	–	–	–	–	18.7	263.7	79.4	133.0	306.1
Total Eurobonds	5,508.2	3,708.8	1,936.7	7,281.6	12,915.0	15,741.7	12,009.2	16,476.9	18,911.9

Foreign bonds	1972	1973	1974	1975	1976	1977	1978	1979	1980
Yankee bonds	1,353.0	1,019.0	3,291.0	6,462.0	10,604.0	7,428.0	5,795.0	4,515.0	3,429.0
Swiss francs	1,014.5	1,535.3	972.4	3,529.0	5,443.6	4,959.3	7,608.8	9,479.5	7,454.7
Deutschmarks	500.0	362.0	253.0	1,089.0	1,288.0	2,181.0	3,789.0	5,379.0	4,839.0
Yen	311.0	271.0	–	67.0	226.0	1,271.0	3,826.0	1,833.0	1,088.0
Luxembourg francs	60.2	39.9	26.3	45.7	37.3	80.3	206.8	208.3	198.3
Dutch guilders	31.0	–	4.0	182.0	597.0	211.0	385.0	75.0	259.0
Others	342.8	427.1	237.7	202.3	78.7	63.7	464.2	476.7	519.7
Total foreign bonds	3,612.5	3,654.3	4,784.4	11,577.0	18,274.6	16,194.3	22,074.9	21,966.5	17,787.7
Total international bonds	9,120.7	7,363.1	6,721.1	18,858.6	31,189.6	31,936.0	34,084.1	38,443.4	36,699.6

Appendix A continued

Eurobond market	1981	1982	1983	1984	1985	1986	1987
US dollars	21,154.8	39,644.6	35,685.4	62,003.7	94,044.1	113,948.5	67,818.2
Deutschmarks	1,227.4	4,498.0	5,625.4	6,060.4	11,195.0	16,686.9	15,988.2
Dutch guilders	507.0	591.1	632.6	658.7	603.1	2,684.6	2,901.9
Other European currencies	1,095.8	829.5	2,128.7	4,430.5	7,644.1	15,707.0	48,912.0
Canadian dollars	690.0	1,239.0	1,177.4	1,983.7	2,870.6	5,175.9	6,750.4
Composite and dual currencies	663.1	788.7	1,795.6	2,742.8	6,799.0	6,698.5	–
Middle East & African currencies	115.9	158.7	–	–	26.1	7.0	–
Far East & Australasian currencies	299.0	466.5	527.8	1,556.3	11,311.0	21,407.9	22,345.3
Total Eurobonds	25,752.9	48,216.1	47,572.9	79,436.0	134,493.1	182,316.3	164,716.0

Foreign bonds	1981	1982	1983	1984	1985	1986	1987
Yankee bonds	7,552.0	5,946.0	4,545.0	5,487.0	4,655.0	6,064.0	2,277.9
Swiss francs	8,709.8	11,611.7	12,952.3	11,493.2	16,646.7	25,715.0	24,207.0
Deutschmarks*	755.8	824.5	998.9	1,052.6	1,942.6	1,958.0	58.3
Yen	2,457.0	3,418.0	3,624.0	3,710.0	5,791.0	4,158.8	0.1
Luxembourg francs	133.1	127.8	101.5	138.4	313.5	602.6	1,360.1
Dutch guilders	479.9	868.6	849.2	1,058.4	1,150.0	1,894.3	25.2
Others	4,931.8	7,008.5	4,457.7	3,629.4	2,636.5	3,540.5	7,388.0
Total foreign bonds	25,019.4	29,805.1	27,528.7	26,569.0	33,135.4	43,933.3	35,316.6
Total international bonds	50,772.3	78,021.2	75,101.6	106,005.1	167,628.5	226,249.5	200,032.6

Appendix A *continued*

Eurobond market	1988	1989	1990	1991	1992
US dollars	81,355.3	125,837.4	69,806.6	85,831.5	109,592.3
Deutschmarks	24,270.6	17,416.4	19,648.6	27,374.7	45,927.9
Dutch guilders	3,649.1	4,427.7	2,074.5	4,346.3	7,677.8
European & other currencies	54,323.4	55,730.5	71,031.1	104,764.8	97,189.5
Canadian dollars	13,214.8	12,970.2	5,298.3	18,264.8	12,428.5
Japanese yen	16,826.3	18,340.0	24,284.5	36,072.6	31,218.3
Total Eurobonds	193,639.5	234,722.2	192,143.5	276,654.7	304,034.3

Foreign bonds	1988	1989	1990	1991	1992
Yankee bonds	1,012.7	2,520.3	1,064.3	1,657.7	2,311.9
Swiss francs	27,060.1	21,313.3	25,158.2	21,338.4	20,510.4
Deutschmarks*	96.8	425.6	1,254.8	58.8	–
Yen	–	–	27.9	–	–
Luxembourg francs	1,556.6	1,644.5	3,545.0	3,114.6	1,302.1
Dutch guilders	223.6	–	–	–	–
Others	3,669.8	6,074.8	5,333.7	4,987.5	3,722.5
Total foreign bonds	33,619.6	31,978.5	36,383.9	31,157.0	27,846.9
Total international bonds	227,259.1	266,700.7	228,527.5	307,811.7	331,881.2

Appendix A continued

Eurobond market	1993	1994	1995	1996	Total 1963–1996
US dollars	156,854.2	159,211.6	128,760.5	276,416.3	1,697,402.3
Deutschmarks	75,363.6	60,377.2	98,982.9	77,301.7	532,381.3
Dutch guilders	13,710.8	16,416.2	19,062.8	21,391.2	105,505.8
European & other currencies	136,629.6	137,868.9	111,159.4	147,824.7	1,026,131.0
Canadian dollars	22,850.1	10,490.2	3,816.7	6,289.1	128,865.5
Japanese yen	41,398.1	64,492.8	73,147.5	55,436.7	419,931.4
Total Eurobonds	446,806.4	448,856.9	434,929.8	584,659.7	3,910,217.3

Foreign bonds	1993	1994	1995	1996	Total 1963–1996
Yankee bonds	1,070.5	2,031.3	2,208.4	1,493.0	108,552.0
Swiss francs	34,866.4	29,213.9	34,508.5	26,456.7	396,241.4
Deutschmarks*	–	8,266.7	18,458.8	33,522.8	91,188.0
Yen	–	–	95.7	228.4	32,511.0
Luxembourg francs	250.8	155.4	–	–	15,269.1
Dutch guilders	–	39.4	–	118.2	8,576.7
Others	6,182.0	7,195.8	19,078.4	30,226.9	124,630.0
Total foreign bonds	42,369.7	46,902.5	74,349.8	92,046.0	776,968.2
Total international bonds	489,176.1	495,759.4	509,279.6	676,705.7	4,687,185.5

* DM foreign bonds are not strictly distinct from DM Eurobonds, though there are some foreign bond issues for specified borrowers. These figures are consequently not reliable and, in other sources, the issues concerned will often be listed under the Euro DM cateogory.

From 1987, the category European and other currencies includes composite and dual currencies, Middle East currencies and Far East currencies, with the exception of the Japanes yen.

Sources: Capital Data, World financial markets – JP Morgan, Banque Internationale a Luxembourg, Nomura International, Deutsche Bank, Amrobank, OECD and Datastream.

N.B. Statistical sources not always consistent.

Appendix B

The chart and annual commentary that follow, highlight the growth in the international bond market between 1963 and 1996.

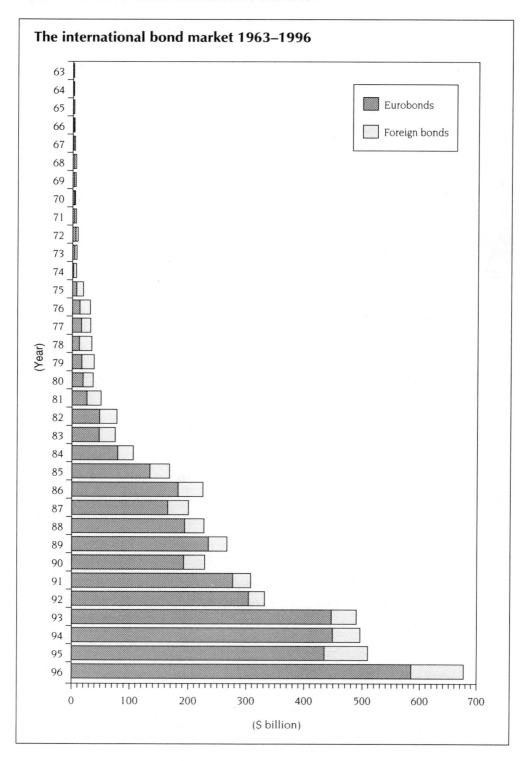

Annual commentary

Year	Commentary	Eurobonds ($ billion)	Foreign bonds ($ billion)
1963	First Eurodollar issue for Autostrade.	0.15	1.78
1964	First DM Eurobond.	0.68	1.42
1965	First Dfl Eurobond, Voluntary Restraint Program.	0.81	1.70
1966	Bond market conditions robust.	1.34	1.73
1967	First Ffr Eurobond, sterling devalues.	1.77	2.14
1968	First Sfr issues, Euroclear founded.	3.09	3.06
1969	ISMA founded.	2.88	2.70
1970	First Samurai issue, first FRN.	2.76	1.71
1971	Cedel Bank founded, Smithsonian Agreement.	3.29	2.84
1972	First Euro-sterling issue.	5.51	3.61
1973	Yom Kippur War, oil begins four fold increase, dollar devalues.	3.71	3.65
1974	IET repealed.	1.94	4.78
1975	First SDR Eurobond.	7.28	11.58
1976	Low interest rates boost bond issuance.	12.91	18.27
1977	First yen Eurobond.	15.74	16.19
1978	Rapid dollar depreciation fosters strong currency sectors.	12.01	22.07
1979	Beginning of EMS, first Volker package.	16.48	21.97
1980	Afghanistan crisis, gold at $850/oz, second Volker package.	18.91	17.79
1981	First zero coupon bond, interest rate swaps popularised.	25.75	25.02
1982	Third World Debt Crisis begins.	48.22	29.81
1983	Boom year for FRNs and partly-paid bonds.	47.57	27.53
1984	US withholding tax removed, markets start globalisation, IPMA founded.	79.44	26.57
1985	Non-dollar markets join in move towards de-regulation.	134.49	33.14
1986	Strong currency sectors boom, perpetual FRNs boom then bust.	182.32	43.93
1987	October stock exchange crash.	164.72	35.32
1988	Markets rebound with loosened credit.	193.64	33.62
1989	Inflationary pressures peak, Berlin Wall tumbles.	234.72	31.98
1990	Interest rates hiked, Kuwait invaded, Reg S and Rule 144A introduced.	192.14	36.38
1991	Gulf War, interest rates abate.	276.65	31.16
1992	Low interest rates lead to record US mortgage re-financing.	304.08	27.85
1993	Emerging markets become new focus of attention.	446.81	42.37
1994	February's increase in interest rates puts markets into reverse.	448.86	46.90
1995	Barings Bank rescued, flight to quality in new issues.	434.93	74.35
1996	Markets recover during period of political and interest rate stability.	584.66	92.05

2

ISSUERS AND INVESTORS

Over the period 1963-96, approximately $4,687 billion (equivalent) has been raised by borrowers in the international bond market. Of this amount, the Eurobond sector alone accounted for more than $3,900 billion. Who borrowed this money and how were they affected by the events which helped to shape the market?

The type of issuers

A variety of issuers use the international and Eurobond markets. Historically, one of the largest issuing groups has been *sovereign entities*. These are chiefly governments borrowing under their own name (ie Kingdom, Republic, Commonwealth or Government), or through their respective ministry of finance, treasury or central bank. In countries such as the UK and France, state-owned or controlled bodies do their own bond issues. Because these bodies are not agencies of their governments, ie not actually part of the government, they frequently carry the guarantee of the sovereign state. This enhances their credit standing. From time to time, wholly-owned state entities issue bonds without an explicit sovereign guarantee. In many such cases, credit support is provided by the issuer's statutes where, for example, the government may be obligated to make good a cash deficiency. Some state-owned bodies are sufficiently creditworthy on their own to issue bonds without the direct support of the sovereign state behind them. Another type of sovereign borrower is the municipal/regional government or authority and its agencies. Here, the power to raise taxes at either the municipal or regional level contributes to the credit standing of the borrower. Certain agencies of these issuers have also used the international bond market. Such agencies include some of the largest utilities in the world, such as Hydro Quebec, and typically borrow with the explicit guarantee of the authority concerned; these issues are usually regarded as being of only slightly lower credit standing than the issues of the guarantor itself.

A related group of issuers are called *international organisations* or *supranationals*. Owned by sovereign states, these entities' credit standing depends in large part on the commitments of support from their various shareholders. For example, the capital of many of the large development banks such as the International Bank for Reconstruction and Development (IBRD, often referred to as the World Bank), is divided into two portions: called or paid-in, and callable. Callable capital represents sums pledged by the shareholders which can be requested for immediate payment to discharge liabilities of the bank, including liabilities in the form of borrowed moneys. Development banks often have restrictions in their charters that limit the amount of debt which each may raise to a set percentage of callable capital. This ties the credit of the international organisations very closely to their shareholders. Development banks which have historically been active borrowers in the international bond market include the Asian Development Bank (ADB), the Inter-American Development Bank (IADB) and the Nordic Investment Bank.

An entire sub-category of supranational issuers has grown out of the European Union (EU). In the past, these have included the EU borrowing under its own name and the Council of Europe, as well as several of the related European institutions such as the European Coal and Steel Community (ECSC), the European Investment Bank (EIB), Eurofima and Euratom. The credit of these borrowers relies in part on the member states of the EU.

In the private sector, *banks* and *industrial* and *commercial corporations* have been frequent issuers of international bonds, although their participation in the market has been characterised by wide fluctuations in the level of activity. Banks have been issuers of fixed-rate bonds and floating-rate notes in their own names and those of their holding companies. Banks in some countries, such as the UK, choose or are required to subordinate the securities they issue to the claims of their depositors.

A wide range of corporate borrowers have raised funds in the international markets in a variety of forms including straight bonds, equity convertibles, warrant bonds and floating-rate notes. Prime corporate names represent a large portion of the total volume of issues. Some of these corporate offerings, particularly those with scarcity value (borrowers which have not come to the market very often), are considered to be of comparable standing to high quality banks, municipal authorities and even many governments.

Borrowers in the market

During the initial years, 1963-67, the Yankee bond market was still a very significant sector of the overall international market, accounting for half of total new issue activity. This performance was achieved despite the imposition of the Interest Equalisation Tax (IET) which forced Western European and other developed country borrowers back to their home capital markets. During the time of the IET, the vast majority of Yankee borrowers were Canadian entities (provincial, municipal and corporate), followed by international organisations of which the US was a member, and developing countries, such as Brazil and Mexico, which enjoyed exemption from this tax.

If the Yankee issues were excluded from the 1963-67 international market graph, one would see a reasonable balance between public and private sector borrowers. This was also true of the Eurobond sub-market (which made up nearly three-quarters of the international market excluding Yankees), but here the balance was slightly in favour of the private sector. In the international market overall, government and other public issuers had a more dominant presence.

During the next period, 1968-73, public organisations or state enterprises re-enforced

Exhibit 2.1
Breakdown by type of borrower, 1963–67

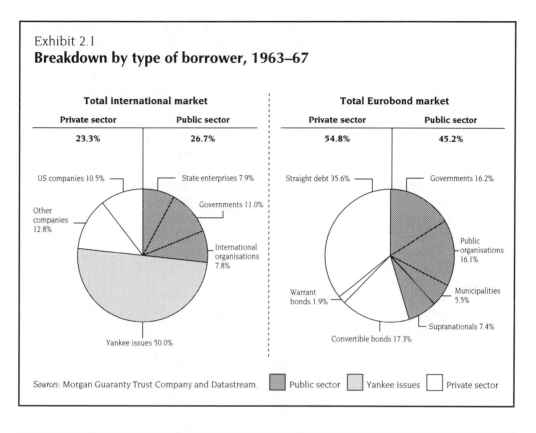

Sources: Morgan Guaranty Trust Company and Datastream.

Exhibit 2.2
Breakdown by type of borrower, 1968–73

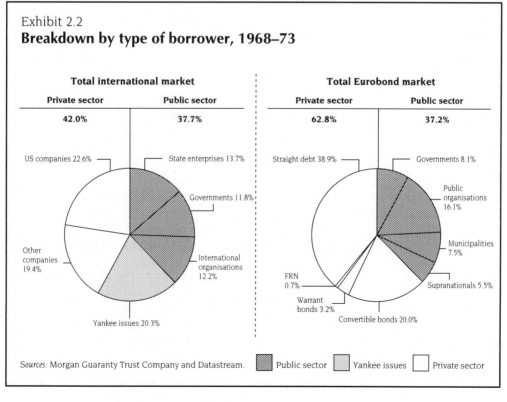

Sources: Morgan Guaranty Trust Company and Datastream.

their position in public sector bond issuance. This was true in both the international and Eurobond markets. Despite the increase in state enterprise offerings, which evidenced a wish by governments to raise more capital through their owned or controlled entities, the public sector overall gave up ground against the private sector. This was particularly true in the Eurobond sub-market (accounting for one-third of all Eurobond issues during the period) . In January 1968, the US Capital Restraint Program became mandatory, forcing many companies overseas to finance their foreign subsidiaries. US stockmarkets were also extremely strong during the year, prompting corporations to opt for dollar-denominated convertible issues. Thus, convertible offerings and warrant bonds rose from 19% to nearly a quarter of all Eurobond financings. The importance of US corporate borrowers was also reflected by the dominance of this category in the international market; a reversal of positions with other companies in 1963-67. The 1968-73 period also heralded the introduction of the floating-rate note, which made a modest contribution towards private sector issuing volume. All these factors forced a reduction in the public sector's share from 53% of the total international market (excluding Yankees) to 47%, and from 45% to 37% in the Eurobond sub-market.

Another development was the relative decline in the importance of Yankee bonds. This was largely due to growth in other sectors of the international market, but the percentage of Yankee issues to total international bonds sank from 50% in 1963-67 to 20% in 1968-73.

Significant reversals of these trends occurred in 1974-77 for Yankee issues and public sector borrowers. With the removal of the IET, European and other developed nation borrowers were again able to gain access to the New York market, and the volume of Yankee bond issues swelled. They accounted for a 30% share of the overall international market, up by half over the preceding period.

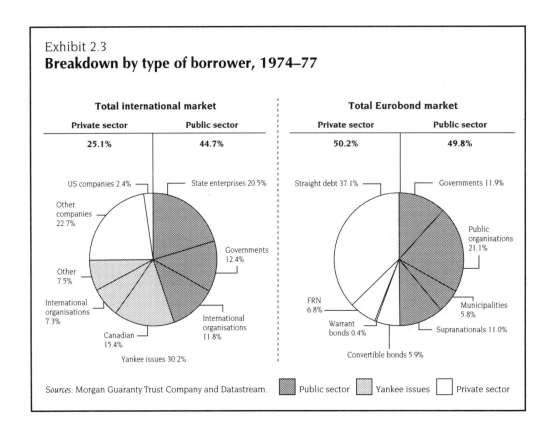

Exhibit 2.3
Breakdown by type of borrower, 1974–77

The public sector also reasserted itself, more than recapturing the market position it had given up in previous years. Indeed, the graph showing the Eurobond sub-market indicates that the public sector increased its market share to account for almost half the total new issue amount, a great improvement over its standing in 1968-73. As for international bonds (excluding Yankees), public sector issues recorded almost twice the volume of the private sector. Unquestionably the major reason for this reversal was the rapid rise in oil prices at the beginning of the period, causing certain nations to run balance of payments deficits which in turn were financed partially through international and Eurobond issues. It was state enterprises or public organisations as well as governments, that were substantial borrowers in the market. This prominence supports the theory that state agencies and other government-owned entities were used as borrowing vehicles for financing payments deficits during the period. Supranational issuers also showed a substantial increase in Eurobond activity (accounting for twice as much market share as in 1968-73). It may be assumed that a significant portion of these borrowings was re-channelled to individual countries requiring financial assistance in balancing their books.

Another factor in this reversal was the reduction in the number of US corporate borrowers in the market. After capital restraints were removed in early 1974, US companies were no longer compelled to finance foreign operations in either the international market or Eurobond sector. In addition, the poor performance of US stock markets discouraged a new wave of convertible issues, and the use of this instrument declined by approximately two-thirds from 20% of all new Eurobond offerings to under 6%. US corporate borrowers accounted for only 2½% of all international issues during this period.

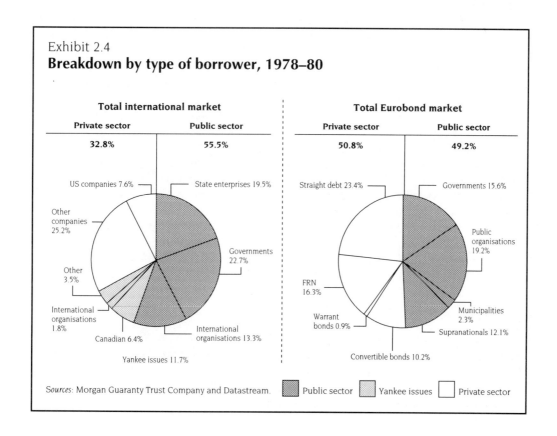

Exhibit 2.4
Breakdown by type of borrower, 1978–80

Sources: Morgan Guaranty Trust Company and Datastream.

US borrowers returned in force to the international markets in the period 1978-80. The openness of these markets, together with the need on the part of the borrowers to diversify capital resources, led to a more than tripling of their share of total international issues.

The private sector was healthy, but in the international market, public sector borrowers still held sway. During this period, governments showed a greater inclination to borrow under their own names, nearly doubling their share of all issues. Supranational borrowings also showed an increase in the international market (excluding Yankees). The amount of issues for these borrowers in New York, however, recorded a sharp decline. This tends to suggest that the international organisations made a conscious shift in their financing strategy, preferring to issue bonds in the lower interest rate non-dollar currency sectors of the Euro- and foreign bond markets.

Within the Yankee sector, the percentage financings of both Canadian and other borrowers showed a decline of approximately one-half. This reduction, together with the fall off in international organisation offerings, led to a drop in Yankee issues as a percentage of total international bonds from 30% to below 12%.

In the Eurobond sub-market, a balance was struck again between the public and private sectors. However, a major difference was the types of instruments used by private sector borrowers. Both convertibles and warrant issues were popular, doubling their share of the market from the previous period. A more radical change, though, occurred with floating rate notes, which jumped from under 7% to over 16% of all Eurobonds. The rapid growth in innovative forms of financing produced a reduction in straight corporate bonds from 37% to 23.4% of the market.

1981-83

During the next period, although public sector Eurobond issues largely kept pace with the private sector, there was a major change in the identity of borrowers in the respective areas. Governments showed a marked decline in issuing activity in the wake of the Third World debt crisis which was precipitated by the near-bankruptcy of Mexico in August 1982. The slack in borrowing was taken up instead by the public organisations which rose from 19% to 23% of all financings. In the private sector, declining interest rates prompted a wave of straight debt offerings which saw this corner of the market advance from 23.4% to 33.5% of total new issues. So strong was this trend that both FRNs and equity-linked instruments declined in relative prominence.

Trends in the Eurobond sub-sector were repeated in the overall international market as private sector borrowers gained in popularity. The return of US companies to the market was reflected in their doubling from 7% to 14% of all offerings. Other nationalities of corporate borrowers also recorded a useful gain, rising from a 25% to nearly 29% share of the market. Yankee issues were rather left behind in the rush and saw their percentage of new issues drop from over 11.5% to some 8.6%. This decline in the importance of Yankee issues confirmed a trend which continued through the 1980s and lasted up to the mid-1990s.

1984-87

So strong was the recovery in corporate borrowing during 1984-87, that Eurobonds were split approximately 60/40 in favour of the private sector. Again, straight debt offerings led the pack, representing nearly 34% of total issuing volume. FRNs also rebounded to virtually equal the past peak achieved during 1978-80. Commercial banks were major issuers during this period as they endeavoured to improve their

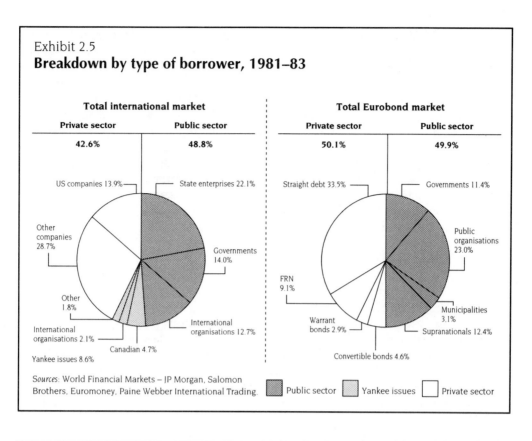

Exhibit 2.5
Breakdown by type of borrower, 1981–83

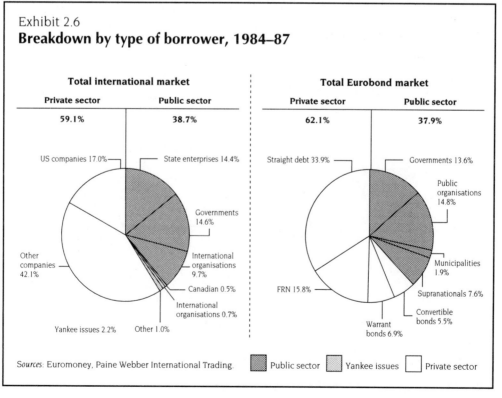

Exhibit 2.6
Breakdown by type of borrower, 1984–87

balance sheet ratios by raising more long-term capital. Although the public sector as a whole was reduced in percentage terms, governments did return to the markets in greater numbers accounting for 13.6% of new issues. Their performance tended to overshadow the issuance record of the other categories of sovereign borrowers.

Again, the international market reflected the broad trends of the Eurobond sector. This was not surprising as Eurobonds accounted for a growing percentage of the international market through the mid-1980s. The liberalisation of national or foreign bond markets encouraged their absorption by the Eurobond sector. Consequently, the overall international market reflected the same 60/40 split of private versus public sector borrowers. The category 'other companies' was responsible for over 42% of all new issues. Such issues, with the Japanese in a prominent position, dwarfed the offerings made by US companies which recorded under 17% market share. The decline in public sector financing was reflected most clearly in the drop of state enterprise issues from 22.1% to 14.4%. Yankee issues suffered a more pronounced decline from 8½% to just over 2% of all new offerings.

1988-89

The progressive dominance of private sector issuers continued during the final years of the 1980s. A buoyant economy (probably overheating) boosted corporate profitability and encouraged rapid expansion, both via takeovers as well as by internal growth. Much of the financing for this was debt-based. Consequently, private sector financings in both the international and the Eurobond markets were split 66/33 over public sector borrowings. Particularly outstanding were the numbers of convertible and warrant

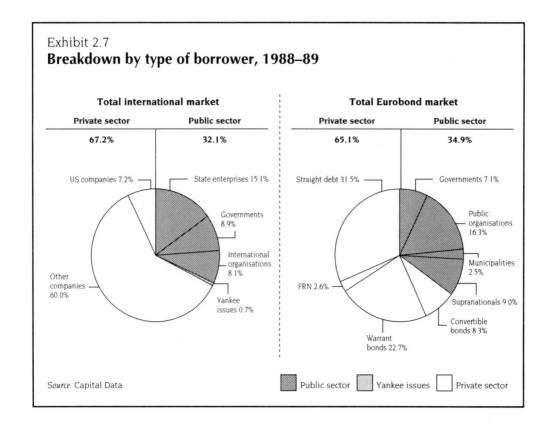

Eurobonds floated over this period: a full 31%. This marked a record level for these sectors. Fuelling these results was the $18 billion of Japanese warrant bonds outstanding at the end of 1988 alone. The growing strength of the Japanese was evidenced also in the massive 60% of the international market accounted for by 'other companies'. This period also witnessed a significant underwriting volume denominated in US dollars. Apparently, non-US companies were sufficiently comfortable with the American currency that they utilised it in preference to their own.

Strong economic conditions also produced healthy revenues for government Treasuries. Thus their funding requirements reduced together with their need to access the bond markets. Yankee issues sunk for the first time in history to under 1% of the international market. The quicker turnaround time associated with the Euromarkets (as well as the relative absence of red tape) proved an irresistible temptation. Only toward the end of the mid-1990s were Yankee issues destined to recover a bit of their former importance.

1990-1993

The early 1990s were characterised by record underwriting volumes, driven in large part by declining interest rate levels. What is curious is the change in the type of borrowers which issued new securities in these years. Both the international and the Eurobond markets reverted to a nearly 50/50 split between private and public sectors. For example, in the Eurobond market governments and public organisations accounted for 34.4% of all financings, up from 23.4% in the final years of the 1980s. Such resurgence can be explained in large part by the need to finance recession-hit

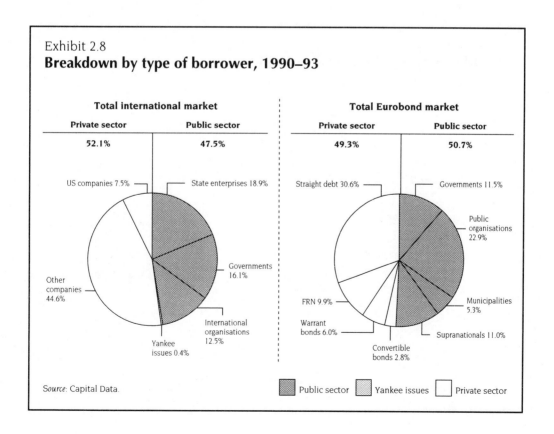

government budgets. The Eurobond sector also evidenced a complementary shift away from corporate borrowing. Especially hard hit were the more exotic warrant and convertible bonds which together shrunk to only 8.8% of the market (down from the previous level of 31%). Plain vanilla issues of straight debt and a resurgent FRN sector both maintained their earlier positions relatively well.

The international market followed the main trends seen in the Eurobond market. The 'other companies' category lost the most ground as Japanese and European issuers waited on the sidelines to see when market conditions might begin to pick up. The Yankee sector showed yet another decline. It should be pointed out, however, that the newly liberalised Rule 144A permitted quasi-private placements in the United States, statistics of which are not included among the SEC-registered Yankee issues.

1994-95

Looked at from afar, the mid-1990s look very similar to the mid-1980s. The private sector recovered its earlier strength by commanding a slightly greater share of both the international and Eurobond markets than it did in the early 1990s. Appearance can, however, be deceptive. 1994 was a very difficult year as the Fed's decision to raise interest rates by ¼% in February heralded the end of a three-year bond rally. Other problems with derivative-based products (symbolised by Orange County's $2 billion loss) and the Mexican peso crisis, all caused investor concern. By the time Barings Bank neared collapse in February 1995, the visible flight to quality seemed more like a stampede. More exotic issuers and issues were shunned. Convertible and warrant Eurobonds totalled a mere 4.5% of the market. Straight debt and traditional FRNs

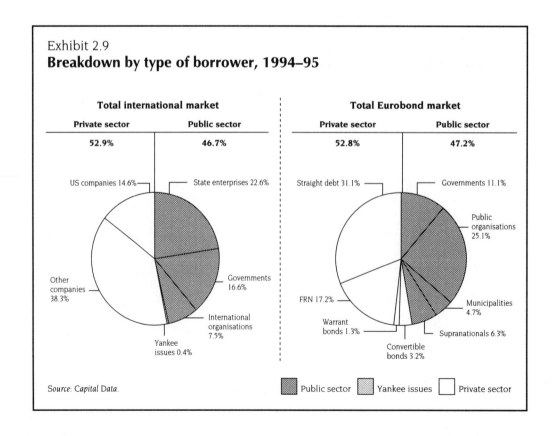

Exhibit 2.9
Breakdown by type of borrower, 1994–95

Source: Capital Data.

became the order of the day, accounting for 48.3% of the Eurobond market, up from 40.5% in the early 1990s.

This radical change in investor sentiment was evident as well in the international market. Here, well-known US companies virtually doubled their market share to 14.6%. Such favourite borrowers like General Electric Capital Corporation were capable of doing a multiplicity of issues, at yield levels cheaper than the US government itself. As in previous periods, the Yankee sector retained its position, albeit at a low level in absolute terms.

1996

The ascendancy of the private sector persisted through 1996. A combination of global political stability, steady-as-you-go policies and low interest rates whetted investor appetite for bonds. Improving fiscal performance in many OECD countries led to a decline in, as well in the need for, public sector borrowing. As a consequence, public sector issuing volume shrunk to 40.8% of the Eurobond market, with the biggest fall in the number of offerings by public organisations and municipalities. The real action was therefore in the private sector where straight issues witnessed another leap in market share to 33.1%. Paradoxically, FRNs were also strong and jumped as well to 21.4% of private sector issues (up from 17.2% in the preceding 1994-95 period). The success of the FRN structure evidenced its increasing acceptability as a medium of international finance.

Trends in the overall international market mirrored those in the Eurobond sub-sector. Government financings (with the exception of international organisations) all

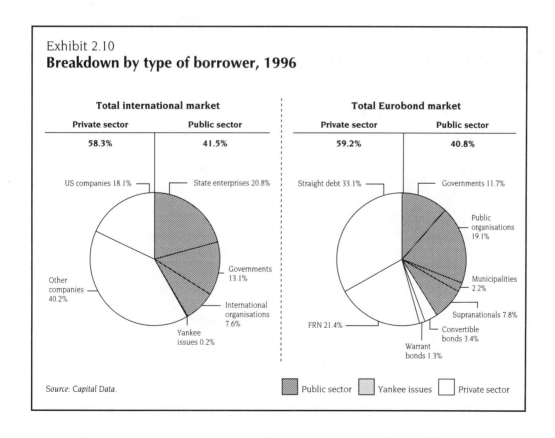

Exhibit 2.10
Breakdown by type of borrower, 1996

surrendered market share to the burgeoning private sector. US corporate issuers were a particular beneficiary with their share of total financings rising to 18.1% during 1996, up from 14.6% during the two preceding years. Yankee issues however, gave up further ground and accounted for a barely-visible 0.2% of the overall market.

Country of borrowers

Where did these borrowers come from? What was the mix between developing country and developed country borrowing? Over the years 1963-96, both the international bond market and the Eurobond sub-market devoted more than 90% of their capital resources to borrowers from North America, Western Europe, Asia (mostly Japanese issuers), Australia/New Zealand and international organisations (whose major shareholders are the industrialised countries of the world).

The bond issuing performance of certain Third World regions has depended extensively on one or two wealthier countries. For example, bond issues for African borrowers in the periods 1963-67 and 1968-73, were almost all for South Africa. In later years, hydrocarbon-rich Algeria became a more important borrower from that continent.

Prior to the Third World debt crisis, certain groups of developing countries did, however, show some progress. For instance, South American borrowers were virtually unknown to the Eurobond sub-market until the period 1974-77, and then gained in activity through 1978-80 when they accounted for 4½% of new issues. In the international bond market, the combined percentage borrowings from South and Central America rose from over 2% in 1963-67 to 4% in 1978-80. Understandably, after

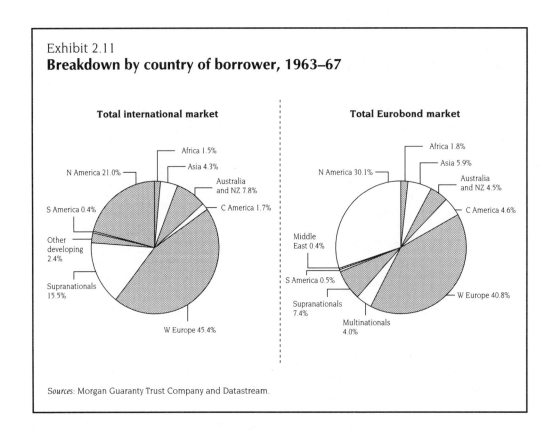

Exhibit 2.11
Breakdown by country of borrower, 1963–67

Total international market

Africa 1.5%
Asia 4.3%
N America 21.0%
Australia and NZ 7.8%
C America 1.7%
S America 0.4%
Other developing 2.4%
Supranationals 15.5%
W Europe 45.4%

Total Eurobond market

Africa 1.8%
Asia 5.9%
N America 30.1%
Australia and NZ 4.5%
C America 4.6%
Middle East 0.4%
S America 0.5%
Supranationals 7.4%
Multinationals 4.0%
W Europe 40.8%

Sources: Morgan Guaranty Trust Company and Datastream.

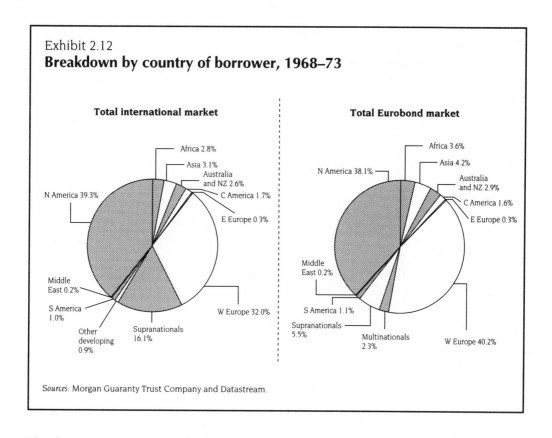

Exhibit 2.12
Breakdown by country of borrower, 1968–73

Sources: Morgan Guaranty Trust Company and Datastream.

the debt crisis, financing resources for Latin America virtually dried up. This was despite the fact that bondholders (because of the difficulty of identifying and negotiating with them) sometimes received preferential treatment to commercial bank lenders. Latin American borrowings dropped to 3% of new issue volume during 1981-83, and further in 1984-87 to 0.1%. Performance in the Eurobond sub-market was equally dismal with 2½% in 1981-83 falling to only 0.1% in 1984-87 as well.

Other regions were also neglected. African borrowings slipped from a historic high point of nearly 3% of total international bonds in 1968-73 to ½% in 1984-87. The bond market overall has remained chiefly the domain of the wealthier countries, though Third World nations have benefited from the growth of supranational agencies, such as the World Bank, whose stated objective is lending capital to lesser-developed countries.

Of the different regional groupings, Asian borrowers have shown the greatest growth, nearly quadrupling their share of international issues from the earliest period through to 1984-87. This reflects the rapid economic expansion of Japan and the Asian region as a whole. Western Europe has remained the largest and most consistent generator of new bond issues, maintaining a fairly stable 30%-50% share of the market. North American borrowers have also been prominent but until recently their involvement has been fairly volatile. In the international market, North American borrowers virtually doubled their participation from 1963-67 to 1968-73. It was during the latter period that US legislation forced American corporations to finance offshore activities overseas. When this legislation was relaxed in the next period, 1974-77, North America's share of the market declined by over a third.

Exhibit 2.13
Breakdown by country of borrower, 1974–77

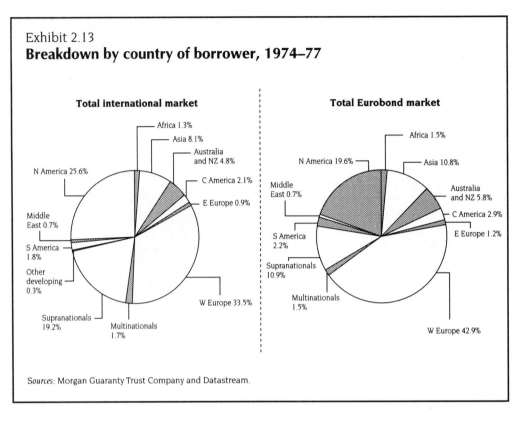

Sources: Morgan Guaranty Trust Company and Datastream.

Exhibit 2.14
Breakdown by country of borrower, 1978–80

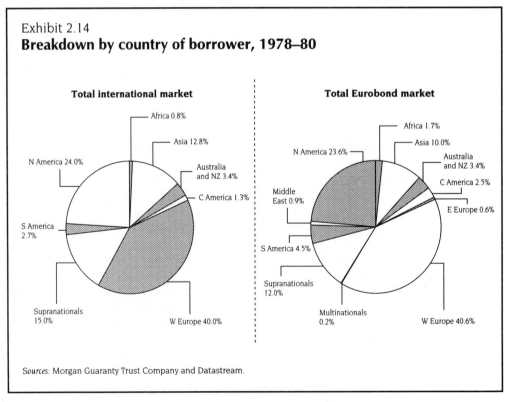

Sources: Morgan Guaranty Trust Company and Datastream.

In the Eurobond sub-market, issues by North American borrowers fell off by nearly 50% in 1974-77 but evidenced a recovery in the next period 1978-80. During both of the periods 1981-83 and 1984-87 North American borrowers stabilised at around 30% of all Eurobonds.

Certain borrower groups issue a greater percentage of international bonds than Eurobonds. As approximately 75%-90% of all international flotations are Eurobonds, the variation cannot be wide. However, depending on the year, Third World borrowers have been significantly more active in issuing international bonds as opposed to Eurobonds. This behaviour may, in part, be explained by the highly name-conscious and conservative nature of investors in the Eurobond market.

During the late 1980s, with a strong global economy and a positive investor attitude, Latin American (Central and South American) issuers were given a warmer welcome by the market, rising from a low of 0.1% of the international market in 1984-87 up to 0.5% in the latter two years of the decade. Other more exotic credits also found favour, especially amongst the so-called 'Tiger' economies of Asia. The greatest growth of all was evident across the entire Asian continent, which saw its share of the markets nearly double to about 30% in both international and Eurobonds. Part of the explanation for this strong performance was the high issuing frequency of Japanese corporations. Their surging stock exchange values encouraged an outpouring of both equity convertible and warrant offerings. The strength of such financings naturally commanded a greater share of the overall markets, forcing a percentage reduction in both the mighty sector for European borrowers and the next most important sector, that for American borrowers.

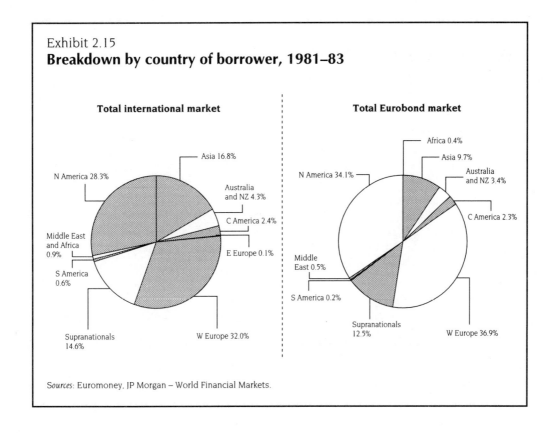

Exhibit 2.15
Breakdown by country of borrower, 1981–83

Sources: Euromoney, JP Morgan – World Financial Markets.

Exhibit 2.16
Breakdown by country of borrower, 1984–87

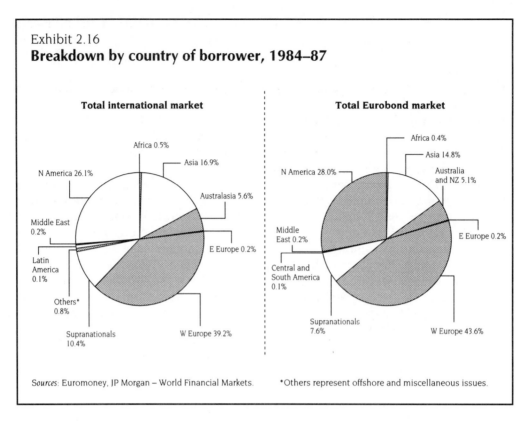

Sources: Euromoney, JP Morgan – World Financial Markets.   *Others represent offshore and miscellaneous issues.

Exhibit 2.17
Breakdown by country of borrower, 1988–89

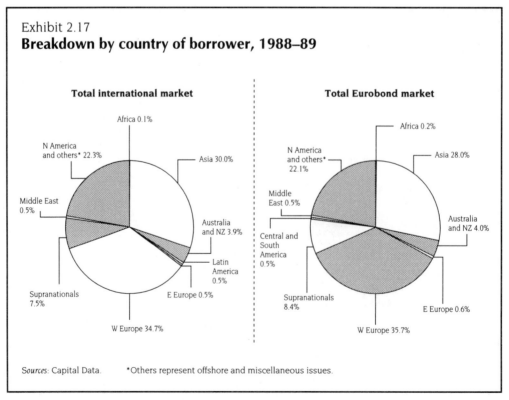

Sources: Capital Data.   *Others represent offshore and miscellaneous issues.

During the next two periods, 1990-93 and 1994-95, the pre-eminence of the Asian borrowers was reversed. In the early 1990s Asian issues slipped to 16.5% and in 1994-95, to 10.8% of all international bonds. An identical trend was evident in the Eurobond sub-sector. The first half of the 1990s was characterised by a deep economic recession which gripped most industrialised or industrialising nations of the world. Hence there was a need to finance government deficits (fuelled by high unemployment and low tax revenues) and a desire by investors to seek refuge in more traditional forms of financial instruments. This latter factor discouraged the issuance of equity-linked bonds which had been a favourite of Japanese borrowers. The consequence of the former point was that Western European issuers dominated the markets with their massive deficit funding requirements. It may be recalled from the earlier breakdown by type of borrower for these two periods that it was governments and state enterprises together with international organisations which extended their control to nearly 50% of both the international and the Eurobond markets. Hence, the greatest growth in issuing demand came from the public sector reacting to the pressure of the financial downturn.

It is also interesting to note the dominant role played by European issuers. During the late 1980s they accounted for 34.7% of the international market, but later increased their position to 44.1% during 1990-93 and to 51.7% in 1994-95. Possibly, as the centre of the Euromarkets is in Europe, this is a natural consequence of geographic proximity. Another explanation is that European borrowers relied quite heavily on their own foreign bond markets. Although these were in the process of being integrated into the wider Euromarket, it is fascinating to note that in the first half of the 1990s European borrowers consistently accounted for some 5% more international bonds (which include foreign bonds) compared with Eurobonds (which exclude foreign bonds). Increasingly, it would seem that the international markets were becoming Europe's private fiefdom.

Not all other countries were shut out, however. American borrowers still accounted for about a quarter of the market. Additionally, certain developing countries also made important strides. The most significant examples were Latin American issuers. This group was responsible for only 0.5% of the international bond market activity in the period 1988-89. However, by the first half of the 1990s their market share increased to 3%-4%. Curiously, their reception appears to have been warmest in the Eurobond sub-sector. In any event, advances such as this helped to underscore the global appeal of the broadening Euromarkets.

1996

Latin American borrowers continued to forge ahead in 1996 accounting for 5.6% of the overall international market and 6.4% of all Eurobonds. Much interest in this part of the world was stimulated by the proven economic success of Chile and the determined efforts of other countries to learn from this example. Some countries, like Argentina, went on an effective 'dollar standard', providing their domestic currencies with new-found strength. High real interest rates proved a magnet to inward investment. However, other developing parts of the world, like Africa and the Middle East, did not see comparable increases in issuing volumes.

North American borrowers in the international market made useful gains together with supranationals. Western European issuers consequently surrendered market share, slipping to 43.5% in 1996 from 51.7% in the period 1994-95. Other gainers were Asian borrowers who advanced to reclaim a larger proportion of international financings.

Exhibit 2.18
Breakdown by country of borrower, 1990–93

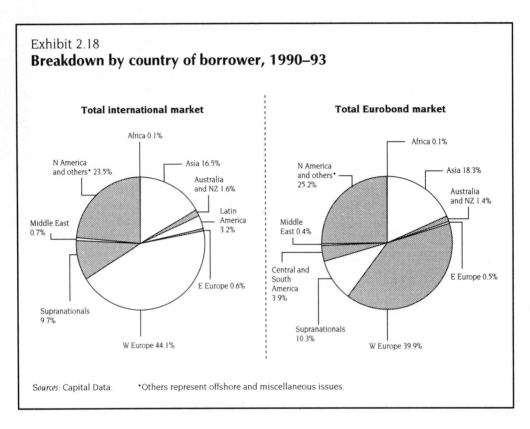

Sources: Capital Data.   *Others represent offshore and miscellaneous issues.

Exhibit 2.19
Breakdown by country of borrower, 1994–95

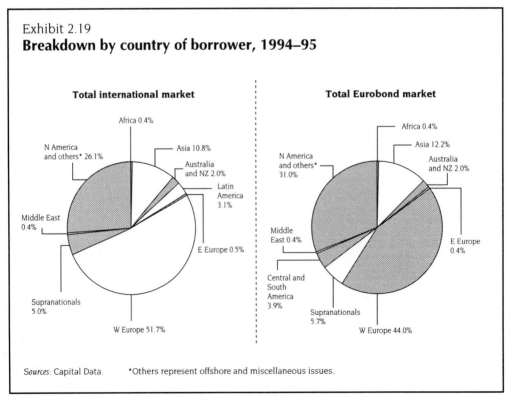

Sources: Capital Data.   *Others represent offshore and miscellaneous issues.

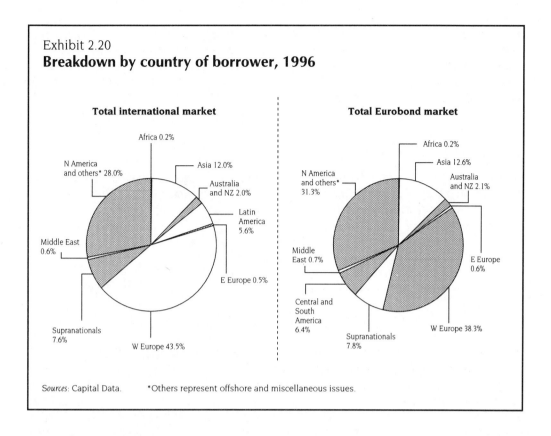

Exhibit 2.20
Breakdown by country of borrower, 1996

Sources: Capital Data.   *Others represent offshore and miscellaneous issues.

Who may borrow?

From the preceding analysis, it is evident that borrowers from developed countries are accorded the warmest welcome by the international bond market. Governments, in particular, have been consistently successful in raising finance. As for corporations, those from industrialised countries have the greatest access to the market. There are other criteria as well.

Deciding who may borrow is a relatively easy task if past issues of a corporate borrower have been rated by one of the two major US agencies: Moody's Investors Service, Inc, or Standard & Poor's Corporation . Ratings from AAA, triple A (the highest grade), to BBB, triple B, are all considered acceptable or investment quality. BB paper is sometimes placeable in the international market by a well-known issuer, but this is rare. Borrowers which have tapped the US market almost always have issue ratings. Pure Eurobond borrowers frequently find ratings helpful, especially if their credit is not well known. The process of obtaining a rating is outlined briefly in Chapter Four.

The majority of new Eurobond issues are rated. However, for non-rated issues the market applies three general criteria on the borrower in question: name, size and past issuing frequency. The first criterion, the borrower's name, is a subtle measure. A borrower can be accepted solely because its name is known to investors in the market. Investors' collective assessment of the quality of the issuer also counts.

The appropriate size is also difficult to define because each investor and investment institution employs its own standards, particularly with reference to country credits. However, corporations wishing to come to the market should generally have around $1 billion or more of revenues, $50 million or more of net income and $1 billion or more of total capitalisation (long-term debt plus shareholders' equity and reserves). Another measure occasionally applied is the number of times fixed borrowing charges, or debt service, are covered by pre-tax, or after-tax, income. For an acceptable credit, pre-tax income should exceed interest charges by a multiple of at least two.

Planning to borrow?

In advance of issuing bonds, a borrower (sometimes together with its bankers) will typically make certain preliminary assessments concerning its financing needs and the best means by which these may be met. The major areas for consideration include the following:

- the amount and nature of the financing requirements;

- the debt policy of the borrower; and

- the strategy for approaching different capital markets.

After establishing that a borrower will meet the credit criteria of the market, it is important to determine the amount of money to be raised. This is best ascertained by preparing projections of future cash requirements under a range of assumptions. Information provided by such studies will assist in deciding issue size and frequency. A related point is the use to which the borrowed funds will be put. Investors have to be told how their moneys are going to be employed. Generally speaking, those best received are corporate bond issues intended to finance productive assets (eg new plant or equipment) which will generate a return sufficient to meet all payments of principal and interest. Another rule of thumb for corporate borrowers is to match whenever possible the maturity of a borrowing with the life of the assets being financed. In this way, short-term borrowing is ideally reserved to acquire stocks or inventory, which will be liquidated in less than a year's time, while fixed assets are financed by long-term debt. Mismatching the maturity of the borrowing with the assets acquired introduces financial risk to a commercial enterprise. It also detracts from a borrower's credit.

A borrower must determine its optimum level of debt. For a corporation, this is sometimes referred to as gearing or leverage, and varies according to the type of business a company is engaged in. A typical industrial concern may, for instance, feel that it can comfortably support a capital structure (shareholders' equity plus long-term borrowings) which is 30% debt. Property companies can be geared higher. The measure of debt capacity for sovereign borrowers, on the other hand, is more difficult to quantify. This is not for want of various ratios but rather because the interpretation of such ratios is more open to question. Generally speaking, a country should be seen to be in control of the maximum level of its external borrowings. Ideally, overall indebtedness should not grow faster than a nation's export earnings available to repay borrowings. A well defined debt policy greatly enhances the credit standing of both public and private sector borrowers. Future financings are easier to arrange if investors perceive that past borrowings have been part of a prudent capital-raising programme. The difficulties of certain Third World debtors has placed even greater emphasis on a conservative approach to borrowing.

Finally, a strategy is usually adopted for timing issues in different sectors of the international capital market. Many borrowers need wide and varied sources of money. One approach is to raise funds from several different types of investors. This usually means tapping a variety of markets and raising funds from different lenders within the same market. Although different market sectors have tended to merge over time there is still sufficient distinction between these sectors and different categories of investors, that borrowing opportunities do remain to this day. As well as providing the most reasonable interest rate, a planned approach can gradually introduce the borrower to new investors and ensure that demand for the borrower's bonds is not swamped through too many issues in a single market. If well managed, a programme of borrowing will preserve the issuer's good name and attract new investors.

Assessing financing alternatives

When deciding a particular financing strategy, a borrower normally evaluates several alternative means of raising the required capital. These may include its domestic or foreign currency bond markets, private placements, convertible and other equity-linked instruments, bank loans or other kinds of borrowing such as project financing, export credits or co-financing with an international agency such as the World Bank. If the borrower opts for foreign currency, it must be sure of an adequate supply of, or access to, this currency. The relative cost of the options presented to the borrower would also have to be explored. For instance, both seven and 10-year fixed rate money might be available, but the cost of extending the maturity for the additional three years could mean a ½% increase in coupon.

There is then the additional question about whether the use of swaps might be advantageous. For example, a natural DM borrower might find the US dollar sector particularly buoyant and then raise money in this market only to swap it (sometimes simultaneously) for DMs. Further complexities arise if there is a choice between floating-rate and fixed-rate financing. The question will always be: which is cheaper. Many active borrowers employ a benchmark-type system. This involves taking all the financing options and converting them (on paper at least) to a common standard which serves as the comparison measuring stick. This common standard is usually a US dollar floating-rate financing. The method of conversion is the use of swaps to arrive at the desired standard. As swap markets are usually very liquid this can be accomplished with some ease. Once all the choices are converted to the common standard an apples-with-apples comparison can be made.

Types of investors

As Eurobonds are bearer instruments, there is no direct means of identifying the ultimate holders of these securities. The banks and other institutions which sell Eurobonds are naturally discreet about the identity of their clients. Nevertheless, it is possible to identify the major categories of investors, both through discussions with banks and institutions, and through examining the characteristics which distinguish Eurobonds from other instruments.

Eurobonds pay interest and principal free of withholding tax and investors may therefore, be attracted to these securities for fiscal reasons. They may also provide attractive opportunities to those who have only a limited choice of investment options in their nations of residence. They are also frequently available in relatively small denominations (eg $1,000 per bond) which makes them suitable for retail investment. The range of currencies available in the Eurobond market allows investors to diversify foreign exchange holdings. Finally, there is the possibility of capital appreciation, particularly through instruments such as convertible and warrant bonds. Given these characteristics it is easy to understand why the groups discussed below have come to dominate the market.

Two major groups of investors may be distinguished: individuals and institutions. In the early days of the Euromarkets, individual investors were relatively active. Over recent years, however, institutions have played an increasingly dominant role. Their new-found prominence is reflected in many trends visible in today's markets. One such is the increased average-size securities trade. In the late 1970s and 1980s individual Eurobond switches averaged between $250,000 and $5 million. Now switches of more than $10 million are commonplace. Such a boost testifies to the growth in institutional investment activity and the complementary commitment of larger capital sums to the market by professional participants. The increase in secondary trading turnover and market liquidity has been correspondingly great. Large sophisticated institutional investors have also brought with them an appreciation of the global opportunities available in the world's capital markets. This in turn has acted to merge or at least realign once fairly separate sectors of the market. The single most important example of this trend has been the gradual realignment of the Eurodollar and domestic US dollar sectors. Historically, prime US corporate borrowers could issue dollar Eurobonds at an interest cost lower than that achievable by the US Government in its own home market (some still do). Now, virtually all new dollar Eurobonds are priced, and subsequently switched on the basis of their yield relationships with or spread over US Treasury securities. Heavy sales of government bonds abroad to help fund the US domestic deficit have also helped to popularise US Treasury securities as the benchmark against which all other dollar bonds are measured.

The different types of investors display different portfolio approaches. Changes in the characteristics of the instruments which have been offered in the Euromarkets reflect, in part, the change in the relative importance of these major investor groups.

The individual investors who participate directly in the Eurobond market are typically people who wish to diversify their currency holdings or to increase interest return or capital appreciation by acquiring securities denominated in different currencies. Individuals who live in countries with underdeveloped capital markets offering few investment opportunities are also attracted, as are some who live in economically/politically unstable countries or who wish to maintain their anonymity. Many of these people have limited time and expertise for the analysis of financial data provided by borrowers. They, therefore, adopt a fairly conservative philosophy, favouring well-known borrowers from developed countries. Furthermore, they tend to hold securities to maturity rather than regularly switching investments.

In Europe, the Swiss have been a significant category of investor in all currencies, and both residents and non-residents have been active buyers of securities through discretionary and non-discretionary Swiss bank accounts. The French have resumed their activity in Eurobond investment and the Spanish have become willing converts (particularly to strong currency DM and Sfr bonds) as foreign investment restrictions have been loosened. Residents of the Benelux countries have consistently favoured foreign currency issues which offered higher coupons than those available in the domestic market. By contrast, the Germans have concentrated chiefly on DM securities, except during periods when their own currency was under pressure on foreign exchange markets. In the UK also, with the greater liberalisation of the markets, the numbers of individual investors have risen. There is now a much greater awareness and participation worldwide in Eurobonds. This feature is best illustrated by the largest nationality of new investors – the Japanese.

Swiss banks are also active purchasers of Eurobond issues. A great many international investors have traditionally maintained custodian accounts with these banks. The importance of such accounts to the Eurobond market is underlined by a somewhat dated estimate that approximately 40%-60% of all Eurobonds eventually find their way into portfolios managed by Swiss banks. Today, even with the enormous growth in private banking, this may prove to be an over-estimate. The majority of those securities held by Swiss banks have been purchased on behalf of individual foreign investors during the last few years, since currency considerations have made such investments relatively unattractive to Swiss residents.

As mentioned previously, institutional investors are playing an increasingly important role in the Eurobond market. This may be attributed in part to the growth in the range and liquidity of instruments and the size of the market, and in part to the increasing number of investors who channel their savings through investment funds and bank trust departments. The trend towards institutional investment has been given a boost by the larger issues being brought to market. This has permitted smaller pricing spreads and increased liquidity in secondary market trading.

Central banks have established themselves as significant investors in the Eurobond market over the past two decades. The massive accumulation of foreign currency reserves by the monetary authorities of oil-producing countries contributed to the growth in this category of investor. The orderly and efficient management of a country's finances (and a certain amount of foreign exchange intervention, as appropriate) is key to the role of central banks, and their investment approach is understandably cautious. Investment strategy differs from central bank to central bank. A few central banks believe that it is prudent to keep virtually all their investments in short-term instruments such as deposits and short-dated government debt. The majority, however, view a portion of their reserves as permanent in that it is unlikely that it would fall below a particular level. The bulk of such banks' reserves are also kept in short-term instruments, the most liquid form, while the permanent core is invested in marketable, longer-term securities. These securities may be actively switched to improve the level of return or to achieve some other defined portfolio objective. It was once the case that many central banks restricted themselves to maturities of five years or less. Now that this has changed there is far greater scope for investment and switching.

Important participants in the market, as both investors and borrowers, are government agencies and international financial institutions. In their investment role they tend to be cautious, matching the currency and maturity of their outstanding obligations, and investing in lower yielding instruments issued by high-quality borrowers. Like central banks, these agencies and institutions have various calls on their money and therefore concentrate on liquid investments. Intermediate-term securities are particularly sought after and switching is more the exception than the rule.

Another significant category of investor is pension funds, particularly those maintained by multinational corporations which may need to hedge foreign currency liabilities. These funds remove the complications of reclaiming tax deducted at source. Insurance funds are also an expanding category of Eurobond investor. Offshore captive insurance companies, ie offshore subsidiaries formed by multinational corporations primarily to write insurance for the group, have grown rapidly in importance as have purely domestic companies, particularly the Japanese life assurance companies.

Investment funds are a significant investor group, but one difficult to generalise about since portfolio strategy will vary with the objectives of particular funds. Funds may, for example, be yield- or growth-oriented and their investment approach will reflect these specific goals. In common with pension and insurance funds, investment funds will quickly adjust their portfolios to suit changing circumstances. They are sophisticated participants in the market and hold large blocks of bonds that they are willing to switch to improve yield or achieve some other investment objective.

Many corporations, particularly multinational corporations, invest liquid assets in the Euromarkets. Treasurers are anxious to preserve liquidity and capital value, and consequently tend to invest in short-term assets, such as Euro-deposits. They will, however, from time to time invest cash balances in bonds or FRNs when a higher return can be obtained but will also have to accept a higher level of risk. Lastly, bank trust departments represent a broad range of investors, including a number of investors referred to in previous categories. The objectives determining their portfolio strategy vary from client to client, making generalisations difficult. Possibly because clients are often individual investors, trust departments typically prefer corporate issues, particularly US ones. Their clients are often yield-conscious and will therefore accept somewhat higher credit risk.

Investment criteria

In selecting a Eurobond portfolio, investors base their choice on a number of specific characteristics of a bond. These characteristics will generally include currency denomination, maturity, type of income generated, credit quality, size of issue and liquidity. Later chapters of this book will explore further these various characteristics and the manner in which they may be analysed and utilised in the creation of different portfolio strategies.

3

NEW ISSUE PROCEDURES AND SYNDICATION

New issue procedures have evolved over time. During earlier periods, it was fashionable to talk about different 'sectors' of the Euromarkets with emphasis given to the unique characteristics of each. More recently, descriptions of the Euromarkets emphasised globalisation, which meant the gradual envelopment of the individual sectors by the sprawling international market. Currently, though, the picture seems to be more one of integration. At its heart is the merger of the US capital market with the Euromarkets. This integration should not really come as any surprise because the US dollar is the major reserve currency and primary medium of exchange for the world. What might be surprising is the fact that integration took so long to occur. However, with the IET, Interest Equalization Tax, penalising non-US issuers if they deigned to raise capital in America from 1963 to 1974 and the ever-present (and seemingly draconian) US securities laws and tax regulations, there were strong forces which held the markets apart for some time. However, regulatory changes over the past few years have helped to bring down the barriers. Near full integration of the markets (which must have been inevitable) has finally been achieved.

With this integration have come a variety of changes which affect the way the Euromarkets operate. The nature of these changes and the practical impact they have had will be discussed more fully in this chapter. On balance, the benefits have outweighed the disadvantages. For instance, Eurobond issuers can now offer securities with tenors of 30 years or longer. This happened because the US market has provided access to structured funds which are suited to these investment parameters. The Euromarkets have also adopted US procedures to suit international circumstances. These techniques have grown in popularity to the point where they have been spread to the domestic national markets, which housed the so-called currency sectors of yore. Thus the process of integration has extended to include most of the major domestic capital markets.

The new issue procedures and syndication approach described in this chapter represent an important norm in the markets. Of course, there are variations on this theme, but it is impressive to see how well-established the norm has become.

Outline of a bond offering
There are three significant dates around which a Eurobond offering is structured: launch, signature and closing.

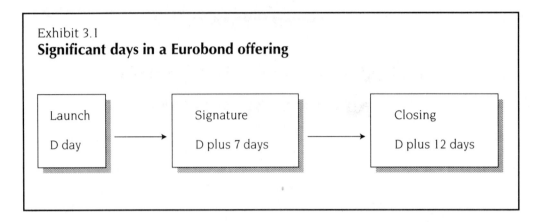

Exhibit 3.1
Significant days in a Eurobond offering

Launch — D day → Signature — D plus 7 days → Closing — D plus 12 days

The above time schedule reflects modern market practice with respect to fixed price offer/re-offer or, at least, pre-priced issues. However, the timing of a new issue can vary enormously. A well-known OECD issuer might compress the timetable sketched out above to, say, 10 days or less. By contrast, a first time issuer or emerging markets borrower might extend the offering formalities out to 5 weeks or more. Having cited this variation, it is instructive now to expand upon the common elements in new issue procedure.

1. Pre-launch
Prior to the launch, a competitive procedure is usually followed which results in the mandate being awarded to one or two bond houses which then become the lead or bookrunning manager(s). Additionally, an issuer's consents will need to be obtained (from corporate officials and/or governmental authorities) and work must begin on the underwriting documentation and the offering circular or prospectus. Drafting also needs to begin on the new issue invitation, be it by screen or by telex. Telephone invitations have to be prepared as well so that there are no material discrepancies between the different forms of invitation. Decisions must also be made about other matters, such as listing, roadshow, the choice between a trustee or fiscal agent and marketing strategy (including private placement sales into the United States). Depending on these decisions, a variety of other wheels must be set in motion.

2. Launch
By launch day the lead manager(s) will have most of the new issue procedural matters well under control. The first form of invitation will probably be either by telephone or screen announcement. These invitations will be made to potential co-managers (the members of the management group). If a particular prospective manager indicates interest in principle in the offering then the lead manager dispatches a more formal invitation telex. At this stage a variety of institutions are mobilised and contractual relations are established with a view to the successful flotation of the new issue. Typically, the institutions approached are all large banks which will form the management group and underwrite the entire issue. On rare occasions a selling group will also be formed to assist in the distribution of securities. Under the rules of IPMA (the International Primary Markets Association, described in Appendix A of this chapter)

the proposed existence of a selling group must be disclosed at the time that co-managers are invited to underwrite the new issue. Managers also need to be informed about the amount of claw-back which can occur from their allotments as a consequence of demand from the selling group. IPMA further specifies that such claw-back should be applied in proportion to the co-managers' respective underwriting commitments.

3. Typical syndicate: the bought deal

A common syndicate structure is referred to as the bought deal. In this structure, co-managers underwrite the entire issue. Bought deals or pre-priced issues first emerged in the Euromarkets in the beginning of 1979 when a number of US issuers took advantage of a window (ie an issuing opportunity) to raise funds before further deterioration occurred. The technique gained greater acceptance in subsequent years as the markets increased in their volatility and as a premium was placed on speed of execution. Additionally, speed was essential as the use of swaps (both currency and interest rate) became widespread and called for both expeditious and precise timing. The need for streamlining also gave impetus to the phasing out of underwriting groups (and, in most cases, of selling groups as well).

A bought deal syndicate structure can be diagrammed as follows:-

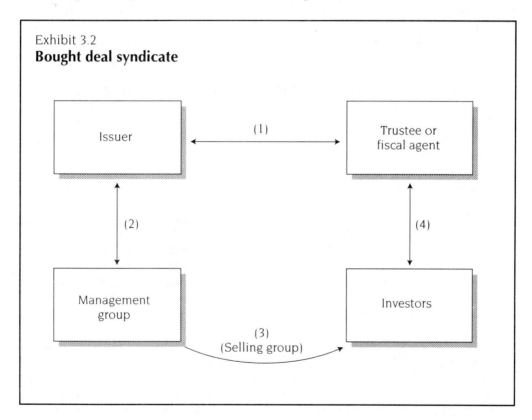

Exhibit 3.2
Bought deal syndicate

Arrows (1) and (4) in Exhibit 3.2 show the commercial and legal relationship of either a trustee or a fiscal agent. In the former case, a trust deed is entered into between the issuer and a professional trustee. Instead of appointing a trustee another approach is to appoint a fiscal agent. A fiscal agent's role is essentially that of a principal paying agent with the added responsibility of looking after the mechanics of an issue.

As there are no separate underwriters, the managers forming the management group commit themselves both jointly and severally to buy the entire issue (arrow (2)), if necessary, ie, if the selling effort fails to place all the securities. The agreement setting out the managers' obligations to the issuer (and vice versa) is usually referred to as the "subscription agreement". The major duty of the managers is to subscribe (or pay for) the new issue securities at the selling price on the closing date.

In a bought deal-type syndicate there is typically an "agreement among managers" which binds members of the management group together. With the IPMA standard forms, however, this contract is deemed to have been signed when the subscription agreement is itself executed by the managers. When bond houses are invited to join a management group, the telex invitation should stipulate the use of this IPMA standard form subscription agreement and the relevant version. At the time of writing the version in common use is version one. In return for accepting an underwriting commitment, the managers are paid a fee which varies according to the credit quality and the maturity of the securities issued. For example, a triple-A rated issuer would be charged approximate fees for the following maturities: two years – $\frac{1}{8}$%, three years – $\frac{3}{16}$%, five years – $\frac{1}{4}$%, and 10 years – 35bp.

Most syndicates market securities directly by managers to investment institutions (arrow (3)). Sometimes, though, a selling group will be recruited. In such instances, relations with the selling group are handled by the managers or by the lead manager on their behalf. Selling group members (or managers acting in their placing capacity) sell to end-investors or act as purchasers themselves. Additional fees are frequently charged to investment accounts controlled by the placing bank. The applicable securities laws of the jurisdiction in which these sales take place dictate the nature of the information to be provided to investors and the potential liabilities which exist. In most cases, an offering circular describing the issuer (and guarantor, if any) and the securities being offered, is distributed. This, and other related documents, must provide accurate and complete information.

4. Documents

Offering circular or prospectus; subscription agreement; agreement among managers; selling group agreement (as needed); trust deed and paying agency agreement or fiscal agency agreement; form of bond and coupon. These documents will be discussed in greater detail in Chapter Four and are referred to only briefly here.

All participants receive the offering circular or prospectus. Prospectus procedures have sometimes loosened with the acceleration of bond issue time schedules and the growing popularity of Euro-MTN issues. Slackness in this area has prompted IPMA to recommend that a draft of the prospectus be sent to co-managers at least two full business days before signature of the formal subscription agreement (or exceptionally a copy may be made available for inspection at the lead manager's London office). In the case of Euro-MTNs, IPMA recommends that a pricing supplement be produced with each new issue (needed in any event to record new issue terms) together with any updated disclosure document. If the prospectus is dated prior to one year before the signature date, then it is highly advisable that such a prospectus be updated. For new issues listed on the London Stock Exchange, this update is essential.

The two-day review period recommended by IPMA does not allow much time to do a thorough review of a borrower's financial position prior to launching a new issue but the recommended policy does mark an improvement over previous practices. The EU has also endeavoured to tighten procedures further through its Prospectus Directive of 1988 which would have required the circulation of a finalised prospectus (which had received the blessing of a competent national authority) before the offering period for the new securities. This suggestion was firmly resisted as a delaying factor which could jeopardise many bond issues which are priced when market conditions are most propitious and must be floated immediately thereafter. It was a major achievement of IPMA, which co-ordinated the representations of industry participants, that Eurobonds were eventually exempted from the Prospectus Directive. The major consideration in this exemption is that Eurobonds are sold exclusively to market professionals.

A subscription agreement is sent to all managers. This document defines the relationship between the borrower and management group or underwriting syndicate. As mentioned above, there is another contract called an agreement among managers, but this is not sent to members of the management group (because it is considered to have been agreed when the subscription agreement is signed). This agreement defines the contractual relationship that exists among the managers (as well as the division of the management fee).

The selling group agreements (to the extent that they are used at all) are either mailed, telexed or incorporated in other documents sent to selling group members. The agreement says simply that participants in the selling group undertake to pay for the bonds they have been allotted and to adhere to prohibitions against sales in specified countries.

A trust deed incorporating a form of bond and coupon (or a different agreement called a fiscal agency agreement) sets out the obligations of the borrower as to payment, default and covenants. It also sets out the mechanics of interest payment and redemption (both optional and mandatory amortisation). The trust deed or fiscal agency agreement is not distributed but normally kept with certain institutions where it can be viewed by any interested party.

5. *Telexes*

Invitation telex to co-managers and (as required) invitation telex to selling group members.

The most important telex is the invitation to co-managers sent by the lead manager. The different points that have to be made in the managers' telex are important. The key clauses are summarised in Chapter Four. The invitation telex is usually preceded by a telephone call or an invitation via a trading screen. A commitment based on these earlier communications is binding except where the subsequent invitation telex reveals basic changes or additions to the commercial terms of the transaction as previously disclosed. Acceptance of the formal invitation telex is also a binding commitment except if there are subsequent material changes or additions to the terms set forth in the invitation telex. All commitments are, of course, still conditional on the signing of the subscription agreement. Sometimes participation commitments are expressed as a range of amounts (or number of units) in which case IPMA recommends that the lower amount should not be less than 75% of the higher amount.

6. *Offering period*

After launch, a sales campaign commences. With equity-linked issues, first time issuers, or borrowers absent from the market for some years, it is often thought wise to plan a syndicate tour, or roadshow, to visit various key financial institutions in cities throughout Europe (or in global issues throughout the world). Lunches and dinners may also be organised to make contact with more investors. Particularly in the case of equity-linked financings, the borrower sends one or two representatives on the tour who are accompanied by a matching team from the lead manager. The purpose of the tour is to tell the borrower's story.

It is vital to be aware of and to comply with the securities regulations of different jurisdictions which may impact upon roadshows. For example, under the United Kingdom Financial Services Act of 1986, only an authorised person under the Act "shall issue or cause to be issued an investment advertisement in the United Kingdom unless its contents have been approved by an authorised person". Most of the marketing materials used or shown during a roadshow would be considered an "investment advertisement". More ominously, under the same Act it is a criminal offence punishable by a fine or up to seven years in jail, or both, "to issue false or misleading information (or to conceal material facts) or to engage in any act or course of conduct which creates a misleading impression, with the purpose of inducing another person to enter into an investment agreement or to exercise or refrain from exercising any rights conferred by an investment".

In the typical pre-priced (or bought deal) offering, IPMA recommends that final allotments are made within the next business day following a new issue's launch. Allotments can, in fact, be made sooner, immediately after the management group is formed. Securities not allotted at that time are retained by the lead manager for its own profit or loss.

As the retail (sales to end-investors) marketing effort progresses, syndicate members give an idea of their interest. They inform the lead manager of their estimate of potential demand. This practice is called 'book-building' and is one of the few remaining new issue procedures which has survived from the classical underwriting approach used in the 1960s and 1970s. Co-managers may ask for a pre-allotment (or protection) on a certain number of bonds (ie for an assured supply of the securities for resale to their end-investors). The granting of protection depends on the strategy adopted for each issue. However, IPMA regulations require that any pre-allotment requested by the co-managers upon acceptance of the syndicate invitation cannot be less than 50% of the expected or minimum underwriting commitment.

During the offering period there are a number of other jobs to do. The necessary documents must be sent to the sponsor or listing agent, which helps in the listing of an issue on the appropriate exchange. Other procedural and administrative chores will also be seen to.

7. Signing day
Over the course of the three days prior to the offering, the lead manager receives indications of investment demand and requests for protection from syndicate members. Analysis of demand is essential to any adjustment in final terms. In spread priced issues (to be discussed later), an excess of demand may lead to a tightening of the yield over the reference security. In particularly popular deals, a decision may be taken to increase issue size. When this happens IPMA recommends that all managers should be offered a share of the increase pro rata to their original underwriting commitment.

The point of analysing orders carefully is to ensure that the offered securities are properly distributed in strong hands and ideally to end-investors. This is not always the case. A lead manager is always afraid that selling group members, or even co-managers, which have exaggerated true demand, will dispose of their excess bonds (dump them) on the secondary market after pricing. Some dumping is inevitable. But immediate and heavy sales cause erratic market performance of the securities, and steep price declines. This reflects badly on the credit of the borrower and offends investors which have bought at the offer price. If a borrower's first issue gets off to a shaky start, its prospects for subsequent issues on fine terms are reduced.

8. *Syndicate stabilisation*

For a number of days after the offering, the syndicate department, in concert with the trading and salesforce of the lead manager, stabilises the market price of the new issue. The quoted price of the securities is usually allowed to move only within a certain range. If there is selling pressure on the new issue as unwanted bonds are dumped on the market, the lead manager may support the price by buying these loose securities. Conversely, if excess buying demand develops, the lead manager can sell bonds into the market to keep the price down. This makes distribution to end-investors easier by smoothing out the trading pattern of the newly offered bonds. If trading in the bonds were left to the market, volatile price movements would attract speculators, while more cautious, long-term investors would wait to see where the price finally settled.

Stabilisation techniques do vary and, where permitted in the syndicate documentation, the lead manager can employ hedging instruments as appropriate provided that the economic consequences of such hedging are included in the stabilisation account. IPMA rules require early disclosure of planned stabilisation and, as detailed below, limit the economic consequences to syndicate members. When the distribution of securities is thought to be complete, the lead manager also needs to contact the managers and selling group as to the precise time the syndicate is to be 'broken', as the term is used in fixed price offer/ re-offer transactions.

The purpose of stabilisation is to promote the orderly distribution of a Eurobond issue. This exercise can potentially be fairly expensive. Consequently, IPMA recommends that the lead manager should not deduct the costs of stabilisation from the syndicate's fees unless this right is reserved at the time of the invitation telex is sent out. In the event that stabilisation costs can be deducted, IPMA recommends that the total of these costs plus other unreimbursed expenses should not exceed the underwriting fee, or 60% of the combined fee (the management and underwriting fee combined). Conversely, profits made on stabilisation need to be credited to syndicate members in an amount up to the level of the deemed underwriting fee. Therefore, underwriting fees can double (less other non-reimbursed expenses), but no more. Stabilisation gains and losses which exceed these limits are for the account of the lead manager. IPMA rules also emphasise that stabilisation of a pre-priced debt issue should be concluded by the closing date. With other forms of offering, stabilisation should be discontinued as soon after the closing as possible, and the syndication account itself ought to be closed within 30 days following the signature date. In no event can the lead manager require the syndicate members to either give up a portion of their entitlement to securities (or accept additional bonds above their commitment) in order to settle a stabilisation position.

9. *Closing*

On the day before closing, managers and selling group members typically pay for their securities through a dollar account set up for this purpose in Euroclear or Cedel Bank. Payment is made in funds which may be used (to earn interest, etc) on the same day as the securities are delivered (the major elements of the closing are designed to take place simultaneously). The securities delivered are typically represented by a global bond, which will be replaced by definitive securities when selling restrictions (if any) are lifted and the bonds themselves are ready. The precise form of the securities to be delivered needs to be disclosed by the lead manager in the invitation telex. It is preferred market practice that definitive securities be delivered at the request of an investor, without expense to the investor. Should a global issue form be used then IPMA recommends that this be exchanged for the definitive securities as soon as possible following 40 days after closing.

At or before the time of closing of pre-priced debt issues the syndicate's fees are paid (for other issues, the payment deadline is 30 days after closing date). Such fees include the underwriting fee and the management fee. This latter fee may be reduced by the 'off the top' percentage claimed by the lead manager and termed the 'praecipium'. When the underwriting and management fees are aggregated (called the 'combined fee'), IPMA's recommendation is that 40% of the total be deemed to represent the management fee. As noted above, underwriting fees are adjusted for the stabilisation profits or losses, in accordance with the designated limitations. Also mentioned above are other 'unreimbursed expenses'. These are the out-of-pocket expenses of the lead manager which have not been repaid by the issuer. The non-reimbursed portion should usually not be charged to the syndicate but, if so, such overspend would be paid out of underwriting fees, and capped at 10% of these fees or 20% of the expense reimbursement in other issues. It is expected that all fees payable are settled promptly. IPMA recommends that late fees accrue interest at the rate of 1% per month (or part thereof) from the date that they are due.

As a prior condition to the closing, certain documents have to be delivered to the syndicate: legal opinions as to the proper incorporation and establishment of the borrower, and legality of the securities issued; confirmation of the listing; approvals and authorisations required for the offering; and a letter from the auditors, plus a further certificate from an officer of the borrower, testifying to the financial position of the borrower at or near the date of the closing. After the closing, the tombstone is distributed to newspapers and financial magazines to announce the completed bond offering. In the weeks following the new issue, the relevant offering documents and closing papers are assembled and bound in book form. This bound volume, often called the 'Bible', is nowadays prepared by the lawyers working on the transaction and can be completed within a week of closing at nominal expense. Bibles are distributed to the borrower and managers as well as other parties such as legal advisers and so on.

Exhibit 3.3
Sample time schedule for a Eurodollar bond issue, ABC Corporation

---

Week of D-7
1. Basic terms and conditions put to competitive tender and mandate awarded.

2. Work begun on:

    a. Offering circular (due diligence investigation).

    b. Subscription agreement.

    c. Syndicate invitations.

    d. Listing application prepared.

    e. Sales material (optional).

3. Other formalities:
    a. Final authorisations and board approvals obtained.
    b. Working party meetings as necessary to prepare documents.
    c. Drafts of documents sent to printers.
    d. Preparation of statistical comparison (ie spread pricing analysis) and other sales materials (optional).

D Day (launch day)
1. Lead manager sends:
    a. Invitations to co-managers.
    b. Invitations to selling group members (optional).
2. Acceptances received from syndicate members.
3. Listing application queries answered.

D+1
1. Allotments made for managers and protection given upon request.
2. Allotments made for selling group members (optional).

D+1 through D+6 (offering period)
1. Indications of syndicate and investor interest are recorded in the book.
2. Pre-allotments are made in the amount of not less than 50% of underwriting commitment.
3. Advertising agency contacted for preparation of tombstone announcement and list of likely newspapers and magazines.

D+5/6
1. All documents for signing (plus draft prospectus) need to be sent to syndicate members for review at least two days prior to signature day (or in exceptional circumstances documentation may be made available for viewing in the lead manager's London office).
2. Final terms review (especially size increase) in response to recorded syndicate subscriptions and investor interest.
3. Printing of final prospectus for signing the following day and to comply with FSA Sect. 149 timing.
4. Trust deed or fiscal agency agreement finalised.

D+7 (signature day)
1. Signature of the subscription agreement.

2. Release of press announcement.

3. Final terms released to listing agent, document and advertising agency for tombstone.

D+7 through D+12 (syndicate stabilisation)
1. New issue supported by syndicate bid until distribution judged complete. Syndicate notified about precise time when trading restrictions will be lifted.

2. Preparation of final copy of tombstone advertisement.

3. Listing application checked to assure listing on or before closing.

4. Closing memorandum reviewed setting out arrangements for closing.

5. Delivery and payment instruction forms received from managers and selling group members.

D+12 (closing day)
1. Co-managers (and selling group members) make payment for securities acquired through accounts with Euroclear or Cedel Bank..

2. Closing documents delivered.

3. Signature of Trust Deed (or Fiscal Agency Agreement).

D+12 through D+40
1. Publication of tombstone advertisement.

2. Preparation of Bible, containing offering documents and closing papers.

3. Selling restriction procedure, as necessary, for 40 days after which definitive securities are delivered.

US-led syndication innovation

The process of Eurobond syndication has undergone sweeping changes during the past few years. A major driving force has been changes in US legislation, particularly the introduction of Rule 144A and Regulation S. Both laws came into force in 1990 and have had a pronounced impact on the Euromarkets. These two pieces of legislation will be discussed in greater detail below. Another factor which has affected the Euromarkets virtually since their inception has been the extreme competitive pressures which cut profit margins and led to the innovations that reduced costs or linked one product sale to that of another. An example of the latter form of innovation is the packaging of swaps with a bond issue, where the bond issue was frequently the loss leader. Efforts have been made to restore profitability to the main line Eurobond business, and in 1989-1990 a new form of discipline known as the 'fixed price offer/re-offer' method was introduced. Although there are variations on this syndication technique today, the approach remains the standard of the market.

Exhibit 3.4
Prospectus front cover

This cover page appears as an example only. The bonds described herein have already been offered for sale.

The fixed price offer/re-offer method is very similar to the syndicate practice employed in the domestic US capital market. Legislative liberalisation, evidenced by Rule 144A and Regulation S, has also served to help integrate the two massive capital markets in the US and Europe. Hence, American pricing practices such as 'spread pricing' and fixed price offer/re-offer have been adopted. Possible new issue maturities in the Euromarkets have also lengthened considerably to correspond closer with those available in America. So strong has this integration become that the new international market practices (themselves modelled on the US) have become adopted as the standard in many of the world's purely domestic capital markets.

To gain a better understanding of these new syndication techniques, it is necessary to give a more detailed description of the market forces and legislative changes which brought them into being.

US *Regulatory Changes*. Following the great stockmarket crash of 1929, there was a need to restore investor confidence. In the United States, the route chosen was a strict regulatory structure which was laid out in two major pieces of legislation: the Securities Act of 1933 (the "Securities Act") and the Securities Exchange Act of 1934 (the "Exchange Act"). Rather than relying on the notion of self-regulation (which is the norm in the Euromarkets), the US securities legislation is enforced by the SEC (Securities and Exchange Commission) which is an agency of the federal government. Not only are violations of securities laws treated as criminal offences, but the SEC can issue its own regulations which have the force of law and can bring actions in criminal courts to enforce either the securities laws or its own regulations. The SEC can be approached for its opinion as to the appropriateness of a certain proposal. If the SEC determines that the proposal will not lead to an enforcement action then it will issue something called a 'no action' letter. While this term sounds somewhat negative, it is frequently greeted with a great sigh of relief by the recipient.

The US securities laws and regulations are designed to protect investors by requiring disclosure of material facts concerning investments which are sold in the markets. Additionally, controls are imposed on securities dealers, the market for securities and specific trading practices. Perhaps the greatest concern for non-US issuers has been the level of mandatory disclosure, especially the imposition of US generally accepted accounting principles (GAAP) as well as the criminal penalties, if a mistake is made. Not only does there have to be proper disclosure in a new issue, but certain publicly held companies (called 'reporting companies') have an ongoing requirement to file full financial statements (as frequently as every three months) with the SEC for public dissemination.

Perhaps understandably non-US Eurobond issuers are reluctant to submit themselves to this type of regime (called 'registration') unless a conscious choice is made to sell securities in the US market. This would seem like an easy thing to determine, but it is not. One problem is that many types of US laws are extraterritorial; they can be held to operate in countries outside the United States. The anti-fraud sections of the US securities laws are no exception. For example, the application of the Securities Act is defined as any sale of a security involving interstate commerce, where interstate commerce is defined as including "trade or commerce in securities or any transportation of communication relating thereto... between any foreign country and any State, Territory, or the District of Columbia." Hence, the rules apply if the securities transaction 'touches' the United States from a country outside its boundaries. The laws may still apply even if the United States or US persons are involved in only a tangential manner.

The extra-territoriality of certain US laws has been something which has dogged the Eurobond market from its inception. However, in the early days the IET (Interest Equalization Tax), which penalised securities of non-US issuers placed in the US market, at least carried with it the presumption that such securities would probably never touch the United States. The IET was, however, abolished in June 1974. Since then the Eurobond market has become an increasingly international affair and has pushed ever closer towards possible conflicts with US securities laws. There has been a corresponding need to seek clear definition and, to be fair, the US authorities have been at pains to be reasonable and to avoid discouraging upstanding foreign issuers from using the US domestic capital market. Their actions have in part been prompted by enlightened self-interest. Nobody would wish to make the US markets uncompetitive, particularly in a growing global economy which has liberalised administrative and regulatory structures.

Actually most common sense people wanted the same thing: a new set of rules which maintained standards whilst allowing for the legitimate distribution of securities. The new rules were termed colourfully the 'safe harbours'. Rule 144A is one such important 'safe harbour'.

Rule 144A. This rule was adopted by the SEC on April 19, 1990 and provided an exemption from registration requirements of the Securities Act for securities sales within the United States to certain Qualified Institutional Buyers (QIBs). In practical terms this allowed certain categories of Euromarket issuers to place securities with large institutions in the United States without any obligation to file a registration statement with the SEC. The theory behind this new regulation is that big institutions are capable of making their own informed investment decisions and, therefore, do not require the same level of scrutiny as is associated with an SEC filing. Issuers wishing to avail themselves of this opportunity are obliged to take steps to ensure that 144A securities are not sold back into the public markets. Hence, re-sales are handled through a closed trading system like PORTAL (Private Offerings, Resale and Trading through Automated Linkages). Use of Rule 144A does not avoid the anti-fraud provisions of the US securities laws, so an issuer's investment banker and counsel will need to do thorough due diligence. Frequently, a 10b-5 letter will be requested from counsel to provide a degree of comfort that satisfactory due diligence has been conducted.

Despite hurdles like due diligence, Rule 144A does provide foreign issuers a new user-friendly access to the US capital markets. The target market, or QIBs, are exciting prospects because they are typically institutions which own or invest $100 million or more in securities (other than those issued by affiliates). Additionally, Rule 144A may be utilised by issuers of ADRs (American Depository Receipts) and preference shares, together with the colourful hybrids of both these types of securities. Finally, the issuance of MTNs (Medium Term Notes) has also been given a significant boost by easy access to the major US domestic investment institutions.

Regulation S. To an extent Regulation S is the offshore counterpart of Rule 144A (and indeed the two new regulations are often utilised together in the same transaction). What Regulation S does is to liberalise and clarify the registration requirements for both US and non-US issuers placing securities outside the United States. Regulation S is another 'safe harbour' and defines three different categories of issuing and selling restrictions depending on the type of issuer (the so-called categories 1, 2, and 3) and the anticipated degree of investment interest in the United States. The great concern here is with something called 'flowback', which is the propensity for securities placed abroad to make their way back to the domestic American capital markets.

Briefly summarised the three categories of Regulation S issuers are as follows:

1. Foreign issuers with no Substantial US Market Interest (SUSMI), securities backed by the full faith and credit of a foreign government and securities sold in certain Overseas Directed Offerings (like non-US foreign bonds) or pursuant to specific employee benefit plans.

2. Reporting issuers and debt securities of any other foreign issuer (whether reporting or not) including asset-backed securities and certain types of preferred stock.

3. Non-reporting US issuers and equity offerings of non-reporting foreign issuers having SUSMI.

The issuers qualifying in category one are allowed the least restrictions in their offering procedures. Those issuers in categories two and three, however, face progressively tougher regimes.

Over the years, investment banks employed a procedure called a 'lock-up' which involved the issuance of a single global bond which was retained for a length of time before it was broken down into normal bearer bonds upon the certification of non-US beneficial interest. With the advent of Regulation S, however, many issues are no longer subject to lock-ups and, if so, the period of selling restriction is reduced from 90 to 40 days.

Furthermore, Regulation S has also relaxed restrictions on sales of securities to US citizens. For example, US citizens residing outside the United States can now be sold these securities. Additionally, discretionary accounts for US persons managed abroad and US fiduciaries managing money for foreigners are all now fair game. Regulation S has also facilitated the continuous offering of securities, like MTNs, by loosening restrictions on the resales of these instruments. Similarly, Regulation S has opened new markets for equity and warrant issues and for various other derivative products.

IRS Tax Rules. Just when you thought it might be safe to emerge from one's harbour, there is another obstacle to face. That is the attitude of the US tax collector, the Internal Revenue Service or IRS. Can the tax man affect securities offerings? Yes. The IRS worry is that most Euromarket securities are in bearer form. That means that no one knows the identity of their beneficial owner.

Prior to Regulation S, the SEC used to ensure (so far as possible) that US citizens did not buy new Eurobonds. With the liberalisation of the securities laws, the IRS grew concerned that this might become a charter for tax evasion. Sanctions are, however, available to the IRS which encourage compliance. As far as issuers go, they can lose their interest deductibility on their coupon bearing debt or face the imposition of excise tax. Investors can also find a 30% withholding tax imposed on interest payments.

IRS regulations in this area stem from the Tax Equity and Fiscal Responsibility Act of 1982 (TEFRA). Most noteworthy amongst these regulations are the so-called 'D Rules', which (if followed) avoid the sanctions noted above. The key objective under the D Rules is that new issue procedures are "reasonably designed" to avoid sales to a "United States person" (a similar safe harbour, called the 'C Rules', applies in specific circumstances to foreign issuers not engaged in interstate commerce or at risk of such engagement, US banks' foreign branches, and certain controlled foreign banks operating outside the United States). Hence, most issuers will tend to follow a sales restriction procedure for 40 days and then issue definitive securities upon certification of non-US beneficial ownership (this would frequently be avoided under the SEC's Regulation S). Additionally, the IRS uses its own definition of US person which includes US citizens resident abroad. There are, though, certain exceptions which loosen the impact of these rules. For instance, Eurobond offerings in jurisdictions which do not by law permit non-US certification (such as in Switzerland) are freed from these disclosure obligations.

Selling restrictions and tax
The issue of selling restrictions has become a primary focus as regulations have changed and national authorities have sought to strengthen securities rules generally. The national laws of the country of domicile of the issuer and guarantor usually have the greatest relevance to selling restrictions. The laws of the country whose currency is used to denominate a bond are also relevant if securities are intended to be sold in that country. Additionally, US selling restrictions are present in virtually all US dollar issues and other currency issues where bond distribution is widespread. IPMA recommends that all national sales restrictions be described in screen, telephone and telex invitations. IPMA proposes the following abbreviated form of disclosure; deleting where appropriate:

"US: |Not/ 144A Eligible/ (Restrictions)|, |Reg. S. 1/2/3|, |TEFRA D/C|"
The key to these simplified codes is as follows:

Not 144A Eligible	144A sales are not permitted
144A Eligible	144A sales by distributors are permitted as part of primary sales
144A Eligible (Restrictions)	144A sales are permitted as part of primary sales, but subject to specific restrictions, e.g. lead manager(s) only
Reg. S 1/2/3	The issuer is a Regulation S Category 1,2, or 3 issuer as appropriate
TEFRA D/C	The Internal Revenue Service 'D Rules' or 'C Rules' as appropriate apply to this issue

---

In the event that a US private placement option is available other than the 144A safe harbour, this option needs to be disclosed as well as "the identity of the managers who can use this option, who can purchase the securities, and what minimum denominations are required to be purchased."

Disclosure must also be made of specific tax aspects of the bond issue. Eurobonds are structured so that they are free of any taxes imposed by the country of the issuer as long as the ultimate investor has no other connection with that country than as a holder of the particular securities concerned. If withholding taxes are imposed then it is typically the responsibility of the issuer to make so-called gross-up payments to ensure that the investor receives his full return. Eurobonds are also assumed to provide anonymity of beneficial ownership. This is not always the case and exceptions include specially targeted registered issues of the US government and government agencies, FRNs of the Kingdom of Belgium and any registered bond. Some US corporate bonds provide protection against certification or identification requirements and certain FRN issues omit this protection but are denominated in such large amounts (eg $50,000 per bond) that their audience is chiefly institutional. Indeed, IPMA specifically states (particularly in recognition of the fact that it is illegal in certain countries) that the "managers of an issue should not be required to divulge the names of any of their customers showing interest in the issue, or the level of interest, unless there are compelling reasons for doing so." To the extent that name disclosure may become necessary then this needs to be stated in the invitation to managers together with the reasons for this requirement.

Because of the importance of tax issues, IPMA recommends the following disclosure language to address specific situations:-

(a) *Taxes*
All payments of principal [premium, if any] and interest will be made free and clear of [country of issuer]withholding and other taxes, subject to customary exceptions. In the event that [such taxes are imposed/certain adverse tax consequences occur], the issuer will pay additional amounts so that [country of issuer] aliens will receive the full amount of principal [premium, if any] and interest which otherwise would have been due [subject to customary exceptions].

(b) *Optional Redemption*
[On or after......the issuer may redeem ..../non-redeemable except] in the event of imposition of certain [country of issuer] withholding taxes the notes [at any time/at the next interest payment date] in whole at [price], plus accrued interest and any additional amounts due up to such date.

(c) US *Information Reporting and Back-up Withholding Taxes (Fixed and Floating Rate Notes)*
Under temporary regulations, payments of principal and interest on the notes to a holder made by the issuer or its paying agents outside the United States will generally not be subject to information reporting or back-up withholding unless the issuer or its paying agent has actual knowledge that the holder is a United States person. With certain exceptions the issuer will be required to redeem the notes at par without additional amounts plus any accrued interest within one year in the event that payments thereon outside the United States should become subject to certain US certification, information or other reporting requirements, the effect of which is the disclosure to the issuer, a paying agent or a governmental authority of the nationality, identity, or residence of a beneficial owner who is a United States alien. If such requirements can be satisfied by the payment of a back-up withholding tax or similar charge, the issuer will have the option to pay the additional amounts in respect of such charges rather than redeem.

Similar disclosure to (c) above is employed with zero coupon bonds. IPMA also states that invitations by screen, telephone, or telex should "disclose whether there is a gross-up provision and tax call possibility, in the latter case with the redemption price. If the tax call can be triggered by events other than the imposition of withholding tax, they should be specified...In the cases of US issuers it should be stated whether there is protection against the imposition of certification or identification requirements." Additionally, IPMA sets forth specific "Principles for Tax Redemption Clauses":-

Optional tax redemption provisions in circumstances where withholding tax has been or will be imposed should comply with the following principles:

1. The right to call only should arise when a change in law or in the application or official interpretation thereof has occurred and, as a result, the issuer has or will become obligated to gross up.

2. Notice of redemption should not be given earlier than the date 90 days before the earliest date on which grossing-up would be required were a payment in respect of the relevant securities then due.

3. An issuer should be required to take reasonable measures available to it to avoid the incidence of withholding tax and the obligation to gross up.

4. An issuer should satisfy the Trustee of its securities (if any) and/or provide certification that the necessary conditions precedent to the right to redeem have been met.

5. In the case of floating rate securities, redemption should be made only on an interest payment date.

US/Euromarket integration

It may seem a wonder why any issuer or investor would ever want to have anything to do with the United States capital market. The fact, though, is that its size and its dynamism make it impossible to ignore. Indeed, a major trend in the development of the international market is its progressive integration with the domestic US market (as many other domestic markets have likewise grown closer to form a truly global capital pool).

This process of integration has naturally been encouraged by Rule 144A and Regulation S (and by the revamped procedures designed to cope with TEFRA D). One can see how practices from one market are being adopted by the other. One example of this mentioned previously is a technique called spread pricing.

Spread pricing is the margin above (or below) the yield of the similar maturity Treasury bond (eg US Treasuries, for dollar issuers) at which a new Eurobond is priced. The yields of Treasury bonds typically form a curve rising gently upwards as they extend out in maturity. Hence, spread pricing is frequently referred to as the spread above the Treasury curve. For example, if the appropriate spread for a five-year Eurobond is determined to be 25bp, and the five-year Treasury bond was yielding 7% at the time, then the Eurobond would be priced to yield 7.25%. If the yield of the Treasury bond jumped up to 7.15%, then the Eurobond would be priced at 7.40% (the spread remaining constant). This technique is a straight adaptation from the procedures of the US domestic capital markets. As a practical matter, spread pricing allows for more 'tightly' priced issues. The lead manager no longer needs to quote a wide range of possible yield levels to allow for market movements. This is because the benchmark Treasury bond will itself move to reflect any change in the market. Thus, the remaining concern is the correct spread over the Treasury curve. There are a number of factors to take into account when determining the proper spread: the credit quality of the issuer, size of the proposed new issue and specific supply/ demand-type market characteristics. Despite these numerous concerns, a new issue's spread can frequently be set in a range not wider than two to three basis points.

Another new issue technique which has been imported from the United States is the 'fixed price offer/re-offer' system. The system was experimented with following the late 1980s when more traditional syndicate practices were breaking down. The problem at that time (and one which continues in a similar form to this day) is that new issue underwriters frequently did not place their allotment of bonds but instead sold them, typically at a discount, into something called the 'grey market', the market which developed in securities prior to their formal issuance. What added to the mystery of the grey market was the anonymity afforded underwriters by the brokers who bought their unwanted bonds. It was naturally very irritating for the lead manager of a new issue to hear of the issue quoted in the grey market at a discount not only to issue price, but on occasion, to a level lower than the combined underwriting and selling fees. Insult turned to injury when grey market bonds were sold back to the lead manager during the process of price support, called stabilisation. Everyone complained about the grey market and nearly everyone took advantage of it when it was in their interest. Typically, too, everyone blamed everyone else for the problems which ensued. Lead managers blamed underwriters for failing in their placement duties and dumping bonds after having collected their fees. Underwriters blamed lead managers for mispricing new issues so badly that the securities could not be placed normally in the market. The old syndication process had hit a crisis point; something had to change.

Fixed Price Offers/ Re-offers. The innovation was fixed price offer/re-offered issues. The intention of this system was to restore discipline in Euromarket syndicates. It worked by requiring the managers of a new issue to sell to end investors at a fixed price, with only modest re-allowances (ie discounts) allowed to special customers. This discipline would be maintained until the syndicate 'broke' or was disbanded. For example, underwriting fees were set at 35 basis points (low by traditional standards, but the habit of grey market discounting often eroded the old fees levels). Ten basis points would then be re-allowed, leaving the managers a net 25 basis points for their efforts and underwriting risk. Under IPMA recommendations, syndicate members which are invited to join a yield basis fixed-price offer / re-offer deal are informed (i) whether the price of the reference security (eg the US Treasury bond) is calculated on its bid, mean or offer price and (ii) the precise timing of the determination of issue yield and price. On all occasions the issue yield is to be calculated as the sum of the yield of the reference security and the spread and, unless the lead manager states to the contrary, the yield calculation shall be determined on the ISMA (International Securities Market Association) standard basis.

The fixed price offer/re-offer system lends itself to short pre-marketing periods which last for only one to two days. After this period investor interest is reported back to the book-running lead manager and the new issue is finally priced on a spread basis. The fixed price offer/re-offer system also has come in for a degree of criticism. This problem arose partly because of its name, 'fixed' price, which conjured up notions of monopolistic practices. The image was taken seriously enough for the Office of Fair Trading (OFT) to take a closer look. At the end of their investigation, the OFT indicated that it would "take no action", the equivalent of issuing a clean bill of health.

A longer lasting problem which still plagues the fixed price offer/re-offer system is the practice of some syndicate members selling bonds at a discount through the broker network. There have been various 'improvements' to the fixed price offer/re-offer system which have been experimented with. Some of these include 'control numbers' (an old idea for tracking the serial numbers of bonds to determine who the discounters are), 'name give-up' (the requirement that sellers of bonds into the stabilisation bid have to disclose the name of the original owner), 'statement of undertaking' (a certificate signed by a firm's compliance officer confirming that discounting had not been indulged in) and 'flexible allotments' (which provides book-running lead managers greater discretion over the allotment of new bonds to individual syndicate members, thus keeping them guessing as to how many they will eventually own). All such innovations have their strengths and weaknesses (and correspondingly, their supporters and detractors). The underlying situation is that the Euromarket securities industry is fairly fragmented as evidenced by the sweeping changes over time in the names of top bond houses. Fierce competition has led to aggressive new issue pricing (frequently required to win a bond mandate in the first place) and, consequently, to a greater propensity towards syndicate indiscipline. The problem of low profitability amongst bond houses has become endemic.

Other syndicate innovations

There have been a number of variations to the normal bought deal syndicate and fixed price offer/re-offer technique which have reflected different trends and pressures in the marketplace. One such practice is the competitive bid, where a number of the more active bond houses are asked to propose terms for a new issue. The lowest bid (ie the cheapest cost of money to the issuer) usually wins. On the other hand, this is not always the case. Certain issuers understand the market as well as, or better than, the bond houses and therefore are reluctant to accept a bargain basement-type of bid which runs a significant risk of failure. This would result in heavily discounted securities and unhappy managers and investors alike. The issuer's reputation would suffer accordingly. An alternative is to 'hit a bogey', that is a realistic yield target set by the issuer for a particular maturity range. Bond houses are asked if they can match or better the target.

Due to the highly competitive nature of the Eurobond market, the tendency is to stretch too far. Commissions have become compressed and the yield spread chosen for pricing is often so narrow that the subsequent discounting of securities eats away at underwriters' commission income much as it did in the days before fixed price offer/re-offer issues became the market norm.

Considerable effort has understandably been invested in finding a way to make bond issues more profitable. The use of swaps (interest rate and currency) linked to bond issues has supplemented revenues. Swaps, of course, require precision timing, particularly if they are linked to a bond issue. As a consequence there has been a trend in many bond houses to merge the swaps desk with the new issue origination team, so that their efforts can be more closely co-ordinated. Following on from this, so-called 'capital market services' groups have emerged which unite individual practitioners from the swaps, origination and syndication areas. Such groups provide a unified approach to new issue proposals, brainstorming together in response to rapidly changing opportunities in the market. As a window (ie opportunity) opens, the capital markets services group swings into action with new issue proposals which are quickly transmitted to prospective clients. The reward for ingenuity and timeliness is a mandate and a strengthened position in the league tables, which record the performance of respective bond houses as a function of the total volume of new issues underwritten.

Frequent issuers need a way to compare one bid from a bond house with another one from a competing house. Also, there is the need to weigh the relative benefits of issuing in one currency sector, say Japanese yen, versus another, say, Deutschmarks. What is needed is a common denominator. The markets have, therefore, developed a benchmark type technique. This involves creating theoretical currency and interest rate swaps so that each competing bid is translated into a margin above or below US dollar Libor. Then the relative merits of one proposal compared to another can be properly evaluated. This benchmarking technique is dependent on the efficiency of the swaps market. However, its use can assist an issuer in identifying particular sector opportunities which can produce significant savings. Additionally, the technique is a useful rationale for choosing a particular new issue option over another. Without a common denominator approach, one would invariably be left with an apples and oranges type of comparison.

For less frequent issuers, the bought deal bid procedure is still commonly followed. Syndication may take somewhat longer and adopts a more market-oriented approach, but overall the result is about the same. First time issuers, for instance, need to spread their name around the market and often will enlist the support of the lead manager to organise a roadshow. As the name implies, this public relations exercise involves a tour of major Euromarket centres where presentations are given to invited institutional guests who are prepared to learn more about the prospective issuer in return for a free lunch. There is some debate about the efficacy of roadshows. Many people decline to attend because they are simply too busy. The problem is that no one has found a better method of introducing a new issuer.

In a later chapter of this book attention will be focused on European Medium Term Notes or Euro-MTNs. Although these will be analysed as a separate type of Euromarket security, they also have had a significant impact on Eurobond procedures. This is because Euro-MTNs are a form of continuous offering of securities which can be used as a launch pad for bond issues. Currently, upwards of 60% of all new Eurobonds are issued off the back of Euro-MTN programmes. The two types of securities have indeed merged into one, for all practical purposes. A driving factor behind this change is the relentless pressure to reduce costs. Euro-MTNs have an advantage here because the documentation for the programme is compiled only once (although disclosure materials need updating) and form the basis for several new issues. There is also a quicker response time because less preparation needs to be done to bring a new issue to market. This provides issuers with greater agility in availing themselves of opportunities in the capital and swaps markets. The trend towards Euro-MTNs has also increased the price and idea competition among bond houses. Rather than changing the course of the Euromarkets, Euro-MTNs have furthered the trends which already characterise it.

Appendix A

The International Primary Market Association

The International Primary Market Association (IPMA) is the main self-regulatory organisation concerned with new issue procedure in the Euromarkets. IPMA is the primary (or new issue) counterpart to the International Securities Market Association (ISMA), which concerns itself more with the secondary market for traded securities. There are other differences as well. For instance, ISMA is a Designated Investment Exchange, whereas IPMA is neither an exchange or a regulator empowered by statute. Its influence grows out of the consensus it can forge amongst market participants. IPMA's rules, therefore, take the form of recommendations which are themselves based on the general agreement of the major securities houses active in the market. IPMA also produces standardised underwriting contracts that embody general principles which form the basis of new issue documentation employed by its members.

IPMA was incorporated under English law on November 26, 1984. It has its head office and secretariat in London, England. The organisation includes three standing committees: the Market Practices Committee, the Legal and Documentation Committee and the Communications Committee. At the time of its establishment, IPMA had only 15 founder members. By the mid-1990s, the membership roll exceeded 100 institutions. Such growth in membership reflects the widespread acceptance of IPMA's recommended practices and procedures as well as the value placed on IPMA by the major institutions comprising the international market itself.

IPMA's basic aim is to uphold standards in documentation, communication and syndicate techniques to the benefit of lead managers and other syndicate members alike. By maintaining such standards, communication and decision-making is greatly facilitated. Nearly all new Eurobonds are now announced in a manner which conforms to the substance of IPMA guidelines (and any material variation must be disclosed at the time a new issue invitation is transmitted). Such standardisation assures market participants of an important level of disclosure and speeds up the process of syndication. Indeed, the new issue procedures described in this book all make careful note of IPMA's recommended procedures.

IPMA also plays an invaluable role as a spokesman for the international primary market. It has been active, for instance, in working with EU regulators mandated with the task of harmonising the European financial markets. IPMA's major contribution has been in curbing certain aspects of over-regulation which would have proved harmful to the primary market. IPMA has also assisted in presenting a positive image of the international markets to institutions and other bodies which were not always fully informed of the benefits being derived. Finally, IPMA has been pro-active in devising procedures for new instruments, most notably international equities and MTNs. Such new securities represent a challenge to established procedures due to their unique characteristics. IPMA has, however, been responsive and has revised its definitions of best practice to accommodate such innovative offerings.

IPMA's market recommendations and standardised underwriting contracts are contained in a volume known as the IPMA Handbook. This work is updated periodically to reflect additions of new recommendations and alterations to existing ones.

4

DOCUMENTATION, EUROBOND LISTING AND RATING

The documentation for a new issue includes the offering circular (or prospectus), underwriting contracts and certain other legal agreements. The underwriting contracts conform to the principles of the IPMA standard forms (although the standard forms themselves are used less frequently). Examples of these standard forms are included as exhibits in this chapter. While certain modifications can be negotiated, care is required when making changes. Clauses of underwriting contracts are often inter-related and minor alterations in one clause could have major repercussions on others. Furthermore, as a general principle, any deviation from standard IPMA procedure or documentation must be disclosed.

The issuer's covenants (which the lead manager believes to be necessary for a successful offering) and the choice of a fiscal agent or trustee are open to negotiation. In addition to the negative pledge clause discussed later in this chapter, the covenants may also include limitations on the activities of the borrower, eg the amount of debt it may raise in the future, as well as requirements such as the provision of financial accounts prepared in accordance with international Generally Accepted Accounting Principles (GAAP). To the issuer, these restrictions and requests for GAAP financial information may seem onerous, and negotiations over them can be tough, the argument often turning on a particular definition or phrase. The lead manager has to understand the borrower's position and look for a workable compromise.

A lead manager may recommend the use of a trust deed instead of the common fiscal agency agreement. This is because a trustee gives the borrower important flexibility, since it has discretion to waive minor defaults and modify certain terms of the trust deed. On the other hand, a trusteeship is usually more expensive than a fiscal agent, and the provisions of a trust deed are more complex and may produce more work for the borrower. The use of a trustee is recommended particularly in the case of corporate borrowers, issues with long maturities, or where there are covenants which require monitoring. However, for uncomplicated short or medium-term issues for prime sovereign borrowers, clearly the fiscal agency route is acceptable.

Offering circular

The one area which, by necessity, must be tailored to the specific needs of an issuer, within the context of listing requirements and standards of good practice, is the offering circular or prospectus. The European Union Prospectus Directive (89/298/EEC) and the Listing Particulars Directive (80/390/EEC) also must be adhered to as they are mandatory for an EU listing. These directives require a standard of disclosure regarding the issuer (eg an assessment of its financial position) and the securities being issued, which is sufficient to enable investors and their advisers to make an informed decision about the quality of the investment.

Apart from setting out the issue and underwriting terms, the offering circular describes the financial condition of the borrower. This, therefore, is a key document. The offering circular provides:

1. A reliable means by which the issuer's creditworthiness can be judged by investors.

2. A clear exposition of the business and financial condition of the borrower, which may improve the marketability of its debt.

3. An opportunity to highlight the positive qualities of the borrower and its operations.

An offering circular is an important means of publicity for a borrower in the bond market. This applies more to lesser-known issuers than to those which borrow in the international market two or more times a year. For some borrowers, a prospectus may be their first chance to communicate with certain groups of investors. The fact that a particular borrower is able to do a public bond issue says a great deal. It is sometimes pointed out that offering circulars are seldom read, as few investors have enough time to look closely at these documents during the brief offering period for a new issue. But the prospectus is often the only current statement on the issuer generally available to the Euromarkets. Because of this it shapes investors' opinions and helps to form the basis of a borrower's reputation.

Due to the general acceleration of Eurobond timetables, the offering circulars of prime borrowers are often only an afterthought. Key financial information may, therefore, have to be communicated in the invitation telex. Obvious shortcomings in such procedures have concerned certain official EU bodies, as well as IPMA. As a consequence, IPMA recommends that where a new issue is to be made as part of an MTN debt programme, the prospectus should be no more than a year old. London listing particulars and other information also require updating. Under current IPMA recommendations the latest draft of the offering circular should be sent to co-managers at least two full business days before signing the subscription agreement. Under exceptional circumstances, the draft might be made available for inspection at the lead manager's London office.

Lead managers sometimes use the offering circular as a selling tool, emphasising without either exaggeration or misrepresentation, the borrower's strong points. A lead manager usually begins by considering what questions investors might have about the issuer. The answers to these questions will figure prominently in the prospectus. Answers to the more awkward questions, which could raise concern with investors, must be given equivalent or greater prominence.

Disclosure in the offering circular involves the borrower, and to a lesser extent the lead manager, in potential liabilities. While there are few court precedents to go on in the international markets, it is widely accepted that borrowers and management syndicates might be sued for negligence if they could be shown to have provided wrong or incomplete information on which investment decisions are based. The scale of these potential liabilities is large, as Eurobond offerings normally range from $50 million to over $1 billion. Lead managers take pains to provide good information and to reduce their own liability wherever possible. In the new issue documentation, the offering circular is agreed to be the primary responsibility of the borrower. This is because the issuer must be considered the best authority on itself.

A lead manager can ask all the right questions but, in the end, it is the borrower which supplies the answers. The underwriters have to rely on the borrower's accuracy when using the offering circular to sell securities. This is why the borrower agrees to indemnify the syndicate managers against liabilities resulting from the prospectus. In spite of this insurance, however, it is not clear that the managers are fully protected (and, if the borrower gets into financial difficulty, the indemnity may not be worth much). As a result bond houses take reasonable steps to avoid any liability.

The name of a lead managing bank is closely identified with each new issue it brings to market. Investors tend to associate the creditworthiness of a borrower with the standing of the lead manager. The usual assumption is that top bond houses would not agree to underwrite a borrower unless certain standards were met. If a problem arises, the managers may well lose their reputations as well as their money. As a result, most reputable bond houses send lawyers with the working parties which visit borrowers to help in the preparation of an offering circular. In certain instances, lawyers will also be asked to give a letter (called a 10b-5) which gives a degree of comfort concerning the disclosure provided in the offering circular.

Due diligence

The process of researching a borrower's fitness to issue bonds in the international capital markets is called *due diligence*. The thoroughness of this investigation will largely determine the quality of the offering circular. It is the best guarantee against liability for misleading information and is also the clearest indication of a firm's character and professional reputation.

Due diligence consists of discussions with the borrower and external checks. All borrowers are involved in this process from the World Bank to emerging market borrowers. Taking corporate credits, as an illustration, a company's outside auditors will usually be consulted. Notes are kept of these meetings and the information used as background material for the prospectus. A due diligence investigation must be tailored to the particular circumstances of the borrower. For instance, service companies, financial organisations and companies with a short operating history may present unique problems. As already stated, the offering circular is the borrower's document. The lead manager only assists in its preparation and sees that it meets the standards of the market. Important information, which could damage the borrower's competitive position but is not of material significance to an investor, may be disclosed on a confidential basis to the lead manager.

Corporate borrowers

The most crucial and time-consuming part of a presentation on corporate borrowers (ie any financing where recourse is to the balance sheet) is the provision of financial information. This information typically includes the latest annual set of audited accounts and the last unaudited interim results as well. It is useful to contact a borrower (and its auditors) concerning these requirements well in advance of scheduling working party meetings, particularly if the issuer's accounting system is sufficiently unfamiliar to the international markets to require supplementary explanation. The key topics of financial disclosure are:

Corporate financial disclosure: main topics

1. Use of proceeds: identification of specific uses to which money raised will be put.

2. Capitalisation: table showing shareholders' equity and short and long-term debt outstanding at a recent date

3. Income statements: usually two years of full consolidated income statements (three years for summary financial information), supported sometimes by management's discussion and analysis.

4. Balance sheets: usually two years of consolidated balance sheets accompanied by notes to financial statements and auditors' report relating to the most recent year.

5. Sources and uses of funds statements: usually two years of such consolidated statements (if they normally appear in the issuer's financial accounts), providing an historical account of the internal generation and external raising of capital and the investment purposes for which it was used.

Financial disclosure fits into an overall presentation on the borrower. This information is normally supported by enquiries into an issuer's business activities. Certain of the major additional points to be discussed with the borrower are:

Corporate due diligence: additional points

1. Industry analysis: the economic and political factors which have a significant impact on the company's industry.

2. Company management: the past track record of management as an indication of their ability to deal with current industry trends.

3. Operational risks: foreign exchange exposure, supplier relations, access to investment capital, impact of inflation and interest rates, actual or threatened litigation, etc.

4. Technological risks: impact of technological development on products and manufacturing processes, inventory and plant obsolescence, patents, licences and research and development.

5. Market/competitive factors: risks relating to product marketing, competitive position, quality of backlog or order book.

6. Foreign operations: size and scope of overseas business.

7. Labour: company track record and policy regarding labour relations.

8. Accounting: review of major policies on which company's financial statements are based.

Sovereign state credits

The analysis of country credit varies markedly from that of a corporation because of the different (qualitative as well as quantitative) assessments which have to be made. Also, nations do not have outside auditors. Performing due diligence for a country is, therefore, often more of an art than a science.

Country due diligence

Most country credit offering circulars follow a set pattern of disclosure:

1. Nation's area and population: size of different age groups, population centres, educational level, national income distribution.

2. Government: form of government, history of political parties, relationship between local and central governments.

3. Membership in international organisations: affiliations with external associations such as the IMF.

4. Economy: performance and management of economy:

    a. gross domestic product: five years of GDP accounts with commentary on significant trends;

    b. investment: five years of accounts showing national investment by sector with commentary on significant trends;

    c. development plans (if any): national planning process and development programmes;

    d. economic sectors: description of chief areas of economy, with relevant statistical data;

    e. price levels and employment: data on historical employment levels and wholesale and retail price indices.

5. Government finance: five years of past national budgets together with draft budget for coming year, summary of tax system and policy towards domestic debt management.

6. Financial system: history and functions of central bank and other financial institutions, data on money supply.

7. Foreign trade/balance of payments: five years of past trade and balance of payments accounts, together with commentary on most recent figures available.

8. International reserves: historical data on holdings of gold and other reserves, history of exchange controls, if any.

9. Public debt: historical data on domestic and external debt obligations of the national government, amortisation table, record of prompt and full payment of debt in past.

Contracts and participation review

Apart from drafting an offering circular, the other important element of documentation is the preparation of underwriting contracts and ancillary legal agreements pertaining to a new bond issue. As mentioned previously, these contracts and agreements conform to the recommendations and principles embodied in IPMA's standard forms and are altered only modestly, say, when tailoring the representations and warranties. There are, also, different acceptable clauses consistent with the IPMA recommendations (eg whether the lead manager will stabilise the issue or not) and the specific version should be highlighted. Additionally, the precise terms of the securities have to be properly understood. Thus, managers have to review the invitation telex, offering circular and underwriting agreements sent to them to ensure the acceptability of the transaction. The credit quality of the borrower will also have to be assessed. But, assuming this is acceptable, the next step is to check syndicate arrangements and review the underwriting contracts (a summary of these procedures is given towards the end of this chapter).

Contracts: *agreement among managers*

The major concern here is the liability or potential costs to a bank of an underwriting. First, how much is the bank being asked to underwrite? Is there any chance that the bank may be required to underwrite more than the stated amount? The IPMA standard form Agreement Among Managers provides a procedure for re-allocating securities from managers who have defaulted in their commitment to take up bonds. Firstly, such unwanted securities go to those non-defaulting managers which have subscribed for bonds in an amount less than their underwriting commitments. Once these subscriptions are filled on a pro rata basis up to the initial commitments, any then surplus bonds may be allocated in excess of (but still proportionate to) the original commitments. This IPMA procedure is significant because it allows bond houses to reduce their underwriting risk by effective placement of securities (so that their subscriptions meet or exceed their initial commitments). Those bond houses which have failed to place securities are the first to be asked to take on any defaulted bonds. IPMA also gives flexibility to lead managers to retain any of the surplus securities for their own account or to locate a third party (which might be an existing manager) to volunteer to subscribe for more bonds.

Secondly, there is also the potential liability relating to the cost of stabilisation, usually borne by the managers. For this reason, IPMA regulations state that this cost allocation must be disclosed and is limited as is more fully described in Chapter Three.

Thirdly, when is the underwriter going to be paid his fees? As mentioned in Chapter Three, fees to co-managers should typically be paid by the closing, with deduction only for the *praecipium* (special compensation for the lead manger). IPMA's rules are intended to protect managers' payments and even provide that interest should be calculated at the rate of 1% per month and charged on late payments after they fall due.

Contracts: selling group agreement

Another major issue for a bank considering an offer to join a management or selling group concerns the restrictions on how the offering can be sold. The most relevant restriction is the prohibition placed on sales in certain nations or to certain nationals. Normally, it is left to the managers and selling group members to ensure that the sales they make are legal. In some countries, no special procedures need to be followed as there are no restrictions on public offerings of foreign currency bonds. Certain selling restrictions do apply in other nations (such as the US and UK) and these have been referred to in Chapter Three. The most stringent restrictions are those of (or modelled after) the US. Therefore, in cases where there are TEFRA D considerations or potential for strong interest from US investors which could prompt flowback to the US, lead managers usually consider precautionary selling restrictions (similar to what was once called a lock-up).

The selling restriction procedure delays distribution of the definitive securities until the offering is completed and the end purchasers can be identified. Firstly, 40 days are allowed to pass – the restricted period – after which definitive securities are delivered, but only upon presentation of a certificate stating that the beneficial owner is not a US person or a beneficiary of a US person, or an entity holding securities for the benefit of a US person. During this 40-day period, those buying securities are credited with a portion of a global bond kept at either Euroclear or Cedel Bank, the bond clearing houses. Lock-up type procedures are always used with US connected issues (and nearly all new issues, in practice). However, IPMA recommends that such procedures be limited to 40 days after closing after which definitive bonds should be made available on an exchange basis. The precise form of the bond to be delivered should be disclosed in the early stages to the co-managers.

Contracts: subscription agreement

The subscription agreement is signed all the managers and the issuer. When executing the subscription agreement, the co-managers also accept to abide by the terms of the IPMA agreement among managers (typically version one), unless notified of variations. Hence, the managers are bound together in the syndicate by virtue of signing the subscription agreement.

When reviewing a subscription agreement, the force majeure 'out clause' should be carefully examined. There are two IPMA versions which grew out of heated debate around the time of the Gulf War. Make sure which version is being used. Issuer's (and guarantor's, if any) covenants and representations and warranties should also be examined. Representations and warranties given by the issuer normally cover its authority and ability to carry out the issue, the validity of the bonds, the availability of necessary consents, and the fact that there has been no adverse change in the issuer's financial condition since the publication of its last audited accounts. The issuer normally covenants to do certain things, such as paying documentary or issue or registration fees or VAT or similar taxes related to the issue. The reimbursement of other expenses is covered in an 'expense letter'. In a separate clause, the issuer is required in the IPMA standard form to indemnify the managers (assume any liability to them) against any claim which results from a matter which has been represented or warranted by the issuer. The typical Euro-indemnity extends to any breach of the representations or warranties (as compared to a US indemnity which is usually restricted to non-disclosure). The issuer's representations and warranties survive (ie must remain true) through to the deal closing.

Issue provisions

The credit on which the offering is based may be direct – a single borrower with no backing from another entity – or it may include a guarantee, where a separate entity agrees to assume the obligations of the borrower, if the borrower fails. The analysis of the credit is dependent on the type of backing for the securities. In the case of a weak issuer, it is important to analyse the guarantor (not the borrower), because the quality of the credit depends on the guarantee and the status of the guarantee itself. Guarantees are either statutory or contractual. Contractual guarantees are usually categorised as either an indemnity or a surety. According to IPMA regulations, an indemnity has the following characteristics:

> "(a) the amount that can be claimed includes all principal, premium and interest (including additional amounts under gross-up provisions) which is due,
>
> (b) the guarantee is valid irrespective of the validity, regularity and enforceability of the bond or note against the borrower,
>
> (c) the guarantee is enforceable whether or not there has been any action taken to enforce the terms of the bond or note against the borrower, and
>
> (d) the guarantee is not affected by any waiver or consent or time or indulgence given by the bond or note holder in respect or non-payment or breach of covenant by the borrower".

A guarantee lacking any of the characteristics (b), (c) or (d) above is normally considered a surety. Indemnities favour the investor and are the norm in the Eurobond market. Sometimes guarantees are statutory (as opposed to contractual). However, the terms of these vary widely, so it is hard to generalise.

In a few issues the credit might be tied to a project financing which may rely for support on certain contracts, eg 'take or pay' and 'throughput' agreements, binding the companies involved in the project. The provisions in these contracts, as well as the financial standing of participants in the project, have to be looked at. All necessary information should be included in the offering circular.

The next question is the ranking of the security being offered. This information will be found in the screen or invitation telex, offering circular, trust deed or form of bond.

Eurobonds typically fall into one of the following ranking categories:

(a) secured,

(b) senior (unsecured, unsubordinated),

(c) subordinated (mainly for certain bank issues and many convertibles), and

(d) junior (deeply) subordinated.

IPMA provides the following standard classifications and descriptions of common varieties of debt ranking. It should also be noted that for banks, deposit notes rank equally with deposits while subordinated or capital notes are normally junior to deposits. Equity notes are often deeply subordinated.

(a) For many debt instruments (ranging from secured to subordinated), such a variety exists that it is difficult to provide standard summaries.

(b) Senior debt for industrials. This may typically be described as follows: "The bonds (or notes) will be direct, unconditional, and unsecured obligations of the issuer and will rank pari passu amongst themselves and (except for....), will rank equally with all other present and future unsecured and unsubordinated obligations of the issuer".

(c) Senior debt for banks. This may typically be described as follows: "The notes will be unsecured obligations of the issuer and will rank pari passu amongst themselves and with all other present and future unsecured obligations of the issuer (other than subordinated obligations), including those in respect of deposits for the time being outstanding with it".

(d) Subordinated debt for banks. This may typically be described as follows: "The notes will be unsecured obligations of the issuer and will be subordinated to the claims of all depositors and other unsubordinated creditors (except for....)".

(e) Subordinated debt in the case of convertibles. This may typically be described as follows: "The obligations will be subordinated and junior in right of payment (to the extent set out in the Trust Deed) to the prior payment in full of amounts then due on senior debt of the issuer".

The status and ranking of secured debt should be spelled out in all communications (screen, telephone invitation and invitation telex) to managers. Senior debt may be described simply, if no peculiarities exist, as 'unsecured and unsubordinated'. For banks the key characteristic is the ranking of the debt relative to their deposits. Subordinated obligations need to be described in a manner which clarifies which creditors have a prior claim, and for debt offerings below subordinated debt (eg bank equity notes) the specific ranking of the securities must be very clearly defined. IPMA also recommends that descriptive adjectives be used in the titles of issues to give a brief indication of the ranking of the securities offered. For example, a floating rate note issue might be named 'floating rate subordinated notes'.

Many Eurobonds are obligations which rank equally (*pari passu*) with other unsecured and unsubordinated indebtedness. Such bonds may, however, benefit from a negative pledge clause, the purpose of which is to assure investors that no other similar borrowings will be granted security and that, if they are, the same security will be extended to the previously unsecured bondholders.

Negative pledge clauses can be drafted in a variety of ways and merit close attention. US issuers, for instance, normally have certain exceptions to their negative pledge commitments which are intended to allow them the necessary flexibility to carry on their business on a day to day basis. Other non-US issuers positively limit the types of securities to which the negative pledge applies (eg to foreign bonds or traded securities). IPMA regulations recognise that there are common exceptions to a negative pledge and there is no need to disclose these. However, the absence of a negative pledge must be disclosed as well as any major variations (ie beyond the common exceptions) to accepted wording.

Ratings of the relevant issue by either Moody's or Standard & Poor's should also be disclosed. Whether or not the relevant issue is itself rated and other of its public debt is, then these other ratings should be disclosed. A statement should also be made about the inferior or superior status of such debt. If between announcement and closing the issuer has been re-rated or placed on the watch list of either agency then a statement should be made noting this fact and indicating the possible outcome (either an upgrade or downgrade).

The question of security is fundamental, as it involves the rights of investors in the event of an issuer's bankruptcy. If a borrower defaults, a secured bondholder has a direct claim on specific assets (plant, property and equipment) of the borrower. These assets can be sold or liquidated, and the proceeds can go towards repaying secured investors. Whatever is left, plus the sale of unsecured assets, goes to satisfy the unsecured creditors, including bondholders. Anything remaining is used to pay subordinated creditors, which may also include other classes of bondholders.

The events of default clause in a bond issue should also be carefully reviewed. An event of default commonly arises if the borrower either voluntarily declares itself bankrupt or if it is forced into involuntary liquidation. Events of default relevant to a securities issue are often qualified by the number of days that can pass after a payment of interest or principal falls due. A similar limit is imposed on the length of time an issuer is allowed to be in breach of one of its covenants.

It is important for underwriters that these grace periods be long enough to give the borrower adequate time to put its house in order, if the breach is one which can be remedied, but not so lengthy that they encourage irresponsibility or prejudice the rights of bondholders. In a standard Eurobond issue, provision is also made for cross-default: repayment can be accelerated if the borrower defaults on any of its other debts. This allows bond investors to commence legal proceedings to protect their interests as soon as other creditors become entitled to take action against a borrower as a result of a default on their loans.

According to IPMA the strongest type of cross-default clause allows the acceleration of a Eurobond (together with accrued interest): "(a) if any indebtedness of the issuer, the guarantor, a significant subsidiary or agency [in the case of sovereign issues] (i) shall become or be capable of becoming repayable prior to the due date by reason of default of the issuer, guarantor, significant subsidiary or agency or (ii) shall not be repaid at maturity, or (b) if any guarantee given by the issuer, guarantor, significant subsidiary or agency shall not be honoured when due and called upon, or (c) if a security for any such indebtedness or guarantee is enforced in favour of the creditors of such indebtedness."

Such a sweeping clause can be cut back in at least six different ways:

"(a) limitation of the level of indebtedness covered: only external indebtedness, indebtedness for borrowed money, publicly issued debt or funded debt.

(b) limitation of whose debt is included: only issuer's and not guarantor's, significant subsidiaries' or agency's.

(c) elimination of immaterial defaults: only defaults in respect of an indebtedness or guarantee which exceeds a threshold which may range from $1 million upwards. The threshold may also be expressed in terms of a percentage of the issuer's net worth or may be on an aggregate basis to cover a succession of small defaults.

(d) limitation of the triggering events: only actual acceleration as opposed to capability of being accelerated.

(e) inclusion of a grace period: they often range from five to 60 days. Many clauses also provide that they are not triggered if and so long as the issuer is contesting the acceleration in good faith. It is sometimes provided that the grace period starts running only after the holders of a specified percentage (10%-25%) have given notice to the issuer.

(f) inclusion of a materiality test: some cross-default clauses provide that they are not triggered unless the trustee certifies in writing that the default is, in his opinion, material."

A lead manager should disclose if a cross-default clause exists and be prepared to say how the clause in question varies from the type described above (eg the threshold default may be $500,000) and how the issuer's cross-default provisions operate in its domestic issues. If a guarantee exists, there should also be disclosure of the applicability of the cross-default to the guarantor's own debt.

Several other points about the mechanics of an issue of securities are worth noting. Mandatory amortisation, ie repayment by instalments, for example, reduces the amount of time bonds will remain outstanding. There are two types of mandatory amortisation: sinking and purchase funds. Both are used to buy back securities from investors. A sinking fund works either according to a set schedule (redeeming specific numbered bonds or series on certain dates) or buying in the market or drawing (by lot) at par a predetermined principal amount of bonds each year. A purchase fund operates according to a defined schedule but securities are only purchased when their market price falls below a specified level, usually par. If the market price remains above the specified level for a certain period of time, normally a year extendible for a further six months, the obligation to buy securities during that period expires. Both methods redeem bonds prior to maturity. The amount of redemption which occurs before the stated final maturity is often calculated as a percentage of the total principal amount. In such a calculation, purchase funds are assumed to be fully used, as though the market price were always below the trigger level. A more common method of measuring redemption is to calculate the average life of the bonds outstanding (again full use of the purchase fund is assumed). This computation is illustrated in Chapter Five.

In many Eurobonds, the issuer is also given the option to redeem securities either in part, or in whole, prior to maturity – optional redemption (also termed a 'call'). This can, for example, help a borrower in a period of falling interest rates to refund an old issue with new securities carrying a lower coupon. But prepayment means a loss of yield to investors. It is, therefore, important to note the number of years (the non-call period) before optional redemption is permitted. Often, a premium is payable by the borrower in the event of early redemption. For instance, a borrower may be required to buy back securities at 101% of face value in order to refund the issue.

Another type of redemption open to the borrower is the call due to changes in taxation, legislation or disclosure requirements. Issue conditions on Eurobonds generally provide that an issuer must pay additional interest, or gross-up, to compensate for the imposition of withholding taxes or other levies during the life of the bond which reduce the return to investors. In that case, the borrower also has the option to redeem the entire issue, usually at par. Eurobonds can also be extendible or lengthened in maturity at the borrower's option, or they can be retractable or capable of being put back to the borrower by the investor prior to the stated maturity. Such features operate at par or at different premiums or discounts. Under IPMA regulations, all put, call and extension provisions should be fully disclosed in all communications concerning the description of the securities.

The mechanics of a convertible bond are slightly different from those of a straight, non-equity linked security, as will be discussed more fully in Chapter Nine. Most important, however, is the conversion formula: the number of shares which may be bought when a bond is converted into equity, and the premium of the conversion price (the share price at which the bonds are convertible) over current stock market price. In the case of convertibles for Japanese issuers, and certain other convertibles, a fixed exchange rate linking the US dollar with another currency is either stated or otherwise built into the terms of the offering. This foreign currency option may have as much speculative appeal as the equity element.

Finally, there are a variety of hybrid bonds and other innovative instruments. The planned new issue may, for example, be comprised of floating rate notes which pay interest as a margin over the Eurodollar deposit rate. With such securities, it is important to determine if there is a level of minimum interest rate or 'floor' being offered, or whether, by contrast, there is a maximum interest rate, or 'cap'. Alternatively, both a floor and a cap may be built into the structure to form a 'collar'. All such features should be fully disclosed.

General arrangements

Other elements of an underwriting position include the fees paid to the management group, terms of underwriting contracts and the key disclosure points in the offering circular. A further figure to research is the expense cap. If the reimbursement is too small, out-of-pocket costs can consume a substantial portion of the management fees.

The time schedule, often found in the invitation telex, includes important information for the syndicate and operations (back office) departments. There are deadlines for the acceptance of the management participation and for indications of interest: requests for bonds. Other key dates are signing date, payment and delivery. The bank should also know the currency of and method of payment required. One would also want to know whether definitive bonds are to be made available at the closing or whether a global bank will take their place for up to 40 days before it is exchanged for definitive securities. In practice, bearer bonds are typically not available at the closing.

Exhibit 4.1
Standard IPMA invitation check list

GUARANTEE:

Contractual:	indemnity	surety
Statutory:	jurisdiction	

RATINGS S&P Moody's other

This issue
other issues

RANKING

Secured & security
Senior
Subordinated
Junior subordinated

NEGATIVE PLEDGE

By issuer: Guarantor: Subsidiaries: all/principal
Type: obligations indebtedness securities
 traded foreign

CALL PROVISIONS

By Issuer: None
 Yes Amount Date Price

By Holder: None
 Yes What Action

TAX

Domestic tax gross up: Tax redemption
Identification protection:
No interest payments in US:

SALES RESTRICTIONS

US: 90 day lock up other termination date
Great Britain:
Issuer's jurisdiction: Jurisdiction of currency:
Private placement: Lead Manager only with Lead Manager permission

EXPENSE CAP

Amount: IPMA: other:

STABILISATION:

IPMA: Other:

FORCE MAJEURE

None Yes Deviations:
Third-party contract conditions

CROSS DEFAULT

None:
Yes: Issuer: Guarantor:
Type:
Domestic issues:

Exhibit 4.2
IPMA standard agreement among managers

Version I
(Managers only – Fixed-Price
Non Equity-Related Issues)

EXPLANATORY NOTE
IPMA Standard Form Agreement Among Managers

A. The IPMA Standard Form Agreement Among Managers Version I is intended for use in fixed-price non equity-related issues where there is no intention to charge stabilisation losses to the Managers. It also assumes that the IPMA Recommendation that cost overruns should not be charged to co-Managers is to be followed. This revision of Version I will apply in respect of all issues using Version I where the Invitation Telex is sent on or after 8 April 1991.

B. This version of the IPMA Standard Form Agreement Among Managers will be used when the Invitation Telex contains the words:

Agreement Among Managers: IPMA Version 1.

C. In the telex requesting each Manager to appoint authorised signatories to execute agreements on its behalf the following language should be

The execution of the Subscription Agreement by or on behalf of all parties will constitute your acceptance of the IPMA Agreement Among Managers Version I subject to any amendment notified to you in writing at any time prior to the earlier of the receipt by the Lead Manager of the document appointing your authorised signatory and the execution of the Subscription Agreement.

The effect of adding these words is that each Manager will become bound by this version of the Standard Form Agreement Among Managers (with the appropriate variations) by virtue of having become bound by the Subscription Agreement.

D. The Agreement contemplates that the Lead Manager will notify each co-Manager of the net amount due from it at Closing (i.e. after deduction of the Combined Commission due to it). In making that notification, the Lead Manager should make an appropriate adjustment for any praecipium.

E. Clause 3 has been amended since Version I was first issued. The previous version was based on existing precedents widely used in the market, which had developed over a long period of time. It was felt that this language had become over-complicated and the new version represents a simplification, whilst retaining the substance of the previous version.

The Terms of the Agreement Among Managers in respect of each issue where this form of agreement has been selected for use are as follows (subject, in the case of each Manager, to any amendment notified to that Manager in writing at any time prior to the time when the Power of Attorney granted by that Manager to the Lead Manager is received by it or, where no Power of Attorney is granted by that Manager, the date on which that Manager signs the Subscription Agreement). Terms used in this Agreement have the meanings assigned to them in the attached Schedule. Where this Agreement Among Managers has been selected for use, it is conditional upon and will take effect upon the execution of the Subscription Agreement for the relevant issue of Securities.

1. OFFERING

The Managers confirm that the Lead Manager, on their behalf, as agents of the Issuer, has offered or will offer the Securities to Managers in the amounts already notified to each Manager by the Lead Manager.

2. UNDERWRITING

The Securities will as between the Managers be severally underwritten by the Managers in the amounts set out in the Commitment Telex.

3. SUBSCRIPTION BY MANAGERS

If any Manager defaults in its obligation to subscribe any amount of Securities offered to it as described in Clause 1, or if the Lead Manager in its absolute discretion believes that any Manager will so default:

(1) the Lead Manager may require each non-defaulting Manager who has agreed to subscribe Securities as a result of offers described in Clause 1 in a principal amount which is less than its Commitment, to subscribe or purchase additional Securities, but so that no non-defaulting Manager shall, under this paragraph (1) and as a result of offers accepted by it as described in Clause 1 be obliged to subscribe or purchase a principal amount of Securities in excess of its Commitment. In exercising its rights under this paragraph, the Lead Manager shall allocate Securities to each non-defaulting Manager to whom the paragraph applies in proportion to their Commitments, subject to paragraphs (4) and (5);

(2) if any Securities remain to be subscribed or purchased after paragraph (1) has been applied, the Lead Manager may require each of the non-defaulting Managers to subscribe or purchase such Securities in proportion to their Commitments;

(3) any Securities to which this Clause relates will be subscribed or purchased by the non-defaulting Managers at the Selling Price, but after deduction of the defaulting Manager's Combined Commission, divided among the non-

defaulting Managers in proportion to the amount of Securities taken up by them under this Clause, which amount shall be notified to each non-defaulting Manager by the Lead Manager;

(4) the Lead Manager may adjust the amount of Securities it requires any Manager to subscribe or purchase under this Clause up or down to such extent as it may deem expedient and equitable so as to ensure that no Manager is required to subscribe or pay for a fraction of any Security;

(5) as an alternative and/or in addition to paragraphs (1) and/or (2), the Lead Manager may, in its absolute discretion, offer any Securities to which this Clause applies to any person (whether or not a Manager) or may retain them for its own account.

4. AUTHORITY TO LEAD MANAGER

Each of the Managers authorises the Lead Manager as its agent and on its behalf to do whatever that Manager is (or all the Managers together are) required or entitled to do under the Subscription Agreement including:

(1) entering into such arrangements with Morgan Guaranty Trust Company of New York, Brussels office, as operator of the Euroclear system and Centrale de Livraison de Valeurs Mobilieres SA as the Lead Manager reasonably believes to be appropriate to effect payment for and delivery of the Global Instrument delivered in respect of the Securities in accordance with the ISMA Primary Market Settlements recommendations;

(2) borrowing for the account of the non-defaulting Managers, for their several accounts in proportion to their respective Commitments, such sum as may be necessary in order that payment to the Issuer can be effected as specified in the Subscription Agreement and the Lead Manager may pay interest at then current rates;

(3) waiving compliance with any of the conditions referred to in the Subscription Agreement in respect of which the right of waiver is reserved.

As an alternative to borrowing under paragraph (2), the Lead Manager may as principal lend, and may charge interest at then current rates on, such sums as are referred to in that paragraph mutatis mutandis on the terms of that paragraph.

Any amounts due from any Manager as a result of any borrowing made on its behalf, or any loan to it, will be paid forthwith upon demand.

5. STABILISATION

(a) Stabilising Manager

Each Manager acknowledges that the Lead Manager is appointed stabilising Manager for the Stabilisation Securities. However, this Clause does not authorise the Lead Manager to carry out stabilisation and/or over-allotment transactions on behalf of the Managers. Any such transactions shall be for the Lead Manager's own account and shall be effected in accordance with applicable laws.

(b) Non-Stabilisation Agreement

No Manager other than the Lead Manager (and any lawful regional stabilising Manager) will effect any transactions (whether in the open market or otherwise) with a view to stabilising or maintaining the market price of the Stabilisation Securities at levels other than those which might otherwise prevail.

6. EXPENSES

(a) Retention

The amount paid by the Issuer or the Guarantor in respect of Managers' expenses shall be retained by the Lead Manager for its own account. The other Managers will not be reimbursed for any of their expenses in connection with the issue of the Securities.

(b) Expenses on Termination

If the obligations of the Managers under the Subscription Agreement to subscribe the Securities are terminated, the Managers agree to contribute (subject to the aggregate amount of such contribution not exceeding the lower of 6% of the Combined Commission and 20% of the amount reimbursable by the Issuer (failing whom the Guarantor) in respect of expenses) in proportion to their respective Commitments in meeting any direct out-of-pocket expenses incurred by the Lead Manager which are not recoverable and/or are not recovered from the Issuer or the Guarantor under the Subscription Agreement.

7. TERMINATION

If any Manager wishes to terminate its obligations to subscribe the Securities under the Subscription Agreement, it shall consult with the Lead Manager who shall, to the extent the Lead Manager considers reasonably practicable, consult with the other Managers. The Lead Manager may in any event, on behalf of the Managers and in its sole discretion, give notice of such termination to the Issuer in accordance with the terms of the Subscription Agreement and shall not be responsible to any Manager for any consequences resulting from any such notice. No other Manager may give any such notice and the Lead Manager may not be required to give, or not to give, such notice.

8. PARTNERSHIP

None of the provisions of this Agreement or any other agreement relating to the Securities shall constitute or be deemed to constitute a partnership or joint venture between the Managers or any of them, or between them (or any of them) and anyone else, and, except as specifically provided, none of the Managers shall have any authority to bind any other Manager in any way.

9. INDEMNITY

The Managers agree, whether or not the Securities shall have been issued and settlement made of all other rights and obligations under this Agreement, to contribute (without regard to the limit set out in Clause 6(b)) in proportion to their respective Commitments towards (a) all expenses incurred by the Lead Manager and not reimbursed by the Issuer or the Guarantor or any other person in investigating or defending any claim or proceeding which is asserted or commenced by any party (including any governmental or regulatory body) in connection with the issue and offering or proposed issue and offering of the Securities (other than any such claim or proceeding as may arise from the gross negligence or wilful misconduct of the Lead Manager) and (b) any liability, including legal fees, incurred by the Lead Manager in respect of any such claim or proceeding, whether such liability shall be the result of a judgment or of any settlement agreed by the Lead Manager (other than any such expense or liability as to which the Lead Manager receives indemnity in the form of payment from any other person or which arises out of the Lead Manager's gross negligence or wilful misconduct). Further, the Managers confirm their authority to the Lead Manager to take such action in that respect on behalf of the Managers as, in its absolute discretion, the Lead Manager considers appropriate. The Lead Manager shall notify the other Managers of any such claim or proceeding and shall (without prejudice to its foregoing authority), to the extent it considers reasonably practicable, consult the other Managers before taking any decision which the Lead Manager at the time believes may have a substantial effect on the outcome of any such claim or proceeding which it then considers material.

10. GOVERNING LAW AND JURISDICTION

This Agreement, as to which time shall be of the essence, shall be governed by and construed in accordance with English law. With respect to any suit, action or proceedings relating to this Agreement ("Proceedings"), each party irrevocably submits to the jurisdiction of the English courts and waives any objection which it may have at any time to the laying of venue of any Proceedings brought in any such court, waives any claim that such Proceedings have been brought in an inconvenient forum and further waives the right to object, with respect to such Proceedings, that such court does not have jurisdiction over such party.

Nothing in this Agreement precludes any party from bringing Proceedings in any other jurisdiction (outside the Contracting States, as defined in Section 1(3) of the Civil Jurisdiction and Judgments Act 1982 or any modification, extension or re-enactment thereof for the time being in force) nor will the bringing of Proceedings in any one or more jurisdictions (outside the Contracting States) preclude the bringing of Proceedings in any such other jurisdiction.

SCHEDULE

Closing Date
The date defined as such in the Subscription Agreement.

Combined Commission
The combined management and underwriting commission set out in the Invitation Telex.

Commitments
The amounts severally underwritten by the Managers as set out in the Commitment Telex.

Commitment Telex
The telex sent to each Manager by or on behalf of the Lead Manager setting out the names and underwriting commitments of all of the Managers. Note: this information may be contained in the Invitation Telex.

Guarantor
The Guarantor, if any, of the issue.

Global Instrument
Includes any global instrument to be delivered by the Issuer, as provided for in the Subscription Agreement.

Invitation Telex
The telex inviting each Manager to participate in the issue.

Issuer
The issuer of the Securities.

Lead Manager
The Manager expressed to be the Lead Manager in the Invitation Telex or as notified by any subsequent telex.

Managers
The parties named as such in the Subscription Agreement.

Power of Attorney
The document from a Manager appointing an authorised attorney to execute the Subscription Agreement.

Securities
The securities to be issued as described in the Invitation Telex.

Selling Price
The price at which the Managers agree to subscribe the Securities under the Subscription Agreement (that is, the gross issue price less any selling concession or commission).

Stabilisation Securities
The securities in respect of which the right to carry out stabilising action has been reserved in any circular or prospectus pursuant to the Conduct of Business Rules of the Securities and Investments Board.

Subscription Agreement
The agreement between the Issuer, the Guarantor (if appropriate), the Lead Manager and the other Managers setting out the terms and conditions upon which the Managers agree to subscribe the Securities.

Exhibit 4.3
IPMA standard subscription agreement

I. Subscription agreement:-

1. INTERPRETATION

Terms used in this document have the same meanings as in the agreement into which they are incorporated (the "Subscription Agreement").

2. THE ISSUE

(A) Subscription

The Managers jointly and severally agree to subscribe the Securities at the Selling Price on the Closing Date, on the terms of the Subscription Agreement. Each Manager has complied, and will comply, with the Selling Restrictions and will indemnify the Issuer against the consequences which may result if it does not do so (unless its failure to do so is based upon legal advice received by it).

(B) Issue

The Issuer agrees to issue the Securities on the Closing Date to the Managers or as they may direct and (if there is one) the Guarantor agrees to give the Guarantee. Each of them will enter into each Specified Document to which it is to be a party, not later than its Specified Date and will obtain any Closing Consents on or before the Closing Date. Each confirms that the Managers may distribute copies of the Disclosure Document, and were authorised to circulate a draft of it, in connection with the offer and sale of the Securities.

3. STABILISATION

Any stabilisation activities described in the Disclosure Document will not be carried out by the Lead Manager as agent for the Issuer or (if there is one) Guarantor and the Lead Manager will not account to them for any resulting profit, nor will they be liable for any loss. No more than the Issue Amount of the Securities will be issued.

4. LISTING

The Issuer agrees that the Securities will be listed on the Stock Exchange and the Issuer and (if there is one) the Guarantor will use all reasonable efforts to obtain and to maintain the listing. If it is unable to do so, having used such efforts, it will use all reasonable efforts to obtain a listing for the Securities on another stock exchange approved by the Lead Manager.

5. REPRESENTATIONS AND WARRANTIES

(A) Warranties

The Issuer (together with the Guarantor (if there is one), on the Agreed Basis) represents and warrants to each Manager that:

(1) Existence: it, and each of its Subsidiaries, exists as a legal entity with full power to own its assets and conduct its business in whatever jurisdiction those assets are located or that business is conducted;

(2) Specified Documents and Securities: the Specified Documents to which it is, or is to be, a party and the Securities are, or (if to be entered into after the date of the Subscription Agreement) will when entered into be, its legally binding obligations, enforceable against it in accordance with their terms (subject to any qualifications in the legal opinions described as Closing Letters);

(3) No Impediments: apart from the Closing Consents (if any), which will be obtained on or prior to the Closing Date, no action or thing (including the obtaining of any consent or licence or the making of any filing or registration) is required to be taken or done for the carrying out of any obligation by it or on its behalf, as contemplated by the Specified Documents. There is nothing which could prevent the carrying out of the transactions contemplated by the Specified Documents and the carrying out of such transactions will not conflict with its constitutional documents (if any) or any of its other obligations or any law to which it is subject;

(4) Disclosure: the Disclosure Document contains all information with respect to it and to it and its Subsidiaries taken as a whole (its "Group") which is material in the context of the issue and offering of the Securities (including all information required by law and the Stock Exchange). The information contained in the Disclosure Document relating to it and its Group is, in all material respects, true, complete and not misleading and has been verified by it through all reasonable enquiries. Nothing has been omitted from the Disclosure Document which (if it had been included) would materially alter the meaning or significance of the information in the Disclosure Document. Where it consists of opinions or intentions, these are honestly held and have been reached after considering all relevant circumstances and are based on reasonable assumptions;

(5) Financial Statements: its Specified Financial Statements were prepared in accordance with accounting principles and in accordance with the laws applicable to it, which have been applied on a consistent basis, except as disclosed in them. They present fairly the financial position and results of itself and its Group. Since the date of the Specified Financial Statements, there has been no material adverse change, or development involving a prospective material adverse change, in such position or results, except as disclosed in the Disclosure Document;

(6) Litigation: there are no pending actions or proceedings against or affecting it

or any of its Subsidiaries or any of its or their properties which, if determined adversely to any such entity, would individually or in the aggregate have a material adverse effect on its condition (financial or other), prospects, results of operations or general affairs or those of its Group, or on its ability to perform its obligations under the Specified Documents or the Securities or (if there is one) the Guarantee or which are otherwise material in the context of the issue of the Securities and, to the best of its knowledge, no such actions or proceedings are threatened or contemplated;

(7) Events of Default: no event has occurred or circumstances have arisen which, had the Securities already been issued, might (whether or not with the giving of notice and/or the passage of time and/or the fulfilment of any other requirement) constitute an event described under "Events of Default" in the Securities;

(8) Other Representations: the Representations (if any) set out in the Subscription Agreement are also part of this Agreement.

(B) Repetition and Indemnity

The representations and warranties in Clause 5(A) must remain true, even though circumstances change, up to and including the Closing Date. The Issuer (and the Guarantor, if there is one, on the Agreed Basis) agrees with each Manager that it will indemnify such Manager and each of its officers or employees and each United States Person who controls such Manager for the purpose of Section 15 of the Securities Act against any consequences, direct or indirect, which such Manager, officer or employee or United States Person may suffer (i) as a result of any of the matters represented or warranted by the Issuer or (if there is one) the Guarantor in relation to the issue not being, or being alleged not to be, as represented or warranted and (ii) notwithstanding that such Manager investigates whether the matters represented or warranted are true.

6. UNDERTAKINGS

The Issuer (jointly and severally with the Guarantor, if there is one):

(A) Taxes

will pay any documentary or issue or registration fees payable in any Specified Jurisdiction in connection with the Specified Documents or the transactions contemplated therein or the Securities and any value added or other similar tax payable in respect of any amount payable to the Managers hereunder; and

(B) Warranties

will promptly notify the Lead Manager if, on any day, it is unable to repeat the representations and warranties in Clause S(A).

7. CONDITIONS

(A) Conditions

The obligations of the Managers to subscribe the Securities are conditional on:

- (1) Listing: the Securities being listed on the Stock Exchange, subject only to the issue of the Closing Security, or the Lead Manager being satisfied that they will be listed shortly after the Closing Date;

- (2) Closing Letters: the Closing Letters having been delivered to the Managers on, and dated as of, their Specified Dates;

- (3) Representations and Warranties: the representations and warranties in Clause 5(A) being true up to and including the Closing Date;

- (4) Performance: each of the Issuer and the Guarantor (if there is one) having complied with all its obligations to be performed under the Subscription Agreement on or by the Closing Date;

- (5) Closing Certificate: the delivery on the Closing Date of a Closing Certificate by the Issuer and (if there is one) the Guarantor; and

- (6) Other Conditions: the satisfaction of the other conditions (if any) set out in the Subscription Agreement.

(B) Waiver

The Lead Manager on behalf of the Managers may, at its discretion and on such terms as it thinks fit, waive compliance with Clause 7(A)(2), (3), (4), (5) and (6).

8. CLOSING

At the Specified Time on the Closing Date and in such place as the Lead Manager may reasonably require, the Issuer will issue to the order of the Managers the Closing Security, duly executed and (if so required) authenticated. Against such delivery, the Managers will pay the Closing Payment in the currency of the Securities for value the Closing Date to such account in the principal financial centre for the currency as the Issuer may specify to the Lead Manager not later than 5 days before the Closing Date. Such payment shall be evidenced by a confirmation by a depositary common to Morgan Guaranty Trust Company of New York, Brussels office, as operator of the Euroclear System and Cedel SA that it has so made that payment.

9. COMMISSION

The Issuer (failing whom the Guarantor, if there is one) agrees to pay the Commission to the Managers.

10. EXPENSES

The Issuer (failing whom the Guarantor, if there is one) will pay to the Lead Manager the Expense Amount, in the manner specified in the Expenses Letter.

11. TERMINATION

(A) Failure to satisfy conditions

The Lead Manager may, by notice to the Issuer at any time before subscription of the Securities, terminate the Subscription Agreement if any of the conditions in Clause 7(A) is not fulfilled or waived. Upon such termination, the parties shall be released from their obligations under the Subscription Agreement, except for those of the Issuer and (if there is one) the Guarantor under Clauses 5 and 10.

(B) Force Majeure

The Force Majeure Clause shall apply as if set out in these Standard Terms.

12. SURVIVAL OF RIGHTS

Performance of the obligations to issue and subscribe the Securities shall not terminate any rights which any party may have under the Subscription Agreement, which shall continue in full force and effect, nor shall any such rights be affected by an investigation made by or on behalf of any of the Managers.

13. COMMUNICATIONS

Any communication shall be given by letter, telex, fax or telephone to the Issuer or (if there is one) the Guarantor or, through the Lead Manager, the Managers, in each case at its Specified Address and to the person specified under Specified Address. Any communication shall be effective (1) in the case of a letter, when delivered, (2) in the case of telex, when sent, provided what purports to be the correct answerback is received at the beginning and end of the telex, (3) in the case of fax, when acknowledged by the addressee specified under Specified Address and (4) in the case of telephone, when made.

14. GOVERNING LAW AND JURISDICTION

(A) Governing Law and Submission

The Subscription Agreement, as to which time shall be of the essence and which may be executed in any number of counterparts, to be taken together as one agreement, shall be governed by and construed in accordance with English law. The Relevant Courts are to have jurisdiction to settle any disputes which may arise out of or in connection with the Subscription Agreement and accordingly any legal action or proceedings arising out of or in connection with the Subscription Agreement ("Proceedings") may be brought in such courts. Each of the Issuer and the Guarantor (if there is one) irrevocably submits to the jurisdiction of such courts and waives any objection to Proceedings in any such courts whether on the ground of venue or on the ground that the Proceedings have been brought in an inconvenient forum. This submission is made for the benefit of each of the Managers and shall not limit the right of any of them to take Proceedings in any other court of competent jurisdiction nor shall the taking of Proceedings in one or more jurisdictions preclude the taking of Proceedings in any other jurisdiction (whether concurrently or not).

(B) Process

Each of the Issuer and (if there is one) the Guarantor irrevocably appoints the Process Agent (if any) as its authorised agent for service of process in England.

II. Agreement definitions:-

(For use with IPMA Standard Terms
for Subscription Agreements)

This Agreement is made on [   ] BETWEEN:

(1) [Name of Issuer] (the "Issuer");

(2) [Name of Guarantor] (the "Guarantor");

(3) [Name of Lead Manager](the "Lead Manager"); and

(4) [Names of the other Managers] (together with the Lead Manager, the "Managers").

This Agreement records the arrangements between the parties in relation to the issue of the Securities.

1. INTERPRETATION

(A) Definitions

"Agreed Basis" means [insert basis on which the warranties are given by the Issuer and the Guarantor, if there is one – e.g. "joint and several". If there is no Guarantor, delete the definition];

"Closing Certificate" means a certificate, dated the Closing Date and signed by a duly authorised officer of the entity giving it, confirming the warranty in Clause 7(A) (3) of the Standard Terms, as at the Closing Date;

"Closing Consents" means [insert details of those authorisations, consents etc. which cannot be obtained until after the signing of the Subscription Agreement, but which are to be obtained on or before the Closing Date];

"Closing Date" means [   ] or such later date as the Issuer and the Lead Manager on behalf of the Managers may agree;

"Closing Letters" and, in relation to each Closing Letter, its "Specified Date" means:

Closing Letter	Specified Date
[Insert details e.g. legal opinions and auditor's comfort letters]	[Date of Letter]

each substantially in the form of the draft signed for identification by [English legal advisers to the Lead Manager] with such changes as may be approved by the Lead Manager;

"Closing Payment" means an amount equal to the Selling Price less the Commission and the Expense Amount;

"Closing Security" means [e.g. the temporary global bond];

"Commission" means a combined management and underwriting commission of [ ] per cent. of the principal amount of the Securities;

"Disclosure Document" means [e.g. the Prospectus/offering Circular/ Listing Particulars] dated [   ] [and [e.g. the draft/preliminary Prospectus/offering Circular/Listing Particulars] dated [   ]]. prepared by the Issuer and the Guarantor (if any) in connection with the issue of the Securities;

"Expense Amount" means the amount specified in the Expenses Letter;

"Expenses Letter" means the letter dated [   ] from [   ] to [   ];

"Force Majeure Clause" means [IPMA Version 1/Version 2] in the form in existence on [date on which Managers were informed of the Version to be used], with the clause relating to expenses being deemed to be Clause 10 of the Standard Terms, and with the Lead Manager referred to being deemed to be the Lead Manager, as defined herein;

"Guarantee" means [the guarantee to be contained in the Trust Deed/the guarantees in the form set out in the Fiscal Agency Agreement/the guarantees to be endorsed/enfaced on the Securities], in the form set out in the Specified Documents;

"Issue Amount" means [insert currency and full principal amount of the Securities];

"Process Agent" means [set out name of Process Agent for Issuer and (if there is one) Guarantor. Do not include for Issuers or Guarantors who have a presence in the United Kingdom];

"Relevant Courts" means [insert courts which are to have jurisdiction];

"Relevant Jurisdiction" means [jurisdiction of incorporation of Issuer and (if there is one) Guarantor];

"Securities" means the [currency, total principal amount and description of the Securities to be issued], and includes, where the context admits, the Closing Security, each in the form set out in the Specified Documents;

"Selling Price" means the issue price of [ ] per cent. of the principal amount of the Securities, [plus accrued interest, if any, from [   ] to the Closing Date], less a selling [concession/commission] of [ ] per cent. of such principal amount;

"Selling Restrictions" means the terms set out in the Schedule to the Subscription Agreement and the additional restrictions set out in Clause 2;

"Specified Address" means [set out the specified address and contact details for each party];

"Specified Documents" and, in relation to each Specified Document, its "Specified Date", means:

Specified Document	Specified Date
[Identify contract, including the Subscription Agreement and the Guarantee, if there is one]	[Date of contract]

each (save for this Agreement) substantially in the form of the draft signed for identification by [English legal advisers to the Managers] with such changes as may be approved by the Lead Manager;

"Specified Financial Statements" means [insert details of the financial statements of the Issuer and, if there is one, the Guarantor which are to be the subject of the warranties, e.g. "contained in the Disclosure Document" or "contained in its annual reports for the years [   ]"];

"Specified Jurisdictions" means any Relevant Jurisdiction and [   ]

"Specified Time" means [insert time for closing] (London time) or such other time as may be agreed between the Lead Manager, on behalf of the Managers, and the Issuer;

"Stock Exchange" means [   ]; and

"Subsidiaries" means [insert definition (including affiliates, if appropriate) relevant to the Issuer/Guarantor, e.g. the definition used by the law of incorporation of the Issuer/Guarantor].

(B) Incorporation of Standard Terms

Except as otherwise provided in this Agreement, the terms of the IPMA Standard Terms for Subscription Agreements dated [   ] (the "Standard Terms") shall apply to this Agreement as if they were set out in it. [Note: Alternatively, attach a copy in a Schedule.]

2. ADDITIONAL AGREEMENTS BY THE MANAGERS

[Set out United Kingdom and other selling restrictions.]

3. ADDITIONAL REPRESENTATIONS AND WARRANTIES

In addition to Clause 5 of the Standard Terms, each of the Issuer and (if there is one) the Guarantor represents and warrants on the Agreed Basis to each of the Managers that:

(l) No Directed Selling Efforts

> Neither it nor its subsidiaries nor its affiliates nor any persons acting on its or their behalf have engaged or will engage in any directed selling efforts (as defined in Regulation S under the United States Securities Act of 1933) with respect to the Securities.

[Insert additional warranties including, if Category 1 under Regulation S is used, the following:

> "[(2)] No Substantial US Market Interest:
>
>> It reasonably believes that there is no substantial US market interest (as defined in Regulation S under the United States Securities Act of 1933) in its debt securities". [Note: if the Issuer is a subsidiary of the Guarantor, only the Guarantor need give this additional warranty.]]

The references in the Standard Terms to the representations and warranties in Clause 5(A) shall be deemed also to include the representations and warranties in this Clause.

4. OTHER TERMS

This Agreement has been entered into on the date stated at the beginning.

[NAME OF ISSUER]
By:

[NAME OF GUARANTOR]
By:

[NAME OF LEAD MANAGER]
By:

[EACH MANAGER]
By:

Listing

It is normal practice to list Eurobonds on one or more stock exchanges. Currently the most common listings are on the Luxembourg Stock Exchange or the London Stock Exchange, although the Irish Stock Exchange is growing increasingly active. The Irish Stock Exchange is not analysed separately in this book due to the facts that (i) until December 1995 this exchange was part of the London Stock Exchange and (ii) except for certain specific issuers, the Irish Stock Exchange follows the same listing rules, procedures and cost structures of the London Stock Exchange which are contained in the Yellow Book. Such rules and procedures do apply for Eurobond issues.

Listing is undertaken chiefly to make securities eligible for the widest possible range of investors. Residents of some countries are prohibited, under foreign exchange regulations and other restrictions, from purchasing unlisted foreign securities. A number of institutional investors also have a self-imposed policy of buying only listed bonds. Listing assists in the initial placement of a new issue and its subsequent marketability. Listing also provides good value to a borrower as an advertising medium. It gives a regular reminder of the borrower's existence to a wide range of executives and professionals who read the financial newspapers and the official price lists where the quotations appear daily.

Investors benefit from listing because the stock exchanges usually require the maintenance of a paying agent in the country of the listing and the supply of current annual reports and other financial information. Prices of listed securities are also quoted and printed on a regular basis in a number of news publications. As a practical matter, though, the prices of listed securities show only modest changes and therefore do not reflect the true volatility of the underlying secondary market.

Curiously enough, the stock exchanges where Eurobonds are listed are rarely used for buying and selling bonds. The real market for securities is maintained instead by professional dealers who trade bonds over the telephone or via computer. Price quotes that are provided by the stock exchanges are often obtained from these professional market-makers. When stock exchanges are used for securities transactions, the amounts involved are small (odd lots) and the margins, differences between market price and price to investor, are wide. The additional costs represented by these wide margins are a disincentive to using the exchanges. Much narrower margins can be found in the dealers' (or over-the-counter) market.

A comparison of fees and documents required for listing on the major stock exchanges follow below.

The Luxembourg Stock Exchange

A listing application for the Luxembourg Stock Exchange must be submitted by one of the Luxembourg banks which is officially recognised by the Luxembourg Stock Exchange. The Luxembourg bank or listing agent acts as a sponsor representing the issuer, and works with the lead manager to gather the documents required for listing. Most of the major Luxembourg banks have specialised departments experienced in preparing listing applications and guiding them through the stock exchange's procedures. Previously, new issues needed to be separately reviewed by the Luxembourg Banking Control Commission, but now this function has been centralised with the stock exchange.

It may be advisable to contact the listing agent a couple of weeks before a new issue is announced so that preparations can be made. For infrequent issuers, and guarantors in particular, a draft prospectus, copies of the last two years' annual reports and copies of the by-laws and articles of incorporation, should be sent to the listing agent a week or two prior to announcement. These go to the stock exchange which reviews the quality of information provided and requests modifications. Standards of disclosure are consistent but not onerous. The review may last two to three weeks. A summary time schedule for an infrequent issuer follows below:

Timetable – Luxembourg

Week of D-21
1. Contact listing agent.

2. Send draft preliminary prospectus for review by the Luxembourg Stock Exchange together with issuer's (and guarantor's, if any) annual reports for past two years, issuer's by-laws and articles of association, and draft underwriting documents.

Week of D-7
1. Receive comments from Luxembourg Stock Exchange.

2. Prepare modifications to preliminary prospectus and notify listing agent of changes made.

3. Receive confirmation from listing agent that modifications are acceptable to the Luxembourg Stock Exchange. Communication usually handled over the telephone.

D Day
All preliminary documents mailed to listing agent. Agent will notify lead manager (announcement) about which documents are required.

D+1 to D+7
1. Final review of documents by Luxembourg Stock Exchange and comments, if any.

2. Modifications, if necessary, are reflected in final prospectus.

D+7
Signing day

Week of D+7
1. All final documents faxed/couriered to listing agent, to be received two days prior to listing. Agent will notify lead manager about which documents are required.

2. Confirmation of listing approval by Luxembourg Stock Exchange. Communication telex to listing agent which passes information to the lead manager.

D+12 (closing)
1. Listing granted and securities free to trade on floor of the Luxembourg Stock Exchange.

Well-known issuers can accelerate the above time schedule. High quality borrowers that have completed a number of bond offerings, for instance, need only an abbreviated review by the Luxembourg Stock Exchange, so the time required is greatly reduced. Fewer documents are needed as information such as company by-laws will already be on file with the Luxembourg Stock Exchange.

The London Stock Exchange

Listing on the London Stock Exchange (LSE) is reasonably straightforward. The LSE's specific listing rules are frequently referred to as the Yellow Book. The major disclosure documentation required by the London Stock Exchange is known as the Listing Particulars. It should be noted, though, that the offering circular lodged with either the London or Luxembourg exchanges is also referred to as listing particulars under the Council of the European Communities Listing Particulars Directive (80/390/EEC). London listing particulars are for the most part broadly descriptive, containing similar information to that which historically had been found in a prospectus. However, there are certain differences. For instance, pictures, charts and graphs are normally discouraged unless the exchange is convinced that this is the only manner in which factual information can be clearly communicated.

Generally speaking, all issuers may seek a listing for their securities on the London Stock Exchange as long as they are properly incorporated and, except in particular circumstances, have published accounts in accordance with their relevant national laws for the preceding three years. The securities also need to be freely transferable. The terms of the securities must also conform to the laws of the country of incorporation and be consistent with the memorandum and articles of association of the issuer. The total market capitalisation of the securities (other than tap issues) needs to be at least £200,000.

A listing is usually applied for by an institution referred to as a listing agent. Historically, this was a London-based broker but now any approved institution (or 'authorised person') regulated under the FSA can perform this role. Additionally, listings may also be made by any European institution authorised under relevant national regulations to participate in securities issues and to provide services related to such issues. The listing agent is responsible for advising the issuer with respect to the application of the Listing Rules and has to lodge a declaration with the LSE (Schedule 4B of the Listing Rules) that all required documents have been supplied and other relevant requirements have been met. The listing agent handles most communications with the LSE, including the lodging of required documentation. Final approval from the LSE is also sought by the listing agent.

Together with the preparation of the listing particulars (or equivalent offering document in the case of sovereign states and local authorities), other materials should be submitted to the Capital Markets and Listing Departments in both draft and final form. The issuer is free to publish his own notice of listing once it is approved. However, the London Stock Exchange will typically prepare a Formal Notice which will appear in the Regulatory News Service, which is the electronic information service operated by the Exchange's Company Announcements Office. This notice will give, inter alias, the nature and country of incorporation of the issuer as well as a description of the securities and the addresses where copies of the listing particulars may be obtained or reviewed by the public. The Formal Notice should be advertised as soon as the listing particulars have been approved but no later than the day when the listing becomes effective.

Following is an example of an approximate timetable for a London listing for a first time corporate issuer. Frequent issuers can accelerate the schedule considerably. Additionally, the LSE is prepared to be flexible in certain instances when this is reasonably justified. For the sake of clarity, the London Stock Exchange exercises an effective two step approval. The first step, which is administered primarily by the Capital Markets Department, concerns itself chiefly with the content and disclosure quality of the listing particulars. Once Formal Approval is obtained for the particulars, the Listing Department assumes responsibility for the remaining listing procedures which include a final check of the particulars and the gathering of other outstanding documentation. Once all procedures have been complied with successfully, then the securities to be listed are "considered for admission by the Exchange".

Timetable – London

D-3 weeks
1. Listing agent approaches London Stock Exchange to commence discussions on specific disclosures in the listing particulars (conforming to the Listing Particulars Directive and other specific information requirements, or omissions, as agreed with the London Stock Exchange – Capital Markets Department).

2. Assembly of other documentation required by The Listing Rules to support the listing application.

D-2 weeks
1. Submit three draft copies of the listing particulars (or equivalent offering document).

2. Prepare draft of Formal Notice describing the issuer and the date and times when the listing particulars may be viewed.

3. Submit any non- applicability letter or omission of information letter or omission of material contract from display letter.

4. Submit 3 copies of other documents to be authorised under Section 154 of the FSA.

D-1 week
1. Signature of subscription agreement.

2. Formal Approval of listing particulars ('stamped') and Formal Notice published.

D-2 days
1. Submit documentation (the '48 hour documents') in final form for review by the Listing Department:

    a. The formal listing application (in accordance with Schedule 3B of The Listing Rules) signed by the issuer.

    b. Three copies of the listing particulars.

    c. A declaration of compliance from the listing agent (in accordance with Schedule 4B of The Listing Rules).

d. A copy of any national newspaper which contains the Formal Notice.

   e. Copies of any letters regarding the omission of information, the 'non-applicability' letter and any letters regarding the omission from display of a material contract.

   f. Copies of the issuer's shareholders' and board's resolutions approving the issue, the listing application and the publication of the associated documents.

   g. Copies of any other documents required by The Listing Rules of which the LSE has informed the issuer or its listing agent.

   h. For first time issuers, copies of: their certificate of incorporation, memorandum and articles of association, annual reports covering the periods contained in the listing particulars and most recent interim report since the date of the last annual report.

   i. Letter from the listing agent regarding any deferred settlement arrangements.

2. Exchange to be advised immediately if any matter arises which has a significant impact on the existing listing particulars, in which case supplementary listing particulars shall be published stating the nature of such matter, giving a responsibility statement and giving a statement that no other significant matter has arisen.

D – day
1. Listing of securities considered for admission by the LSE.

2. Payment of listing fee due by 9:00 am.

D-day until D + 5
1. Copies of the listing particulars continue to be available at the offices of the listing agent and paying agent in sufficient quantity to satisfy public demand.

2. Other documents to be submitted:

   a. A statement of the number of securities which were in fact issued.

   b. A written request for refund of fees if the number of securities issued was less than that applied for.

   c. A final copy of the Formal Notice (when only a draft had been previously lodged with the LSE).

   d. An executed copy of the trust deed or fiscal agency agreement, as appropriate.

   e. A copy of the temporary document of title and any definitive document, together with a declaration from the securities printers, as requested.

   f. A certified copy of every expert opinion contained within the listing particulars.

   g. Any letter, report, valuation or like document referred to in the listing particulars.

As noted previously, the above timetable may be shortened for frequent issuers. This is particularly true for continuous offerings such as Euro-MTNs. Once such a programme has been established with full listing particulars, new particulars need not be lodged for issues during the subsequent 12 months (except for supplementary particulars to reflect significant changes in an issuer's credit standing). For each new issue within the 12-month period, a pricing supplement must be submitted to the exchange showing the final terms of each new issue. Also, the listing charges need to be paid, and there must be a confirmation of the number of securities that have finally been issued. There are similar modifications of procedure to reflect the special circumstances of state guaranteed debt, convertible debt and warrants and direct issues by sovereign states and their regional and local authorities.

Exhibit 4.4
Listing fees of major stock exchanges

Initial listing: (assuming $50 million, seven-year issue in US dollar equivalents and rounded to nearest $50)[1]

Item	Luxembourg US$	London US$
Admission/listing fee	750	3,000
Listing agent's fee	1,500/3,000	4,000[3]
Annual charge/total cost[2]	500/4,000	–
Prospectus review fee	750/1,500	–
	3,500/9,250	7,000

1. Fees to be paid in local currency. It is emphasised that the indicative fees vary widely as a consequence of the type of issuer (new or established), the nature of the offering and the amount of the work required.
2. Indicative fee which will vary in accordance with the size and the maturity of the offering. This maintenance fee is reduced for the second and subsequent listings for the same borrower.
3. Indicative fee only, actual cost will depend on the amount of work required and the relationship between the issuer and the listing agent.

Exhibit 4.5
Summary of documents required for listing on major stock exchanges[1]

	Item	Luxembourg	London
1.	Preliminary prospectus (listing particulars)	2 copies	3 copies
2.	Final prospectus (listing particulars)	40 copies to be with listing agent before the business day preceding first listing	3 copies, one of which is to be signed by official(s) of issuer/guarantor. 1 signed copy of the listing particulars
3.	Execution copy of each final prospectus from guarantor and issuer	2 copies from each	1 signed copy
4.	Copies of borrower's by-laws and articles of incorporation	3 certified copies of issuer's, and 3 of the guarantor's, statutory documents to be with listing agent 3 working days before listing	1 copy
5.	Copies of annual reports for last three years	2 copies from issuer and guarantor	1 copy from issuer and guarantor, together with the recent interim report
6.	Copies of underwriting contracts	2 copies of all underwriting and related contracts	Offering or invitation telexes and other similar documents need not be submitted
7.	Copies of fiscal and paying agreement (trust deed), subscription agreement, warrant agreement agency	2 conformed copies	1 conformed copy
8.	Resolutions of borrower/guarantor authorising issue/guarantee and necessary government and other consents	2 certified copies	1 certified copy
9.	Listing application or letter of application	1 copy addressed to the Société de la Bourse de Luxembourg	1 copy signed by official(s) of issuer and 1 copy signed by partner or director of sponsor
10.	Expert opinions	n/r	1 copy of the opinion of experts referred to in the listing particulars (if any) and 1 copy of their consent

123

Exhibit 4.4 *continued*

Item	Luxembourg	London
11. Specimen bond certificates	3 specimens	1 copy of any temporary document of title and any definitive documents of title
12. Announcements	n/r	Copies of the Formal Notice and any advertisement or announcement relating to the admission of listing

n/r = not required

1. Requirements may be reduced for second and subsequent issues of certain borrowers which have already obtained listing.

Ratings

A guide to the credit standing of those borrowers who have issued bonds in certain domestic markets is provided by bond rating agencies. The best known of these agencies are Moody's Investors Services, Inc. and Standard & Poor's Corporation, both incorporated in the US, but operating internationally. The ratings are assigned to debt instruments issued by particular borrowers (and not specifically to the borrowers themselves). The rankings are as follows:

Standard & Poor's	Moody's	Definitions
AAA	Aaa	Highest quality; minimum investment risk
AA	Aa	High quality; little investment risk
A	A	Good quality; favourable investment characteristics
BBB	Baa	Medium quality; some speculative characteristics
BB	Ba	Lower medium quality; speculative characteristics
B	B	Low quality; very speculative characteristics
CCC	Caa	
CC	Ca	Poor quality; default may or has already occurred
C	C	

In an effort to fine tune its debt grading systems, Standard & Poor's sometimes modifies its ratings from AA to CCC by the addition of a plus or a minus sign to show relative standing within the major rating categories. In the case of subordinated debt of an issuer, the rating will move one step lower than the senior debt in the investment categories BBB or better. For example, if senior debt were rated A, then subordinated debt of the same borrower would carry an A- rating. A two step reduction applies for subordinated debt where senior debt is in the more speculative grades, BB or lower, or where the subordination is more substantial. Moody's utilises a similar system of rating modifiers within the categories Aa through B, with the numbers 1, 2 and 3 replacing the + and − signs.

Some 60%-90% of new Eurobond issues have ratings or, alternatively, refer to the ratings of comparable debt in the respective domestic market. IPMA dictates that all ratings should be disclosed during the course of a new bond issue and the ranking of the domestically rated debt relative to the new issue, if this is not rated itself.

Different types of ratings

There are two general types of ratings; public and private. The public rating is used with public bond issues and is quoted widely in the financial press as well as in the marketing efforts for a new issue. A private rating is more confidential and normally associated with the private placement of debt. In such circumstances, knowledge of the rating is restricted to the borrower, its bankers, the agencies and whichever of the lenders the borrower wishes to inform. However, it is important that awareness of a private rating remains carefully restricted.

The rating process often concerns international bond issuers for reasons of confidentiality and worries that a prime rating might not be obtained. The agencies are aware of these concerns, and their procedures allow borrowers to halt the process at a number of points without adverse impact on reputation or prestige.

Initial opinion

It is possible to obtain from the rating agencies an initial opinion as to a borrower's possible rating. This opinion is based on publicly available information and the review may be completed in a few days. Normally, no charge is made for this service and a borrower is not obliged to continue with the rating process if the indication does not meet expectations.

Preliminary comments

If a borrower elects to proceed with the rating process and a formal presentation is made, the agencies will make known their preliminary comments. If these are unsatisfactory, the borrower can choose to halt the process before the formal rating is awarded.

Acceptance/rejection of rating

If the rating process is completed and a rating is awarded, it is still up to the borrower to accept or reject this rating. Rejecting a rating means that it will not become public knowledge and the approach to the agencies will itself remain confidential.

General procedures

There are a number of steps which are normally taken when getting a rating:

1. **Selection of financial adviser.** Sometimes an international borrower will

retain an investment bank before approaching the rating agencies. The presentation made to the agencies should be directed towards those criteria which the agencies normally employ when evaluating comparable credits. It is not important to produce a 'flashy' presentation but rather to address the fundamental credit issues typically raised by the agencies. Frequently, too, issuers choose to approach the agencies on their own. This option has certain advantages because the issuer will always have better access to information on itself than a third party financial adviser. There may also be cost savings.

2. **Selection of a real or hypothetical financing.** The agencies rate individual issues and not borrowers per se, although the ratings for similar classes of debt of a particular borrower usually remain the same (assuming the borrower's financial position does not change materially). Therefore, to get a rating, one has to have an issue. If a borrower has plans for an issue, this may be used to acquire a rating. If an actual financing is not planned, a hypothetical one may be chosen which best reflects the likely terms (amount, maturity, repayments and so on) of a possible future financing.

3. **Choice of a rating agency.** Normally, both Moody's and Standard & Poor's are approached for ratings. If only one is approached, it is possible that the market may assume that the other agency gave a low rating which was subsequently rejected.

4. **Preparation for rating presentation.** A presentation is usually compiled for the agencies by the borrower either on its own or with its financial adviser. Such a presentation, for a corporate borrower, includes detailed information about its current environment and financial position, as well as projected financial statements, a description of the securities to be rated and a statistical comparison with rated borrowers in the same industry. For sovereign state borrowers, the information relates more to their national and international economic activities and prospects. The agencies will give a preliminary indication of their reaction to the presentation.

5. **Formal rating review.** If the preliminary comments of the agencies are accepted, the borrower can elect to proceed with a more formal review. Such a review involves an in-depth analysis of the presentation given to the agencies and, frequently, requests for further information or clarification of information already submitted. Sometimes, in addition, the agencies will usually wish to send representatives to visit the borrower to study its facilities and have discussions with its senior officials. In addition, the agencies will take an active role in reviewing the offering documents, trust deed or fiscal agency agreements and so forth.

6. **Awarding of rating.** The borrower and its financial adviser(s), if any, are notified of the rating as soon as it is determined. If the rating is acceptable, no further action is required. If the rating is below expectations, the borrower may choose to reject it or re-open discussions with the agency involved. Appeals are usually made on the basis of the credit weaknesses identified by the agency. If the ensuing dialogue is unsuccessful in improving the agency's assessment of the borrower, there is always the option of rejecting the rating.

Typical time schedule
The numbers indicate the number of weeks prior to the awarding of the rating.

Week 10
Borrower decides to obtain rating.

Week 10 to Week 9
Borrower selects/decisions taken concerning:

1. Financial adviser(s);

2. Actual or hypothetical financing; and

3. Rating agencies to approach.

Week 9 to Week 6
Borrower and financial adviser(s) compile information for rating agency presentation.

Week 6 to Week 4
Agencies receive presentation and begin informal review. Agencies relay preliminary comments to borrower and financial adviser(s). Borrower decides whether to proceed with formal rating process.

Week 4 to Week 1
Agencies proceed with formal review and request clarification and additional information. Agencies visit borrower.

W-week
Agencies communicate rating to borrower which accepts or rejects or re-opens discussions.

Estimated expenses
The following estimates assume a first time public rating for a corporate issue.

Moody's (range)	approx. $10,000-$60,000
Standard & Poor's	approx. $40,000

The above fees are indications only and will vary according to the circumstances and the difficulty of the rating work involved. It is useful to seek a rating quote from the agency(ies) once the scale of the task is more clearly known. Please note the above figures are also subject to an annual monitoring fee.

5

BOND TRADING AND PORTFOLIO MANAGEMENT

The following chapter sets out to discuss the chief characteristics of bonds and their trading behaviour in the secondary market.

It is often surprising to learn that, despite the existence of well-established, efficient international stock exchanges, most bond trading takes place in an over-the-counter market; over telephones and screens and fax and telex machines between individuals employed by firms located around the world. This practice has grown up in part because international bond professionals are scattered geographically and often are not located where securities are listed.

The firms which commit their own capital are called market-makers. The individuals who buy and sell securities are called dealers in the UK and Europe, and traders in the US. A continuous secondary market in securities is maintained by the bond dealers employed by various investment houses. Their contribution is essential.

Investors who buy bonds need to know that these securities can be sold again before they mature, should they need their money back. Few individuals or institutions can afford to commit money for between five and thirty years with no option to sell or liquidate their holdings. Even if investors do not need their money back, they may find other investments which are more attractive. What the secondary bond market provides is both a ready way of putting a price to older or seasoned bonds and a place where bonds can be sold or traded. By providing these services, the secondary market balances a borrower's desire for long-term money and investors' needs for liquidity. Without it, the international bond market would be a far more limited source of capital.

In brief, the secondary bond market gives a price to securities so that they can be bought and sold prior to maturity. There are a number of reasons why bond prices fluctuate in the secondary market. Four major factors are:

1. Interest rates. If the general level of interest rates in a particular currency changes, for example, as a result of government intervention, bond price levels will adjust so that all securities of a similar maturity and quality give a comparable return.

2. Currency. If the underlying currency of a bond loses value relative to other major currencies, the action of investors selling the weak currency securities will have a depressing effect on the price of these securities.

3. Bond characteristics. If a bond changes with respect to one of its unique characteristics, this alteration will be reflected in its price. If, for instance, its credit deteriorates, its price will decline.

4. Technical factors. Bond prices can be affected by certain forces, apart from those mentioned above, which are peculiar to the workings of the market. For example, in the ordinary course of trading a large short may develop in a specific issue and cause abrupt price rises as dealers rush to cover their positions.

Which market?

Before beginning an examination of each of these factors, it is important to establish what is meant by the term market. In the past there was not just one international bond market, but a collection of different markets and within these a series of further divisions or partitions. Such distinctions have all but faded away over time. Perhaps one distinction which has lasting power is the separation between the primary or new issue from the secondary market for bonds. Failure to appreciate this distinction can lead to some confusion.

Primary versus secondary markets

There are frequently differences in yield between new issues and seasoned issues of the same borrower, with similar maturities. Such differences or spreads or differentials can range from a few basis points to 100 basis points or more. One cause of these spreads is that new issues often offer investors a modest yield premium over seasoned issues as an incentive to purchase the new securities. Eurobond offerings represent a significant increase in the supply of securities traded in the market and, therefore, a comparable demand must be encouraged.

From practical experience, a number of observations can be drawn:

- The primary market is subject to somewhat greater volatility than the secondary market.

- From time to time, substantial discrepancies, that is up to two percentage points, tend to develop between primary and secondary market bond yields. This occurs most often when the market is moving at its fastest.

- New issues appear on average to give a marginally better yield return than bonds trading in the secondary market.

These above observations suggest certain insights into investor behaviour. First, many bondholders tend to remain holders, and despite the growing tendency to swap securities, once bonds have been placed in firm hands their price volatility drops appreciably. Second, investors appear to need coaxing to buy newly issued securities. The yield premium noted above is, therefore, paid to attract investor interest (this is particularly true in a large offering where a substantial volume of securities has to be placed). Third, investors show a preference for outstanding issues with low coupons. This is because of fiscal advantages (the tax differential and sometimes lower rates typically applicable to capital gains) and the reduced probability of optional redemption by the borrower. Finally, from a banker's perspective, it is understandable why new issue spread pricing (against an actively traded benchmark security like the US Treasury) has become so popular. The secondary market price for seasoned bonds is often not a good guide for what is happening in the primary market.

While it is possible to speak in generalities about the relationship between the primary and secondary markets, these do not always hold true for individual bond issues. For example, new issues do not always offer a yield premium over seasoned issues. In the case of an outstanding issue trading at a small discount, investors might well prefer the increased current income offered by a slightly higher coupon on a new issue. As a result, little or no premium need be offered. The new issue might also be larger in volume and therefore attract a greater proportion of institutional investors.

Interest rates

Shifts in interest rate levels are a key factor in determining bond performance. Indeed, the purpose of the bond market is to price securities so that their yields correspond to the changing levels of interest rates. The exact relationships may not appear immediately clear, but as the general level of interest rates change, the prices of outstanding bonds must adjust accordingly. They cannot remain static. For example, if the level of seven-year interest rates increases from 8% to 8½%, investors will switch out of their old 8% coupon seven-year bonds and purchase the new securities being offered with ½% higher interest. This switching will continue until the fall in price of the old securities equates their return with that on the newly issued bonds, or, more typically, bond dealers will mark down securities prices to adjust for the new interest levels expected by investors. As an axiomatic principle, the price movement of a security is inversely related to its return. In the preceding example, the price of an older security fell, with the effect that its return was increased. Had its price risen, its return would have dropped. Another word for the return provided by a bond is yield, which includes investor return both by way of the interest coupon and the price of the security (eg capital appreciation or depreciation as in the calculation of yield to maturity).

Interest rate levels generally vary for different maturities of securities. The most common distinction is that between long-term rates (those that correspond to bond yields) and short-term rates (interest returns provided by 'money market' instruments or credit facilities which have an initial maturity of one year or less). Long-term rates have clear significance to bond investors and issuers because it will be these rates which determine the yield levels (and therefore prices) at which securities will be bought and sold. The general trend in long-term rates corresponds to the level of inflation in society. According to classical theory, they should remain at a slight premium over the inflation rate.

Short-term interest rates, on the other hand, are more susceptible to direct government intervention. Indeed, certain key rates such as that for US Federal Funds (the overnight rate of interest for deposit balances held within the US Federal Reserve System) are employed to regulate monetary growth and influence the rate of inflation. Such rates can provide clues to government policy (and the future of inflation). They can also assert a direct influence over longer-term rates and, by extension, the bond market. In this way they are seen as a key indicator of all interest rates.

The relationship between short- and long-term rates is highly complex. However, certain relationships can be clearly detected. When short-term rates rise to the point where they exceed long-term rates, there is a general tendency to attract funds out of the long-term bond market and into higher yielding short-term securities or bank deposits. The effect of selling bonds to buy short-term securities is to depress the price of the bonds (and thus increase their yield).

Rising short-term interest rates also have a pronounced impact on the market for new bond issues. This is because almost all bond houses finance their holdings of long-term securities thorough short-term borrowings. When short-term rates are lower than the coupons offered by bonds, the bond houses benefit from the differential, called a 'positive carry'. However, when the relationship is reversed and it costs more to fund bond positions than is received back in coupon return from the long-term securities (a 'negative carry'), the bond houses stand to make substantial losses. As a natural reaction, they tend to sell off their inventories of bonds. This causes price declines and increases in yield. New offerings are also discouraged because bond houses are reluctant to hold quantities of long-term securities in their inventories if this produces a net financing loss.

Currency

Bonds in the international markets are denominated in a wide variety of currencies. As values of these currencies fluctuate on the foreign exchange markets, so, too, will the attractiveness of the related securities. This is self-evident. What is really surprising is the volatility of foreign exchange rates and their impact on total bond yield. In the past, a number of foreign borrowers have been tempted to raise Sfr fundings due to the low coupon rates. What they did not fully expect is that the appreciation of the underlying currency (which had the effect of increasing the total debt outstanding) frequently more than offset the interest savings.

It is little wonder then that issuers, particularly dollar-based borrowers, approach foreign currency bond markets with great caution. While some issuers have made savings, others have paid the price of borrowing in a rapidly appreciating currency. A lesson to be learned from this experience is the importance of matching the currency of borrowing with that already generated in revenues by the issuer. For example, a corporate treasurer should borrow Sfr if his company earns income in that currency or another equally strong European currency. If the Sfr appreciates so will the value of the issuer's Sfr revenues. The loss on one is compensated by the gain on the other. Alternatively, the foreign exchange exposure can be offset by doing a currency swap or hedging by using the forwards or options markets as described in Chapter Six.

Bond characteristics

There are numerous characteristics of bonds which have a substantial impact on trading performance in the secondary market. By varying each of these characteristics, a new pattern of performance emerges.

Maturity and amortisation

One of the important variables is maturity. The relevance of maturity to borrowers is obvious; less clear, perhaps, is what it means to investors. First, from the average investor's point of view, the longer the maturity, the greater the perceived risk and the higher the expected return. Furthermore, and more subtly, the longer the maturity the greater the price volatility. This is explained later in this chapter. A similar effect can be observed with coupon levels, because low coupon bonds are more price volatile than high coupon bonds. These are natural characteristics of all bonds and not features unique to Euro-securities. Where the significance lies for investors is in portfolio strategy. For example, if interest rates and yield levels are predicted to rise, investors will act defensively and shorten the average maturity of their portfolios and concentrate on buying high coupon bonds. It is important for borrowers to understand these patterns of investor behaviour when structuring new issues during different points in the interest rate cycle.

Maturity is one of the most basic bond characteristics, and issuers have been highly inventive in this area, particularly in structuring features which alter maturity through various forms of repayment.

Two examples of bonds with varying maturities are bonds which may be extended at the option of investors (called extendibles) and bonds which may be repaid, again at the option (this time called a put) of the investors, prior to maturity (called retractables). Retractable bonds favour borrowers because, in practice, investors often do not bother to request the earlier maturity. On the other hand, retractable bonds, for this very reason, are that much less saleable and have to offer something of a yield premium in order to encourage investment. Both forms of securities are similar, however, in the sense that they give investors a choice between short and long maturities. This provides an investor with the opportunity of electing to extend or retract according to the level of and outlook for interest rates at the time such a decision is made.

Bonds may also be partially redeemed prior to maturity. This feature is called amortisation. There are two classical forms of amortisation: sinking fund and purchase fund. The sinking fund is an obligation of the borrower to repay or retire a set amount of bonds in certain 12-month periods before maturity. Sinking funds normally require that the borrower buy back its bonds at par (100% of principal amount) by the last day of each of these periods. Bonds bought this way are selected by lot and the bondholders notified well in advance through published advertisements of the date set for this redemption. Borrowers are also given the flexibility to purchase bonds in the secondary market to satisfy their sinking fund obligations, giving them the advantage of possibly buying bonds at a discount rather than at par. These open market purchases may either be made by the borrower or by a bank acting on its behalf. Normally, banks charge a fee calculated on the principal amount of the bonds purchased.

Whoever does the buying, an attempt is made to acquire the bonds at the lowest price possible. Sometimes a borrower will also reserve the right to double the sinking fund amount in any year, called an option to double. The purchase of these additional securities cannot normally, however, be used to reduce the sinking fund commitment in subsequent years.

A less common type of amortisation, the purchase fund, is similar to a sinking fund, with the difference that a purchase fund operates only if the secondary market price of an issue falls below a certain level, usually par. If, for instance, the price is continually above par, no securities need be bought back. Purchases which are made are at the going market price at that time. A borrower normally retains the services of a bank, the purchase agent, to operate its purchase fund, and the fee charged is usually calculated on the principal amount of all bonds acquired.

A typical purchase fund requires that a certain number of bonds be bought during specified six or 12-month periods before maturity. If, however, the purchase agent is unable to acquire the set number of bonds during a particular period, it is usually allowed an additional six months to buy the remaining bonds. If the purchase agent still cannot acquire the remaining bonds during the additional six months, then this obligation lapses. Like a sinking fund, a purchase fund permits the borrower to buy bonds in the open market and credit these bonds towards fulfilling subsequent purchase fund obligations.

In theory, purchase funds favour investors because they only operate at prices below par, whereas sinking funds may be used by borrowers to acquire at par bonds which are trading at a premium. Purchase funds are sometimes used in the early years of an issue to help market offerings which are hard to sell. As a result, they have come to be associated with complex financings or financings which require the additional liquidity provided by the workings of such funds.

As for secondary market performance, both these types of amortisation support the price of a bond when it is trading at a discount. A sinking fund also has the effect of lowering the premium at which a bond might trade, as bonds purchased are acquired at par. This form of amortisation has a dampening effect on above par trading. While a purchase fund acts to support the price of a security trading below par, a sinking fund both supports the price when trading is at a discount and restrains it when trading is at a premium, thus tightening a security's price range around par. Both types of funds also give liquidity to an outstanding issue. A flurry of trading activity often occurs in a previously quiescent security when these funds begin to operate.

Practical experience suggests that despite the structural advantages of a purchase fund, investors seem to prefer sinking funds. The certainty of a specific amortisation schedule has definite appeal. The presence of sinking and purchase funds serves to encourage investor confidence.

Amortisation can be optional as well as mandatory. A borrower is frequently given the alternative to buy back a part or all of his bonds in the open market at the then prevailing price. The borrower may also be given the power to force investors to have their bonds repaid at par or at a slight premium. This option, referred to as a call, usually begins some years after the securities have been issued and continues through to maturity. The option of calling a bond is most important when an outstanding issue is trading well above par and the borrower would like to refund it with a new, lower coupon offering. Thus, bonds trading at high premiums often perform erratically or in a depressed fashion in the secondary market, particularly as a call date approaches.

The borrower is usually provided a third type of optional amortisation: the right to call an issue if withholding or other taxes affecting the securities are imposed. The fact that Eurobonds pay their interest free of all withholding and related taxes is crucial to their popularity. If such taxes are imposed during the life of an issue, the borrower is almost always required to make gross-up payments (additional interest payments to make the net after-tax payments equal to the earlier non-taxed payments). In such an event, the borrower is typically given the choice between making the gross-up payment or calling all of the outstanding issue. Although such an event might seem so improbable as to be of academic interest only, several bond issuers and investors were faced with this prospect in the Spring of 1987. At that time the US government was altering its double taxation treaty with the Netherlands Antilles which had been used as an issuing base for many US corporations. The impact was that withholding tax would have had to be paid on certain existing Eurobonds. Because many of the affected securities were trading above par and the news suggested that borrowers would be free to repay these bonds at par only, secondary market prices dropped precipitously. The situation corrected itself, however, when a specific exception was made for the affected securities by the US Government.

Credit quality

Credit quality is of interest to an investor because it is a key determinant of the relative terms of a bond. An investor's assessment of a borrower's ability to meet all required payments in a timely manner influences, among other things, the rate of return he demands.

Investors in the Euromarkets will, in general, accept only those bonds issued by borrowers of a high credit standing. Borrowers which have successfully issued bonds in the Euromarkets include: supranational institutions, governments, government guaranteed entities, state-owned entities, municipal and regional authorities and agencies, major banks and large industrial and commercial corporations. The minimum acceptable credit standing, however, varies with the instrument the borrower wishes to issue; equity-linked securities, for instance, have been successfully issued by corporations whose credit standing was less than would be acceptable to investors in the straight debt sector of the market. Among issuers of straight debt, longer maturities are usually restricted to the highest grade of borrowers.

A guide to the credit standing of those borrowers who have also issued bonds in certain domestic markets is provided by bond rating agencies. The best known of these agencies are Moody's Investors Services, Inc., and Standard & Poor's Corporation, both incorporated in the US, but operating internationally. The ratings are assigned to debt instruments issued by particular borrowers (and not specifically to the borrowers themselves). The rating of bond issues is discussed in greater detail in Chapter Four.

Good quality credits generally trade at a lower yield and, therefore, at a higher price than poorer credits. Investors simply require a higher return for placing their money with borrowers which may not repay their debts. For top quality credits there is less risk and thus no need for the premium. When the market is stable the premium remains moderate, say, 1%-1½%, but this differential can widen as interest rates grow more volatile and are on the rise. During such periods of uncertainty, credit quality is naturally of greater concern.

Higher grade bonds typically appeal to a wide range of investors and are therefore actively traded. This makes them quite responsive to shifts in the general level of interest rates. By contrast, lower quality bonds tend to be poor traders and respond in a rather lethargic manner.

Liquidity

The liquidity of a security, or the ease with which it can be purchased or sold without materially affecting the market price, is a major priority for investors who may wish to use invested moneys, or adjust their portfolios, prior to maturity. The liquidity of a security is related to several factors, including the age and amount outstanding in an issue as well as its currency of denomination. In general, the larger the issue the greater its liquidity. Institutional investors, who normally trade in large blocks of securities, often restrict their investments to those issues which will allow them to trade their holdings without affecting the price. Liquidity is also related to the currency of an issue. The small number of participants in relatively minor currency sectors such as Austrian schillings may mean that transactions will tend to affect price. In general, the older a security, the less liquid it is likely to be.

The average size of Eurobond offerings has increased markedly since 1963, as is shown more graphically in Chapter Eight. Inflation has been an important factor in this trend over the period. Historically, as the purchasing power of money fell through inflation, corporate profitability typically was reduced forcing the funding of operations through debt rather than retained earnings. Thus, the average size of an issue has tended to grow. Another factor contributing to the trend more recently has been the increasing depth and maturity of the market, together with the growing volume of funds available to it, particularly from institutional investors.

Complexity and reputation

Occasionally, issues of relatively good quality borrowers perform less well than might be expected. For example, warrant bonds are typically poor traders once their warrants have been removed or stripped off. This is no reflection on the credit quality or standing of the borrower but reflects rather the simple fact that the warrants are frequently the most attractive elements of these financings to investors. Additionally, the ex-warrant bonds usually are left with below-market coupons once the warrants are stripped, which depresses prices.

Investors also tend to shy away from issues which have been poorly handled or, for other reasons, had a difficult time coming to the primary market. Individual issuers acquire reputations which reflect the initial reception they get from investors. A warmly received offering engenders a certain amount of goodwill, which continues to benefit it in the secondary market. In contrast, an unsuccessful new issue will tend to trade at the lower end of the range expected on the basis of its fundamentals.

Over time, issuers become typecast as to their quality. This impression or name is slow to change, yet is sufficiently important to dilute the effect of many of the other influences discussed above. As a result, a poor quality name, for instance, will often trade at a discount despite a relatively high current coupon.

Technical factors

Significant price changes also occur as a result of technical factors. These include influences which are external to a bond issue itself but still have an effect on trading performance. A good example is short covering. From time to time, dealers or other market professionals will sell securities they do not own in anticipation of a future price decline which will permit them to buy those securities needed for delivery later, at a lower cost basis than the original transaction. If all goes well, the trader will collect the difference between the first sales price and the lower cost to him when purchasing bonds in the secondary market. If things do not go as planned, the dealer will still have to buy bonds in the market to cover his short and make the delivery of securities required in the first transaction. The price in the secondary market might then be at the same level or higher than the initial sales price. And, if things go really badly the act of covering the short will push the price further upwards. Thus, short covering in a specific issue may have the effect of pushing up its price and depressing its yield out of line with general market levels.

Portfolio management

The purpose of portfolio management is to maximise the return on securities holdings subject to investment constraints laid down by the investor. As mentioned previously, one element of bond return is the interest or coupon which is paid. The other element is price appreciation (for securities selling at a discount relative to their face value) or depreciation (for premium priced securities). The price of a bond, also called its quote, is expressed as a percentage of its principal amount. Thus, a bond with a par value of $1,000, selling at 99% is worth $990. The bond market is made up of buyers and sellers, so securities are quoted as having two prices: the bid – what people are prepared to pay, and asked – what people wish to receive for bonds.

The combination of interest return and price appreciation (or depreciation) is called yield. When talking about yields, market professionals customarily use the expression basis point, which is equal to one-hundredth of 1%. If yield levels increase from 8% to 8.50%, then the gain has been 50 basis points.

There are a number of ways to calculate and express yield. Each has its own particular use and shortcomings. The major definitions of yield follow below.

Current yield

The current yield (also called the interest, income or flat or running yield) is the simplest measure of the return on a security. It is expressed as a percentage and is computed by multiplying the annual coupon amount by 100 and dividing by the purchase price of the related security, ie the current yield of a bond with a 9% coupon selling at 97% is:

$$\frac{9\% \times 100}{97\%} = 9.28\%$$

Redemption yield

Current yield does not take into account any capital gain or loss which may be realised on the redemption of a fixed interest security at maturity. Redemption yield considers both the coupon yield and this capital gain or loss. It does this by discounting all the expected cash flows from the bond.

Redemption yield is used to calculate the discount rate which would make the present value of a bond's future cash flows equal to the price of that bond. Such price (called the 'gross price') is the aggregate of the quoted price (called the 'clean price') plus any accrued interest. The general formula for redemption yield is as stated below:

$$P = \sum_{i=1}^{n} CF_i \times v^{L_i}$$

Source: ISMA

P is the gross price of the bond and n represents the number of future cash flows. CF_i equals the i th cashflow and L_i is the time in years to the i th cashflow; v is the annualised discount factor.

The International Securities Market Association (ISMA) specifically recommends use of this general formula to all but non-ISMA securities (ie certain national domestic market instruments). ISMA also recommends the following Redemption Yield Principles:-

- Unless otherwise specified redemption yields are quoted with an annual compounding period, irrespective of how many coupon periods per annum a bond may have.

- Compound interest is always used for the entire life, even when there is one period to redemption.

- If the bond accrues interest on a 360-day year then the calendar for all yield calculations consists of a 360-day year.

- Unless otherwise specified, yields are calculated from the assumed value date, not the settlement date (if different) or the trade date.

Annual interest compounding is the norm in the Euromarkets. If an alternative approach is used, then ISMA's rules require that a specific description be given as to the method which is employed. It is important to take careful notice of this presumption in favour of annual compounding. An interesting comparison can be made of annual compounding with a common alternative, semi-annual compounding.

Annual versus semi-annual compounding

Although a coupon is described as annual (paying interest only once a year), its yield to maturity may theoretically be calculated on either an annual or semi-annual basis. The reason for this is that international bonds can carry either annual or semi-annual (paying interest twice a year) coupons.

The calculation of yield can be adjusted to assume that interest is paid and reinvested either annually or semi-annually. The two assumptions can be applied to either type of coupon. The effect of applying semi-annual discounting is to lower the yield of an annual coupon. This is because an annual coupon is worth less than a semi-annual once. While an annual coupon pays interest only once a year, a semi-annual coupon pays every six months, allowing the holder to pick up additional interest income on their investment of the six-month coupon (assuming that the investor avails himself of the opportunity to earn interest on interest, and a suitably high return can be earned on a short-term investment). For example, take two coupons, one annual and the other semi-annual, which both bear nominal interest at 10% per annum ($100 a year). Interest can be reinvested at 10% per annum.

In the case of the annual coupon, the investor is left at the end of the year with $100. The holder of the semi-annual coupon has, however, received two payments of $50 each totalling $100, permitting him to earn half a year's interest, say, $2.50, on the first of these payments. Thus, the semi-annual coupon is worth $2.50 more than the annual coupon, despite the fact that both bear the same nominal rate of interest.

	10% annual coupon	10% semi-annual coupon $50 paid and reinvested	10% interest on interest	
Six months' time				
	$100 paid	$50 paid	$2.50 paid	= $102.50 paid
One year's time	$100 paid	$100 paid +	$2.50 paid	

The assumptions used in compounding (or more specifically, discounting) reflect expectations about the timing of interest payments. Semi-annual discounting assumes that interest is paid twice a year and when applied to an annual coupon, has the effect of lowering yield to the extent that interest is not being earned on a six-monthly coupon payment. Conversely, annual discounting assumes payment of interest only once a year and has the effect of raising yield when applied to a semi-annual coupon, to reflect the extra value of the six-monthly compounded interest. There is need for using both methods of discounting when comparing the specific merits of alternative means of investing or borrowing. US domestic bonds, Yankee bonds and Japanese Eurobond convertibles typically pay interest semi-annually, while in Europe annual coupons are standard.

In the international markets, securities can pay interest on a quarterly and even a monthly basis. Just as semi-annual coupons may be valued more highly than annual coupons (when measured from the perspective of annual discounting), these more frequent interest payments also represent an increase in yield. It is critical when comparing different securities or different investment opportunities, to factor in the yield impact of interest payment or coupon frequency. Additionally, the precise formula for interest payment can have a surprising effect on yield. For example, floating rate notes typically pay interest on the basis of the actual number of days elapsed over a year of only 360 days. This formula has the effect of giving a floating rate note investor a bonus of five days' extra interest per year (or six days in the case of a leap year). This translates out to 14 extra basis points more yield assuming a 10% semi-annual coupon.

Delay days

In virtually all securities, interest payments have a delay feature. In the case of Small Business Administration (SBA) pool certificates, for example, interest payments are subject to a 60-day delay. This means that while interest payments have accrued, investors do not receive their money until 60 days following their purchase. Once interest payments begin to be received, the interest fixing formula applies to an earlier period. The effect of this initial delay is to shift the whole interest payment schedule forward in time by some two months. Therefore, at maturity, there will still be run-off payments to be made even though the capital value of the investment has been reduced to zero. The yield impact of this delay feature is greater than would be ordinarily expected. This reflects the importance of the time value of money. As an example , if an SBA certificate was paying 9⅞% throughout its 20-year weighted average maturity, the 60-day delay would result in a reduction of approximately 27 basis points per annum.

The calculation of yield to maturity relies on a number of assumptions, including the timing of coupon payments and reinvestment of proceeds (eg interest payments). It is assumed that the investment rate corresponds to the coupon on a bond. This is often not the case, particularly during times of high interest rates which are generally expected to decline. In such circumstances, re-investment will probably be at a lower rate than the coupon level. This means that the actual return to the investor may be lower than that estimated by the yield to maturity computation.

Yield to average (or equivalent) life/yield to first call

Another shortcoming with the calculation of yield to maturity is that many bonds are either partly or entirely repaid prior to their stated maturity. Partial repayment occurs through the operation of sinking or purchase fund provisions under which the issuer is obliged to buy back bonds in accordance with prearranged conditions during the life of an issue. As a result, the bonds, on average, are outstanding for a shorter period of time than if the entire principal amount were paid back at maturity. Therefore, sinking and purchase funds reduce an issue's maturity or life. The effective maturity or average life of an issue is calculated mathematically as in the following example: assume a $50 million seven-year issue with a $5 million sinking fund operating in years three through six.

(a) Year end	(b) Principal repayment	(c) Bond years (a) x (b)	(d) Average life (c) ÷ (b)
1	$0	0	
2	0	0	300/50 = 6 years
3	5	15	
4	5	20	
5	5	25	
6	5	30	
7	30	210	
Total	$50	300	

An average life calculation provides a weighted average of the different maturities of all the bonds in a particular issue. The calculation may not be relevant to an investor who owns bonds in only two or three issues. But a more substantial investor will find that the larger his portfolio, the more its average life will approximate those of the issues which comprise it. For this reason bonds are normally quoted on two bases: yield to maturity and yield to average life. It should be said, too, that yield to average life assumes that the redemption of bonds will conform to a fixed schedule. This overlooks the fact that purchase funds can operate only when issue price is below a set level (usually par) and annual purchases are, therefore, difficult to predict with accuracy. In both sinking and purchase funds, the borrower retains the right to acquire bonds in the secondary market. This also confuses the question of an issue's effective maturity. It is ISMA convention to calculate redemption yield to average life for bonds with a sinking fund, but not for bonds with a purchase fund.

A further complication arises with serial issues in which specific series of numbered bonds are due for redemption at different times. Working out maturity is easy if only one series is held. However, if more than one series is owned then maturity should be calculated according to the weighted average of the holdings of the different series (eg four bonds of five years maturity and six bonds of seven years maturity equals a weighted average maturity of (4 x 5) + (6 x 7)/10 bonds = 6.2 years.

Another factor which can reduce issue life is the right given to the borrower in many longer-term financings to repay or call all outstanding bonds. Issues are typically called when they are trading at a healthy premium over par and the borrower feels that the indebtedness can be refinanced by floating a new issue with a lower coupon. When these circumstances prevail, the effective maturity of a bond may not be either its final maturity or average life, but rather its next call date. With issues trading at high premiums, market professionals will calculate yield to first call. This computation takes into consideration both the length of time until call date and the redemption price to be paid when early calls are made. Where an issuer is permitted to prepay, it is customary to exact a penalty in the form of a redemption premium to compensate investors for being taken out of an attractive investment. This is because borrowers will, as a rule, only prepay when interest rates are moving (or have moved) in their favour and thus to the disadvantage of investors. Redemption premiums typically start at around 2% and decline by, say, ¼% per annum.

ISMA also recognises another convention which is termed 'life to put'. A put option allows an investor to literally put his securities back at or after a specific period of time. Usually, this would happen if interest rates had gone up and the put option enables the investor to get his money back, typically at 100% or par, and then reinvest in higher yielding securities. Because of this early redemption feature, it is customary to calculate yield to the put date.

Duration

A further refinement to yield is to adjust not only for variations in maturity (say, due to call or put provisions) but also for the impact of the coupon payments. This measure is called duration. The analysis looks at a bond as a series of cashflows: both interest payments and principal repayments. Duration summaries all these cashflows in a single figure which is similar to the average life calculation for a bond.

If a bond is viewed as a series of cashflows, then duration is the weighted average of the maturities of each of the cashflows discounted back to their present value at the time of the bond's issuance (or purchase).

To see how this works, the last example of the $50 million seven-year issue with a $5 million sinking fund (and assuming an 8% annual coupon) may be modified as follows:

Exhibit 5.1
Calculation of bond duration

(a) Year end	(b) Interest payment	(c) Principal payment	(d) Cash-flow (b) + (c)	(e) Present Value of Cashflow	(f) (a) x (e)
1	$4.0	$0	$4.0	$3.7040	3.7040
2	$4.0	$0	$4.0	$3.4280	6.8560
3	$4.0	$5	$9.0	$7.1460	21.4380
4	$3.6	$5	$8.6	$6.3210	25.2840
5	$3.2	$5	$8.2	$5.5842	27.9210
6	$2.8	$5	$7.8	$4.9140	29.4840
7	$2.4	$30	$32.4	$18.8892	132.2244
Totals				$50.000*	246.9114

* Computational discrepancy due to rounding.

The calculation above computes the weighted average of the present values of both the interest and principal cashflows from the bond. The sum total (the F column) is then divided by the value of the bond to obtain the bond's duration (ie 246.9114 ÷ 50 = 4.94 years). Typically, the yield to maturity of the bond is employed to provide the discount factors used to calculate the present values of the respective cashflows. In the example above, the coupon rate of 8% is employed as the discount factor because the bond is assumed to be priced at par or 100%.

Compare how the earlier average life calculation of the bond was determined to be six years, while its duration is actually less than five years. Duration is now widely accepted as the more accurate way of expressing the effective average maturity of a bond because it takes into account all aspects of a bond's cashflow.

According to ISMA, duration (which is also called Macaulay Duration) may be calculated using the following formula:

$$D = \frac{1}{P} \times \sum_{i=1}^{n} CF_i \times L_i \times V^{L_i}$$

Source: ISMA

In the above formula D equals duration, while n is the number of future coupon and capital cashflows. CF_i represents the ith future cashflow and L_i, the time in years to the ith cashflow. V is the annualised discounting factor and P equals the gross price (clean price plus accrued interest).

Why is duration an important measure of maturity? Another way of saying maturity is the word 'exposure', that is the period of time one is at risk holding a bond. If interest rates go up, for instance, the price of the bond will go down so that its yield adjusts upwards in proportion to the new higher interest levels. The longer the duration of a bond the more one is exposed to the risk of adverse interest rate movements.

An interesting characteristic about bonds (and other securities) is that high coupon bonds have a shorter duration than low coupon bonds with otherwise identical terms. For example, if the annual coupon on the $50 million seven-year issue were 12% (not 8%) than its duration would contract from 4.94 years to 4.57 years. This effect is created by the greater present value of high interest payments in the early years of the 12% coupon bond. By contrast, the lower coupon of a bond the greater the duration. According to ISMA, a zero coupon bond has a duration equal to its maturity or seven years.

Price sensitivity
Duration is not only a measure of risk exposure but also of price sensitivity. Price sensitivity is the amount of change in price for a set movement in interest rates (or yield). This can be expressed computing what is known as 'modified duration' as represented by the following equation:-

$$\frac{\Delta \text{Price}}{\Delta \text{Yield}} = - \frac{\text{Duration} \times (\text{Price}/100)}{(1+\text{Yield}/100)}$$

Source: Based on Dattatreya and Fabozzi, *Active Total Return Management of Fixed Income Portfolios*, Probus Publishing Company, Chicago 1989.

Modified duration (ie duration divided by 1 + yield/ 100) can be solved as follows:-

$$\frac{100 \times \Delta \text{Price} / \Delta \text{Yield}}{\text{Price}} = - \frac{\text{Duration}}{(1+\text{Yield}/100)}$$

Source: Ibid.

The negative sign on the right hand side of the equation (the modified duration) indicates that any change in price will move in an opposite direction to a change in yield. The higher the yield moves, the lower the price drops and vice versa. The left side of the equation signifies the percent movement in price per 100 basis points (ie 1%) change in yield. Hence, the modified duration is represented as the alteration in price for each 1% movement in yield. Yield is itself divided by 100 which converts it to a decimal and assumes annual discounting (200 would be used instead if one were solving for semi-annual discounting).

Using the terms of the $50 million seven-year issue, modified duration may be computed.

$$\text{Modified duration} = - \frac{4.94 \text{ [i.e. Duration]}}{(1+8\%/100)}$$

$$= - \frac{4.94}{1.08}$$

$$= - 4.57$$

Putting the left and right sides of the equation together, what is being said is that for each 1% movement in yield the price of the $50 million seven-year bond will change by approximately 4.57% in the opposite direction. For example, if interest rates dropped 1% from 8% to 7%, one could expect that the $50 million seven-year bond would rise in price from, say, par or 100% to 105% (rounded upwards). The word approximately is used repeatedly because this equation is an estimate only and because duration itself changes as yields move. This characteristic was noted previously in that low coupon (ie low yield) bonds have relatively longer durations while high coupon (high yield) bonds have shorter durations.

Dollar duration

Modified duration measures the percentage change in the price of a bond for each one per cent shift in interest rates. Another meaningful measure, called dollar duration, measures instead the actual change in price (expressed in dollars) for each one per cent shift in interest rates. The equation for dollar duration may be expressed simply as:-

$$\frac{\text{Modified duration} \times \text{Price}}{100}$$

Returning again to the example of the $50 million seven-year bond issue, its dollar duration is calculated as follows:-

$$\frac{4.57 \times \text{Price}}{100}$$

If the price of this bond was par or 100% then the bond's dollar duration would equal its modified duration. If, however, its price dropped to 90% then the dollar duration would be:-

$$\frac{4.57 \times 90\%}{100}$$

$$= \$4.11$$

At the 90% price level, a one per cent movement in interest rates produces an alteration in actual price of approximately $4.11.

Dollar duration is a more commonly used measure than modified duration because one can add dollar amounts. The percentage amounts of modified duration are not additive. Similarly, the dollar duration of a number of bonds can be added together to calculate the dollar duration of an entire portfolio of investments. This analysis is useful in estimating the price volatility of the portfolio in various interest rate scenarios. Individual bonds can likewise be analysed and added to the portfolio to achieve stated objectives. For instance, in an environment of uncertainty or rising yield levels, an investor would most likely select 'defensive' bonds which displayed a low dollar duration. If yield levels were expected to fall then the opposite investment strategy would be appropriate. Furthermore, more sophisticated investment strategies can also be implemented as more is known about the price/yield performance of bonds.

Convexity
As previously mentioned, duration alters as coupon or yield levels change. This is a characteristic of bond performance known as convexity. This is most easily understood in a graphic representation and again the $50 million seven-year bond issue can be used as the example. In the graph below, the price of the bond is marked on the Y-axis in dollars and the yield, expressed in percents, is found on the X-axis. The straight line is the dollar duration estimated at different levels of price and yield. Its 'negative' slope reflects the inverse relationship between price and yield. The higher the yield, the lower the price. Notice, though, that the actual yield to maturity of the $50 million seven-year bond does not follow the dollar duration line precisely. Instead, it is slightly bowl shaped or 'convex'.

It was noted earlier that duration (including modified duration and dollar duration) was an estimate only of bond performance, specifically price/yield sensitivity. Now it can be seen that at higher yield levels, say the 12%-14% range, the bond trades at a higher price level than dollar duration would indicate; indeed the

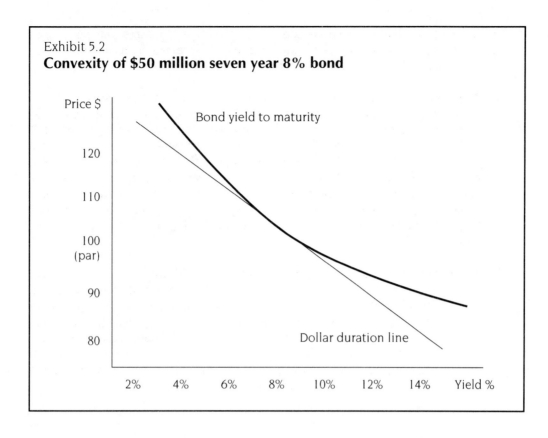

Exhibit 5.2
Convexity of $50 million seven year 8% bond

discrepancy increases as yield levels themselves increase. Additionally, the bond's actual price performance also improves at lower yield levels at a faster rate than dollar duration. At all yield levels the estimated price level as calculated by dollar duration is equal to or lower than the bond's actual yield to maturity. An understanding of a bond's convexity gives rise to a number of interesting portfolio investment strategies.

The yield curve
When determining the maturity structure of his portfolio, an investor must consider the prevailing relationship between yield and maturity.

This relationship is often depicted in graphic form as a yield curve, which plots yield on the vertical axis and maturity on the horizontal axis. Such curves, which consider only two characteristics of a bond, have significance only when other characteristics are held more or less constant; that is, they are appropriate only when plotted for similar instruments available in a range of maturities such as UK government bonds (Gilts) or US Government Treasury securities.

Yield curves may be drawn by choosing about a dozen bonds of comparable credit standing and other characteristics but with different maturities. Their yields are then plotted on a graph together with the yields of shorter-term investments such as Euro-deposits or certificates of deposit. Next, a smooth line is drawn, passing through or coming near to as many of the yield points as possible (achieving the best fit). Yield curves represent the structure of interest rates at a particular point in time. The smooth line may change its position in the space of a month or two, and can also assume a different shape.

The shape of the yield curve shows the current structure of interest rates and gives an indication of how investors expect interest rates to move in the future. This can be explained by examining the four basic yield curve shapes.

1. **The positive yield curve** is one in which short-term interest rates are lower than long-term rates. A higher yield is normally paid to investors as compensation for the perceived risk of investing money for a longer period. A more steeply sloped positive yield curve occurs when investors expect a general rise in interest rates. If investors believe that an increase is imminent, they will sell their long-term securities, forcing prices down and yields up. They will also make short-term investments, forcing short-term rates down. This process will continue until the differential between short-term and long-term rates is large enough to compensate for the possibility of a rise in rates.

2. **The negatively sloped or reverse (or inverse) yield curve** is one where yield declines as maturity extends. It usually occurs when investors expect short-term interest rates to fall. If investors think that such a decline is imminent they will be willing to lock themselves into a long-term rate which is less than that available on short-term instruments. A reverse yield curve does occur occasionally. It can often result from government intervention in the capital markets to achieve objectives such as reducing inflation or supporting the external value of its domestic currency.

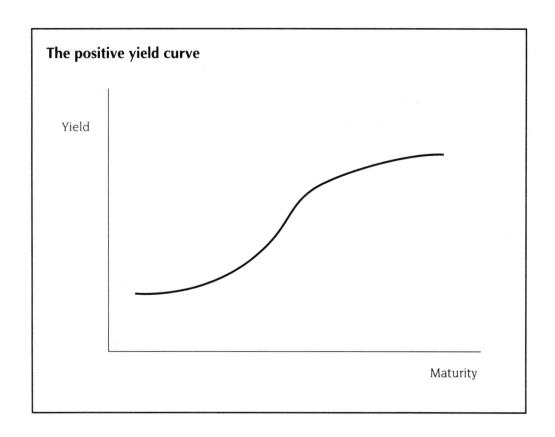

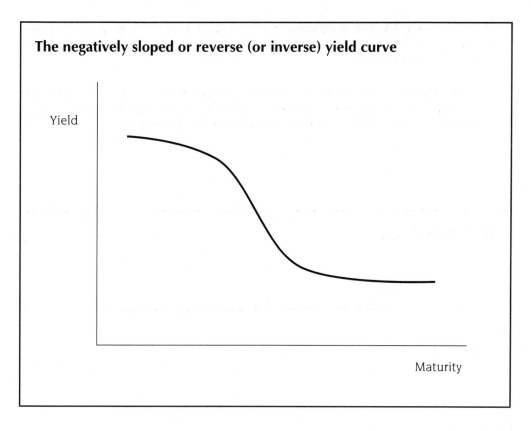

The negatively sloped or reverse (or inverse) yield curve

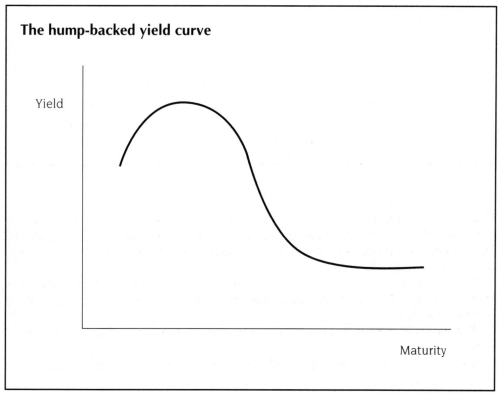

The hump-backed yield curve

3. **The hump-backed yield curve** occurs under tight monetary conditions when investors anticipate lower interest rates in the long run but expect increases in the medium-term.

4. **The flat yield curve** appears when the outlook for interest rates is similar to the prevailing interest rate levels. A flat yield curve can also occur when a reverse yield curve is changing to a positive curve or vice versa.

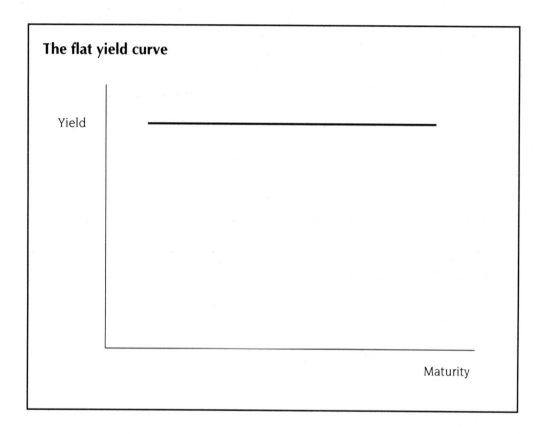

Yield curves can also be used to identify trading anomalies between securities of similar credit standing. If, when plotted on a yield curve, a security lies above the curve it may be said to be relatively cheap. Conversely, if it lies below the line it may be said to be relatively expensive.

In the example shown on the next page, security A is overvalued compared with securities C and D which have similar maturities, whereas security B is undervalued compared with security E.

The anticipated shape of the yield curve in the future also influences investors' portfolio strategy.

There are four possible ways in which a yield curve can change its shape and position.

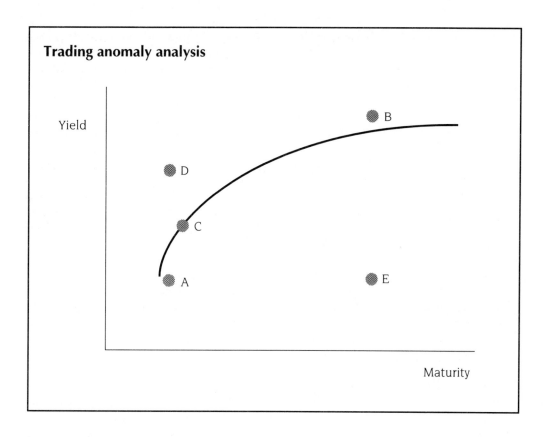

Yield curve changes

Shape of curve	Position of curve
1. Stays the same	Stays the same
2. Stays the same	Moves up or down
3. Changes	Stays the same
4. Changes	Moves up or down

The investment strategy suggested for each of these possibilities will depend on the initial shape of the yield curve. The following strategies assume that the yield curve is initially positive.

- If an investor predicts either that the yield curve will remain stationary or move lower while retaining a positive slope, then he is better off investing long-term. An additional bonus of such a strategy is that, as fixed rate coupon securities reach maturity, they will begin to trade like short-term investments. This means that they will rise to a price premium because short-term rates are lower than long-term rates in a positive sloping yield curve. (Bond yield is inversely related to price; the lower the yield the higher the price.) The strategy of holding securities for this effect is called riding the yield curve.

- If an investor believes that the yield curve will retain its positive slope but move higher as a result of rising interest rates, the investor should sell his bonds, invest short-term (for instance, in bank deposits) and reinvest later at a higher yield once interest rates have risen.

- If the investor believes that short-term rates will soon rise, creating a negative yield curve, he is better off investing short-term until the rate adjustment has occurred and then investing long-term. If it appears, however, that the shift in short-term rates is a prelude to generally rising interest rates along the whole maturity spectrum, then the investor is well advised to keep his money in short-term instruments. This will allow him to roll over his investments, reinvesting every six months or so and taking advantage of the predicted rise in short-term rates. In the process he also retains the option to invest long-term when he has decided that these rates have peaked.

- If the initial yield curve has a negative slope, then the choice of strategies depends on the investor's predictions about long-term rates. If, for instance, he believes that the rise in short-term rates is only temporary, then he will invest long-term. Alternatively, if he expects a rise in long-term rates, then he should hold short-term investments until this has occurred.

Securities switching

There are times when an investor will wish to consider changes between securities holdings to improve portfolio performance. This type of activity is known as switching or swapping. The use of the computer has made it easier to monitor the characteristics of securities and highlight possible switching opportunities.

A common type of switch involves trading different currency bonds to realise gains on foreign exchange movements. Within a single currency sector, though, the time lag/anomaly switch is pre-eminent. The purpose behind this switch is to sell a security which is trading at an historically high price relative to another issue and to reverse the switch at a later date when market movements have adjusted the yield spread to a more normal trading pattern. This is also sometimes called a basis swap. Ten-year IBM Eurobonds might, for example, have displayed an historical yield premium over similar maturity US Treasury bonds of 25 basis points. An anomaly switch might be considered if the following yield relationship was subsequently located in the market:

		Price	Yield
Buy	IBM 10% 10-year Eurobonds	97.6%	10.40%
Sell	US Treasury Bonds 10% securities	100%	10.00%
	Differential		0.40%

The rationale for making the switch would be to exploit an aberration in the market where the normal gap between IBM bonds and US government securities had increased to an unusually wide margin. This switch could be reversed as soon as the normal trading pattern reasserted itself, with the trader collecting 15 basis points profit for his effort. Caution needs to be exercised with such swaps because historical relationships do alter fundamentally over time and spread differentials may vary due to different influences, such as the absolute level of interest rates, (generally speaking, the higher the interest rates, the greater the spreads). Comparisons are, however, now greatly facilitated by screen-based information systems which literally graph out specific relationships as they have evolved through time during different periods in the market.

There are other types of switches used to alter the composition of an investment portfolio, namely, the yield improvement switch, the quality switch, the sector switch and the volatility improvement switch. Most of these can be difficult to achieve, though, as the market moves quickly to iron out anomalies. Whereas five years ago it might have taken a couple of days to realign issues, now such adjustments take place in a couple of minutes of trading.

Yield improvement switch

This is one of the most fundamental switches, and involves selling a security in order to purchase a similar quality security with a higher current yield or yield to maturity. As a hypothetical example, consider the purchase of an 11½% Société Nationale des Chemins de Fer Français (SNCF) issue due 2002 and the purchase of an 11⅛% Electricité de France (EdF) issue due 2003:

			Price	Yield to maturity
Buy	SNCF 11½%	due November 15, 2002	103⅝%	10.57%
Sell	EdF 11⅛%	due January 25, 2003	107½%	9.42%
		Differential		1.15%

Such a switch would mean an increase in yield to maturity of 115 basis points together with a pick-up in current yield of 75 basis points. However, adjustment must be made for accrued interest. For example, if the switch was made with a value date of May 15, 1997, the SNCF security would have 180 days of accrued interest (ie interest earned but not yet paid on a bond), while there would be 110 days of accrued interest on the EdF security. In this instance, the adjusted price of the SNCF is 109.38% (103.63% + [180/360 x 11.5]) and the adjusted price of the EdF issue is 110.9% (107.50% +[110/360 x 11.13]). If all the sale proceeds are reinvested, 101.4 SNCF bonds could be purchased for every 100 EdF bonds sold (110.90%-109.38% x 100). When the yield to maturity of the SNCF issue is adjusted for the larger number of bonds, the improvement in the yield increases to 1.30% (101.4/100 x 10.57% − 9.42%).

Quality switch

This involves switching between securities with different credit ratings. Usually, the investor switches to improve the quality of his portfolio, and this may involve loss of yield. However, higher quality securities tend to perform well in bull markets and have greater resistance to capital loss in bear markets. An example of a quality switch is:

			Price	Yield
Buy	Campbell Soup 10½%	due September 4, 2005	104½%	9.66%
Sell	Beatrice Finance 10½%	due September 15, 2004	95%	<u>11.52%</u>
		Differential		(1.86%)

Beatrice Finance has a moderate credit rating, whereas Campbell Soup is a top grade credit. Executing the switch would lead to a loss in yield of 186 basis points and involve new money of some $95.00 per bond in order to retain the same number of bonds, assuming the income is not to be reinvested.

Sector switch
A sector switch involves the replacement of an issue with another issue of a different category; for example, switching between corporate and government issues. As an example consider two reasonable quality credits:

			Price	Yield
Buy	GMAC 7⅝%	due November 11, 2001	93⅛%	9.55%
Sell	New Zealand 7⅝%	due September 3, 2001	95⅛%	<u>9.02%</u>
		Differential		0.48%

Such switches may provide a yield increase or a yield loss depending on whether the bond purchased is of a lower quality than the bond sold.

Volatility improvement switch
The volatility of a security – the percentage price movement for a 1% change in yield – is potentially a valuable ingredient in swaps and other forms of portfolio management. There are two basic factors which influence a security's volatility: coupon and maturity. The effect of these factors may be summed up as follows:

A. Coupon
The lower the coupon, the greater the price fluctuation for a set change in yield.

B. Maturity
The longer the maturity, the greater the price fluctuation for a set change in yield.

Securities' volatility can be illustrated showing the percentage price movement resulting from an alteration in yield over a range of coupons and maturities. In Exhibit 5.3, the change of yield is assumed to be from 10% to 9%.

Exhibit 5.3
Bond price movement per 1% yield change (10% to 9%)

	Coupon[1]			Maturity[2]	
Coupon (%)	Price Movement	Change in price as a %	Years	Price movement	Change in price as a %
4	54.36 to 59.71	9.8	5	92.43 to 96.13	4.0
6	69.59 to 75.80	8.9	7	90.27 to 94.95	5.2
8	84.80 to 91.93	8.4	10	87.72 to 93.56	6.7
10	100.00 to 108.08	8.1	15	84.80 to 91.93	8.4

1 Assumes 15-year maturity.
2 Assumes 8% coupon.

It is clear from Exhibit 5.3 that more leverage (in this case, greater price movement) can be obtained from a low coupon and a long maturity. During times of falling interest rates, an investor can maximise his potential for profit by purchasing bonds with these characteristics. One may, for instance, consider a swap undertaken to extend maturity during a time of generally falling interest rates:

			Price	Yield
Buy	9½% securities	due 2011	96.63%	9.96%
Sell	9½% securities	due 2002	98.25%	9.96%
		Differential		0.00%

The swap in which the securities due 2002 are exchanged for the securities due 2011, involves no increase in yield but it does generate cash ($16.20 per security), because of the lower price paid for the long maturity securities. An impressive gain is also realised after interest rates have fallen, say by 2%.

			Price	Yield
Buy	9½% securities	due 2011	112.73%	7.96%
Sell	9½% securities	due 2002	106.17%	7.96%
		Differential		0.00%

If the investor continued to hold the securities due 2002, he would have achieved a price increase from 98.25% to 106.17%, an increase of 8.1%. His decision to invest longer-term, however, produced a better return. The securities due 2011 increased in price from 96.63% to 112.73%, a gain of 16.7%.

An understanding of a security's volatility can also be useful in times of rising interest rates, when prices of all securities are falling. On such occasions, there is little hope of capital gains. Nevertheless, losses can be kept to a minimum through the adoption of a defensive portfolio strategy, ie by moving from volatile securities to those which are less volatile.

			Price	Yield
Buy	10% securities	due 2006	104.69%	9.21%
Sell	4% securities	due 2006	68.86%	9.21%
			Differential	0.00%

In this case, a low coupon is exchanged for the higher one. Additional money must be raised to make the switch, but the current yield is increased by 0.72% after adjusting for the new money. The point of the swap is to buy the defensive value of the high coupon; assuming a 2% rise in interest rates, the two securities would trade as follows:

			Price	Yield
Buy	10% securities	due 2006	93.38%	11.21%
Sell	4% securities	due 2006	60.10%	11.21%
			Differential	0.00%

The loss on the low coupon security would have been 68.86% to 60.10% or a decline of 12.7%, while the higher coupon security would have declined from 104.69% to 93.38%, a more modest loss of 10.8%.

Shortening maturity can also be used as a defensive strategy, and this often has more pronounced effects than increasing the coupon.

Miscellaneous switches
In addition to the switches mentioned above, the investor may wish to swap securities for many other reasons. These could include:

(a) Average life switch. The replacement of a security with another for an improvement in average life and yield to average life.

(b) Call provision switch. The replacement of a security for an improvement in call features. If a bond is called at less than its market price the investor sustains a capital loss. When interest rates are falling, the borrower has an incentive to call outstanding securities, and conversely, the investor has the incentive to switch to other bonds in order to avoid the possibility of capital loss on redemption.

6

Forwards, futures, options and swaps

Since the difficulties related to Orange County and Bankers Trust (not to mention the near collapse of Barings Bank in February 1995), the word 'derivatives' has acquired a somewhat sinister connotation. Misused, of course, derivatives can be highly dangerous, particularly because of their high gearing or leverage characteristics which will be discussed below. Derivatives, however, are an everyday part of financial life. For example, callable bonds (securities which may be redeemed by the issuer or borrower prior to their maturity) have been in existence since the beginning of modern day capital markets. What makes the bonds 'callable' is an in-built (called an 'embedded') derivative: an option exercisable by the issuer to call or redeem his bonds at a set price(s) and on a specific date(s) in the future. Because derivatives are an everyday feature of financial life it is important to understand them and to learn how to use, not abuse, them.

Forwards, futures, options and swaps are all types of derivatives. The purpose of this chapter will be to discuss each of these in turn with particular emphasis on their use in managing risk (or hedging) with respect to securities holdings. The subject of derivatives is highly complex and frequently relies on the application of advanced mathematics. A certain amount of arithmetic explanation is unavoidable. However, for the most part, the description below will be confined to general principles. An interested reader is invited to consult the numerous specialised texts available in the market to gain further details about these intricate but fascinating instruments.

To begin, it is helpful to be clear about who the participants are in derivatives. Typically, they fit into three categories: hedger, speculator, and arbitrageur. The hedger is the individual who will be dealt with chiefly in this chapter. He is the person who uses other securities to 'lay off' or reduce the risk of holding bond positions (eg US government bonds used to hedge Eurobonds). Also, hedgers use derivatives because of the advantages in liquidity, gearing and flexibility that they offer. The speculator, by contrast, uses derivatives voluntarily and exposes himself to risk (by betting on the future direction of the market) with a view to making a gain. The arbitrageur also seeks profit but avoids risk and instead exploits anomalies between prices of the same instruments in different markets or different instruments in the same markets.

Therefore, arbitrageurs are indifferent to the direction of the price in either market, only to the relative position of the price in one market vis-à-vis the other market. As part of this activity, he may also make money through the creation of derivative-based or structured products intended for on-sale to third part clients.

Hedging – general observations

Hedging is used to reduce risk. This simple assertion, however, essentially begs the question of what is risk. Risk is not only a complex subject but it is also relative. What is risk for one investor may not be for another. For example, a Libor-based floating rate note is a suitable investment for an international bank which likewise funds itself with Libor deposits. However, a US pension fund might find the same investment fairly risky given the different nature of its liabilities and investment objectives. Risk is also disparate. In transferring interest rate risk from one participant to another via a derivative, other risks may be generated (eg counterparty risk).

Usually, what a bond investor wishes to achieve by hedging his portfolio is something called 'immunisation': the reduction of price and reinvestment risks. The word 'reduction' is used because there is almost no such thing as a perfect hedge. All one can strive to do is to match the characteristics of one's portfolio as closely as possible to the hedging instruments available in the market. The greatest threat to a holding of fixed coupon bonds is a change in interest rates which may adversely affect the price on the bonds. The best way to hedge these securities is to match their dollar duration (as described in Chapter Five) with hedging investments (eg interest rate futures) which have the same or a similar dollar duration. There are also certain compensating factors when interest rates increase. For instance, if interest rates do rise, fixed coupon bonds will suffer a drop in price (a capital loss). On the other hand, the coupon payments and capital repayments, if any, will be capable of reinvestment at the new higher interest rate levels. Hence, if securities are initially selected on the basis that their weighted average duration matches forecast liabilities (or targeted investment objectives) then the risk of interest rate movement can be minimised.

Hedging instruments can be constructed and traded in a variety of ways. Their related terminology can also be rather confusing. This subject will be discussed in the section of the chapter dealing with options.

Sometimes an investor may not wish to hedge his entire investment but only an element of it. For instance, the investor may be dollar-based (ie have US dollars as his currency of account) but be attracted to buy bonds in the UK sterling sector where the yields may be attractively high, say, at the 10% level whereas US dollar yields are lower or, say, 4%. Were this the case, then the investor might investigate hedging instruments available in the forward, futures or options markets. The different risk / reward exposures might be diagrammed as follows (assuming a starting exchange rate of $1.60/£).

The investor has three choices. He may decide to keep his UK sterling position completely unhedged (as represented by the solid line). If sterling appreciates against the US dollar, say, moving to $1.70/£, then the investor will enjoy both the 10% yield together with the 6.25% capital appreciation (in dollar terms) of the currency gain, producing a total return of 16.25% (in dollar terms) for the year overall. If sterling depreciated, however, the 10% yield would be eaten away by the loss in currency value. Were sterling to drop to, say, $1.50/£ then the investor's total return (yield less capital depreciation) for the year would similarly slip to 3.75%. Alternatively, the investor

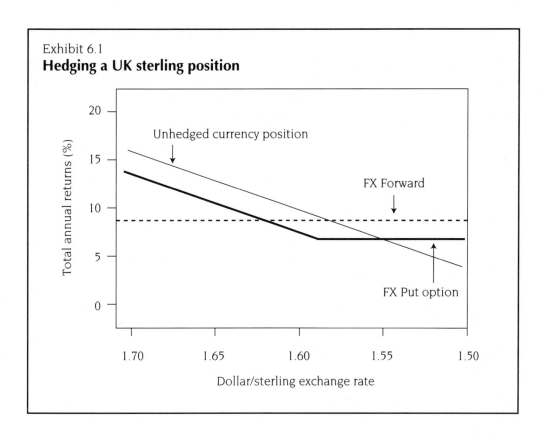

might fix the rate of exchange for one year in the foreign exchange (FX) markets by using a foreign currency 'forward'. As noted on the graph, this strategy locks in a fixed yield for the entire year irrespective of any movement in $/£ exchange rates. The FX forward line lies slightly lower than the 10% yield level because it is assumed that the one year $/£ rate is at a discount to the current (or spot) rate. Such forward premiums/discounts will be discussed later in this chapter. The third alternative is the acquisition of a put (which allows the investor to sell or put his sterling at a fixed dollar exchange rate at any time during the year). A put is an option which is similar to an insurance policy. One does not use it unless there is difficulty. In this case, the put option protects the investor in the event that sterling drops lower than a predetermined level, say, $1.58/£. After that point, the option has the effect of locking in that exchange rate so that the total return may be maintained at that lower yet still acceptable level. Because the investor is not obliged to employ the option, it can use the option when it wants to and can still enjoy a good portion of the capital gain if sterling appreciates above $1.60/£. The gain will, however, not be as great as that produced by an unhedged position because all options have an initial purchase cost (called a premium) which must be paid by the investor.

Foreign exchange hedging is a very useful technique for borrowers (or issuers) as well. Given the volatility of foreign exchange markets, many issuers have been reluctant to borrow in currencies to which they do not have ready access via their business revenues. Sometimes there is little alternative because specific bond sectors as defined by currency (eg the Deutschmark bond sector) close from time to time, forcing borrowers to find other sources of funds. One solution to this problem is to issue in a currency to which they have only limited access and then enter into foreign exchange forward contracts to lessen or eliminate the exposure to that currency.

The foreign exchange forward contracts allow borrowers to fix now the rate at which one currency can be converted into another at a predetermined time in the future. The exchange rate of the currency in which the bonds are issued against the currency in which the issuer requires funds can be determined at the time a financing is arranged, so that it applies throughout the life of that financing.

By way of example, Roylease Ltd a subsidiary of The Royal Bank of Canada, set out some time ago to raise five-year funds in Canadian dollars. At that time, the Canadian dollar domestic market was fairly unreceptive, and the rates obtainable in that market were, to say the least, unattractive. The Euro-Canadian dollar market was shut. Roylease, therefore, explored other ways of raising five-year fixed rate funds in Canadian dollars. A Eurodollar bond was a possibility, but at that moment the US dollar sector was weakening appreciably. One market which was open, however, was the Deutschmark or DM sector, and Roylease arranged a private placement denominated in that currency. Roylease was, thus, incurring a DM liability, which it did not want. It therefore entered into a series of foreign exchange forward contracts whereby it hedged all its DM liabilities – principal and interest payments into either US dollars or Canadian dollars – in accordance with its exact requirements.

The forward exchange markets are volatile, and extreme care had to be taken to ensure that the DM private placement and the foreign exchange forward contracts were entered into at precisely the same moment in order to fix the cost of funds. As a technical point, all the hedging and foreign exchange contracts were done through the forward markets, and those which were ultimately hedged into Canadian dollars were arranged by way of a swap into US dollars first. The cost of funds in the DM private placement was a little under 7% based on a coupon of 6¾% and the standard private placement commission. The cost of hedging those Deutschmarks into US dollars was about 3½% percentage points and then a further 50 basis points into Canadian dollars. Thus, the overall cost of borrowing was a little under 11%, a figure acceptable to Roylease and, at that stage, considerably cheaper than any other alternative.

This kind of currency hedged financing based on the relative attraction of particular bond markets is generally available up to seven to 10 years. Ideally, all such schemes are carried out in currencies which have active forward markets. There are other forms of sophisticated currency exchanges which can also be arranged to produce an effect similar to forward foreign exchange hedging. However, the key in all these transactions is that the various different elements must be fixed simultaneously to ensure the cost of borrowing.

A major advantage of currency/bond hedging is the reduction in borrowing costs without a corresponding increase in foreign exchange risk. Such schemes also permit borrowing in a currency where there is good investor demand, thus giving the financing an improved chance of success. This is better than trying to get money out of a rather unreceptive market, and helps to preserve a borrower's good name.

Forward Foreign Exchange Operations

A bond investor may often purchase foreign currencies in either the spot or forward foreign exchange market to reduce implicit foreign exchange exposure through holdings of securities denominated in different currencies.

Foreign currencies may be purchased on the interbank spot market for delivery in two business days' time. On that day, termed the settlement date, parties to the transaction exchange currencies.

Foreign exchange may also be purchased on the forward market for delivery on a specified date which is more than two days hence. In the forward markets, the absolute forward exchange rate is not quoted directly, but as a premium to or a discount from the spot rate. Exhibit 6.2 illustrates how spot rates and forward differentials are generally quoted.

Exhibit 6.2
Typical foreign exchange quotation

	Spot	1 month	2 months	3 months	6 months	12 months
UK$/US$	1.6861/71	8.9/8.5	21.8/21.3	35/34	82/81	195/192
US$/DM	1.5392/99	32.1/31.9	60.2/58.2	86.5/84.5	176/172	354/348
US$/Sfr	1.3070/80	40.5/40.0	76/75	111/108	220/218	432/428
US$/Ffr	5.2215/25	102.5/100	184.5/181	265.5/260	525/515	1066/1056

The forward rate for any given period is found by subtracting the premium of the forward price from the spot or, in the case of a discount, adding it to the spot price. A premium occurs if interest rates are lower in the swapped currency compared to those in the reference currency; a discount occurs if the opposite is the case.

This is normally an easy calculation but one thing to remember is that the $/£ exchange rate (called cable) is quoted in terms of the number of US dollars which it takes to purchase one UK pound. With most other exchange rates, the reverse is the case. For example, in the table above, the $/DM, $/Sfr and $/Ffr rates are all quoted in terms of the amounts of these currencies which is required to purchase one US dollar.

Let us begin with a normal illustration (remembering always that the reverse will be the case with UK sterling). Typically, if a currency is trading at a premium then its price will be higher on the left side of the quote than the right side of the bid/asked quote. The reverse is the case for a discount. Again, looking at the above table, one can see that the DM, Sfr and Ffr are all trading at a premium, as their interest rates are all lower than dollar rates. When calculating the forward value of a currency trading (as mentioned above) one simply deducts the premium from the spot price. So, the dollar value of, say, six-month Deutschmarks would be 1.5392 less .0176 or 1.5216.

Because sterling interest rates are higher than those in the US, one would expect to see it trading at a discount to the US dollar. However things are different in Britain. Thus, what would otherwise be a discount appears to be a premium (ie the left-hand quote being higher that the right-hand quote). It is in fact trading at a discount because the premium is always deducted from the spot rate, and sterling's spot rate is calculated as the amount of US dollars needed to purchase one pound. Hence, when the premium is deducted that is equivalent to saying that fewer dollars are needed to acquire a pound. The spot rate today may be $1.6861/£. But, were we to purchase pounds in the three-month forward market we would only need to pay $1.6826 (ie $1.6861 less $0.0035).

In the above examples, it has been assumed that the investor has acquired the non-dollar currency (and sold dollars). Thus, the left hand side of the bid/asked quote was used. If the reverse were the case then the right hand side of the quote would be employed. Two opposite six-month Ffr transactions can be illustrated as follows:

	Buy	Sell
$/Ffr spot	5.2215	5.2225
Deduct forward	−.0525	−.0515
Six month price	5.1690	5.1710

The forward premium or discount reflects the interest differentials on bank deposits in different currencies. An investor always has the alternative of exchanging his domestic currency immediately and investing the foreign currency proceeds, or investing his domestic currency and exchanging the principal and interest at maturity.

As an example, consider the sale of the US dollar six-month forward against the DM. Suppose, six-month Eurodollar deposits are paying 5.5369% per annum, whereas one-month Euro-DM deposits are paying 3.25% per annum. The US dollars will be sold today but not delivered for six months. Therefore, these dollars can continue to earn interest at 5.5369% . On the other hand, interest of 3.25% is forgone on the DM. The net position is an interest gain of 2.2869% (5.5369% less 3.25%) annualised or 1.1435% for the half year. This US dollar interest gain can be translated into a foreign exchange forward value (a premium in this case) by multiplying the US dollar percentage gain by the current spot exchange rate. If the spot rate of exchange is $1/DM1.5392 then the discount is 1.5392 x 0.0114 = 0.0176. The forward rate of exchange is obtained by subtracting the discount from the spot rate giving $1/DM1.5216. So, fewer DM can be bought in six months' time to compensate for the additional interest earned in holding the US dollars for that period. The reverse would be true if the deposit rates for the currency sold were lower than that of the currency bought.

Forward operations in foreign exchange can be useful in investment management for a variety of reasons. Most importantly, investments in securities denominated in foreign currency represent an exposure to any future weakness in that currency. To reduce this exposure, foreign currency should be sold forward against the base currency of the portfolio. This operation is known as hedging. While the foreign currency risk can be reduced by this hedging, the investor incurs a commitment to provide foreign currency sold for delivery on a particular future date. If the investor does not have the foreign currency to meet this commitment, the forward position will have to be closed prior to the delivery date. In the event that the foreign currency has been weak in relation to the base currency, it can be bought back at a lower price and money will have been made for the portfolio. If, however, the investment judgement has been wrong and the foreign currency has strengthened, a loss will be realised when the forward operation is closed. Alternatively, the investor may wish to take up the foreign currency, in which case he will have to provide the foreign exchange on delivery date. If this involves selling securities to raise the foreign exchange, a risk of capital loss could arise.

An investor may also wish to purchase a currency which he predicts will show strength in the future, but for the time being remain in high yielding assets denominated in a different currency. In this case, if he feels that the foreign exchange value of a currency over a certain period will outperform the existing interest rate differential between the two currencies, then he should buy the strong currency in the forward market. Of course, when one takes a view on the future course of the markets, one becomes a speculator not a hedger.

Futures and options

In essence, a future, like a forward, is a contract (or obligation) to buy or sell an asset at a fixed price and at a set date in the future. The forward contract is traded on the over-the-counter market, while a future is bought and sold on an exchange. The buyer of a future agrees contractually to acquire the specified asset (pork bellies or an amount of US dollars) at some future date. The assets which are bought and sold in the futures markets typically take the form of specified standard parcels or quantities, each of which is referred to as a contract.

By contrast, an option is the right (not an obligation) to buy or sell an asset at a set price at a set time or during a set period. When it is used, an option is said to be 'exercised', and the dates on which it may be used are the 'exercise date' or 'period'. With the so-called European-style options, the exercise date occurs only on the expiry date of the option (ie at the end of the option's life). American-style options may, however, be exercised at any time during their life prior to their expiry date.

Futures and options have a number of characteristics in common with forwards and sometimes can be used interchangeably in hedging operations. However, they are sufficiently dissimilar to merit separate descriptions.

Futures

As mentioned above, a future is a contract to buy or sell a standard amount of a specified asset at a fixed date in the future and pay/receive the purchase price. A buyer of a futures contract is said to be 'long' the contract, while a seller of the contract is said to be 'short'. Contracts are typically traded on an organised futures exchange and the transaction is handled through the related clearing corporation. This relieves each party to the contract (there are always two) from having to worry about the performance or the credit stranding of the other. The detailed function of the exchanges and their related clearing houses will be discussed in the next section of this chapter.

Futures contracts are usually purchased with a downpayment termed a margin which may need to be topped up with margin calls or variation margin if the contract value drops below a certain level. An investor in futures may wait until the expiry day and then take (or make) physical delivery. Alternatively, it is possible to 'close out' the contract by acquiring an offsetting (opposite) position in the same contract. If, say, one was long 1,000 pork bellies, one would close this out by selling a contract for the same amount.

Futures contracts can exist for a wide variety of asset categories. Pork belly (or bacon) futures have the advantage of a tangible underlying commodity and therefore are reasonably easy to comprehend. Futures contracts can apply to currencies and interest rates in much the same way as pork bellies. All one needs is a standardised amount of a specified financial instrument, such as the US government's benchmark 30-year bond, where price moves can be employed as a barometer of rising or falling interest rates. The government bond contract, thus, can be bought or sold to hedge against rate movements. Interest rate futures are particularly useful to investors and other market professionals who wish to reduce the risk of holding bonds by creating positions (long or short) which offset the effect of interest rate fluctuations on securities held in portfolio.

Established exchanges for futures and options

Dealings in derivatives can be handled in one of two ways: either (i) between principals in what is termed the over-the-counter market or (ii) on an exchange. Concentrating for a moment on exchange-executed transactions, there are always two counterparties (the buyer and the seller). This relationship gives rise to two potential problems. One problem is that each party is exposed to the credit risk of the other. Also the buyer would have to find the original seller to close out the transaction prior to expiry. The latter problem is addressed by transferring the performance obligations of both of the parties to a clearing house (usually by a form of transfer called 'novation') at frequent intervals, usually daily. This means that the buyer looks to the clearing house which is associated with an exchange for performance of the delivery obligations while the seller looks to it for performance of the payment obligations. This process is described as the clearing house 'standing in the middle of the contract' and allows the buyer and the seller to close out by entering into an equal and opposite trade with another exchange member.

The former problem of credit risk is addressed in part by the members of the clearing house supporting it financially. This financial support is further enhanced by a downpayment (an initial margin) which is paid by both buyer and seller. (To pay the full purchase price would negate the point of the futures contract, because the parties might as well do a spot trade). Since the price of the underlying asset may subsequently move, thus increasing the risk of default by one of the parties, the party against which the price has moved is asked to pay further amounts ('margin calls') representing the amount by which the price has moved or varied. This additional margin is called variation margin.

In London, futures and options are traded primarily on the London International Financial Futures and Options Exchange (LIFFE). LIFFE owes its origins to the major commodities futures exchanges located in Chicago in the US. The two primary exchanges in Chicago are the Chicago Board of Trade (CBOT) and the Chicago Mercantile Exchange (CME). These two exchanges have been the forerunners in trading financial products and are increasingly integrated with the Euromarkets. These exchanges and the products they offer will be discussed below.

The CBOT was established in 1848 and is the world's oldest and largest futures and options exchange. At the time of its establishment, the CBOT concentrated primarily in contracts involving agricultural products. Its location in Chicago made it ideally sited to service the 'bread basket' of the US. By 1975, the CBOT expanded into financial contracts when trading commenced in US Treasury bond futures. In 1982, options on futures were initiated on a pilot programme basis. By 1996, the annualised volume of contracts on the CBOT was running at some 225 million and covered the main areas of agricultural futures and options, financial futures and options, metals futures and options and insurance futures and options. As will be mentioned later, the CBOT has established a link with LIFFE to specialise in the trading of long-term Euro-debt products. There are a number of examples of this type of cooperation. One such is the planned introduction of a euro-denominated government bond timed to correspond with the formation of the 'euro' (the single European currency) scheduled for 1999.

Chicago Board of Trade products

US Treasury bond. Futures and options on US Treasury bonds having a maturity of (or non-callable for) at least 15 years. Contracts are quoted with a face value of $100,000 or multiples thereof. Flexible options can also be acquired with a minimum amount of 100 contracts of $100,000 each. The strike price is expressed as an absolute level or relative to the underlying futures contract.

10-year US Treasury note. Futures and options on US Treasury notes having a maturity of between 6½ and 10 years. Contracts are quoted with a face amount of $100,000 or multiples thereof. Flexible options can be acquired on the 10-year US Treasury note in a manner similar to the US Treasury bond.

Five-year US Treasury note. Futures and options on US Treasury notes having an original maturity of not more than five years and three months and a remaining maturity of not less than four years and three months as of the first day of the delivery month. Contracts are quoted with a face value of $100,000 or multiples thereof. Flexible options are also available on the five-year US Treasury note.

Two-year US Treasury note. Futures and options on US Treasury notes that have an original maturity of not more than five years and three months and a remaining maturity of not less than one year and nine months from the first day of the delivery month but not more than two years from the last day of the delivery month. Contracts are quoted with a face value of $200,000 or multiples thereof, and flexible options are also available.

30-day Fed Funds. Futures contracts determined as 100 minus the monthly average overnight Fed Funds effective rate for the delivery month. For example, a 5 1/8% rate equates to 94 7/8. Contracts are quoted in a unit size of $5 million.

Brady bond index. Futures and options calculated as $1,000 times the CBOT Argentina, Brazil or Mexico Bond Index. Price is quoted in points with one point equal to $1,000.

As noted previously, the other main Chicago futures and options exchange is known as the Chicago Mercantile Exchange or CME. Importantly, the three-month Eurodollar futures contract traded on the CME is now the most actively traded futures contract in the world. Banks and investment banks have found the flexibility of Eurodollar futures useful for several purposes, such as hedging longer-term liabilities with combinations of Eurodollar contracts of different maturities strung together ('strips'). The market has grown such that market participants have requested contract months extending out to 10 years. The CME has since added several short-term interest rate products including one-month Libor, three-month Euro-yen and Fed funds rate futures contracts. The CME also lists options on futures for many of these instruments. With the growth of emerging markets, the CME has added a Growth and Emerging Markets Division through which Brady bond futures are traded

Chicago Mercantile Exchange products
Three-month Eurodollar. Futures and options are based on the London Eurodollar time deposit market having a principal value of $1 million with a three-month maturity. The final settlement price is determined by a random sample of 16 reference

banks from a list of no less than 20 that are major participants in the London Eurodollar market.

One-month Libor. Futures and options are based on the London Eurodollar time deposit market having a principal value of $3 million with a one-month maturity. The final settlement price is determined by a random sample of 16 reference banks from a list of no less than 20 that are major participants in the London Eurodollar market.

Brady bonds. Futures and options are based on securities created under the Brady Plan by former US Treasury Secretary Nicholas Brady to reduce the claims on debtor nations and to create vehicles which could be used to pay off their sovereign debt. The Brady bonds created under this plan gave debtors and lenders latitude to utilise a variety of characteristics, with par and discounts and varying degrees of collateralisation. The CME trades futures based on Argentine FRB, Brazilian C, Brazilian EI, and Mexican par Brady bonds. Each futures contract is valued at $1,000 times the price of the respective Brady bond. Final settlement is determined by a random selection of four brokers from a list of no less than four that are active participants in the market for Brady bonds.

Federal Funds rate index. Futures are based on a one-month average of the daily Federal Funds effective rate. Bids and offers shall be quoted in terms of the IMM Federal Funds rate index: 100.000 minus the average and having a principal value of $3 million. The final settlement price is determined by the Clearing House as 100.000 minus the average daily Federal Funds rate for the IMM Federal Funds calculation period for the contract month, which begins with the termination of the trading date for the preceding contract month including all succeeding days prior to the termination of the trading date for the current contract month.

13-week Treasury bill. Futures and options are based on US Treasury bills and have a face value at maturity of $1 million. 13-week Treasury bill futures call for delivery at the expiration of US Treasury bills with 13 weeks remaining to maturity.

In Europe, the LIFFE exchange was founded in 1982 and today is constituted as a Recognised Investment Exchange under the Financial Services Act 1986 and is accountable to the Securities and Investment Board (SIB). Although only second in importance to the Chicago exchanges, LIFFE maintained daily turnover of some £150 billion during 1996.

LIFFE *products*

Treasury bonds. Contracts on long-term US Government securities which are based on the benchmark 30-year US Government bond. Such contracts are traded in conjunction with the similar product offered by the CBOT. Under a co-operative arrangement, both futures and options on this contract will be dealt via open outcry on the floors of both exchanges. A similar reciprocal arrangement applies to LIFFE's German government bond (Bund) contract.

Three-month Eurodollar. An interest rate futures contract in the amount of $1 million based on the Libor deposit rate determined quarterly and quoted by a random sample of 16 designated banks. Options are also sold on the three-month Eurodollar futures contract.

Long gilt. Futures contracts specify the delivery of £50,000 nominal value of a notional gilt with a 12% coupon and having a residual maturity of between 15-25 years.

There are a variety of other contracts (including both interest and other financial futures) available at LIFFE. These include:

FT-SE (Financial Times Stock Exchange Index or Footsie) 100 Future. Average level (divided by 10) of the FT-SE 100 Index between 11.10 am and 11.20 am on the last trading day of the current month.

Three-month Euro-yen. A fungible contract linked with the Tokyo International Financial Futures Exchange (TIFFE).

Three-month sterling interest rate. Traded in units of £500,000 based on the rates for three-month sterling deposits offered to prime banking names and quoted by a random sample of 16 from a list of designated banks.

Returning to the question of how to hedge a bond portfolio; assuming an investor's Eurobond holdings totalled $20 million and had on average demonstrated a volatility which was three-quarters that of the standard 30 year Treasury bonds (note that the minimum residual maturity deliverable into the CBOT contract is 15 years, so only 30-year original maturity bonds can be used in this contract). Then a hedge (or cross-hedge because the instruments are not the same but have a demonstrated trading relationship) could be made by selling short $15 million of the Treasury bonds (150 contracts). In this way, offsetting positions would be created which lessened the impact of interest rate increases. Had the investor gone short with physical bonds, an offsetting position could have been created by going long in the futures market. In the case of the futures market short sale, if interest rates were to rise, both the value of the securities sold short and those held physically would decline. Assuming that the interest rate increases took place in October 1997 and the Treasury bonds had been sold for delivery in December 1997, the futures position might be closed out in November together with a corresponding sale of Eurobonds with the following results:

Eurobonds ($ thousand)		Treasury bonds ($ thousand)	
Purchase amount	$20,000	Sale amount	$15,000
Price decline 5%	(1,000)	Price decline 6%	(900)
Sale proceeds	$19,000	Delivery amount	$14,100

Due to the rise in interest rates, only $14.1 million of the Treasury bonds need to be delivered in December, 1997. This compares with the $15 million originally contracted. The difference, or $0.9 million, is earned by the investor who initiated the short sale. This gain may be set against the $1 million portfolio loss (if both the physical and futures positions are closed simultaneously). Thus the investor's profit and loss account would appear as follows:

	Transaction account, November 1996 ($ thousand)
Loss on Eurobonds	$(1,000.0)
Gain on futures short sale	$ 900.0
Brokerage commissions ($30 per future contract)*	$ (4.5)
Net loss	$(104.5)

* Example only

Although the investor has made a net loss, it is substantially less than would have been incurred had his Eurobond holdings been left unhedged. Furthermore, by hedging the investor has preserved flexibility to sell his old Eurobonds (offsetting capital loss with capital gain) and to reinvest in higher coupon bonds which reflect the new market yield levels. High coupon bonds increase current income to the investor. This investment flexibility is important because there is a natural tendency not to sell bonds which have declined in capital value, as this necessitates realising a capital loss. Freedom to set gains against losses means that securities can be traded more easily to achieve other portfolio objectives, such as maximising current income.

Futures contracts are acquired on margin, which means that only a fraction of the total notional amount of a contract need be put up in cash at the time the agreement is undertaken. Members of exchanges are all subject to the same margin requirements. Margin cover does, however, vary from one member's client to another, according to credit standing. Very substantial institutional investors need put down only 1½%-2% of the total contract value.

Hedging in the futures market is not perfect, particularly in the case of cross-hedging with different but related securities. In the example mentioned, the US Treasury bond market might have moved at a slower rate than the Eurobond market, or the long maturity Treasury bond could have reacted differently from the shorter maturity Euro-securities (eg if the yield curve changed its shape). So, it is difficult to eliminate all risk. What can be achieved, though, is a reduction of risk, or to put it another way, the substitution of basis risk for interest rate risk. The basis risk is simply the differential value between interest rate futures and bonds held in portfolio. There is also basis risk between the actual Treasury bond and the Treasury bond contract. Basis risk can be quantified by studying the market performance of a financial commodity, such as Treasury bonds or contracts, against holdings of a single issue of securities or multi-issue securities (average portfolio performance). Over time, basis risk will prove to be far lower than that associated with interest rate movement, particularly as arbitrageurs are always present to smooth out market irregularities. It is for this reason that the futures market is used for the transfer of risk.

Another interesting application of futures hedging is in new bond issues, where co-managing underwriters may be holding substantial quantities of securities for a limited period of time during the distribution period. The potential damage caused by rising interest rates can be minimised by making short sales in the appropriate futures market. This transfer of risk should free the underwriters' attention to concentrate exclusively on the job of placing bonds. An alternative approach is to bypass the futures market and create a short position in the actual US Treasury bond market. This necessitates borrowing bonds to make delivery. There is a cost associated with borrowing bonds, internal procedures to comply with, and the difference in liquidity between the futures market and that for physical securities. These factors must be borne in mind when deciding which hedging technique to use.

Options

As mentioned previously, purchasing an option confers the right but not the obligation to acquire or sell an asset at a specific price. This non-obligatory aspect of an option is the major advantage it has over a future. Additionally, options benefit from greater flexibility, allowing investors or issuers to fine tune their hedging needs with greater precision. For example, an option's price varies markedly depending on whether it is 'in' or 'out of the money' (ie whether or not the exercise price of the option represents real or intrinsic value in relation to the underlying securities' contract; this relationship will be diagrammed later). If the option's exercise price is deep in the money because of its high intrinsic value then the option will be relatively costly but it will also provide nearly complete protection against adverse market moves. By contrast, the investor may only want to protect against market movement beyond a certain point. In such circumstances, an option can be acquired which is out of the money, with no intrinsic value at present (and only the prospect of future value in the event of a pronounced market movement) but which is also considerably less expensive. Because of the flexibility of options, they can be used in a variety of sophisticated financing structures. This chapter will provide some indication of the wide variety of option-based products which are currently available to market participants.

Returning to terminology, the right to buy at a pre-agreed price is known as a call option. The right to sell is known as a put. One can buy either a call or a put, in which case one would be 'long' the call or the put. Alternatively, one can sell (or 'write') a call or a put in which case one would be 'short' the call or the put. Although long and short positions in options sound similar, their financial implications are dramatically different. If an investor buys a call or a put, his downside is limited to the price (called a 'premium') paid for the option. No more can be lost, and if things work out and the market moves as expected, the upside has no bounds. By contrast, however, the writer of an option can only earn the premium, so his upside is capped. The downside, however, is unlimited.

Options are highly geared instruments. Gearing here does not refer to borrowing but instead to the inherent dynamics of the instrument. For example, assume one were predicting a fall in interest rates. One could buy a bond and, with a rise in the market of 10%, its par value of $1000 would increase to $1,100. Alternatively, one might purchase a call option exercisable at a price (the 'strike' or 'exercise' price) of, say, 101% and this option might itself cost $50. Its gain would be calculated as follows:-

Appreciated price		$1,100
Less: Strike price		$1,010
Less: Option cost		$ 50
Option profit		$ 40
	divide by	$ 50 (original investment amount)
	equals	90% capital gain on the option
		(NB. only 10% gain on the bond)

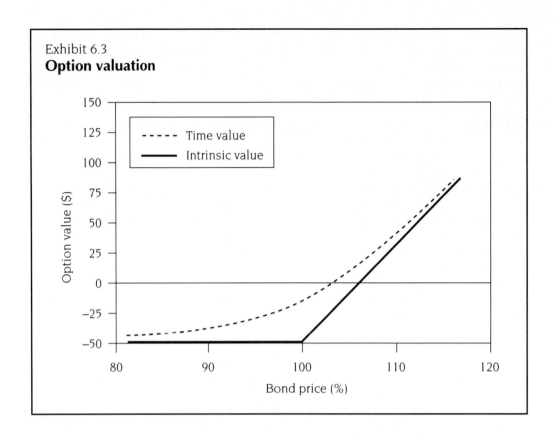

Exhibit 6.3
Option valuation

It is important to note that options are tradable instruments and can be bought or sold without having to take physical possession of the underlying assets. Many options are traded (by a novation mechanism) on exchanges, in which case (like futures) there is little risk of performance or credit exposure. There are also options which are not exchange traded, known as over-the-counter or OTC options. Such instruments usually are tailored or created to meet specific needs, however the identity of the counterparty is of much greater concern.

The valuation of options is a subject of much learned discussion. An industry standard valuation approach is known as the Black-Scholes model after the individuals who created it. With variations used in certain circumstances, this model is still among the most popular valuation approaches in use today. Leaving aside the mathematics, the theoretical value of an option at a set point in time may be diagrammed as below. The following example assumes a strike price of 101% for receipt of a long-term bond with the call option priced at a premium of $50.

Following the solid line representing the intrinsic value of the option, it can be seen that the option only begins to rise from its floor value of minus $50 (its original cost or premium) when the bond price advances past the strike price of 101%. Break-even is achieved when the price of the bond reaches 106% at which point the original premium is recouped.

Interestingly, though, options rarely trade at their intrinsic value and, indeed, as the dotted line shows, are almost always valued more highly than solely their intrinsic value. This extra value above the intrinsic value line is often referred to as 'time value', which reflects the probability of the option gaining in intrinsic value prior to its expiry date. The market will pay more for an option than for the underlying security because of the gearing benefits of the option as identified above and because of the limited downside. Note that the difference between time value and intrinsic value is greatest when the exercise price is approached. That is because this is the area where probabilities increase that the option may gain quite quickly in geared value. The difference between time and intrinsic value will also increase as a function of any volatility in the price of the underlying security. This is because volatility also raises the probability that gains will be made swiftly in intrinsic value. A depressing effect, however, is felt when the option's expiry date nears. This effect is called 'time decay' because the option loses value as it runs out of time (and therefore probability) to make gains in intrinsic value.

There are a variety of ways that options may be used to hedge or enhance the yields of bonds and other securities. One of the most popular strategies is known as the 'covered call'. This involves writing or selling a call option against an asset already owned. The writing of the option produces premium income. As noted earlier, option writing can be very risky because the downside is unlimited. In the case of a covered call, however, the option writer already holds the underlying asset, and if the option buyer exercises the call, the writer can deliver the asset to fulfil his obligations under the contract. By contrast, writing an option without owning the underlying asset would be termed a 'naked' call. In any event, the writing of a covered call involves little or no risk because if the call value increases that means that the underlying asset will have also appreciated so that the writer can offset losses on the written option with the gains realised on the appreciation of the underlying asset. If the market does not move or goes down, then the writer will have benefited from the premium income which he would have lost had he not written the option in the first place.

Bond values can be safeguarded by another strategy known as the 'protective put'. This involves buying an interest rate put option (ie going long the put) as a form of insurance for a portfolio of bonds. Investors are almost always long bonds and this strategy is typically deployed if there are fears that interest rates might rise and so undermine the capital values of the bonds. If these fears materialise, the bonds will drop in price but this will be compensated for by an increase in the value of the put. Alternatively, the put can be exercised and the bonds delivered at the strike price. Naturally, the put costs money, as any insurance policy does. However, the avoidance of major loss is frequently worth the premium paid.

A further strategy is called the 'currency option' hedge and takes advantage of the fact that an option confers the right but not the obligation to enter into a specific transaction. Consequently, an option is ideally suited for a situation the outcome of which is uncertain. Suppose a syndicate of major underwriting houses is competing in a bid for a new Australian dollar Eurobond issue. The houses might be tempted to fix an Australian $/US$ forward rate in advance of the bidding. However, what if they do not win their request to underwrite the issue? Then they would be left with a forward contract which would represent a major risk exposure (because it confers an obligation as well as a right), unless the contract was unwound at a price. A better approach is to acquire an FX option and only exercise it if the bid is accepted. Should the bid not succeed then the option can always be resold on an exchange. When a hedging exercise such as the above is contemplated, it is useful to compare the price of the premium of the option against alternative forms of insurance, like the forward markets. It is also helpful to gauge the transferability and liquidity of the respective markets for these instruments to ensure that, if not required, the instruments can be unwound or otherwise disposed of with minimum penalty.

A final variation on the above theme is something called a 'futures option' which as the name implies bridges both the futures and the options markets. Purchase of this option gives the owner the right (but not the obligation) to buy or sell a particular contract at a set price during the lifetime of the option. This type of strategy gives the hedger access to the futures market without acquiring the normal obligation associated with that market. Additionally, a futures option buyer does not need to put up any initial margin or meet subsequent margin calls, as the payment of the option premium is a one-time, all-inclusive charge.

Creative options

As noted previously options are highly flexible instruments and their scope for innovation, particularly in the OTC markets, seems to have no bounds. Based on the fundamental put and call structures, a vast range of customised products have been created. Their exotic names, 'Bermudan', 'barrier', 'up-and-in', 'quantos' and so forth convey the imagination which has contributed to their creation. These instruments are meant for the most sophisticated investors only. Specifically, they have been tailored to meet the highly specialised needs of market professionals. It is worthwhile noting, however, that the option market is highly innovative and continues to invent new products. Important savings can be made in cost and extra flexibility can be achieved in timing and in other investment objectives such as asset diversification and currency hedging.

Bond swaps

Bond swaps, both currency and interest rate, are the fastest growing sector of the Eurobond market. Their significant increase in importance during the 1980s and 1990s has had a radical and probably lasting impact on the market. It has been estimated that at certain peak periods during the mid-1990s some 80% to 90% of all Eurobonds were tied to swaps of one form or another. Swaps have been created to enhance the value (to both the issuer and the investor) of bond issues, and new issues have also been devised to take advantage of swap possibilities. The International Swaps and Derivatives Association (ISDA) has estimated that at mid-year 1996 there were some $15.6 trillion (notional) of interest rate swaps outstanding, $1.3 trillion (notional) of currency swaps and $4.9 trillion (notional) of interest rate options (eg caps, collars, floors and swaptions). The notional amount of a swap is the total principal amount of the cash flows affected by a swap. Typically, though, it is the difference between cash flows which is swapped. Hence, the 'at risk' amount is only 1%-4% of the notional amount.

To define things simply, a swap is the exchange of cashflows between two parties. The cashflows may differ in one or more of timing, currency and method of determination. Many times swaps may be linked to financings such as bond issues or commercial lending. The following discussion will highlight the use of bonds in creating swaps. Attention will be drawn as well to the basic types of currency or interest rate swaps as a variety of these may be used to support (or as the chief impetus for) bond issues. The history of swaps will also be noted to illustrate certain of the basic issues which have shaped the swap market as we know it today. The complexity of the swap market is such that its treatment in this chapter must be considered introductory only. Further detailed study is recommended for those who wish to understand the innovative financial and legal structures which support the modern swap.

Swaps: a general perspective

Swaps may be used by both investors and issuers to achieve specific financial objectives. These may include reducing risk by hedging either assets or liabilities, raising funds in otherwise blocked markets or gaining other benefits, such as a reduction in the cost of borrowing. Swaps are not a zero sum game; parties on both sides of a swap can be winners at the same time. This is because swaps exploit anomalies in the capital market itself rather than the relative advantages of one group of market participants over another. Inefficiencies do exist between different sectors of the world's capital markets which give rise to financing or investment opportunities. It is these opportunities which swaps are engineered to exploit. There is rarely any cost to society of swaps. Indeed, by making the markets more efficient, swaps secure a better allocation of savings and investment than would otherwise be the case. Furthermore by reducing differences between distinct financing/investment sectors, swaps contribute to the progressive unification of the world's capital markets. It is useful to picture a swap as a bridge connecting once isolated corners of the market. The bridge is the conduit of financing and investment ensuring the most economic and efficient distribution of capital. Unlike certain (usually short-lived) innovations in the Eurobond market, the development of swaps has made a discernible contribution towards encouraging and facilitating world capital flows.

Currency swaps

The use of currency swaps dates back to the 1960s and early/mid-1970s when precursors called parallel loans were used to free up funds which were otherwise blocked by exchange controls. An example of such controls was the tax called the 'investment dollar premium' applied by the UK government prior to 1979 to discourage outward capital investment from the country. In order to fund offshore operations at a reasonable cost (while at the same time complying with the law) companies of different nationalities agreed to finance their respective subsidiaries in their own home countries.

In the example below a UK based parent company lends pounds sterling to a UK subsidiary of a US company in the UK. In return, the US parent of the UK subsidiary lends dollars to the UK company's subsidiary in the US. It is important to note that both financings take place without transferring capital across national boundaries in violation of exchange control provisions. The arrows in this and further diagrams in the chapter signify the direction of the flow of funds.

The two parallel loans would be in the same equivalent amounts and they would normally be bullet maturities, so at the end of their term (which would be the same date in both cases) they would be repaid in full. Maturities would usually range from five to 10 years and the applicable interest rates would approximate to the long-term rates prevailing for the given time period in the relevant currencies in each country. Another important ingredient in parallel loans was the usual inclusion of a right of set-off clause which allowed each subsidiary (in this example) to set-off payments due by it against payments not received by its parent. Thus, if the US subsidiary failed to pay the UK parent, this would relieve the UK subsidiary from its own obligation to pay. In this manner, the different parties would endeavour to reduce their exposure to credit risk. Likewise, they might also request a top-up provision (ie additional payments or repayments of one of the loans) to compensate for significant shifts in exchange rate parities (and resulting differences in the loan amounts outstanding).

One difficulty with parallel loans was the fact that they were two separate loans, typically evidenced by separate sets of documentation. This created the possibility, in

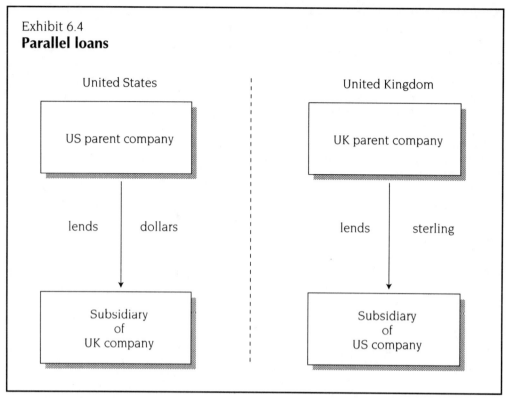

Exhibit 6.4
Parallel loans

certain jurisdictions, that a default by one party in making payments would not relieve the other of its obligations under the other loan. Consequently, a more simple form of currency swap was developed so that the exchange occurred between the two parent companies with the funds then on-lent to their respective foreign subsidiaries. The advantage of this arrangement was that the transaction could be agreed in a single contract, thus clarifying the mutual conditionality of the obligation to pay (ie if one did not pay, the other did not have to either). This new type of financing was termed a back-to-back loan.

A more recent evolutionary development is called a currency swap. This swap functions in a similar manner to the earlier two types of financings but its structural differences have important mechanical and other implications as well as suggesting different evolutionary variations. The currency swap is not an exchange of loans but rather a mutual sale of equivalent amounts of two currencies with the mutual obligation to enter into an equal and opposite transaction at some predetermined time in the future at the same exchange rate as the initial sale. Rather than paying two separate interest payments, typically only the difference (the interest differential) between the respective interest payments in different currencies is paid. The structure may be diagrammed as follows below.

In this example it has been assumed that sterling interest rates are higher than dollar rates, so that the interest differential is payable by the US company to the UK company. It is also assumed that the two parent companies choose to use their acquired foreign currency to fund their offshore operations by way of inter-company loans.

Because the agreement is between two parties only, the right of set-off is clearer and top-up provisions can easily cover the possibility of major shifts in currency values and loan amounts.

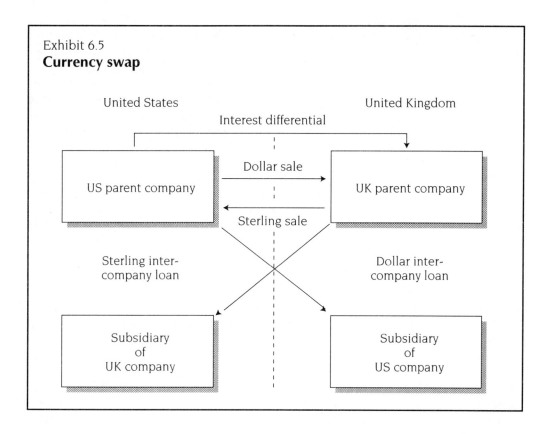

Exhibit 6.5
Currency swap

The transaction is structured as a sequence of purchase and ultimate resales, and each step, if properly documented, is conditional on satisfactory performance by the other party. This degree of conditionality is absent in a parallel loan and makes the straight currency swap a contingent commitment rather than a fixed obligation. Hence, it is possible to account for it as an off-balance sheet item with beneficial gearing or debt ratio implications.

Currency swaps can also be structured so that the initial exchange does not take place at all but there is a commitment to swap currencies at a fixed exchange rate some time in the future. The arrangement is similar to a forward foreign exchange contract and might be used to hedge the value of foreign assets back into ones domestic currency (eg by setting the rate of exchange now which will apply in some years time). Mechanically, this future exchange can be settled by each party paying in full the gross amount which was agreed to be swapped. Alternatively, only the amount of currency appreciation/depreciation of one currency need be paid at the end of the swap term. This is the net change in value of one currency relative to the other. Settlement of this net amount is called alternative performance.

Currency swaps are some of the most imaginative examples of financial engineering in the international capital market today. Frequently, these swaps are custom designed to suit the preferences of a specific client. One whole category of currency swaps which gained general acceptance due to a transaction tailored to suit IBM and the World Bank, is now known as an exchange of borrowings. In 1981, IBM had several bond issues outstanding in DM and Sfr. Due to the strength of the US dollar at the time, the company thought it was prudent to switch these liabilities into US dollars, which would also serve to crystallise the foreign exchange gains which had been achieved already in US dollar terms. The World Bank had the complementary requirement to raise funds in DM and Sfr, which were two currencies widely used in its own programme of development lending. What the World Bank did was to issue Eurodollar bonds of the appropriate maturity and exchange the proceeds of the bonds immediately for DM and Sfr. It then entered into an agreement to pay all the future interest and principal repayments of IBM's DM and Sfr borrowings in return for IBM making all repayments on the World Bank's US dollar obligations on the Eurodollar bonds. Both sets of obligations were in equivalent amounts and for the same maturities. Economically, the two issuers had exchanged their entire borrowings. For IBM, the swap allowed it to convert its DM and Sfr obligations into US dollar denominated debt at an exchange rate which it considered highly advantageous. The resulting foreign exchange gain was reflected in the reduced cost of borrowing which was well below market levels. For the World Bank, it obtained the DM and Sfr funding it required to maintain its own lending programme without overstretching the German and Swiss capital markets with large capital raising exercises.

In the case of the IBM/World Bank swap, fixed rate interest payments in one set of currencies were exchanged for fixed rate payments in another. The same basic principle can, however, be applied to cross currency exchanges which link fixed and floating rate payments or floating with floating rate payments. Complex swaps which link two or more relatively exotic currencies are usually routed through the US dollar Eurocurrency market (ie one leg of the transaction involves swapping into US dollars from one exotic currency and then swapping out again into the other currency). The US dollar market is widely used because almost all borrowers have available to them Eurodollar credit lines and these can be deployed to do floating rate for fixed rate swaps into almost all the world's convertible currencies. With the highly liquid Eurodollar employed as the common denominator, these individual currency swaps can be linked together to achieve unusual currency swap combinations such as Belgian francs for New Zealand dollars. This type of structuring is known as a circus swap which is an approximate acronym for combined currency interest rate swap.

Interest rate swaps
An interest rate swap is similar to a currency swap without the beginning and ending foreign exchange rate fixings. A classic example of an interest rate swap is the exchange by a commercial bank of a fixed rate interest payment for a floating rate payment provided by a good credit but little-known industrial borrower. Typically, the commercial bank will have obtained its fixed rate funds from a bond issue floated in the public market. The industrial corporation might have wanted fixed rate financing but was denied this type of funding because of its lack of name recognition in the public bond market. What the corporation will have available to it are Eurodollar credit facilities (with interest payments tied to Libor) which it might exchange for the fixed rate of interest which the bank obtained from its bond issue. What this and other interest rate swaps do is to exploit the relative financial strength of different parties in different markets. An example of this type of swap may be diagrammed as follows below.

The first important aspect of the transaction to note is that the commercial bank only exchanges interest payments with the industrial corporation. Both organisations remain primarily responsible to their own creditors to which they pay interest periodically and principal at maturity. Mechanically what has happened is that the bank and the corporation have both borrowed similar amounts of money for the same maturity. They then sign a contract which binds each one to exchange periodic

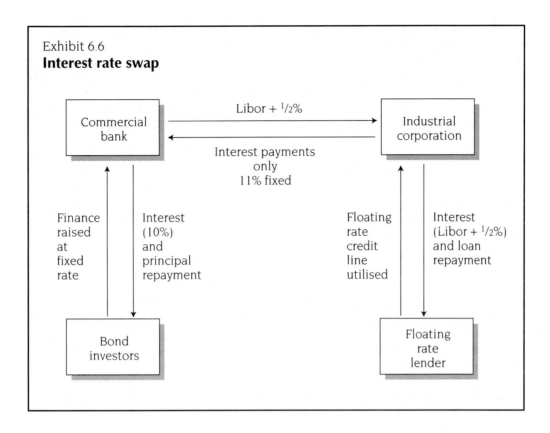

payments that are determined on the same basis as the other's interest cost. In the example above the industrial borrower pays a fixed rate of 11% but receives Libor + ½% which is sufficient to cover its interest expense to its floating rate lender. The commercial bank receives the 11% fixed payment but only has to pay 10% on the Eurobonds it issued. The saving of 1% essentially represents a reduction in the cost of its floating rate interest expense from Libor+½% to Libor–½%.

From the bank's point of view it is happy to enter this swap because it is receiving sub-Libor funding. This matches its assets (ie loans) better than with the Eurobond finance because such assets themselves pay interest on the basis of some margin over Libor. Further, the long-term maturity of the Eurobond, which still remains in place, helps to stabilise its funding base and closes the gap between its maturity of assets (frequently long-term) and its maturity of liabilities (frequently short-term deposits). The industrial corporation is also delighted with the swap because fixed rate financing is better suited to its assets (ie plant and machinery) which do not necessarily go up and down in earnings capacity in line with short-term interest rates. The corporation is also prepared to pay 11% fixed because it would probably have had to pay more than this, if it was able to float a Eurobond at all.

Sometimes the two entities will enlist the assistance of an intermediary (typically another commercial bank or a merchant or investment bank) which will initiate and process the swaps. The intermediary stands between the two entities in the swap channelling the two types of interest payments in both directions and collecting a percentage fee (or a generous bid/offered spread) for services rendered. Such services have value because the intermediary will typically be active in the market and be able to match the requirements of one party fairly precisely with the preferences of another. The intermediary will also absorb much of the credit risk that the swapping entities have to each other. If, for example, the industrial corporation defaults on its payments, the intermediary will still be obliged to maintain the swap with the commercial bank. Naturally, the intermediary will hasten to reduce its own exposure by structuring its relationship with the two swapping parties so that its liability to make interest payments to the respective parties is conditional on their maintaining their complementing payments on a punctual basis. Thus, if the industrial corporation stopped paying its fixed rate interest, it would also lose the floating rate payments which the intermediate was making available to it. This interest rate swap relationship might be diagrammed as follows below.

The presence of the intermediary means that neither swap party need have a direct relationship with the other. This provides important flexibility should, for example, one partner wish to terminate its half of the swap without notifying the other party. The intermediary might also initiate a swap by having only one party in the first instance and then hold an open position until a partner with complementing requirements can be located. This process is known as 'warehousing'.

There are several types of structures which can be developed from these simple examples of interest rate swaps. Among these is the zero coupon swap which typically exchanges floating rate payments with a single lump sum fixed payment at the end of its term. The lump sum payment is usually made to a party which has issued a zero coupon bond. Swaps can also have special features such as puts/calls and extendibility. Such features are frequently built into a swap because the underlying financing has similar features. For instance, a swap party may want the freedom to put or terminate a swap because the same party has a bond issue with a similar put

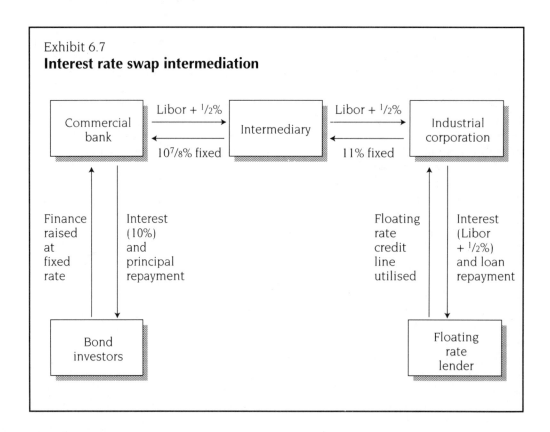

Exhibit 6.7
Interest rate swap intermediation

provision linked to the swap. Swap parties seeking special features usually must pay for these with a premium interest rate and/or a modest penalty percentage payable when the feature is exercised. Swaps can be deferrable in anticipation of improved interest rates in the future or the notional amount can be enlarged in the event that, say, debt warrants are exercised and the issuer requires a greater notional amount of swap (into floating rate funds) to utilise with the increased (fixed rate) debt outstanding.

Swaps can also be tailored to meet the unique characteristics of underlying securities. For instance, it is common for some forms of securities to pay and/or repay principal over the course of their lifetime. Thus, hedging such securities requires a swap which reduces in amount in a proportionate manner. This is called an 'amortising' swap. In some instances, too, the principal amount of the hedged security might increase or step up, in which case an 'accreting' swap would be required. In other instances, accreting and amortising swaps can be tied to an interest rate index to create different forms of synthetic instruments. Swaps can also incorporate put and call features which provide unwind flexibility in the event of liquidity requirements or a change of outlook on the market. Naturally, a price must be paid for this extra flexibility. Finally, swaps can link wholly disparate investments (for example, bonds with equities or bonds with commodities) or different indices within the same category of investment (for example, Libor-based debt with long-term fixed rate debt) or differences in interest rates in different currency markets (known as 'differential' swaps). Options can even be constructed with a swap as the underlying asset. These instruments are sometimes referred to a 'swaptions'.

Another important category of swap is named the basis swap which permits swap parties to exchange one form of floating rate interest for another. A US corporation may want to reduce its exposure to the commercial paper market and therefore swap an appropriate amount of this type of interest payment for an equivalent amount of, say, US Treasury bill interest payment. Similar swaps structured by banks are designed to hedge against too great an exposure to one or another type of short-term interest payment. Likewise, different periods of interest fixings: one month, three month and six month, may be exchanged for one another to fine tune the structure of liabilities.

Caps/mini-maxi FRNs and dual currency bonds. As mentioned at the beginning of this chapter, swaps have had a substantial impact on the Eurobond market. Not only have bond issues been improved through swapping but whole new designs of issues have been created to take advantage of swapping opportunities. A good example of this is the introduction of interest caps on FRNs.

Caps were first employed in the early 1980s when interest rates were high and also quite volatile. The cap represented the maximum level beyond which a floating rate payment could not go. This type of insurance had obvious value to those institutions, like US Savings and Loans, which had long-term fixed rate interest paying assets (eg mortgages) and had financed these with short-term deposits. The profitability of these institutions obviously varied dramatically with the level of short-term interest rates, and any pronounced rise in such rates might even threaten their viability. Hence the attraction of an instrument which could place a ceiling on interest costs on their short-term borrowings. Indeed so great was the demand for these caps that a shortage occurred which prompted a flurry of capped Euro-FRNs which were first brought to market in early 1985. The issuers of these FRNs were typically commercial banks which were not as concerned with volatile interest rates because their loan assets typically paid interest on the basis of a Libor-plus margin (without any cap on how high this formula would go). What the bank issuers would do is to swap their stream of capped floating rate payments for uncapped Libor payments at a discount to the normal rate

The division of an instrument like a capped FRN into its component parts frequently unlocks hidden value. This process, called differentiation, seeks to sell consumers precisely what they want and thereby to exact a premium price. For the Savings and Loans whose very survival seemed to depend on gaining protection against high short-term interest rates, the rate cap commanded just such a premium. The effect of this on the issuers of capped FRNs was to secure them floating rate funding at a highly privileged (ie low) rate.

Mini-maxi (or 'collared') floating rate notes marked a further variation on the traditional FRN formula in response to a swap opportunity. Under the terms of one of these issues the interest rate formula might be set at, say, Libor + ⅜% subject to a maximum rate of 10% and a minimum of eight per cent. The issuers would then swap normal floating rate interest against a fixed interest rate, say, 10½% as diagrammed below.

The effect of the interest rate swap was to create sub-Libor funding for the issuer. If short-term rates rose to 10% or higher, the interest cost on the FRN would remain at a constant 10% while the fixed rate of interest (received from the counterparty) provided income at 10½%. The ½% savings could be viewed as a discount on the Libor interest payment to the swap counterparty. Should interest rates fall so that the FRN formula were set at 8½% then a full 2% discount would be realised on the floating rate interest payment.

Another bond instrument which was created to exploit advantages in the swap market was the dual currency bond. These securities were designed to satisfy a perceived appetite by investors for high coupon issues in a strong currency. They were

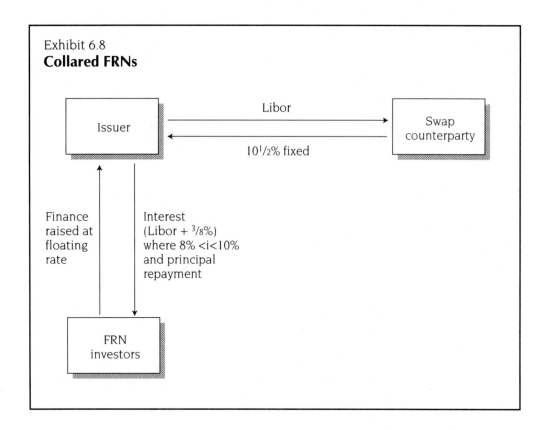

Exhibit 6.8
Collared FRNs

dual currency because the coupon would be in one currency, say, Sfr and the principal amount in another, say, US dollars. In such examples the coupon payments were typically hedged back to US dollars using forward foreign exchange contracts, so that the financing was essentially US dollar denominated. The premium pricing of these sought-after instruments more than offset the cost of forward FX cover. Indeed, certain of these financings were ultimately swapped for floating rate interest to create sub-Libor funding.

Secondary market for swaps
Swaps have been criticised for creating illiquid exchanges of instruments. Certain of this criticism is indeed justified because many complicated swaps involve bonds or other instruments which have difficulty being traded again without unwinding the swaps. Many swaps can be and are unwound, however, on a regular basis. This is easier with interest rate rather than currency swaps as the latter combines foreign exchange movements (which influence the principal amounts outstanding) together with interest rate changes. Conceptually, though, the process is similar and involves the arrangement of new swaps which effectively reverse the original swaps. Interest rate swaps can also be reversed by agreement between the parties and the making of a lump sum cash adjustment which brings the fixed rate payments in line with expected market levels. The ease of unwinding interest rate swaps has encouraged the development of a secondary market in these exchanges.

Interest rate swaps are frequently unwound in order to realise a capital gain. This practice has supported the growth in swap trading. As a parallel development, there has been pressure on intermediary banks since the introduction of interest rate swaps in 1981, to take positions in these exchanges when counterparty interest could be found for only one side of a transaction. This might happen, for instance, when a fixed rate bond issue had been floated but not enough floating rate payers could be located to match its entire principal amount. In such an event, the intermediary might feel obliged to accept part or all of the fixed rate payment and to provide floating rate funds (the other side of the swap) from its own resources. In this way, the intermediary would act as principal at least for the time being. It would no doubt surrender this role as soon as an appropriate counterparty could be found.

The intermediary would also be assuming significant risk. This could arise if yield levels moved up and the fixed rate payments no longer matched market expectations. The chances then of locating a proper counterparty to exchange this fixed rate payment for floating rate funds, would be thin indeed. Instead the intermediary would have to make some cash payment which augmented the fixed rate return so that it rose to market levels. Alternatively, the practice is nowadays for the intermediary to go short on US Treasury securities of a similar maturity and offset the possible loss on the fixed payment with a complementary gain on the short position in US Treasuries. If the situation were reversed and the intermediary was paying (instead of receiving) fixed rate interest then the proper hedge would be for it to acquire (or go long) US Treasuries.

US government securities are used for hedging purposes because of the depth and efficiency of their market. Indeed, such hedging techniques have become so popular that US Treasuries are the new benchmark rate against which fixed rate elements of all swaps are judged. This has significant implications for the pricing of swaps as all exchanges are now done on the basis of their yields relative to US Treasuries. Assume, for example, that the fixed rate payment boasts a healthy spread over the US Treasuries of comparable maturity. This healthy spread can be divided between the various participants in the swap, creating amongst other things a bigger discount below Libor for the floating rate payer. There is another possibility as well. The fixed rate payment (which was obtained by issuing a Eurobond) is not the same thing as the yield level paid by US government securities. Indeed the difference between the two yield levels (the basis risk) can widen or narrow. The truly successful intermediary will be aware of this dynamic and schedule bond issues and swaps to correspond with periods when the spread is narrow, which means that the market does not expect a large yield premium of the bond over the comparable US Treasuries. If the transaction is executed at this time, then all participants should be happy. The fixed rate payer will feel he has a good bond yield relative to the US government's own securities and the floating rate payer will be satisfied that the transaction has been executed at established market levels. One possibly discontented group might be the bond investors. While long-term spread relationships (between the bond and US Treasuries) remain fairly stable, the Eurobond market itself can be quite volatile. It is possible that the spread relationship is attractive at the same time that investors in the Eurobond market are demanding higher yields. Such contradictory influences (and different standards of measure) can lead to highly unpopular bond issues. This is one of the great challenges currently facing the market as a whole.

Despite the problems, the interest rate swap market has gained substantial new liquidity. Intermediaries are now prepared to make an active 'book' in transactions not only for their own customers but also with a view to trading positions with fellow participants in the swap market. Such positions can be held not only to collect the arrangement fees associated with a concluded swap but also in anticipation of future market moves which could improve spread relationships. As intermediaries grow more accustomed to positioning swaps, it has become increasingly easy for established swap parties to unwind their positions at will. Furthermore, Eurobond issuers also have greater flexibility when bringing new bond offerings to market. They can now raise finance at the most opportune moment to themselves and not have to worry about concluding a swap transaction on a simultaneous basis.

The interest rate swap market is divided into two sectors: the short interbank end and the long or securities end. The short end involves maturities of three years or less and is dominated by both US and non-US banks, although the market is itself centred in New York. Increasingly, short-term UK sterling, yen and DM markets are increasing in liquidity.

Prices can be volatile but the general thrust is improved control over and management of liabilities. At the longer end of the swap market, one begins to overlap with Eurobonds, as it is these securities which provide the essential fixed interest payments. Here prices and yields relative to US Treasuries are relatively stable and market-making can be conducted in a somewhat less frantic environment.

The process of positioning and trading interest rate swaps has provided several new advantages to this form of financial intermediation. Indeed, the greater efficiency of this form of financing has also led to a discernible reduction in fees and interest spreads. Currency swaps are possible candidates for market-making but their complexity involving a great number of variables has detracted from their popularity. Positioning is also much more risky. The key to the interest rate swap market is the universal acceptability and liquidity of the US Treasury market which affords a good vehicle for hedging purposes. Hedging in other currency markets is possible but their respective government bond markets do not offer such good proxies as US government securities. The relative expense of operating in these markets is also a factor.

Relationship to the Eurobond market

As noted previously, swaps are frequently arranged through the issuance of a fixed rate Eurobond. Because the swap itself represents much of the value-added to the bond issuer, it is this part of the transaction which receives most of the attention. Thus, the bond issue frequently takes a back seat to considerations affecting the swap. Participants in the bond market, similarly, refer to many swap-driven issues.

An example of the predominance of the swap market is the now established practice of spread pricing where the relationship of bond yields to US government securities is currently all-important. The old practice of yield pricing (adjusting the coupon and other pricing terms and commissions to produce an acceptable market yield) is now almost forgotten. As mentioned previously, this has led to several unsuccessful bond issues. The cost is illiquidity in the bond market. As investors become increasingly alienated because of mis-priced issues, retail demand dries up and in turn discourages professional market makers from committing capital for the purpose of trading securities.

Credit has to be given to the swap market, though, for finding creative solutions for bond issues which encountered difficulties of their own. Mention will be made in Chapter Nine of the problem of unwanted warrant bonds once the warrants have been stripped off. Practitioners in the swap market have been ingenious in structuring interest rate swaps with these securities (exchanging their fixed rate of interest for floating rate payments from a counterparty) and then selling these securities repackaged with the floating rate payments, to commercial banks which are eager to acquire such assets. It is true that these bonds will never trade again but also they will not be left to languish in the market. In this way, swaps assist the bond market by underpinning the value of certain securities.

Another example of repackaging involves perpetual FRNs which experienced a sharp fall in value and pronounced illiquidity in late 1986 and early 1987. In March 1987, Morgan Guaranty formed a financing company called Pacific Securities Ltd which raised funds to acquire from its own and other portfolios, holdings of perpetual FRNs issued by the Australian bank, Westpac. These were acquired at prices which ranged up to 88% of their face value. Indeed, even better bargains were driven with those bond houses eager to get them off their books. The total amount spent of $114 million was funded by the issuance by Pacific Securities of $130 million of 15-year FRNs (priced at the generous level of ½% over Libor) and by $24 million of 15-year zero coupon bonds. The $40 million of over-funding was then deposited with Westpac in a manner that only 35 basis points of interest was paid each year and the remainder rolled up to repay the $130 million of FRNs in 15 years' time. The interest payment on the FRNs was met by the 35 basis point deposit interest taken together with the 15 basis point income paid on the original Westpac perpetuals.

The zeros were structured to be paid back in 15 years not with cash but with the Westpac perpetual FRNs themselves. Their full face amount of $130 million was the speculative attraction for investors in the zeros. As long as the perpetuals retained at least 55% of their face value in 15 years' time then the investors will have made a good deal more than on zero coupon (or stripped) US Treasury bonds.

The repackaging of bond issues is a clear example of the impact of the swap market on Eurobonds. Other instances can also be seen such as the recent IPMA recommendation against using the failure to agree a swap as an out clause in terminating a new bond issue prior to closing. While this is no absolute prohibition against this practice, any contractual provision to this effect must be clearly spelled out.

Accounting, tax and documentation

Thus far in this chapter certain major issues have been touched on which affect the structuring of swaps. These include the handling of credit exposure, the right of set-off and one aspect of credit exposure – the making of top-up payments in the event that currency movements lead to unequal loan outstandings (in parallel loans and back-to-backs). There are numerous other issues chiefly dealing with accountancy (is the swap on or off-balance sheet? How to account for foreign exchange gains or losses? etc) and tax (what payments are tax deductible and which are subject to tax? and which form: income, capital gains or withholding? etc). Answers to such questions require substantial background information which is beyond the scope of this introductory chapter. Furthermore, even with this background information, when doing a swap one is almost always well advised to seek specialist professional assistance due to the highly complicated and frequently changing national approaches to these matters as well as the unique character of individual swaps. The complexities are not all bad news. Indeed, they often provide arbitrage opportunities, the stuff profitable swaps are made of!

There has, however, been consistent progress in the area of standardising swap documentation. Interest rate swaps are, for the most part, less complex than currency swaps and therefore are more susceptible to standardised agreements. Much good work has been done in this area. This chapter will conclude with an Appendix A which contains the 1992 ISDA Master Agreement which is now the industry standard. Included as well is a commentary on the Master Agreement by Clifford Chance.

Appendix A

Commentary on the 1992 ISDA Master Agreement

(Multicurrency – Cross Border)

History
In the early days of the swaps markets, transactions were documented by individual ("stand-alone") agreements. These lengthy agreements were based on banking loan precedents and varied widely in both their terminology and the complexity of their provisions. Consequently, the negotiation of their terms was both time consuming and expensive.

As the swaps markets in both the US and Europe evolved, a consensus on terminology and market conventions emerged. This allowed the International Swaps Dealers Association ("ISDA") (which subsequently changed its name to the International Swaps and Derivatives Association to reflect the broadening ambit of its members' interests) to produce the 1986 Code of Standard Wording, Assumptions and Provisions for Swaps. The Code was not an agreement between the parties to a swap but an initial effort to simplify documentation by setting down standard terms and phraseology which could be incorporated into swap agreements.

In 1987, ISDA published its Interest Rate and Currency Exchange Agreement which could be used to document interest rate and currency swaps in fifteen currencies. Reflecting the continued innovation in the markets, in 1989 Addenda were produced to enable the 1987 Agreement to be used for interest rate caps, collars and floors. In the following year ISDA published Addenda for use with option transactions.

In 1992 the 1987 Agreement was revised to reflect changes in market practice and the broader range of transactions reflected in the 1989 and 1990 Addenda. The result of this exercise were two new master agreements – the 1992 ISDA Master Agreement (Local Currency – Single Jurisdiction) and the 1992 ISDA Master Agreement (Multicurrency – Cross Border). The latter agreement is the one most commonly found in the Euromarkets today and is commonly referred to as the 1992 ISDA Master.

The 1992 ISDA Master
The 1992 ISDA Master uses a "Master, Schedule and Confirmation" format which is very common in the world's derivatives markets. The Master Agreement itself consists of 18 pre-printed pages which set out the legal relationship between two parties and the terms which are likely to be common to all subsequent transactions between the parties. Its provisions deal with the general obligations of the parties, representations, taxation, events of default and the methodology to be followed on early termination following a default. Several other administrative matters are also addressed including the law which governs the agreement and the courts of which country are to have jurisdiction to hear any disputes arising from the 1992 ISDA Master.

The 1992 ISDA Master is pre-printed to save each parties the time consuming task of checking its provisions in detail. If the parties wish to amend any provisions of the 1992 ISDA Master Agreement, this can be done in the 6 page Schedule which is attached to each Master. By using the Schedule the parties can tailor the 1992 ISDA Master Agreement to their particular requirements and quickly identify those provisions of the Master Agreement which have been varied.

Single agreement

The third element of what is described as the "ISDA documentation architecture" is the Confirmation. The Confirmation records the economic terms of each swap transaction between two parties. Therefore, each swap transaction generates one confirmation. Since most of the standard provisions are set out in the 1992 ISDA Master and Schedule, the Confirmation can be very brief – typically it consists of a few pages. The 1992 ISDA Master Agreement, Schedule and each swap transaction and its related Confirmation are expressed to form a single agreement between the parties. This has several advantages. Firstly, it means that the parties need only enter into one Master and Schedule between them. Thereafter, they can do as many swaps as they want recording the terms of each one in a Confirmation. One Master and Schedule can have several hundred swap transactions documented under it. Since the parties need only agree the economic terms of each transaction and record them in a Confirmation, individual swaps can be documented and concluded cheaply and quickly. The second advantage is that by making the ISDA Master, the Schedule and all the swap transaction a single agreement, it prevents a phenomenon known as "cherry-picking". This can occur where the liquidator or bankruptcy trustee of a bankrupt party to a 1992 ISDA Master Agreement seeks to disclaim unprofitable contracts previously entered into by the bankrupt counterparty whilst enforcing profitable ones against the other party. Clearly, if two parties had entered into several swap transactions, subsequent market movements could result in some of the swaps being valuable to the bankrupt party whilst others were unprofitable. Since the situation for the non-bankrupt party is a mirror image (ie contracts which are profitable to the bankrupt party are unprofitable to the non-bankrupt one) it would be at a disadvantage if the liquidator of the bankrupt party "cherry picked" the profitable contracts and required those to be performed whilst disclaiming the bankrupt's obligation to perform on the others. By making all the swap transactions part of a single agreement, the liquidator cannot pick and choose individual swaps, he must either accept or disclaim the entire agreement.

Definitions

The ease of documenting swap transactions under the 1992 ISDA Master Agreement is further facilitated by the publication of books of definitions by ISDA. The book "The 1991 ISDA Definitions" include standard definitions for various floating rates, the basis for calculating fixed and floating rate payments and definitions of several currencies. These definitions can be incorporated by reference into the overall agreement between the parties, allowing them to use the defined terms contained in the book as a convenient short-hand in the Confirmations to record complex economic concepts.

Multiproduct agreement

It is a tribute to the robustness and flexibility of the ISDA Architecture that it has kept pace with the innovations in the derivatives markets. The 1992 ISDA Master Agreement can be used to document not only currency and interest rate swaps but also commodity and equity swaps as well as foreign exchange transactions and currency options, forwards and options over interest rates, bonds, equities, commodities and equity indices (such as the S&P 500 and FTSE). ISDA facilitates the documentation of this broad range of products by publishing a series of definitional booklets. In addition to the 1991 ISDA Definitions, the series currently include:

- **1992 FX and Currency Option Definitions** – containing definitions relevant to foreign exchange, spot and forward transactions as well as currency options.

- **1992 US Municipal Counterparty Definitions** – containing definitions which are appropriate to transactions with Municipal institutions in the US.

- **1993 ISDA Commodity Derivative Definitions** – for use with commodity swaps, forwards and options.

- **1994 ISDA Equity Option Definitions** – containing definitions applicable to options over equity indices and shares.

- **1996 ISDA Equity Derivative Definitions** – containing definitions applicable to options and swaps over shares, baskets of shares and indices.

Work is currently underway on the "1997 Definitions" which will facilitate documentation of options over government bonds. The 1991 ISDA Definitions booklet is also currently being revised to reflect the expansion of the swaps markets into new currencies and new products. Each definitional booklet contains sample forms of the Confirmations applicable to the type of transactions covered by the definitions. Of course, if there is not a sample form of confirmation suitable for the particular transaction contemplated by two parties, they can always prepare one themselves and use it with the 1992 ISDA Master and Schedule. In this way, the ISDA documentation has been able to keep pace with innovations in the derivatives markets. Exotics like credit derivatives, tax and inflation swaps can all be documented under the ISDA documentation architecture.

Credit support documents

As credit analysis and risk management techniques have become more sophisticated so participants in the derivative markets have become more aware of the need to control their credit exposure to their counterparties. Since all derivatives are a contract between the parties which involve some futurity of performance, there is always a risk that a counterparty may fail to perform its obligations either as a result of its bankruptcy or adverse market movements. Derivative agreements therefore need to address the possibility of non-performance of one of the parties to the transactions.

One solution is to use some form of credit support technique. These techniques can vary from a guarantee being provided by a better quality credit (eg a parent company or a commercial bank) to one party providing cash or liquid securities (such as US T-bills) to the other to support its future performance obligations. If the party providing the cash or securities (commonly referred to as "collateral") fails to perform its obligations under the derivative transaction(s), the other party can apply the collateral itself (or sell the collateral and apply the proceeds) in satisfaction of those obligations. This "collateralisation" of derivative transactions is increasingly common since it minimises the credit risk to the party receiving collateral and allows it to deal with counterparties of a lesser credit quality that it would otherwise be able to do if the transactions were not collateralised. Collateral may be provided by only one party to a transaction ("one way collateral") or by both parties, collateral being given and returned depending on whether a party would suffer a loss if the other failed to perform ("two-way collateral").

Historically, collateralisation has been documented by agreements tailored for specific transactions. This caused similar problems to those encountered in documenting swaps under stand-alone agreements in the early days of that market. Therefore, ISDA has recently produced a series of "Credit Support Documents" which facilitate parties collateralising their transactions under a 1992 ISDA Master Agreement. Each of the Credit Support Documents is designed for use with a 1992 ISDA Master, Schedule and Confirmations. Because they dovetail into the ISDA documentation architecture there is no risk of mismatches between the provisions of the derivative transactions and the collateral documents. Like the 1992 ISDA Master, each of them consists of a pre-printed standard form documents which can be tailored to the parties requirements by use of an accompanying schedule. Currently, there are four Credit Support Documents:

- **A 1994 Credit Support Annex (subject to New York law only)**. This serves as an Annex to a 1992 ISDA Master Agreement which is governed by New York law.

- **A 1995 Credit Support Annex (Transfer – English law)**. Like the New York law Credit Support Annex, the English version "bolts on" to an ISDA Master where the 1992 ISDA Master is governed by English law.

- **A 1995 Credit Support Deed (Security Interest – English law)**. Unlike the other two Credit Support Documents, the Credit Support Deed is a stand-alone document and not an Annex to the ISDA Master. However, it is still compatible with and cross references to the ISDA documentation architecture.

- **A 1995 Credit Support Annex (Loan and Pledge – Japanese law).** Again this Credit Support Document operates as an Annex to the ISDA Master.

Which Credit Support Document should be used depends on a number of complex legal issues which are beyond the scope of this commentary. Parties considering using any of the Credit Support Documents should seek suitable legal advice as to which one is the most appropriate in the circumstances.

Summary
The ISDA documentation architecture has made and continues to make enormous contributions to the efficient and rapid recording of frequently complex derivative transactions. The scope of its structure and its flexibility has enabled it to keep pace with a rapidly evolving market and to provide a medium through which sophisticated financial concepts can be easily expressed. Indeed, although ISDA's purpose has been to provide the means through which market participants can articulate their innovative financial ideas, there is a strong case for arguing that in providing this means in a readily accessible and standardised format, the ISDA documentation in itself has assisted in promoting the growth and liquidity of this significant sector of today's financial markets.

(Multicurrency-Cross Border)

International Swap Dealers Association, Inc.

MASTER AGREEMENT

dated as of ....

.... and ....

have entered and/or anticipate entering into one or more transactions (each a "Transaction") that are or will be governed by this Master Agreement, which includes the schedule (the "Schedule"), and the documents and other confirming evidence (each a "Confirmation") exchanged between the parties confirming those Transactions.

Accordingly, the parties agree as follows:-

1. Interpretation

(a) **Definitions.** The terms defined in Section 14 and in the Schedule will have the meanings therein specified for the purpose of this Master Agreement.

(b) **Inconsistency.** In the event of any inconsistency between the provisions of the Schedule and the other provisions of this Master Agreement, the Schedule will prevail. In the event of any inconsistency between the provisions of any Confirmation and this Master Agreement (including the Schedule), such Confirmation will prevail for the purpose of the relevant Transaction.

(c) **Single Agreement.** All Transactions are entered into in reliance on the fact that this Master Agreement and all Confirmations form a single agreement between the parties (collectively referred to as this "Agreement"), and the parties would not otherwise enter into any Transactions.

2. Obligations

(a) **General Conditions.**

(i) Each party will make each payment or delivery specified in each Confirmation to be made by it, subject to the other provisions of this Agreement.

(ii) Payments under this Agreement will be made on the due date for value on that date in the place of the account specified in the relevant Confirmation or otherwise pursuant to this Agreement, in freely transferable funds and in the manner customary for payments in the required currency. Where settlement is by delivery (that is, other than by payment), such delivery will be made for receipt on the due date in the manner customary for the relevant obligation unless otherwise specified in the relevant Confirmation or elsewhere in this Agreement.

(iii) Each obligation of each party under Section 2(a)(i) is subject to (1) the condition precedent that no Event of Default or Potential Event of Default with respect to the other party has occurred and is continuing, (2) the condition precedent that no Early Termination Date in respect of the relevant Transaction has occurred or been effectively designated and (3) each other applicable condition precedent specified in this Agreement.

(b)   **Change of Account.** Either party may change its account for receiving a payment or delivery by giving notice to the other party at least five Local Business Days prior to the scheduled date for the payment or delivery to which such change applies unless such other party gives timely notice of a reasonable objection to such change.

(c)   **Netting.** If on any date amounts would otherwise be payable:-

    (i) in the same currency; and

    (ii) in respect of the same Transaction,

by each party to the other, then, on such date, each party's obligation to make payment of any such amount will be automatically satisfied and discharged and, if the aggregate amount that would otherwise have been payable by one party exceeds the aggregate amount that would otherwise have been payable by the other party, replaced by an obligation upon the party by whom the larger aggregate amount would have been payable to pay to the other party the excess of the larger aggregate amount over the smaller aggregate amount.

The parties may elect in respect of two or more Transactions that a net amount will be determined in respect of all amounts payable on the same date in the same currency in respect of such Transactions, regardless of whether such amounts are payable in respect of the same Transaction. The election may be made in the Schedule or a Confirmation by specifying that subparagraph (ii) above will not apply to the Transactions identified as being subject to the election, together with the starting date (in which case subparagraph (ii) above will not, or will cease to, apply to such Transactions from such date). This election may be made separately for different groups of Transactions and will apply separately to each pairing of offices through which the parties make and receive payments or deliveries.

(d)   **Deduction or Withholding for Tax.**

    (i) **Gross-Up.** All payments under this Agreement will be made without any deduction or withholding for or on account of any Tax unless such deduction or withholding is required by any applicable law, as modified by the practice of any relevant governmental revenue authority, then in effect. If a party is so required to deduct or withhold, then that party ("X") will:-

(1) promptly notify the other party ("Y") of such requirement;

(2) pay to the relevant authorities the full amount required to be deducted or withheld (including the full amount required to be deducted or withheld from any additional amount paid by X to Y under this Section 2(d)) promptly upon the earlier of determining that such deduction or withholding is required or receiving notice that such amount has been assessed against Y;

(3) promptly forward to Y an official receipt (or a certified copy), or other documentation reasonably acceptable to Y, evidencing such payment to such authorities; and

(4) if such Tax is an Indemnifiable Tax, pay to Y, in addition to the payment to which Y is otherwise entitled under this Agreement, such additional amount as is necessary to ensure that the net amount actually received by Y (free and clear of Indemnifiable Taxes, whether assessed against X or Y) will equal the full amount Y would have received had no such deduction or withholding been required. However, X will not be required to pay any additional amount to Y to the extent that it would not be required to be paid but for:-

(A) the failure by Y to comply with or perform any agreement contained in Section 4(a)(i), 4(a)(iii) or 4(d); or

(B) the failure of a representation made by Y pursuant to Section 3(f) to be accurate and true unless such failure would not have occurred but for (I) any action taken by a taxing authority, or brought in a court of competent jurisdiction, on or after the date on which a Transaction is entered into (regardless of whether such action is taken or brought with respect to a party to this Agreement) or (II) a Change in Tax Law.

(ii) **Liability,** If:-

(1) X is required by any applicable law, as modified by the practice of any relevant governmental revenue authority, to make any deduction or withholding in respect of which X would not be required to pay an additional amount to Y under Section 2(d)(i)(4);

(2) X does not so deduct or withhold; and

(3) a liability resulting from such Tax is assessed directly against X,

then, except to the extent Y has satisfied or then satisfies the liability resulting from such Tax, Y will promptly pay to X the amount of such liability (including any related liability for interest, but including any related liability for penalties only if Y has failed to comply with or perform any agreement contained in Section 4(a)(i), 4(a)(iii) or 4(d)).

(e) **Default Interest; Other Amounts.** Prior to the occurrence or effective designation of an Early Termination Date in respect of the relevant Transaction, a party that defaults in the performance of any payment obligation will, to the extent permitted by law and subject to Section 6(c), be required to pay interest (before as well as after judgment) on the overdue amount to the other party on demand in the same currency as such overdue amount, for the period from (and including) the original due date for payment to (but excluding) the date of actual payment, at the Default Rate. Such interest will be calculated on the basis of daily compounding and the actual number of days elapsed. If, prior to the occurrence or effective designation of an Early Termination Date in respect of the relevant Transaction, a party defaults in the performance of any obligation required to be settled by delivery, it will compensate the other party on demand if and to the extent provided for in the relevant Confirmation or elsewhere in this Agreement.

3. Representations

Each party represents to the other party (which representations will be deemed to be repeated by each party on each date on which a Transaction is entered into and, in the case of the representations in Section 3(f), at all times until the termination of this Agreement) that:-

(a) **Basic Representations.**

(i) **Status.** It is duly organised and validly existing under the laws of the jurisdiction of its organisation or incorporation and, if relevant under such laws, in good standing;

(ii) **Powers.** It has the power to execute this Agreement and any other documentation relating to this Agreement to which it is a party, to deliver this Agreement and any other documentation relating to this Agreement that it is required by this Agreement to deliver and to perform its obligations under this Agreement and any obligations it has under any Credit Support Document to which it is a party and has taken all necessary action to authorise such execution, delivery and performance;

(iii) **No Violation or Conflict.** Such execution, delivery and performance do not violate or conflict with any law applicable to it, any provision of its constitutional documents, any order or judgment of any court or other agency of government applicable to it or any of its assets or any contractual restriction binding on or affecting it or any of its assets;

(iv) **Consents.** All governmental and other consents that are required to have been obtained by it with respect to this Agreement or any Credit Support Document to which it is a party have been obtained and are in full force and effect and all conditions of any such consents have been complied with; and

(v) **Obligations Binding.** Its obligations under this Agreement and any Credit Support Document to which it is a party constitute its legal, valid and binding obligations, enforceable in accordance with their respective terms (subject to applicable bankruptcy, reorganisation, insolvency, moratorium or similar laws affecting creditors' rights generally and subject, as to enforceability, to equitable principles of general application (regardless of whether enforcement is sought in a proceeding in equity or at law)).

(b) **Absence of Certain Events.** No Event of Default or Potential Event of Default or, to its knowledge, Termination Event with respect to it has occurred and is continuing and no such event or circumstance would occur as a result of its entering into or performing its obligations under this Agreement or any Credit Support Document to which it is a party.

(c) **Absence of Litigation.** There is not pending or, to its knowledge, threatened against it or any of its Affiliates any action, suit or proceeding at law or in equity or before any court, tribunal, governmental body, agency or official or any arbitrator that is likely to affect the legality, validity or enforceability against it of this Agreement or any Credit Support Document to which it is a party or its ability to perform its obligations under this Agreement or such Credit Support Document.

(d) **Accuracy of Specified Information.** All applicable information that is furnished in writing by or on behalf of it to the other party and is identified for the purpose of this Section 3(d) in the Schedule is, as of the date of the information, true, accurate and complete in every material respect.

(e) **Payer Tax Representation.** Each representation specified in the Schedule as being made by it for the purpose of this Section 3(e) is accurate and true.

(f) **Payee Tax Representations.** Each representation specified in the Schedule as being made by it for the purpose of this Section 3(f) is accurate and true.

4. Agreements

Each party agrees with the other that, so long as either party has or may have any obligation under this Agreement or under any Credit Support Document to which it is a party:-

(a) **Furnish Specified Information.** It will deliver to the other party or, in certain cases under subparagraph (iii) below, to such government or taxing authority as the other party reasonably directs:-

(i) any forms, documents or certificates relating to taxation specified in the Schedule or any Confirmation;

(ii) any other documents specified in the Schedule or any Confirmation; and

(iii) upon reasonable demand by such other party, any form or document that may be required or reasonably requested in writing in order to allow such other party or its Credit Support Provider to make a payment under this Agreement or any applicable Credit Support Document without any deduction or withholding for or on account of any Tax or with such deduction or withholding at a reduced rate (so long as the completion, execution or submission of such form or document would not materially prejudice the legal or commercial position of the party in receipt of such demand), with any such form or document to be accurate and completed in a manner reasonably satisfactory to such other party and to be executed and to be delivered with any reasonably required certification,

in each case by the date specified in the Schedule or such Confirmation or, if none is specified, as soon as reasonably practicable.

(b) **Maintain Authorisations.** It will use all reasonable efforts to maintain in full force and effect all consents of any governmental or other authority that are required to be obtained by it with respect to this Agreement or any Credit Support Document to which it is a party and will use all reasonable efforts to obtain any that may become necessary in the future.

(c) **Comply with Laws.** It will comply in all material respects with all applicable laws and orders to which it may be subject if failure so to comply would materially impair its ability to perform its obligations under this Agreement or any Credit Support Document to which it is a party.

(d) **Tax Agreement.** It will give notice of any failure of a representation made by it under Section 3(f) to be accurate and true promptly upon learning of such failure.

(e) **Payment of Stamp Tax.** Subject to Section 11, it will pay any Stamp Tax levied or imposed upon it or in respect of its execution or performance of this Agreement by a jurisdiction in which it is incorporated, organised, managed and controlled, or considered to have its seat, or in which a branch or office through which it is acting for the purpose of this Agreement is located ("Stamp Tax Jurisdiction") and will indemnify the other party against any Stamp Tax levied or imposed upon the other party or in respect of the other party's execution or performance of this Agreement by any such Stamp Tax Jurisdiction which is not also a Stamp Tax Jurisdiction with respect to the other party.

5. Events of Default and Termination Events

(a) **Events of Default.** The occurrence at any time with respect to a party or, if applicable, any Credit Support Provider of such party or any Specified Entity of such party of any of the following events constitutes an event of default (an "Event of Default") with respect to such party:-

(i) **Failure to Pay or Deliver.** Failure by the party to make, when due, any payment under this Agreement or delivery under Section 2(a)(i) or 2(e) required to be made by it if such failure is not remedied on or before the third Local Business Day after notice of such failure is given to the party;

(ii) **Breach of Agreement.** Failure by the party to comply with or perform any agreement or obligation (other than an obligation to make any payment under this Agreement or delivery under Section 2(a)(i) or 2(e) or to give notice of a Termination Event or any agreement or obligation under Section 4(a)(i), 4(a)(iii) or 4(d)) to be complied with or performed by the party in accordance with this Agreement if such failure is not remedied on or before the thirtieth day after notice of such failure is given to the party;

(iii) **Credit Support Default.**

(1) Failure by the party or any Credit Support Provider of such party to comply with or perform any agreement or obligation to be complied with or performed by it in accordance with any Credit Support Document if such failure is continuing after any applicable grace period has elapsed;

(2) the expiration or termination of such Credit Support Document or the failing or ceasing of such Credit Support Document to be in full force and effect for the purpose of this Agreement (in either case other than in accordance with its terms) prior to the satisfaction of all obligations of such party under each Transaction to which such Credit Support Document relates without the written consent of the other party; or

(3) the party or such Credit Support Provider disaffirms, disclaims, repudiates or rejects, in whole or in part, or challenges the validity of, such Credit Support Document;

(iv) **Misrepresentation.** A representation (other than a representation under Section 3(e) or (f)) made or repeated or deemed to have been made or repeated by the party or any Credit Support Provider of such party in this Agreement or any Credit Support Document proves to have been incorrect or misleading in any material respect when made or repeated or deemed to have been made or repeated;

(v) **Default under Specified Transaction.** The party, any Credit Support Provider of such party or any applicable Specified Entity of such party (1) defaults under a Specified Transaction and, after giving effect to any applicable notice requirement or grace period, there occurs a liquidation of, an acceleration of obligations under, or an early termination of, that Specified Transaction, (2) defaults, after giving effect to any applicable notice requirement or grace period, in making any payment or delivery due on the last payment, delivery or exchange date of, or any payment on early termination of, a Specified Transaction (or such default continues for at least three Local Business Days if there is no applicable notice requirement or grace period) or (3) disaffirms, disclaims, repudiates or rejects, in whole or in part, a Specified Transaction (or such action is taken by any person or entity appointed or empowered to operate it or act on its behalf);

(vi) **Cross Default.** If "Cross Default" is specified in the Schedule as applying to the party, the occurrence or existence of (1) a default, event of default or other similar condition or event (however described) in respect of such party, any Credit Support Provider of such party or any applicable Specified Entity of such party under one or more agreements or instruments relating to Specified

Indebtedness of any of them (individually or collectively) in an aggregate amount of not less than the applicable Threshold Amount (as specified in the Schedule) which has resulted in such Specified Indebtedness becoming, or becoming capable at such time of being declared, due and payable under such agreements or instruments, before it would otherwise have been due and payable or (2) a default by such party, such Credit Support Provider or such Specified Entity (individually or collectively) in making one or more payments on the due date thereof in an aggregate amount of not less than the applicable Threshold Amount under such agreements or instruments (after giving effect to any applicable notice requirement or grace period);

(vii) **Bankruptcy.** The party, any Credit Support Provider of such party or any applicable Specified Entity of such party:-

(1) is dissolved (other than pursuant to a consolidation, amalgamation or merger); (2) becomes insolvent or is unable to pay its debts or fails or admits in writing its inability generally to pay its debts as they become due; (3) makes a general assignment, arrangement or composition with or for the benefit of its creditors; (4) institutes or has instituted against it a proceeding seeking a judgment of insolvency or bankruptcy or any other relief under any bankruptcy or insolvency law or other similar law affecting creditors' rights, or a petition is presented for its winding-up or liquidation, and, in the case of any such proceeding or petition instituted or presented against it, such proceeding or petition (A) results in a judgment of insolvency or bankruptcy or the entry of an order for relief or the making of an order for its winding-up or liquidation or (B) is not dismissed, discharged, stayed or restrained in each case within 30 days of the institution or presentation thereof; (5) has a resolution passed for its winding-up, official management or liquidation (other than pursuant to a consolidation, amalgamation or merger); (6) seeks or becomes subject to the appointment of an administrator, provisional liquidator, conservator, receiver, trustee, custodian or other similar official for it or for all or substantially all its assets; (7) has a secured party take possession of all or substantially all its assets or has a distress, execution, attachment, sequestration or other legal process levied, enforced or sued on or against all or substantially all its assets and such secured party maintains possession, or any such process is not dismissed, discharged, stayed or restrained, in each case within 30 days thereafter; (8) causes or is subject to any event with respect to it which, under the applicable laws of any jurisdiction, has an analogous effect to any of the events specified in clauses (I) to (7) (inclusive); or (9) takes any action in furtherance of, or indicating its consent to, approval of, or acquiescence in, any of the foregoing acts; or

(viii) **Merger Without Assumption.** The party or any Credit Support Provider of such party consolidates or amalgamates with, or merges with or into, or transfers all or substantially all its assets to, another entity and, at the time of such consolidation, amalgamation, merger or transfer:-

(1) the resulting, surviving or transferee entity fails to assume all the

obligations of such party or such Credit Support Provider under this Agreement or any Credit Support Document to which it or its predecessor was a party by operation of law or pursuant to an agreement reasonably satisfactory to the other party to this Agreement; or

(2) the benefits of any Credit Support Document fail to extend (without the consent of the other party) to the performance by such resulting, surviving or transferee entity of its obligations under this Agreement.

(b) **Termination Events.** The occurrence at any time with respect to a party or, if applicable, any Credit Support Provider of such party or any Specified Entity of such party of any event specified below constitutes an Illegality if the event is specified in (i) below, a Tax Event if the event is specified in (ii) below or a Tax Event Upon Merger if the event is specified in (iii) below, and, if specified to be applicable, a Credit Event Upon Merger if the event is specified pursuant to (iv) below or an Additional Termination Event if the event is specified pursuant to (v) below:-

(i) **Illegality.** Due to the adoption of, or any change in, any applicable law after the date on which a Transaction is entered into, or due to the promulgation of, or any change in, the interpretation by any court, tribunal or regulatory authority with competent jurisdiction of any applicable law after such date, it becomes unlawful (other than as a result of a breach by the party of Section 4(b)) for such party (which will be the Affected Party):-

(1) to perform any absolute or contingent obligation to make a payment or delivery or to receive a payment or delivery in respect of such Transaction or to comply with any other material provision of this Agreement relating to such Transaction; or

(2) to perform, or for any Credit Support Provider of such party to perform, any contingent or other obligation which the party (or such Credit Support Provider) has under any Credit Support Document relating to such Transaction;

(ii) **Tax Event.** Due to (x) any action taken by a taxing authority, or brought in a court of competent jurisdiction, on or after the date on which a Transaction is entered into (regardless of whether such action is taken or brought with respect to a party to this Agreement) or (y) a Change in Tax Law, the party (which will be the Affected Party) will, or there is a substantial likelihood that it will, on the next succeeding Scheduled Payment Date (1) be required to pay the other party an additional amount in respect of an Indemnifiable Tax under Section 2(d)(i)(4) (except in respect of interest under Section 2(e), 6(d)(ii) or 6(e)) or (2) receive a payment from which an amount is required to be deducted or withheld for or on account of a Tax (except in respect of interest under Section 2(e), 6(d)(ii) or 6(e)) and no additional amount is required to be paid in respect of such Tax under Section 2(d)(i)(4) (other than by reason of Section 2(d)(i)(4)(A) or (B));

(iii) **Tax Event Upon Merger.** The party (the "Burdened Party") on the next succeeding Scheduled Payment Date will either (1) be required to pay an additional amount in respect of an Indemnifiable Tax under Section 2(d)(i)(4) (except in respect of interest under Section 2(e), 6(d)(ii) or 6(e)) or (2) receive a payment from which an amount has been deducted or withheld for or on account of any Indemnifiable Tax in respect of which the other party is not required to pay an additional amount (other than by reason of Section 2(d)(i)(4)(A) or (B)), in either case as a result of a party consolidating or amalgamating with, or merging with or into, or transferring all or substantially all its assets to, another entity (which will be the Affected Party) where such action does not constitute an event described in Section 5(a)(viii);

(iv) **Credit Event Upon Merger.** If "Credit Event Upon Merger" is specified in the Schedule as applying to the party, such party ("X"), any Credit Support Provider of X or any applicable Specified Entity of X consolidates or amalgamates with, or merges with or into, or transfers all or substantially all its assets to, another entity and such action does not constitute an event described in Section 5(a)(viii) but the creditworthiness of the resulting, surviving or transferee entity is materially weaker than that of X, such Credit Support Provider or such Specified Entity, as the case may be, immediately prior to such action (and, in such event, X or its successor or transferee, as appropriate, will be the Affected Party); or

(v) **Additional Termination Event.** If any "Additional Termination Event" is specified in the Schedule or any Confirmation as applying, the occurrence of such event (and, in such event, the Affected Party or Affected Parties shall be as specified for such Additional Termination Event in the Schedule or such Confirmation).

(c) **Event of Default and Illegality.** If an event or circumstance which would otherwise constitute or give rise to an Event of Default also constitutes an Illegality, it will be treated as an Illegality and will not constitute an Event of Default.

6. Early Termination

(a) **Right to Terminate Following Event of Default.** If at any time an Event of Default with respect to a party (the "Defaulting Party") has occurred and is then continuing, the other party (the "Non-defaulting Party") may, by not more than 20 days notice to the Defaulting Party specifying the relevant Event of Default, designate a day not earlier than the day such notice is effective as an Early Termination Date in respect of all outstanding Transactions. If, however, "Automatic Early Termination" is specified in the Schedule as applying to a party, then an Early Termination Date in respect of all outstanding Transactions will occur immediately upon the occurrence with respect to such party of an Event of Default specified in Section 5(a)(vii)(1), (3), (S), (6) or, to the extent analogous thereto, (8), and as of the time immediately preceding the institution of the relevant proceeding or the presentation of the relevant petition upon the occurrence with respect to such party of an Event of Default specified in Section 5(a)(vii)(4) or, to the extent analogous thereto, (8).

(b) **Right to Terminate Following Termination Event.**

(i) **Notice.** If a Termination Event occurs, an Affected Party will, promptly upon becoming aware of it, notify the other party, specifying the nature of that Termination Event and each Affected Transaction and will also give such other information about that Termination Event as the other party may reasonably require.

(ii) **Transfer to Avoid Termination Event.** If either an Illegality under Section 5(b)(i)(1) or a Tax Event occurs and there is only one Affected Party, or if a Tax Event Upon Merger occurs and the Burdened Party is the Affected Party, the Affected Party will, as a condition to its right to designate an Early Termination Date under Section 6(b)(iv), use all reasonable efforts (which will not require such party to incur a loss, excluding immaterial, incidental expenses) to transfer within 20 days after it gives notice under Section 6(b)(i) all its rights and obligations under this Agreement in respect of the Affected Transactions to another of its offices or Affiliates so that such Termination Event ceases to exist.

If the Affected Party is not able to make such a transfer it will give notice to the other party to that effect within such 20 day period, whereupon the other party may effect such a transfer within 30 days after the notice is given under Section 6(b)(i).

Any such transfer by a party under this Section 6(b)(ii) will be subject to and conditional upon the prior written consent of the other party, which consent will not be withheld if such other party's policies in effect at such time would permit it to enter into transactions with the transferee on the terms proposed.

(iii) **Two Affected Parties.** If an Illegality under Section 5(b)(i)(1) or a Tax Event occurs and there are two Affected Parties, each party will use all reasonable efforts to reach agreement within 30 days after notice thereof is given under Section 6(b)(i) on action to avoid that Termination Event.

(iv) **Right to Terminate.** If:-

(1) a transfer under Section 6(b)(ii) or an agreement under Section 6(b)(iii), as the case may be, has not been effected with respect to all Affected Transactions within 30 days after an Affected Party gives notice under Section 6(b)(i); or

(2) an Illegality under Section 5(b)(i)(2), a Credit Event Upon Merger or an Additional Termination Event occurs, or a Tax Event Upon Merger occurs and the Burdened Party is not the Affected Party,

either party in the case of an Illegality, the Burdened Party in the case of a Tax Event Upon Merger, any Affected Party in the case of a Tax Event or an Additional Termination Event if there is more than one Affected Party, or the party which is not the Affected Party in the case of a Credit Event Upon Merger or an Additional Termination Event if there is only one Affected Party may, by not more than 20 days notice to the other party and provided that the relevant Termination Event is then continuing, designate a day not earlier than the day such notice is effective as an Early Termination Date in respect of all Affected Transactions.

(c) **Effect of Designation.**

(i) If notice designating an Early Termination Date is given under Section 6(a) or (b), the Early Termination Date will occur on the date so designated, whether or not the relevant Event of Default or Termination Event is then continuing.

(ii) Upon the occurrence or effective designation of an Early Termination Date, no further payments or deliveries under Section 2(a)(i) or 2(e) in respect of the Terminated Transactions will be required to be made, but without prejudice to the other provisions of this Agreement. The amount, if any, payable in respect of an Early Termination Date shall be determined pursuant to Section 6(e).

(d) **Calculations.**

(i) **Statement.** On or as soon as reasonably practicable following the occurrence of an Early Termination Date, each party will make the calculations on its part, if any, contemplated by Section 6(e) and will provide to the other party a statement (1) showing, in reasonable detail, such calculations (including all relevant quotations and specifying any amount payable under Section 6(e)) and (2) giving details of the relevant account to which any amount payable to it is to be paid. In the absence of written confirmation from the source of a quotation obtained in determining a Market Quotation, the records of the party obtaining such quotation will be conclusive evidence of the existence and accuracy of such quotation.

(ii) **Payment Date.** An amount calculated as being due in respect of any Early Termination Date under Section 6(e) will be payable on the day that notice of the amount payable is effective (in the case of an Early Termination Date which is designated or occurs as a result of an Event of Default) and on the day which is two Local Business Days after the day on which notice of the amount payable is effective (in the case of an Early Termination Date which is designated as a result of a Termination Event). Such amount will be paid together with (to the extent permitted under applicable law) interest thereon (before as well as after judgment) in the Termination Currency, from (and including) the relevant Early Termination Date to (but excluding) the date such amount is paid, at the Applicable Rate. Such interest will be calculated on the basis of daily compounding and the actual number of days elapsed.

(e) **Payments on Early Termination.** If an Early Termination Date occurs, the following provisions shall apply based on the parties' election in the Schedule of a payment measure, either "Market Quotation " or "Loss", and a payment method, either the "First Method" or the "Second Method". If the parties fail to designate a payment measure or payment method in the Schedule, it will be deemed that "Market Quotation" or the "Second Method", as the case may be, shall apply. The amount, if any, payable in respect of an Early Termination Date and determined pursuant to this Section will be subject to any Set-off.

(i) **Events of Default.** If the Early Termination Date results from an Event of Default:-

(1) *First Method and Market Quotation*. If the First Method and Market Quotation apply, the Defaulting Party will pay to the Non-defaulting Party the excess, if a positive number, of (A) the sum of the Settlement Amount (determined by the Non-defaulting Party) in respect of the Terminated Transactions and the Termination Currency Equivalent of the Unpaid Amounts owing to the Non-defaulting Party over (B) the Termination Currency Equivalent of the Unpaid Amounts owing to the Defaulting Party.

(2) *First Method and Loss*. If the First Method and Loss apply, the Defaulting Party will pay to the Non-defaulting Party, if a positive number, the Non-defaulting Party's Loss in respect of this Agreement.

(3) *Second Method and Market Quotation*. If the Second Method and Market Quotation apply, an amount will be payable equal to (A) the sum of the Settlement Amount (determined by the Non-defaulting Party) in respect of the Terminated Transactions and the Termination Currency Equivalent of the Unpaid Amounts owing to the Non-defaulting Party less (B) the Termination Currency Equivalent of the Unpaid Amounts owing to the Defaulting Party. If that amount is a positive number, the Defaulting Party will pay it to the Non-defaulting Party; if it is a negative number, the Non-defaulting Party will pay the absolute value of that amount to the Defaulting Party.

(4) *Second Method and Loss*. If the Second Method and Loss apply, an amount will be payable equal to the Non-defaulting Party's Loss in respect of this Agreement. If that amount is a positive number, the Defaulting Party will pay it to the Non-defaulting Party; if it is a negative number, the Non-defaulting Party will pay the absolute value of that amount to the Defaulting Party.

(ii) **Termination Events.** If the Early Termination Date results from a Termination Event:-

(1) *One Affected Party*. If there is one Affected Party, the amount payable will be determined in accordance with Section 6(e)(i)(3), if Market Quotation applies, or Section 6(e)(i)(4), if Loss applies, except that, in either case, references to the Defaulting Party and to the Non-defaulting Party will be deemed to be references to the Affected Party and the party which is not the Affected Party, respectively, and, if Loss applies and fewer than all the Transactions are being terminated, Loss shall be calculated in respect of all Terminated Transactions.

(2) *Two Affected Parties*. If there are two Affected Parties:-

(A) if Market Quotation applies, each party will determine a Settlement Amount in respect of the Terminated Transactions, and an amount will be payable equal to (I) the sum of (a) one-half of the difference between the Settlement Amount of the party with the higher Settlement Amount ("X") and the Settlement Amount of the party with the lower Settlement Amount ("Y") and (b) the Termination Currency Equivalent of the Unpaid Amounts owing to X less (II) the Termination Currency Equivalent of the Unpaid Amounts owing to Y; and

(B) if Loss applies, each party will determine its Loss in respect of this Agreement (or, if fewer than all the Transactions are being terminated, in respect of all Terminated Transactions) and an amount will be payable equal to one-half of the difference between the Loss of the party with the higher Loss ("X") and the Loss of the party with the lower Loss ("Y").

If the amount payable is a positive number, Y will pay it to X; if it is a negative number, X will pay the absolute value of that amount to Y.

(iii) **Adjustment for Bankruptcy.** In circumstances where an Early Termination Date occurs because "Automatic Early Termination" applies in respect of a party, the amount determined under this Section 6(e) will be subject to such adjustments as are appropriate and permitted by law to reflect any payments or deliveries made by one party to the other under this Agreement (and retained by such other party) during the period from the relevant Early Termination Date to the date for payment determined under Section 6(d)(ii).

(iv) **Pre-Estimate.** The parties agree that if Market Quotation applies an amount recoverable under this Section 6(e) is a reasonable pre-estimate of loss and not a penalty. Such amount is payable for the loss of bargain and the loss of protection against future risks and except as otherwise provided in this Agreement neither party will be entitled to recover any additional damages as a consequence of such losses.

7. Transfer

Subject to Section 6(b)(ii), neither this Agreement nor any interest or obligation in or under this Agreement may be transferred (whether by way of security or otherwise) by either party without the prior written consent of the other party, except that:-

(a)   a party may make such a transfer of this Agreement pursuant to a consolidation or amalgamation with, or merger with or into, or transfer of all or substantially all its assets to, another entity (but without prejudice to any other right or remedy under this Agreement); and

(b)   a party may make such a transfer of all or any part of its interest in any amount payable to it from a Defaulting Party under Section 6(e).

Any purported transfer that is not in compliance with this Section will be void.

8. Contractual Currency

(a)   **Payment in the Contractual Currency.** Each payment under this Agreement will be made in the relevant currency specified in this Agreement for that payment (the

"Contractual Currency"). To the extent permitted by applicable law, any obligation to make payments under this Agreement in the Contractual Currency will not be discharged or satisfied by any tender in any currency other than the Contractual Currency, except to the extent such tender results in the actual receipt by the party to which payment is owed, acting in a reasonable manner and in good faith in converting the currency so tendered into the Contractual Currency, of the full amount in the Contractual Currency of all amounts payable in respect of this Agreement. If for any reason the amount in the Contractual Currency so received falls short of the amount in the Contractual Currency payable in respect of this Agreement, the party required to make the payment will, to the extent permitted by applicable law, immediately pay such additional amount in the Contractual Currency as may be necessary to compensate for the shortfall. If for any reason the amount in the Contractual Currency so received exceeds the amount in the Contractual Currency payable in respect of this Agreement, the party receiving the payment will refund promptly the amount of such excess.

(b) **Judgments.** To the extent permitted by applicable law, if any judgment or order expressed in a currency other than the Contractual Currency is rendered (i) for the payment of any amount owing in respect of this Agreement, (ii) for the payment of any amount relating to any early termination in respect of this Agreement or (iii) in respect of a judgment or order of another court for the payment of any amount described in (i) or (ii) above, the party seeking recovery, after recovery in full of the aggregate amount to which such party is entitled pursuant to the judgment -or order, will be entitled to receive immediately from the other party the amount of any shortfall of the Contractual Currency received by such party as a consequence of sums paid in such other currency and will refund promptly to the other party any excess of the Contractual Currency received by such party as a consequence of sums paid in such other currency if such shortfall or such excess arises or results from any variation between the rate of exchange at which the Contractual Currency is converted into the currency of the judgment or order for the purposes of such judgment or order and the rate of exchange at which such party is able, acting in a reasonable manner and in good faith in converting the currency received into the Contractual Currency, to purchase the Contractual Currency with the amount of the currency of the judgment or order actually received by such party. The term "rate of exchange" includes, without limitation, any premiums and costs of exchange payable in connection with the purchase of or conversion into the Contractual Currency.

(c) **Separate Indemnities.** To the extent permitted by applicable law, these indemnities constitute separate and independent obligations from the other obligations in this Agreement, will be enforceable as separate and independent causes of action, will apply notwithstanding any indulgence granted by the party to which any payment is owed and will not be affected by judgment being obtained or claim or proof being made for any other sums payable in respect of this Agreement.

(d) **Evidence of Loss.** For the purpose of this Section 8, it will be sufficient for a party to demonstrate that it would have suffered a loss had an actual exchange or purchase been made.

9. **Miscellaneous**

(a) **Entire Agreement.** This Agreement constitutes the entire agreement and understanding of the parties with respect to its subject matter and supersedes all oral communication and prior writings with respect thereto.

(b) **Amendments.** No amendment, modification or waiver in respect of this Agreement will be effective unless in writing (including a writing evidenced by a facsimile transmission) and executed by each of the parties or confirmed by an exchange of telexes or electronic messages on an electronic messaging system.

(c) **Survival of Obligations.** Without prejudice to Sections 2(a)(iii) and 6(c)(ii), the obligations of the parties under this Agreement will survive the termination of any Transaction.

(d) **Remedies Cumulative.** Except as provided in this Agreement, the rights, powers, remedies and privileges provided in this Agreement are cumulative and not exclusive of any rights, powers, remedies and privileges provided by law.

(e) **Counterparts and Confirmations.**

(i) This Agreement (and each amendment, modification and waiver in respect of it) may be executed and delivered in counterparts (including by facsimile transmission), each of which will be deemed an original.

(ii) The parties intend that they are legally bound by the terms of each Transaction from the moment they agree to those terms (whether orally or otherwise). A Confirmation shall be entered into as soon as practicable and may be executed and delivered in counterparts (including by facsimile transmission) or be created by an exchange of telexes or by an exchange of electronic messages on an electronic messaging system, which in each case will be sufficient for all purposes to evidence a binding supplement to this Agreement. The parties will specify therein or through another effective means that any such counterpart, telex or electronic message constitutes a Confirmation.

(f) **No Waiver of Rights.** A failure or delay in exercising any right, power or privilege in respect of this Agreement will not be presumed to operate as a waiver, and a single or partial exercise of any right, power or privilege will not be presumed to preclude any subsequent or further exercise, of that right, power or privilege or the exercise of any other right, power or privilege.

(g) **Headings.** The headings used in this Agreement are for convenience of reference only and are not to affect the construction of or to be taken into consideration in interpreting this Agreement.

10. **Offices; Multibranch Parties**

(a) If Section 10(a) is specified in the Schedule as applying, each party that enters into a Transaction through an Office other than its head or home office represents to the other party that, notwithstanding the place of booking office or jurisdiction of incorporation or organisation of such party, the obligations of such party are the same as if it had entered into the Transaction through its head or home office. This representation will be deemed to be repeated by such party on each date on which a Transaction is entered into.

(b) Neither party may change the office through which it makes and receives payments or deliveries for the purpose of a Transaction without the prior written consent of the other party.

(c) If a party is specified as a Multibranch Party in the Schedule, such Multibranch Party may make and receive payments or deliveries under any Transaction through any office listed in the Schedule, and the office through which it makes and receives payments or deliveries with respect to a Transaction will be specified in the relevant Confirmation.

11. Expenses

A Defaulting Party will, on demand, indemnify and hold harmless the other party for and against all reasonable out-of-pocket expenses, including legal fees and Stamp Tax, incurred by such other party by reason of the enforcement and protection of its rights under this Agreement or any Credit Support Document to which the Defaulting Party is a party or by reason of the early termination of any Transaction, including, but not limited to, costs of collection.

12. Notices

(a) **Effectiveness.** Any notice or other communication in respect of this Agreement may be given in any manner set forth below (except that a notice or other communication under Section 5 or 6 may not be given by facsimile transmission or electronic messaging system) to the address or number or in accordance with the electronic messaging system details provided (see the Schedule) and will be deemed effective as indicated:-

(i) if in writing and delivered in person or by courier, on the date it is delivered;

(ii) if sent by telex, on the date the recipient's answerback is received;

(iii) if sent by facsimile transmission, on the date that transmission is received by a responsible employee of the recipient in legible form (it being agreed that the burden of proving receipt will be on the sender and will not be met by a transmission report generated by the sender's facsimile machine);

(iv) if sent by certified or registered mail (airmail, if overseas) or the equivalent (return receipt requested), on the date that mail is delivered or its delivery is attempted; or

(v) if sent by electronic messaging system, on the date that electronic message is received,

unless the date of that delivery (or attempted delivery) or that receipt, as applicable, is not a Local Business Day or that communication is delivered (or attempted) or received, as applicable, after the close of business on a Local Business Day, in which case that communication shall be deemed given and effective on the first following day that is a Local Business Day.

(b) **Change of Addresses.** Either party may by notice to the other change the address, telex or facsimile number or electronic messaging system details at which notices or other communications are to be given to it

13. Governing Law and Jurisdiction

(a) **Governing Law.** This Agreement will be governed by and construed in accordance with the law specified in the Schedule.

(b) **Jurisdiction.** With respect to any suit, action or proceedings relating to this Agreement ("Proceedings"), each party irrevocably:-

(i) submits to the jurisdiction of the English courts, if this Agreement is expressed to be governed by English law, or to the non-exclusive jurisdiction of the courts of the State of New York and the United States District Court located in the Borough of Manhattan in New York City, if this Agreement is expressed to be governed by the laws of the State of New York; and

(ii) waives any objection which it may have at any time to the laying of venue of any Proceedings brought in any such court, waives any claim that such Proceedings have been brought in an inconvenient forum and further waives the right to object, with respect to such Proceedings, that such court does not have any jurisdiction over such party.

Nothing in this Agreement precludes either party from bringing Proceedings in any other jurisdiction (outside, if this Agreement is expressed to be governed by English law, the Contracting States, as defined in Section 1(3) of the Civil Jurisdiction and Judgments Act 1982 or any modification, extension or re-enactment thereof for the time being in force) nor will the bringing of Proceedings in any one or more jurisdictions preclude the bringing of Proceedings in any other jurisdiction.

(c) **Service of Process.** Each party irrevocably appoints the Process Agent (if any) specified opposite its name in the Schedule to receive, for it and on its behalf, service of process in any Proceedings. If for any reason any party's Process Agent is unable to act as such, such party will promptly notify the other party and within 30 days appoint a substitute process agent acceptable to the other party. The parties irrevocably consent to service of process given in the manner provided for notices in Section 12. Nothing in this Agreement will affect the right of either party to serve process in any other manner permitted by law.

(d) **Waiver of Immunities.** Each party irrevocably waives, to the fullest extent permitted by applicable law, with respect to itself and its revenues and assets (irrespective of their use or intended use), all immunity on the grounds of sovereignty or other similar grounds from (i) suit, (ii) jurisdiction of any court, (iii) relief by way of injunction, order for specific performance or for recovery of property, (iv) attachment of its assets (whether before or after judgment) and (v) execution or enforcement of any judgment to which it or its revenues or assets might otherwise be entitled in any Proceedings in the courts of any jurisdiction and irrevocably agrees, to the extent permitted by applicable law, that it will not claim any such immunity in any Proceedings.

14. Definitions

As used in this Agreement:-

"Additional Termination Event" has the meaning specified in Section 5(b).

"Affected Party" has the meaning specified in Section 5(b).

"Affected Transactions" means (a) with respect to any Termination Event consisting of an Illegality, Tax Event or Tax Event Upon Merger, all Transactions affected by the occurrence of such Termination Event and (b) with respect to any other Termination Event, all Transactions.

"Affiliate" means, subject to the Schedule, in relation to any person, any entity controlled, directly or indirectly, by the person, any entity that controls, directly or indirectly, the person or any entity directly or indirectly under common control with the person. For this purpose, "control" of any entity or person means ownership of a majority of the voting power of the entity or person.

"Applicable Rate" means:-

(a)   in respect of obligations payable or deliverable (or which would have been but for Section 2(a)(iii)) by a Defaulting Party, the Default Rate;

(b)   in respect of an obligation to pay an amount under Section 6(e) of either party from and after the date (determined in accordance with Section 6(d)(ii)) on which that amount is payable, the Default Rate;

(c)   in respect of all other obligations payable or deliverable (or which would have been but for Section 2(a)(iii)) by a Non-defaulting Party, the Non-default Rate; and

(d)   in all other cases, the Termination Rate.

"Burdened Party" has the meaning specified in Section 5(b).

"Change in Tax Law" means the enactment, promulgation, execution or ratification of, or any change in or amendment to, any law (or in the application or official interpretation of any law) that occurs on or after the date on which the relevant Transaction is entered into.

"consent" includes a consent, approval, action, authorisation, exemption, notice, filing, registration or exchange control consent.

"Credit Event Upon Merger" has the meaning specified in Section 5(b).

"Credit Support Document" means any agreement or instrument that is specified as such in this Agreement.

"Credit Support Provider" has the meaning specified in the Schedule.

"Default Rate" means a rate per annum equal to the cost (without proof or evidence of any actual cost) to the relevant payee (as certified by it) if it were to fund or of funding the relevant amount plus 1% per annum.

"Defaulting Party" has the meaning specified in Section 6(a).

"Early Termination Date" means the date determined in accordance with Section 6(a) or 6(b)(iv).

"Event of Default" has the meaning specified in Section 5(a) and, if applicable, in the Schedule.

"Illegality" has the meaning specified in Section 5(b).

"Indemnifiable Tax" means any Tax other than a Tax that would not be imposed in respect of a payment under this Agreement but for a present or former connection between the jurisdiction of the government or taxation authority imposing such Tax and the recipient of such payment or a person related to such recipient (including, without limitation, a connection arising from such recipient or related person being or having been a citizen or resident of such jurisdiction, or being or having been organised, present or engaged in a trade or business in such jurisdiction, or having or having had a permanent establishment or fixed place of business in such jurisdiction, but excluding a connection arising solely from such recipient or related person having executed, delivered, performed its obligations or received a payment under, or enforced, this Agreement or a Credit Support Document).

"law" includes any treaty, law, rule or regulation (as modified, in the case of tax matters, by the practice of any relevant governmental revenue authority) and "lawful" and "unlawful" will be construed accordingly.

"Local Business Day" means, subject to the Schedule, a day on which commercial banks are open for business (including dealings in foreign exchange and foreign currency deposits) (a) in relation to any obligation under Section 2(a)(i), in the place(s) specified in the relevant Confirmation or, if not so specified, as otherwise agreed by the parties in writing or determined pursuant to provisions contained, or incorporated by reference, in this Agreement, (b) in relation to any other payment, in the place where the relevant account is located and, if different, in the principal financial centre, if any, of the currency of such payment, (c) in relation to any notice or other communication, including notice contemplated under Section 5(a)(i), in the city specified in the address for notice provided by the recipient and, in the case of a notice contemplated by Section 2(b), in the place where the relevant new account is to be located and (d) in relation to Section 5(a)(v)(2), in the relevant locations for performance with respect to such Specified Transaction.

"Loss" means, with respect to this Agreement or one or more Terminated Transactions, as the case may be, and a party, the Termination Currency Equivalent of an amount that party reasonably determines in good faith to be its total losses and costs (or gain, in which case expressed as a negative number) in connection with this

Agreement or that Terminated Transaction or group of Terminated Transactions, as the case may be, including any loss of bargain, cost of funding or, at the election of such party but without duplication, loss or cost incurred as a result of its terminating, liquidating, obtaining or reestablishing any hedge or related trading position (or any gain resulting from any of them). Loss includes losses and costs (or gains) in respect of any payment or delivery required to have been made (assuming satisfaction of each applicable condition precedent) on or before the relevant Early Termination Date and not made, except, so as to avoid duplication, if Section 6(e)(i)(1) or (3) or 6(e)(ii)(2)(A) applies. Loss does not include a party's legal fees and out-of-pocket expenses referred to under Section 11. A party will determine its Loss as of the relevant Early Termination Date, or, if that is not reasonably practicable, as of the earliest date thereafter as is reasonably practicable. A party may (but need not) determine its Loss by reference to quotations of relevant rates or prices from one or more leading dealers in the relevant markets.

"Market Quotation" means, with respect to one or more Terminated Transactions and a party making the determination, an amount determined on the basis of quotations from Reference Market-makers. Each quotation will be for an amount, if any, that would be paid to such party (expressed as a negative number) or by such party (expressed as a positive number) in consideration of an agreement between such party (taking into account any existing Credit Support Document with respect to the obligations of such party) and the quoting Reference Market-maker to enter into a transaction (the "Replacement Transaction") that would have the effect of preserving for such party the economic equivalent of any payment or delivery (whether the underlying obligation was absolute or contingent and assuming the satisfaction of each applicable condition precedent) by the parties under Section 2(a)(i) in respect of such Terminated Transaction or group of Terminated Transactions that would, but for the occurrence of the relevant Early Termination Date, have been required after that date. For this purpose, Unpaid Amounts in respect of the Terminated Transaction or group of Terminated Transactions are to be excluded but, without limitation, any payment or delivery that would, but for the relevant Early Termination Date, have been required (assuming satisfaction of each applicable condition precedent) after that Early Termination Date is to be included. The Replacement Transaction would be subject to such documentation as such party and the Reference Market-maker may, in good faith, agree. The party making the determination (or its agent) will request each Reference Market-maker to provide its quotation to the extent reasonably practicable as of the same day and time (without regard to different time zones) on or as soon as reasonably practicable after the relevant Early Termination Date. The day and time as of which those quotations are to be obtained will be selected in good faith by the party obliged to make a determination under Section 6(e), and, if each party is so obliged, after consultation with the other. If more than three quotations are provided, the Market Quotation will be the arithmetic mean of the quotations, without regard to the quotations having the highest and lowest values. If exactly three such quotations are provided, the Market Quotation will be the quotation remaining after disregarding the highest and lowest quotations. For this purpose, if more than one quotation has the same highest value or lowest value, then one of such quotations shall be disregarded. If fewer than three quotations are provided, it will be deemed that the Market Quotation in respect of such Terminated Transaction or group of Terminated Transactions cannot be determined.

"**Non-default Rate**" means a rate per annum equal to the cost (without proof or evidence of any actual cost) to the Non-defaulting Party (as certified by it) if it were to fund the relevant amount.

"**Non-defaulting Party**" has the meaning specified in Section 6(a).

"**Office**" means a branch or office of a party, which may be such party's head or home office.

"**Potential Event of Default**" means any event which, with the giving of notice or the lapse of time or both, would constitute an Event of Default.

"**Reference Market-makers**" means four leading dealers in the relevant market selected by the party determining a Market Quotation in good faith (a) from among dealers of the highest credit standing which satisfy all the criteria that such party applies generally at the time in deciding whether to offer or to make an extension of credit and (b) to the extent practicable, from among such dealers having an office in the same city.

"**Relevant Jurisdiction**" means, with respect to a party, the jurisdictions (a) in which the party is incorporated, organised, managed and controlled or considered to have its seat, (b) where an office through which the party is acting for purposes of this Agreement is located, (c) in which the party executes this Agreement and (d) in relation to any payment, from or through which such payment is made.

"**Scheduled Payment Date**" means a date on which a payment or delivery is to be made under Section 2(a)(i) with respect to a Transaction.

"**Set-off**" means set-off, offset, combination of accounts, right of retention or withholding or similar right or requirement to which the payer of an amount under Section 6 is entitled or subject (whether arising under this Agreement, another contract, applicable law or otherwise) that is exercised by, or imposed on, such payer.

"**Settlement Amount**" means, with respect to a party and any Early Termination Date, the sum of:-

(a)   the Termination Currency Equivalent of the Market Quotations (whether positive or negative) for each Terminated Transaction or group of Terminated Transactions for which a Market Quotation is determined; and

(b)   such party's Loss (whether positive or negative and without reference to any Unpaid Amounts) for each Terminated Transaction or group of Terminated Transactions for which a Market Quotation cannot be determined or would not (in the reasonable belief of the party making the determination) produce a commercially reasonable result.

"**Specified Entity**" has the meaning specified in the Schedule.

"**Specified Indebtedness**" means, subject to the Schedule, any obligation (whether present or future, contingent or otherwise, as principal or surety or otherwise) in respect of borrowed money.

"Specified Transaction" means, subject to the Schedule, (a) any transaction (including an agreement with respect thereto) now existing or hereafter entered into between one party to this Agreement (or any Credit Support Provider of such party or any applicable Specified Entity of such party) and the other party to this Agreement (or any Credit Support Provider of such other party or any applicable Specified Entity of such other party) which is a rate swap transaction, basis swap, forward rate transaction, commodity swap, commodity option, equity or equity index swap, equity or equity index option, bond option, interest rate option, foreign exchange transaction, cap transaction, floor transaction, collar transaction, currency swap transaction, cross-currency rate swap transaction, currency option or any other similar transaction (including any option with respect to any of these transactions), (b) any combination of these transactions and (c) any other transaction identified as a Specified Transaction in this Agreement or the relevant confirmation.

"Stamp Tax" means any stamp, registration, documentation or similar tax.

"Tax" means any present or future tax, levy, impost, duty, charge, assessment or fee of any nature (including interest, penalties and additions thereto) that is imposed by any government or other taxing authority in respect of any payment under this Agreement other than a stamp, registration, documentation or similar tax.

"Tax Event" has the meaning specified in Section 5(b).

"Tax Event Upon Merger" has the meaning specified in Section 5(b).

"Terminated Transactions" means with respect to any Early Termination Date (a) if resulting from a Termination Event, all Affected Transactions and (b) if resulting from an Event of Default, all Transactions (in either case) in effect immediately before the effectiveness of the notice designating that Early Termination Date (or, if "Automatic Early Termination" applies, immediately before that Early Termination Date).

"Termination Currency" has the meaning specified in the Schedule.

"Termination Currency Equivalent" means, in respect of any amount denominated in the Termination Currency, such Termination Currency amount and, in respect of any amount denominated in a currency other than the Termination Currency (the "other Currency"), the amount in the Termination Currency determined by the party making the relevant determination as being required to purchase such amount of such other Currency as at the relevant Early Termination Date, or, if the relevant Market Quotation or Loss (as the case may be), is determined as of a later date, that later date, with the Termination Currency at the rate equal to the spot exchange rate of the foreign exchange agent (selected as provided below) for the purchase of such other Currency with the Termination Currency at or about 11:00 a.m. (in the city in which such foreign exchange agent is located) on such date as would be customary for the determination of such a rate for the purchase of such other Currency for value on the relevant Early Termination Date or that later date. The foreign exchange agent will, if only one party is obliged to make a determination under Section 6(e), be selected in good faith by that party and otherwise will be agreed by the parties.

"Termination Event" means an Illegality, a Tax Event or a Tax Event Upon Merger or, if specified to be applicable, a Credit Event Upon Merger or an Additional Termination Event.

"Termination Rate" means a rate per annum equal to the arithmetic mean of the cost (without proof or evidence of any actual cost) to each party (as certified by such party) if it were to fund or of funding such amounts.

"Unpaid Amounts" owing to any party means, with respect to an Early Termination Date, the aggregate of (a) in respect of all Terminated Transactions, the amounts that became payable (or that would have become payable but for Section 2(a)(iii)) to such party under Section 2(a)(i) on or prior to such Early Termination Date and which remain unpaid as at such Early Termination Date and (b) in respect of each Terminated Transaction, for each obligation under Section 2(a)(i) which was (or would have been but for Section 2(a)(iii)) required to be settled by delivery to such party on or prior to such Early Termination Date and which has not been so settled as at such Early Termination Date, an amount equal to the fair market value of that which was (or would have been) required to be delivered as of the originally scheduled date for delivery, in each case together with (to the extent permitted under applicable law) interest, in the currency of such amounts, from (and including) the date such amounts or obligations were or would have been required to have been paid or performed to (but excluding) such Early Termination Date, at the Applicable Rate. Such amounts of interest will be calculated on the basis of daily compounding and the actual number of days elapsed. The fair market value of any obligation referred to in clause (b) above shall be reasonably determined by the party obliged to make the determination under Section 6(e) or, if each party is so obliged, it shall be the average of the Termination Currency Equivalents of the fair market values reasonably determined by both parties.

IN WITNESS WHEREOF the parties have executed this document on the respective dates specified below with effect from the date specified on the first page of this document.

| .... | .... |
| (Name of Party) | (Name of Party) |

By: ....

By: ....

Name:

Name:

Title:

Title:

Date:

Date:

(Multicurrency-Cross Border)

International Swap Dealers Association, Inc.

SCHEDULE
of the
Master Agreement

dated as of ....

between.. and ....
                    ("Party A")   ("Party A")

Part 1. **Termination Provisions.**

(a)   **"Specified Entity"** means in relation to Party A for the purpose of:-

   Section 5(a)(v),..

   Section 5(a)(vi),...

   Section 5(a)(vii), ...

   Section 5(b)(iv), ...

   and in relation to Party B for the purpose of:-

   Section 5(a)(v)..

   Section 5(a)(vi),...

   Section 5(a)(vii), ...

   Section 5(b)(iv), ...

(b)   **"Specifed Transaction"** will have the meaning specified in Section 14 of this Agreement unless another meaning is specified here ....
   ....

213

(c) The **"Cross Default"** provisions of Section 5(a)(vi) will/will not * apply to Party A
will/will not * apply to Party B

If such provisions apply:-
"Specified Indebtedness" will have the meaning specified in Section 14 of this Agreement unless another meaning is specified here ....

....

"**Threshold Amount**" means ....

....

(d) The **"Credit Event Upon Merger"** provisions of Section 5(b)(iv)
will/will not* apply to Party A
will/will not* apply to Party B

(e) The **"Automatic Early Termination"** provision of Section 6(a)
will/will not* apply to Party A
will/will not* apply to Party B

(f) **Payments on Early Termination.** For the purpose of Section 6(e) of this Agreement:-

(i) Market Quotation/Loss* will apply.

(ii) The First Method/The Second Method* will apply.

(g) **"Termination Currency"** means .... if such currency is specified and freely available, and otherwise United States Dollars.

(h) **Additional Termination Event** will/will not apply*. The following shall constitute an Additional Termination Event:- ....

....

....

....

For the purpose of the foregoing Termination Event, the Affected Party or Affected Parties shall be:-..

....

———————
(*Delete as applicable.)

Part 2. **Tax Representations.**

(a) **Payer Representations.** For the purpose of Section 3(e) of this Agreement, Party A will/will not* make the following representation and Party B will/will not* make the following representation:-

It is not required by any applicable law, as modified by the practice of any relevant governmental revenue authority, of any Relevant Jurisdiction to make any deduction or withholding for or on account of any Tax from any payment (other than interest under Section 2(e), 6(d)(ii) or 6(e) of this Agreement) to be made by it to the other party under this Agreement. In making this representation, it may rely on (i) the accuracy of any representations made by the other party pursuant to Section 3(f) of this Agreement, (ii) the satisfaction of the agreement contained in Section 4(a)(i) or 4(a)(iii) of this Agreement and the accuracy and effectiveness of any document provided by the other party pursuant to Section 4(a)(i) or 4(a)(iii) of this Agreement and (iii) the satisfaction of the agreement of the other party contained in Section 4(d) of this Agreement, provided that it shall not be a breach of this representation where reliance is placed on clause (ii) and the other party does not deliver a form or document under Section 4(a)(iii) by reason of material prejudice to its legal or commercial position.

(b) **Payee Representations.** For the purpose of Section 3(f) of this Agreement, Party A and Party B make the representations specified below, if any:

(i) The following representation will/will not* apply to Party A and will/will not* apply to Party B:-

It is fully eligible for the benefits of the "Business Profits" or "Industrial and Commercial Profits" provision, as the case may be, the "Interest" provision or the "other Income" provision (if any) of the Specified Treaty with respect to any payment described in such provisions and received or to be received by it in connection with this Agreement and no such payment is attributable to a trade or business carried on by it through a permanent establishment in the Specified Jurisdiction.

If such representation applies, then:-

"Specified Treaty" means with respect to Party A ....

"Specified Jurisdiction" means with respect to Party A ....

"Specified Treaty" means with respect to Party B ....

"Specified Jurisdiction" means with respect to Party B ....

(ii) The following representation will/will not* apply to Party A and will/will not* apply to Party B:-

_____

(*Delete as applicable.)

Each payment received or to be received by it in connection with this Agreement will be effectively connected with its conduct of a trade or business in the Specified Jurisdiction.

If such representation applies, then:-

"Specified Jurisdiction" means with respect to Party A ....

"Specified Jurisdiction" means with respect to Party B ....

(iii) The following representation will/will not* apply to Party A and will/will not* apply to Party B:-

(A) It is entering into each Transaction in the ordinary course of its trade as, and is, either (1) a recognised U.K. bank or (2) a recognised U.K. swaps dealer (in either case (1) or (2), for purposes of the United Kingdom Inland Revenue extra statutory concession C17 on interest and currency swaps dated March 14, 1989), and (B) it will bring into account payments made and received in respect of each Transaction in computing its income for United Kingdom tax purposes.

(iv) Other Payee Representations:- ....

....

....

....

N.B. The above representations may need modification if either party is a Multibranch Party.

Part 3. **Agreement to Deliver Documents.**

For the purpose of Sections 4(a)(i) and (ii) of this Agreement, each party agrees to deliver the following documents, as applicable:-

(a) Tax forms, documents or certificates to be delivered are:-

Party required to deliver document	Form/Document/ Certificate	Date by which to be delivered
....	....	....
....	....	....
....	....	....
....	....	....
....	....	....

(*Delete as applicable.)

(b) Other documents to be delivered are:-

Party required to deliver document	Form/Document/ Certificate	Date by which to be delivered	Covered by Section 3(d) Representation
....	....	....	Yes/No*
....	....	....	Yes/No*
....	....	....	Yes/No*
....	....	....	Yes/No*
....	....	....	Yes/No*

Part 4. **Miscellaneous.**

(a) ***Addresses for Notices.*** For the purpose of Section 12(a) of this Agreement:-

Address for notices or communications to Party A:-

Address: ....

Attention: ....

Telex No.: .... Answerback: ....

Facsimile No.: .... Telephone No.: ....

Electronic Messaging System Details: ....

Address for notices or communications to Party B:-

Address: ....

Attention: ....

Telex No.: .... Answerback: ....

Facsimile No.: .... Telephone No.: ....

Electronic Messaging System Details: ....

(b) ***Process Agent.*** For the purpose of Section 13(c) of this Agreement:-

Party A appoints as its Process Agent ....

Party B appoints as its Process Agent ....

_____

(*Delete as applicable.)

(c) **Offices.** The provisions of Section 10(a) will/will not* apply to this Agreement.

(d) **Multibranch Party.** For the purpose of Section 10(c) of this Agreement:-

Party A is/is not* a Multibranch Party and, if so, may act through the following offices:-

....
....
....
....

Party B is/is not* a Multibranch Party and, if so, may act through the following offices:-

....
....
....
....

(e) **Calculation Agent.** The Calculation Agent is ...., unless otherwise specified in a Confirmation in relation to the relevant Transaction.

(f) **Credit Support Document.** Details of any Credit Support Document:- ....
....
....
....

(g) **Credit Support Provider.** Credit Support Provider means in relation to Party A,
....
....
....

Credit Support Provider means in relation to Party B,
....
....
....

(h) **Governing Law.** This Agreement will be governed by and construed in accordance with English law/the laws of the State of New York (without reference to choice of law doctrine)*.

_____

(*Delete as applicable.)

(i) **Netting of Payments.** Subparagraph (ii) of Section 2(c) of this Agreement will not apply to the following Transactions or groups of Transactions (in each case starting from the date of this Agreement/in each case starting from ....*)

....
....
....

(j) **"Affiliate"** will have the meaning specified in Section 14 of this Agreement unless another meaning is specified here..

....
....
....

Part 5. **Other Provisions.**

(*Delete as applicable.)

7

REGULATIONS AND BACK OFFICE

General

The regulatory regime affecting Eurobonds and other Euro-securities has undergone a sea change over the past decade. The Euromarkets still enjoy a valuable element of self-regulation but national and supranational bodies have become increasing proactive in determining the rules by which investment firms conduct their businesses. Regulation has manoeuvred its way into all areas of finance. Central banks, for example, have set down new guidelines for measuring capital adequacy and liquidity. Ratios of bank lending to total capital have been reduced. Stock exchange listing requirements have likewise been stiffened. Actions which were once virtually unregulated are now viewed as crimes, albeit white collar ones, but crimes all the same and punishable by fines or imprisonment or both. A good example is insider trading. This was not even against the law in certain European countries until quite recently. The notion of money laundering has been known to people for some years but only since 1993 has 'assistance' been punishable by a fine and up to 14 years in jail in the United Kingdom.

It is fair to add that some of the new laws and regulations have been imposed so quickly that there is honest debate about the meaning and efficacy of certain provisions. Additionally, the criminalisation of various activities involves the application of judicial procedures which are not only lengthy and expensive but which also involve jurors who may or may not have background experience (or understanding) of the complex workings of the financial community. Changes are bound to be made in the overall approach. Furthermore, the cost of compliance should be reasonable. Otherwise people will find shortcuts to reduce expenses and remain competitive.

Institutional deregulation stands in sharp contrast to what is normally viewed as the trend towards deregulation in the international markets. The two trends do, though, complement each other. Deregulation has largely concentrated on the liberalisation of capital flows and other market mechanisms which used to separate the various sectors of the Euro-markets. The driving force here has been self-interest as much as idealism. For instance, in the first half of the 1990s, funding requirements created by large national deficits encouraged many countries to liberalise their domestic markets to facilitate foreign investment. Frequently, market liberalisation was presented on a quid pro quo basis to encourage, for example, a redistribution of national payment surpluses. In any event, deregulation of the international markets has become a fact of life and is leading inevitably to a single pool of global capital.

From this perspective it is easy to see why national and supranational regulators are keen to maintain some hold over the markets before they grow entirely out of control. If the old mechanisms of market regulation are being cleared away then others need to be found. Hence, the new interest in the regulation of institutions and (in certain instances) individuals. Additionally, as markets do converge there is a natural tendency to level (usually upwards) the degree of regulation. To do otherwise would encourage transnational interference or put a brake on the process of integration altogether.

Additionally, financial collapses such as BCCI, Barlow Clowes and Barings have left national and international authorities with little choice but to do something, anything. The option of inaction is really not a possibility because the so-called 'responsible' bodies are frequently reminded of their position due to the overhanging threat of litigation. Hence, as financial institutions ready themselves to compete in an increasingly unified global market, they will also need to prepare themselves for the stricter regulatory regime which will come hand-in-hand with liberalisation in the international markets.

Current securities regulations

Typically the three main bodies of regulations which affect the securities industry are those relating to residence of the issuer, the residence of the securities firm and the national markets into which the securities are proposed to be sold. Sometimes, other laws come into play. One case in point are the US securities and tax laws, which are discussed in Chapter Three. American law is important because of its extra-territorial reach and because the US capital markets (and investors) enjoy a unique status due to their size and significance.

The majority of Euro-securities are launched from the London market and, therefore, this is a reasonable starting point. Since the passage of the Financial Services Act 1986 (the "Act"), participants in the Eurobond market have had to be either "authorised persons" or "exempted persons". The conduct of investment business without compliance with the Act is a criminal offence. In practice, though, compliance is rarely a problem because nearly all entities involved in the underwriting and distributing of securities are members of the Securities and Futures Authority (SFA). This is a self-regulatory organisation (SRO) which imposes a code of conduct and specific rules on its members. It also has the power to censure, fine and disqualify from business both institutions and individuals. The SFA also maintains a complaints procedure on behalf of investors and an indemnity fund to meet at least part of certain claims against failed financial houses.

Another relevant aspect of the Act is the impact it has on 'advertisements'. This word has a very broad meaning and can cover almost any prospective investment communication. All advertisements must be approved by an authorised person, say a member of the SFA. This approval is based essentially on due diligence and a careful assessment of the accuracy of the disclosure of the advertisement. Specifically, an SFA member which approves an investment advertisement must (i) apply appropriate expertise and (ii) have reasonable grounds to show that the advertisement conveys accurate information and is not misleading. Section 47 of the Act goes further. It makes it a criminal offence to provide false or misleading information (or to conceal material facts) or to create a misleading impression during the course of marketing an investment or with a view to encouraging or discouraging an investor from exercising any rights associated with the investment. Violation of Section 47 is punishable by a maximum of seven years' imprisonment or a fine or both.

What specific relevance does this have to the Eurobond market? Given the catch-all definition of advertisement, nearly any aspect of a new issue which involves the UK will fall under the Act. For example, a roadshow organised from another European centre which toured through the London investment community would be covered by the Act. Hence, considerable care must be taken that presentations are given to only those potential investors whose interest may be solicited in accordance with the law. These are investors which are deemed to be sufficiently expert to understand the investment risks involved. They include authorised and exempted people, governmental authorities and substantial companies, unincorporated associations and trusts. Similarly, offering memoranda are frequently viewed as a form of advertisement, so their distribution needs to be restricted to this same group of sophisticated investors.

When selling securities careful attention also needs to be paid to the category of investor being approached. Generally, different rules apply to different types of investors, with the ones least able to look after their own interests provided the greatest protection under the regulations. Closely allied to this is the notion of suitability. Derivative-based products would obviously be unsuitable when it comes to widows and orphans. Likewise, all private clients must be treated with the highest standards of professionalism (unless they specifically forgo this extra protection by way of written declaration). Additionally, the Eurobond house needs to have an effective way of determining the category into which each client fits. Files should be kept (confidentially) on the client's financial circumstances. Otherwise, it would be impossible to make a judgement on the suitability of a particular investment. Finally, there are rules concerning the hours during which unsolicited telephone calls can be made. The regulations come down to common sense and courtesy but they should be learned when implementing a marketing campaign. Likewise, the stabilisation of a new issue is governed by applicable rules, which when followed, represent little impediment to normal new issue procedure.

The other most relevant aspect of UK securities laws derives from the Public Offers of Securities Regulations 1995 (the POS Regs). These regulations prohibit offers for sale to the public unless a prospectus has been prepared in compliance with the contents requirements of the regulations. The prohibition does not apply where offers are made only to professionals. Otherwise, the best idea is to seek a listing on the London Stock Exchange, because Part IV of the Financial Services Act 1986 removes a listed document from the scope of the regulations once the listing has been obtained.

Additionally, a London listing confers an exemption from the rules mentioned previously regarding advertisements because the Financial Services Act does not apply to those documents consisting of listing particulars. Care, however, must be exercised when applying for a London listing. Under Section 146 of the Act, it says that:-

> "in addition to information specified in the listing rules, the listing particulars shall contain all information as investors and their professional advisers would

reasonably require, and reasonably expect to find there, for the purpose of making an informed assessment of:

(a) the assets and liabilities, financial position, profits and losses, and prospects of the issuer of the securities; and

(b) the rights attaching to those securities."

The POS Regs include a provision identical to that above, which also reflects the position in Common Law. Hence, the above disclosure guidelines are equally applicable to non-London listed transactions. Indeed, Luxembourg listing imposes a specific overriding disclosure obligation. If there is a disclosure violation, say of Section 146, then the parties responsible will be liable for claims for compensation by any investor who sustains a loss as a consequence of any untrue or misleading statement (or omission of a material matter).

Generally speaking, care must be taken that the issuer is in compliance with its own domestic regulations. Any authorisation from relevant authorities should be obtained at an early stage as this will doubtless be included in the issuer's representations and warranties in the foundation documents to the underwriting. In most cases, written evidence of such permissions will need to be delivered as a condition precedent to closing.

As regards selling restrictions in new issues, underwriters and selling group members are typically expected to know and abide by the laws of the jurisdictions where sales are made. Specific language in new issue documentation will usually describe specific sales restrictions in the jurisdiction of the issuer and the jurisdictions of the United Kingdom and the United States. Other specific laws may be referred to if securities distribution is specially intended for other individual countries.

The regulatory requirements relating to listing are detailed in Chapter Four.

Before leaving this section on regulation, it is worth mentioning the increasingly stringent (and complex) rules imposed on nearly all international banks with respect to capital risk weighting. These rules were first proposed by the Basle Committee on Banking Regulations and Supervisory Practices in their report of July 11, 1988. The proposals were in effect guidelines which OECD central banks pledged themselves to implement as a first step, with the central banks of other nations following suit in fairly short order. It is fair to say, however, that a degree of latitude is given to individual central banks to interpret the guidelines and to implement them in a practical manner.

The Basle Committee recommended that a bank's capital should be at least 8% of its *risk weighted assets*. In practice, though, most central bank regulators impose a higher percentage, say 12%-15%, depending on the bank. The effect of risk weighting is to allocate a varying proportion of a bank's capital to support different categories of asset. In theory, more capital is needed to back up a risky asset. Hence, with an unsecured corporate loan the guidelines require that it be 100% risk weighted. This means that an amount of capital, say 12% of the amount of the loan, must be allocated to support the loan. If an asset is 50% risk weighted, then the capital allocated need be only 6% of the asset booked, and so on. The effect of these rules is to ensure that a bank's capital does not become overstretched, and thereby run a risk for depositors. A distinction is typically drawn between different types of bank capital. For instance, 'tier 1' might comprise equity which in turn constitutes , say, half of the total capital requirement; while the other half might be 'tier 2' or, say, subordinated debt. Once again, the specific guidelines are left to the individual central banks to set. Frequently, too, central banks will impose other guidelines which require that certain liquidity ratios are maintained.

These guidelines have a clear impact on the profitability of a bank. For instance, if a bank's balance sheet were used to acquire only 100% risk weighted assets then it would be greatly limited in its asset growth. At a 50% risk weighting, a bank could manage to hold twice the amount of assets. It follows then that the higher the risk weighting the more a prospective asset will need to return to justify the amount of capital being allocated. The calculations of precise risk weighting sometimes are complex to make (and understand). Distinctions are, for instance, sometimes made on the basis of the maturity and the fixed or floating rate nature of the asset being acquired. Holding structures are also looked at. Different rules apply for those assets which are booked (ie held as loans) and for those which form part of a trading portfolio. Risk weighting is essentially a feature of risk control and certain institutions have been able to gain a degree of flexibility (say, in netting off opposing derivative exposures) from their central bank regulators after proving the efficacy of their internal control procedures.

The importance of banks to the international markets and their increasing degree of regulation make considerations such as risk weighting of fundamental importance. The day has arrived when the question is being raised not whether a deal is right on its own merits, but whether it can obtain a low risk weighting. Sometimes, too, it is difficult to know at the outset what the eventual risk weighting will be. In such circumstances, one needs to assemble as much information as possible in the beginning and then advocate a certain approach with the relevant central bank regulators at the appropriate time.

Back office

The notion of the back office as rather dull and uneventful is rapidly changing. The independence of the back office (where settlements and accounting goes on) from the more front-line traders, is essential if proper controls are to be maintained. If the two departments are merged or under the control of a single individual then disaster can strike. One need only look at what happened at Barings in Singapore and Daiwa Bank in New York. Increased emphasis has rightly been placed on the administrative side of the securities business. Additionally, a host of new regulations have recently been introduced which standardise trading practices and settlement procedures.

The lead regulator of the secondary market (where trading goes on) is the International Securities Market Association (ISMA). There is a separate appendix to this chapter dealing with ISMA. It is sufficient now, however, to point out that in February 1988 ISMA was made a Designated Investment Exchange (DIE) for the purposes of the Financial Services Act 1986 and in April of that same year, the UK Secretary of State for Trade and Industry approved ISMA as an International Securities Self-Regulating Organisation (ISSRO) for the purposes of the Act. Virtually all international bond houses are members of ISMA. Consequently, the settlement procedures for secondary market trades are all done to ISMA standards. As may be seen in Chapter Five, ISMA has even standardised the definitions and formulae for yield to maturity and other calculations for a variety of Euro-securities. While ISMA endeavours where possible to resolve problems between market participants using mediation, it also reserves a variety of other sanctions such as the imposition of fines or the suspension of members, to assure compliance. The rules of ISMA apply to Eurobonds denominated in all the major currencies of the world; to bond, equity, currency and other international warrants; and to FRNs, MTNs and dual and multiple currency bonds. All transactions involving these securities must follow ISMA rules unless agreed in writing to the contrary.

One of the most valuable contributions of ISMA has been the determination of normal bond settlement procedures.

Bond settlement – accrued interest

Bonds are bought and sold on a with or 'cum' coupon basis. However, during the six- or 12-month interval before another coupon comes due, a particular security may have changed hands on several occasions. Past holders of the bond must be paid their share of the interest coupon by the person who acquires the security from them. Interest amounts, or accrued interest, are calculated not on the basis of the trade day but on the value day. According to ISMA rules the value date for a new issue is the closing date for the transaction or three business days following the trade date, whichever is the later. Normally the value date for a transaction effected on or after closing will be the third business day following the trade date. Business day is defined as a day when Euroclear, Cedel and the cash market for the currency of settlement are open for business.

The calculation of accrued interest for fixed rate and convertible Eurobonds assumes a year of 360 days comprised of 12 months of 30 days each. This calculation starts from and includes the day on which the last interest coupon was paid (or the day from which interest is to accrue for a new issue) and extends up to but excludes the value date of the transaction. The calculation may be illustrated as follows: 25 bonds ($25,000) of a Eurobond issue are sold on November 15 (value day November 18) at a price of 97½%. The issue carries a coupon of 9% payable annually on October 15.

		$
Principal ($25,000) x price (97½ %)	=	24,375.00
Accrued interest for 33 days $25,000 x $\dfrac{9.00}{100}$ x $\dfrac{33}{360}$	=	+ 206.25
Amount paid to seller		24,581.25

If the value date falls on the 31st day of a month, it is counted as though it were the 30th day of the same month. Thus, if the value date is moved from July 30 to July 31 (in a transaction involving a bond which paid interest on June 15), the accrued interest would still be calculated over 45 days. July 31 in this example would be treated as though it were July 30. In the case where value date corresponds to a coupon payment date, the vendor retains the coupon and no accrued interest calculation is made. Interest is also not accrued when the value date coincides with the day of issue or where bonds are in default, in which case the bonds are traded 'flat'. The market or quoted price for securities are referred to as the clean or flat price. Once accrued interest is added on, this makes it the 'gross price' or 'dirty price'.

Floating rate notes are an outstanding exception to the above-noted accrued interest rules. Under ISMA regulations accrued interest on FRNs is calculated on the actual numbers of days elapsed divided by 360 (or by 365 in a Euro-sterling issue, including leap years) beginning on the date of the last coupon payment up to but excluding the value date of the transaction. If the value date falls on the 31st of a month, that date is counted as the 31st (and not brought back to the 30th as with other Eurobonds).

The table below illustrates different calculations of accrued interest. In this example, the FRNs shown are assumed to be US dollar denominated:-

Figure 7.1
Accrued interest calculation

	Interest accrues from coupon date	Value date	Straight and convertible bonds	Floating rate notes Normal year	Leap year
1.	30.10	28.2*	118	121	121
2.	30.10	29.2*	119	–	122
3.	30.12	28.2*	58	60	60
4.	30.12	3.3*	63	63	64
5.	31.12	28.2*	58	59	59
6.	31.12	29.2*	59	–	60
7.	20.1	31.3	70	70	71
8.	31.1	31.3	60	59	60
9.	1.2	6.3	35	33	34
10.	15.2	6.3	21	19	20

Numbers of days of accrued interest for

* Following year calculations made in cases 1 through 6.

From the above table it is evident that the day count for accrued interest is not always higher for FRNs than for straight (or convertible) Eurobonds, even though straights (and convertibles) assume 30-day months. The major anomaly occurs with the month of February where this latter calculation still assumes a 30-day month, while FRNs count the actual days elapsed: either 28 or 29 in a leap year. As a final word on accrued interest calculations, fractions of cents are always rounded up if the third decimal point is five or more. Thus $24,581.245 becomes $24,581.25 and $24,581.244 stays as $24,581.24.

Settlement Procedures
Except for certain limited exceptions, ISMA members are obliged to report transactions through ISMA's Trade Confirmation and Risk Management System (TRAX). TRAX is a real time trade confirmation system which provides swift and accurate trade reporting for internal, interbank and regulatory reporting purposes. TRAX operates globally, 24 hours a day. According to TRAX it has over 290 subscribers

and processes on average over 30,000 transactions a day valued in excess of $200 billion. Launched in 1989 by ISMA, TRAX will at no additional cost provide trading reports as required by specific regulators such as the SFA, the Bank of England, Deutsche Börse, LIFFE and the Amsterdam Stock Exchange. TRAX also interfaces with both major bond clearing houses: Euroclear and Cedel Bank. The transaction-matching function performed by TRAX fulfils much of what is needed to prepare settlement instructions.

As a practical matter, the TRAX system can take the form of a stand-alone PC or be networked into a central system. Within 30 minutes of a transaction being agreed between counterparties each is obliged to enter the details of the trade conforming to a set format into the TRAX system. There is no convention as to which of the counterparties enters information first. The TRAX system itself searches through its own files until it locates the complementary halves of the trade. Once the matching has been accomplished both parties receive confirmation reports that the transaction has been concluded properly.

On receipt of a confirmation report from TRAX, ISMA recommends that its contents are checked by both counterparties to the trade and any error or omissions reported immediately. The party at fault should then amend its settlement instructions. As an extra procedural step, at least one of the trade counterparties can request an additional confirmation from one of the clearing houses (Euroclear or Cedel Bank) to augment the TRAX confirmation. In the case of confirmations generated in the distribution of a new bond issue, these are conditional on the closing of the bond issue.

Bond transactions are normally settled in accordance with the operating procedures of the relevant clearing house, usually on a delivery-versus-payment basis. This means that securities are exchanged only when the purchase amount is made available in cash, credit or collateral. ISMA rules state that the consideration amount may differ by up to $25 (or the equivalent in another currency) and the settlement will still be deemed effective. Such instruction should be given to the relevant clearing house.

Clearing – general

In the secondary market, settlement is almost always made inside the clearing systems. Settlement inside is simply a matter of book entries, whereas settlement outside typically requires a telegraphic transfer of funds and physical delivery of bonds in a particular financial centre. Securities can be delivered in either definitive form (the printed bonds themselves) or in global form (a temporary certificate representing the whole of an issue). Global bonds typically exist only in the first few months of certain new issues. They are subsequently replaced by definitive bonds. When securities are in definitive form they may be transferred physically, for example, in and out of clearing systems. A global bond, however, must be retained within the systems and transfers can only be effected on a book entry basis between accounts within the systems and between the systems themselves. Temporary accounts are arranged for those investors or underwriters which are not normally participants in one of the two systems.

The clearing systems have a right to refuse receipt of securities for a variety of reasons. These include damaged bonds, missing coupons or warrants, insufficient funds for payment, lack of proper instructions, registered bonds not properly authenticated and so on. In the event of a refusal, all parties have to contact each other to resolve the matter expeditiously. Additional penalty interest may be payable to the seller if the refusal is judged to be the responsibility of the buyer. The interest payable is calculated on the current market rates and not the coupon of the bond. If the seller is at fault, corrected delivery instructions must be issued.

Under ISMA rules, it is the responsibility of the seller (or its clearing house) to present the bonds to the buyer indicating (i) the identity of the seller, (ii) the identity of the buyer, (iii) the value date of the transaction; and (iv) the amount of funds required to be paid in exchange for the securities. It is the seller's job to collect the money it is owed. The seller also is obliged to make 'good delivery'. Mutilated bonds, temporary certificates (when definitives are already available), missing or incorrect coupons or warrants and called or drawn securities (say, by way of sinking fund operation); are all 'bad delivery'. The seller having caused the bad delivery is responsible for the cost of return and the related insurance cover.

Bad delivery frequently gives rise to a refusal of delivery procedure. This takes the form of a registered letter to the party making bad delivery citing the ISMA rules violated and stating the precise reason for the refusal. If the seller was responsible for bad delivery then it must issue corrected instructions to its clearing house or replace the impaired securities. In the event that a buyer is late in making his payment or pays too little, the seller has the right to claim interest on the net amount outstanding. This claim is usually equivalent to the funding costs (the overdraft rate) incurred due to the lack or partial payment of the settlement account. ISMA recommends that interest claims of less than $100 (or its equivalent) should not give rise to a claim.

If delivery is still not made after five business days from the value date, then the buyer has the right to issue the seller with a 'buy-in pre-advice notice' by telex. The definition of a business day is, as before, a day when Euroclear and Cedel Bank and the cash market of the currency of the securities are open for business. Situations can arise when the seller is late in delivering because it is in turn a buyer of the same securities and it has suffered a delay in their delivery. In such an event, the seller passes on the buy-in pre-advice notice to that delaying third party.

The buy-in pre-advice notice needs to be dispatched by 10:00 am London time and has to conform to the designated ISMA notice as set forth below:

"To the international securities settlements manager -

We hereby give pre-advice under the Association's rule 451 of our intention to issue a buy-in notice against your firm on (date – two business days after the date of the pre-advice notice) to close out the contract between us of which details are given below, by means of a buy-in application of the Association's buy-in rules, unless delivery is made on or before that date.

The details of the contract between us are as follows:

Trade date:

Settlement date:

Nominal amount:

Security description:

Price:

Net amount:

Delivery details:

Your attention is drawn to the fact that unless delivery is made as specified above we are obliged under the Association's rule 452.2 to issue a buy-in notice two business days after the date of this pre-advice. We intend to instruct (buy-in agent) to effect the buy-in.

Please inform us if you have any disagreement."

In the case of a 'pass-on' situation (ie in the event of a follow-on trade), reference to the pass-on should be made at the end of the buy-in pre-advice notice. If the situation is not resolved within the allotted time, a 'buy-in' notice is issued by 10:00 am London time. This notice sets forth the contract terms as listed in the earlier notice and states that it is intended to buy-in the securities by a designated agent on the fifth business day following the date of the notice. The defaulting seller still has up until the last day before the appointed buy-in to make good delivery. If the seller still fails to perform the buy-in agent (which should be a 'reporting dealer' in the issue in question and which can have no affiliation with the original buyer) then moves to acquire "in the best available market for guaranteed delivery on the normal value date all or any part of the securities". Partial buy-ins can be supplemented by future buy-ins. Once the buy-in is completed, the original buyer needs to notify the seller of the quantity purchased and the price paid. In the case of a 'pass-on' situation, this confirmation is passed along to the final defaulting member as evidence that the 'close-out' procedures have been successfully concluded. Any monetary difference between the originally contracted settlement amount and the buy-in amount needs to be settled between the original buyer and seller at the earliest opportunity.

The reverse situation involves a default by the purchaser to pay for his securities in full in a timely manner. The remedy for this is a procedure called a 'sell-out'. The sell-out procedure works like a buy-in. After five days following value date, the seller issues a 'sell-out pre-advice notice' prior to 10:00 am London time on the relevant date. ISMA recommends that the notice conforms to the following wording:

"To the international securities settlements manager –

We hereby give pre-advice under the Association's rule 481 of our intention to issue a sell-out notice against your firm on (date – two business days after the date of the pre-advice notice) to close out the contract between us of which details are given below, by means of a sell-out application of the Association's sell-out rules, unless delivery is accepted on or before that date.

The details of the contract between us are as follows:

Trade date:

Settlement date :

Nominal amount :

Security description :

Price :

Net amount :

Delivery details :

Your attention is drawn to the fact that unless payment is made as specified above or delivery is accepted we are obliged under the Association's rule 481.2 to issue a sell-out notice two business days after the date of this pre-advice. We intend to instruct (sell-out agent) to effect the sell-out.
Please inform us immediately if you have any disagreement.

If payment is not properly made after two business days by the purchaser, then a sell-out notice will be sent. This telex repeats the terms of the contract which the seller intends to close out by way of an appointed sell-out agent and informs the purchaser that the sell-out date will be the fifth business day following the date of the notice. As with the buy-in procedure, the purchaser still has four days in which to effect payment and accept delivery. If there is still no performance after this time, then the sell-out agent will "sell on the sell-out day in the best available market all or any part of the securities". The sell-out agent should be a 'reporting dealer' in the particular issue in question but it must not be affiliated with the original seller. Once the sell-out has been completed, the original seller needs to notify the purchaser of the quantity sold and the price received. Any monetary difference between the originally contacted purchase amount and the price obtained by selling out the securities, plus any interest adjustment to compensate for net funding costs over the sell-out period, needs to be settled between the trade counterparties as soon as possible.

Interaction with the primary market
The major self-regulatory body for the Eurobond primary market is the International Primary Market Association (IPMA) whose rules and standard form agreements are described in detail in Chapters Three and Four. There is naturally an overlap between the primary and secondary markets. At this juncture, ISMA has initiated certain significant rules. During the discussion of buy-in and sell-out procedures there was mention of institutions called 'reporting dealers'.

Reporting dealers are members of ISMA who apply for one or more market sectors in which they undertake to maintain a two-way market. Each reporting dealer is responsible for either a representative number or percentage of securities in the nominated sector in specified trading sizes. Reporting dealers also undertake to abide by the rules as may apply from time to time in the respective market sectors relating to, amongst other things, the spreads (ie bid/offered margins) on which securities may be traded. Reporting dealers are called 'reporting' because at the end of each week they submit a list of the securities for which they make a two-way market, and at the end of each trading day, the dealers report the closing bid and offer quotes for each security on their list at the end of the preceding week.

Reporting dealers also play an important role in new issues. This is because maintenance of an effective two-way market is essential to proper securities distribution. Hence, IPMA builds into its own rules the provision that all its members who lead or co-manage international securities issues should register as reporting dealers under ISMA rules from the day following allotments. Lead managers are expected to remain registered for at least 12 months while co-managers should maintain their registration for at least six months.

ISMA also specifies that the shipment and related insurance costs for newly issued securities is properly for the account of the allottee (the manager or selling group member acquiring the bonds).

ISMA has also promulgated general rules and definitions which are helpful in the market. The term 'round lot' is defined as $100,000 (or the equivalent in other currencies). Typically, quoted prices on screens between reporting dealers will apply to these round lots. Pricing is more discretionary for small trade sizes, sometimes called odd lots. When making a market in multiple currency bonds, the reporting dealer must specify in which currency settlement for that bond will be made. When an investor makes a so-called 'time limit' order to buy or sell securities at a specific price or the best price achievable in the market, such order may be cancelled within the time limit. However, the client must accept the execution of any part of the order which was concluded before the cancellation notice was given. An exception to this rule is specific 'all or none' orders, which are self explanatory.

Members of ISMA are also obliged to report to the responsible trustee or fiscal agent any securities it believes to be lost, stolen or forged. The member also will be informed by ISMA as its board may recommend to cease trading in an issue of securities where forgeries are known to be in circulation. Naturally, national legal and regulatory authorities will also be notified.

Calculation of yields to maturity and other yields conform to an ISMA standard. Examples of such formulae may be found in Chapter Five of this book. Deviation from these standard definitions must be clearly disclosed as well as the precise alternative method chosen.

Euroclear, Cedel Bank and other clearing systems
For safety's sake and ease of transfer, Eurobonds are usually deposited in the Euroclear system or Cedel Bank (formerly known simply as Cedel), both of which cover the major sectors of the international securities market. Effective links exist between the German Effektengiro, Euroclear and Cedel Bank which permit the settlement of transactions between these systems.

Euroclear was founded in Brussels in December 1968 by the Morgan Guaranty Trust Company, which soon afterwards sold the system while still furnishing the day-to-day services under contract. At the end of 1996, there were approximately 2,600 participants in the Euroclear system, from throughout the international market. Euroclear is run as a utility for its members; it does not set out to make a profit from its services.

Cedel Bank was established in Luxembourg in September 1970 and commenced operations in 1971 as a multi-shareholder alternative to Euroclear, which was at the time wholly owned by Morgan Guaranty. Cedel Bank currently has 96 shareholders from 19 counties and about 2,000 participants from 84 countries.

The two systems present a simple solution to the problem of securities deliveries. The risks of destruction, loss, theft and delay are reduced by retaining the securities in depositary banks and by effecting transfers between members by simple book entry.

Risks are further reduced by the simultaneous transfers of cash and securities on the agreed settlement date. The two systems have been linked since 1980 by an 'electronic bridge' which enables members to make simultaneous book entry transfers against payment with members of the other system. The two systems also maintain co-operative links with other settlement systems in over 30 domestic markets. Euroclear and Cedel Bank make daily net cash settlements and from time to time make net securities realignments.

The physical security certificates deposited in either the Euroclear system or Cedel Bank are held in their respective network of depository banks which provide custody services and are located in major financial centres. Euroclear and Cedel Bank deposit all securities of a specific issue with a single depository, usually acting as a paying agent for the issue. Cedel Bank records the certificate numbers of all securities in its system and therefore can offer both fungible and non-fungible accounts to its participants. A non-fungible account is an account where certificate numbers are made available to the participants. It can be valuable for control purposes and can be a significant factor in detecting lost, stolen or fraudulent securities. This type of account currently represents about 3% of all securities deposits within Cedel Bank. The more popular, fungible account makes no attempt to identify the ownership and location of individual securities. Instead, the account holder is credited with a certain number of bonds which may be drawn out of a pool of securities. All that is known is the name of the issue and quantity of bonds which are owned of each. The attraction of this anonymous system which, for instance, permits underwriters to off load bonds from a new issue with impunity, is obvious. Euroclear has been very successful despite offering only fungible accounts.

Although the two systems have their differences, competitive pressures have forced them to become increasingly alike. First, Morgan Guaranty surrendered the major part of its shareholding in Euroclear to numerous other banks to counter the criticism of a potential conflict of interest, and to move in the direction of the multi-shareholder Cedel Bank. Within the past few years, Cedel Bank has arranged with a number of its shareholder banks to enable it to provide credit lines for financing the Eurobond and other securities positions of its participants. Alternatively, members may arrange financing from a bank of their choice, subject to approval by Cedel Bank's Credit Committee. In the past, one of the major attractions of Euroclear over Cedel Bank had been its relationship with Morgan Guaranty, which permitted it to finance bond positions (historically providing funding of up to 70%-90% of the market value of securities retained in the system; currently it is difficult to generalise, however, about the percentage funding due to the fact that Euroclear now handles a total of some 85,000 different types of securities). From time to time there are, in fact, differences in the rates of interest which are charged. But these differences have not been substantial. Cedel Bank does, however, pay interest on credit balances in all currencies irrespective of size or duration, whereas certain currencies do not attract credit interest in Euroclear. Both systems do provide comparable services which allow borrowing and lending of securities to other participants in the system.

Transactions between members of Euroclear and members of Cedel Bank are facilitated by the so-called electronic bridge allowing exchanges by means of simple book-keeping entries. The services provided by the two systems are further supported by communications which allow members to send authenticated instructions and to receive reports. In addition to the conventional mail, telex and SWIFT, Euroclear also provides Euclid, and Cedel Bank has its equivalent called Cedcon, which are both computer-based systems of programmes and files that allow users to communicate instructions quickly and efficiently to the clearing systems' own computers. This enables subscribers to transmit instructions to and receive transaction status reports from the clearing systems. One of the problems encountered in bond settlements has been the task of reconciling counterparty confirmations. In conjunction with ISMA, Euroclear and Cedel Bank have established a trade matching and confirmation system. This system, TRAX – described previously – is designed to reduce the clerical burdens of checking incoming confirmations and the exposure to possible failed settlements.

In addition to serving the secondary market, Euroclear and Cedel Bank are also used in new issue placements. Both systems are employed in closing operations. For legal and practical reasons, underwriters rarely take physical delivery of their securities and, instead, have them deposited in a common depository of the two systems. At the time of closing, the issues are physically delivered in global form and are then credited to the accounts of participants within Euroclear or Cedel Bank. The lead manager notifies the clearer in advance of these allocations. The information provided usually includes the date of closing, the procedure for making payment and recipient of payment, closing agent of the issue, paying agents and a final copy of the offering memorandum. Communications with Euroclear and Cedel Bank are handled by telex or data transmissions which are made through network information services using computer facilities of both the clearing systems and the participants.

In 1986 both systems expanded their services to handle the increasingly important clearing of international equity offerings and secondary market trading. Both systems have adopted an approach of expanding their services on a country-by-country basis. By the mid-1990s, each system covered most major, primarily European markets with plans to include all important international markets in the near future. The systems offer book entry against payment settlement services, and either free or against payment cross-border delivery services to the domestic markets. Equities are eligible for the electronic bridge. Equities are sub-deposited with local depository banks or clearing systems. The full range of custody, cash clearing and communication services are available for equity securities.

Finally, Cedel Bank is currently getting a 17A exemption under the US Securities Act 1934 which will enable it to clear and provide settlement services for US equity, debt and government securities. Under this exemption, Cedel Bank will also be able to offer credit facilities to fund holdings of such securities. These securities, together with those traditionally cleared via Cedel Bank, will form part of Cedel Bank's new Global Credit Support Service (GCSS) which provides risk management services to cross-border markets.

The secondary market: growth and importance

The secondary market in securities has grown enormously as shown in Exhibit 7.2 below. Trading volume rose particularly fast during the middle of the 1970s as a number of market-making firms were attracted to the business because of the decline in interest rates and the related profits to be made in trading activities.

Growth throughout the 1980s was substantial as well. Statistical data from Exhibit 7.2 shows moreover that from 1989 to 1996 there has been a marked change in the composition of the instruments being traded. The major trend has been the growth in domestic bonds traded internationally which have displaced the historically pre-eminent Eurobonds. For example, in 1989 Euroclear and Cedel Bank cleared just over

US$2 trillion of Eurobonds compared with US$1.3 trillion of domestic securities. By 1996, the annual Eurobond volume had risen to US$5.8 trillion, but the domestic securities turnover had mushroomed to US$31 trillion. The category 'Others' refers to money market and other floating rate instruments and warrants. If these are excluded from the analysis, straight Eurobonds accounted for only 12% of total secondary market trading in the international markets.

The above considerations provide the clearest evidence of the globalisation of the world's markets and the integration of various national markets into one global pool of capital. Much of this integration has been driven by arbitrage and derivative trading. The trends, though, are obvious. Cross-border investment is the dominant theme of the day.

Exhibit 7.2
Market turnover: trading volume, 1972–96* ($ billion equivalent)

	1972	1973	1974	1975	1976	1977	1978	1979	1980
Euroclear	11.0	11.1	8.2	14.3	37.0	65.2	77.1	102.8	167.0
Cedel Bank	6.0	10.2	8.1	14.2	29.7	38.6	39.7	54.7	80.3
Total	17.0	21.3	16.3	28.5	66.7	103.8	116.8	157.5	247.3

	1981	1982	1983	1984	1985	1986	1987**	1988**
Euroclear	258.4	519.5	613.3	1,029.5	1,457.1	1,978.3	3,000.0	3,000.0
Cedel Bank	155.1	332.0	392.3	519.5	762.2	1,207.4	1,080.0	1,080.0
Total	413.5	851.5	1,005.6	1,549.0	2,219.3	3,185.7	4,080.0	4,080.0

	1989	1990	1991	1992	1993	1994
Euroclear						
Eurobonds	1,306.2	1,333.7	2,035.2	2,802.2	3,483.0	3,486.1
International domestics	786.2	1,122.7	1,915.9	4,614.0	10,021.5	13,453.8
Others	1,265.1	1,417.4	1,608.6	2,210.1	3,570.2	4,654.8
Sub-total	3,357.5	3,873.8	5,559.7	9,626.3	17,074.7	21,594.7
Cedel Bank						
Eurobonds	700.3	836.7	1,221.1	1,377.6	1,173.7	1,134.7
International domestics	491.3	704.3	1,149.7	2,268.2	3,376.8	4,379.7
Others	543.6	889.1	965.6	1,086.5	1,203.1	1,515.7
Sub-total	1,735.2	2,430.1	3,336.4	4,732.3	5,753.6	7,030.1
Grand total	5,092.7	6,303.9	8,896.1	14,358.6	22,828.3	28,624.8

Exhibit 7.2 *continued*

	1995	1996*
Euroclear		
Eurobonds	3,472.3	4,277.2
International domestics	15,807.1	22,736.6
Others	5,476.1	6,823.7
Sub-total	24,755.5	33,837.5
Cedel Bank		
Eurobonds	1,323.7	1,567.0
International domestics	6,029.5	8,330.6
Others	2,088.5	2,499.2
Sub-total	9,441.7	12,396.8
Grand total	34,197.2	46,234.3

Sources: Euroclear and Cedel Bank.

NB: Data inconsistencies required re-calculations on the basis of porportionate composition of different types of instrument.

* Annualised results based on actual data for the first nine months of the year.

** Data available in rounded figures only.

Appendix A

International Securities Market Association

The Eurobond market has a self-regulatory body known as the International Securities Market Association or ISMA. ISMA was founded under the laws of Switzerland in February 1969 and, until January 1, 1992 was known by the name of the Association of International Bond Dealers or AIBD. ISMA is located in Zurich, Switzerland. By the mid-1990s, it had some 890 members including virtually all the major financial institutions active in both the primary and secondary sectors.

The basic purpose of ISMA is to encourage high standards of professionalism among its members and to resolve technical difficulties, particularly in the area of Eurobond settlements, ie payment and delivery. To this end, it makes and enforces rules governing the way business is conducted in the international market, and represents its members in their dealings with governmental bodies, multi-national institutions and other entities which have an interest in the orderly development of the international bond market.

The stated objectives of ISMA are :

1. To promote good relations amongst its members and to provide a basis for joint examination and discussion of questions relating to the international securities markets and to issue rules and to make recommendations governing their operations.

2. To provide services and assistance to participants in the international securities markets.

ISMA generally interprets the above provisions in terms of the following more specific objectives:

1. The implementation and enforcement of a regulatory framework governing the orderly functioning of the international securities market;

2. The encouragement of improvements in the international securities market and the provision of services and assistance to its participants;

3. The examination and resolution of technical problems affecting the international securities market; and

4. The enhancement of relations between its members and related national and international capital markets.

ISMA is governed by a 16 member board. Members of the board are typically elected at the annual general meeting, the exceptions to the rule being the Chief Executive and Secretary General, who is an ex officio member of the board.

ISMA's strategy is defined by the board which also determines matters of policy and approves amendments to ISMA's rules and recommendations. ISMA has been organised around a regional structure since 1974. This enables members to meet regularly in 13 regional groupings with a view to discussing matters particular to that area of the market.

ISMA has been at the forefront not only in setting professional standards for market participants but also in providing an arbitration and reconciliation service to settle disputes amicably amongst its members. ISMA also monitors pricing of international securities through its TRAX price reporting system. Trades are required to be reported into TRAX within 30 minutes.

In February 1988, ISMA was designated a DIE or Designated Investment Exchange by the UK Securities and Investments Board. In April of that same year, the UK Secretary of State for Trade and Industry approved ISMA as an International Securities Self-Regulating Organisation (ISSRO) for the purposes of the UK Financial Services Act 1986.

8

EUROBONDS AND THEIR CURRENCY SECTORS

As noted previously, Eurobonds are defined in the EU Prospectus Directive (89/298/EEC) as meaning transferable securities which:

- are to be underwritten and distributed by a syndicate at least two of the members of which have their registered offices in different states, and

- are offered on a significant scale in one or more states other than that of the issuer's registered office, and

- may be subscribed for or initially acquired only through a credit institution or other financial institution.

By comparison, foreign bonds are issues undertaken by non-domestic borrowers whose securities are underwritten and sold by a syndicate of institutions within a particular domestic jurisdiction. The distribution of such securities takes place almost entirely within that domestic jurisdiction.

The term 'international market' combines both Eurobonds and foreign bonds.

In earlier chapters of this book, there has been discussion of the various ways that different market sectors have been merged together to form a truly global capital market. Largely, this has been due to the liberalisation of old foreign bond markets (ie the removal of withholding taxes and other fiscal and regulatory obstacles). As a consequence, foreign bond markets have declined in importance. This may be noted in the table below which charts the percentage contribution of foreign bond issues to the entire volume of international bonds through the 1980s and mid-1990s.

Exhibit 8.1

Year	1980	1981	1982	1983	1984	1985	1986	1987	1988
Foreign bonds as a percentage of international bonds	40.5	49.3	38.2	36.7	25.1	19.8	19.4	17.7	14.8

Year	1989	1990	1991	1992	1993	1994	1995	1996
Foreign bonds as a percentage of international bonds	12.0	15.9	10.1	8.4	8.7	9.5	14.6	13.6

Irrespective of blips in certain years, the progressive shrinkage of the foreign bond market is a clear trend. So, what then are these newly pre-eminent Eurobonds? It has already been noted that they are obligations to repay money over a period of time at a determined rate of interest. It is also known that these securities are chiefly in bearer form which obfuscates beneficial ownership. Probably the best way to describe Eurobonds further is with reference to their key characteristics.

Maturity

The maturity of a Eurobond, like any bond, is the date at which its full principal amount is due for repayment. The subject of maturity is a complex one and is described in further detail in Chapter Five. The present discussion will focus rather on the evolution of the maturities of Eurobonds over past years. The tables below summarise the changes in both average maturities and specific maturity ranges from the early days of the market to the present time.

The average maturities of Eurobonds have varied significantly over the period 1963-96. Maturities tended to be quite long when the market was developing. During the first three years, maturities of 15 years and more were commonplace. Such long maturities reflected investors' relative confidence in the future. When this confidence diminished, as it did in the mid-1970s, average maturities began a steep decline. The 1980s brought with them a new sense of stability and occasionally 10 year issues became the norm. The rising level of inflation towards the end of the 1980s once again eroded investor confidence and caused average maturities to drop to the six to seven-year range. Such short maturity Eurobonds dominated the market during the recessionary years of the early 1990s, with a gradual improvement towards the middle of the decade.

Ironically, the integration of the Euromarket with the US market has made longer-term issues possible, but the Eurobond statistics do not reflect a major move in that direction. Part of the explanation for this discrepancy may be that the shorter and medium-term issues still remain a hot favourite of the Euromarkets. While there may have been a number of well-publicised long-term issues, these were more than outweighed by the shorter maturity financings. It is worth noting as well that the increasingly popular MTN programmes have been used as launch pads for short-term

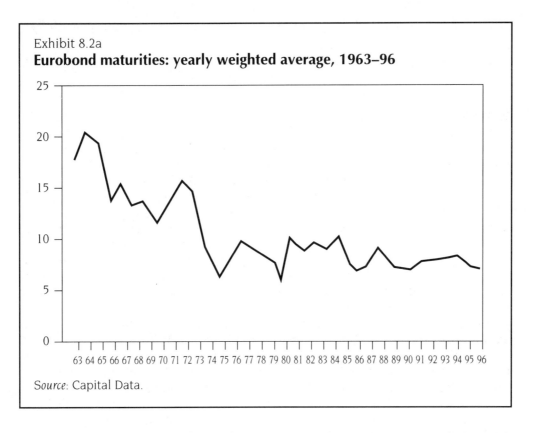

Exhibit 8.2a
Eurobond maturities: yearly weighted average, 1963–96

Source: Capital Data.

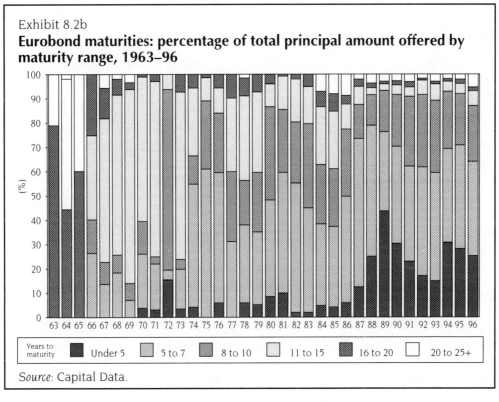

Exhibit 8.2b
Eurobond maturities: percentage of total principal amount offered by maturity range, 1963–96

Source: Capital Data.

241

(virtual commercial paper-type) financings, which have had the effect of bringing down the weighted average maturity.

A lesson to be learned from the above analyses is that the Eurobond market is still very much oriented towards short to medium-term financings.

Issue size

The liquidity of a Eurobond, or the ease with which it can be purchased or sold without materially affecting the market price, is a major priority for investors who may need immediate access to invested moneys, or to adjust their portfolios, prior to maturity. The liquidity of a Eurobond is related to several factors, including the age and amount outstanding in an issue as well as its currency of denomination. In general, the larger the issue the greater its liquidity. Institutional investors, who normally trade in large blocks of securities, often restrict their investments to those issues which will allow them to trade their holdings without affecting the price.

Liquidity is also related to the currency of an issue. The small number of participants in relatively minor currency sectors such as Swedish kronor or Austrian schillings may mean that transactions will tend to affect price. In general, the older a security, the less liquid it is likely to be.

The average size of Eurobond offerings has increased markedly since 1963, as is shown in Exhibit 8.3. Inflation was an important factor in this trend during the mid-1970s to the early 1980s. Historically, as the purchasing power of money fell through inflation, corporate profitability also was reduced forcing the funding of operations through debt rather than retained earnings. Thus, the average size of an issue has tended to grow. Another factor contributing to the trend more recently has been the increasing depth and maturity of the market, together with the growing volume of funds available to it, particularly from institutional investors.

During 1987 there was an uncharacteristic drop in average issue size. This may have been a reflection of the erosion of investor confidence following the October equity market crash. However, by 1988 the Eurobond market was again scoring record average issue volumes. There was a particularly large leap in 1992 which corresponded with declining interest rates and greater investor confidence in overall economic stability. The market experienced a shock, however, when rates began to edge up again in the first half of 1994 causing another drop in new issue size. This trend continued in 1995 with the near collapse of Barings Bank and lingering questions surrounding certain Third World borrowers. By 1996, the average size of Eurobonds exceeded $150 million. This may be seen as a particularly noteworthy achievement when compared to the average issue size at the market's beginning, which was just above $10 million per new issue.

The chart on the following page gives a graphic depiction of the changes in issue size from 1963 through 1996:

Global bonds

Another factor contributing to the growth in the average size of Eurobonds was the development of new offering techniques which produced in the vernacular – global bonds. Actually, global bonds are just like any other bonds except that they are offered in different key capital markets simultaneously. This invariably leads to multiple stock exchange listings, separate regulatory compliance by nation and individual selling groups tailored to penetrate separate geographic areas. Sometimes there is an overall global co-ordinator, but frequently, too, the real power will reside with the geographic representative responsible for their part of the world.

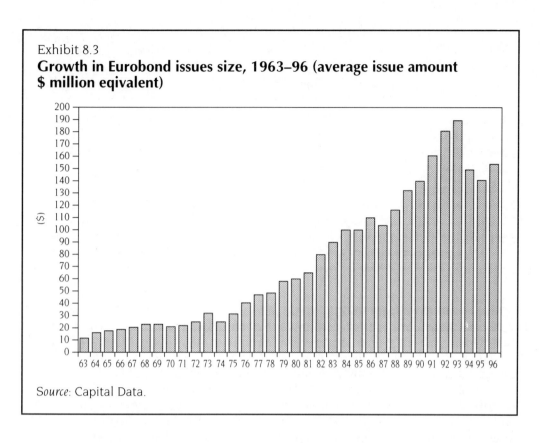

Exhibit 8.3
Growth in Eurobond issues size, 1963–96 (average issue amount $ million eqivalent)

Source: Capital Data.

Global offerings have become an important aspect of the equity markets. Large privatisation issues, such as those during the Thatcher years, did much to popularise this approach. In theory, a global issue should strengthen the market for securities by reaching out to a broad cross-section of the world's investors. Additionally, there is the advantage of diversifying an issuer's geographic investor base; thus minimising the impact of, say, recession in one country or one part of the world. The drive towards global issues also owes much to the sense of prestige conferred upon an issuer. In any event, this sub-sector, which opened only in 1989, has shown significant growth ever since. This is illustrated in the table below:

Exhibit 8.4
Growth in global bonds by currency 1989-96 ($ millions)

Year	1989	1990	1991	1992
US dollar	1,500	9,160	9,574	16,106
Deutschmark	–	–	–	–
Japanese yen	–	–	–	3,789
Canadian dollar	–	1,071	4,392	3,995
Others	–	148	475	1,211
Total	1,500	10,379	14,441	25,101

243

Exhibit 8.4 *continued*

Year	1993	1994	1995	1996
US dollar	28,947	42,975	61,089	105,961
Deutschmark	1,844	4,817	7,710	7,200
Japanese yen	3,833	6,503	–	1,040
Canadian dollar	6,891	3,563	–	921
Others	689	2,760	1,189	1,137
Total	42,204	60,618	69,988	116,259

Source: Capital Data. Other currencies include the New Zealand dollar, Australian dollar, Finish markka, Swedish krona, Danish krone, Ecu and French franc.

One of the surprising characteristics of global bonds is their mushroom-like growth over the past few years. First introduced in 1989, these offerings accounted for over 16% of the Eurobond market by 1995. Another interesting feature is the dominant role played by the US dollar. Perhaps this is to be expected given the near-universal acceptability of this currency. As the market has matured, dollar globals have accounted for between 70% and 90% of all such underwritings. In 1993 there was the greatest diversity of currencies. This may be attributed to the generally buoyant and optimistic tone of the markets which led to greater experimentation on the part of investors. By 1994 and 1995, however, the market's mood had changed appreciably and whole sub-sectors, like the important Japanese yen, dropped off the radar screen. It was in these times, especially in 1995, that the dollar again asserted its dominance. This is somewhat paradoxical, though, because it was the tightening of dollar interest rates which soured the Eurobond market so thoroughly during the first half of 1994.

The trend towards the reassertion of the US dollar sector persisted through 1996 with its percentage contribution to the market rising to 91.1%, up from 87.3% the year before. Volume was also up substantially, gaining by approximately two-thirds during the course of 1996. At that level, nearly 20% of all Eurobonds were structured as global offerings.

The Eurodollar bond sector

The origins of the Eurobond market were closely associated with the international role of the US dollar in the 1950s and 1960s. As the dollar grew in popularity and increased rapidly as the primary international reserve asset, a continuing demand for it among borrowers outside the US prompted the establishment of an expatriate US dollar (Eurodollar) bond market. It was able to draw liquidity from the ready supply of offshore US dollar funds which already formed the basis of the Eurodollar deposit market that had been growing rapidly since the mid to late-1950s. Various US banking regulations unwittingly encouraged both developments, in particular the US Interest Equalization Tax, (IET), which was applied to certain foreign borrowings in the US, and had the effect of forcing European borrowers back to their domestic capital markets.

With increased maturity, the Eurobond market has broadened to incorporate other currencies, and although the US dollar has lost ground, it is still the single most important issuing currency. The removal of the IET in the first half of 1974 again gave non-US borrowers access to the domestic US market. A decline was experienced in Eurodollar bond volume during that year, but this was part of a general market movement, and with the market's eventual recovery Eurodollar bonds reasserted themselves as the most active sector through the early to mid-1980s.

During the latter part of the 1980s, industrial expansion in countries like Japan led to a proliferation in bonds denominated in yen. Given its strength on foreign exchange markets, Japan could also afford to run a low interest rate regime which attracted borrowers, as did the substantial volume of capital available for investment. Other so-called hard currencies, primarily the Deutschmark, benefited from similar fundamentals and attracted issuers by the droves. None of the hard currency sectors has ever recorded a greater volume of financing than the US dollar. However, during certain periods, say of dollar weakness, other currency sectors have proved more than capable of taking up the slack. Indeed, it is an important strength of the Eurobond market that it has such an ample reservoir of different currencies to suit both investors and issuers at all points of the economic and interest rate cycles.

Investment regulations
There is no central authority ultimately responsible for regulating the flow of dollar denominated issues to the market. Most Eurodollar bonds, however, have been listed on either the London or Luxembourg stock exchanges. Both exchanges have broadly similar requirements regarding disclosure of information (discussed in detail in Chapter Four).

Dollar Eurobonds are not registered with the Securities and Exchange Commission

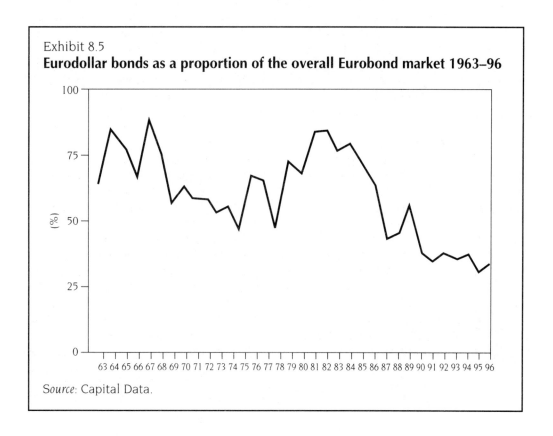

Exhibit 8.5
Eurodollar bonds as a proportion of the overall Eurobond market 1963–96

Source: Capital Data.

(SEC), and US citizens and residents are not offered the securities in the course of their initial distribution. In fact, since relatively few Eurobonds denominated in any currency are registered with the SEC, US citizens and residents are similarly restricted with regard to purchases of such securities in the course of their initial distribution (except as outlined in Chapter Three). Bonds also may not be offered or sold in the U.K., other than to persons whose ordinary business it is to buy or sell shares or debentures. Other nations have their individual restrictions.

Form of offering, listing and payment/delivery

The US dollar sector of the Eurobond market follows closely the standard offering procedures set out in Chapters Three and Four. Because of the size of the Eurodollar bond market as well as its highly competitive nature, issuing procedures are standardised and simplified to allow for accelerated time schedules.

Foreign dollar bond (Yankee bond) market

The foreign sector of the US domestic bond market, known as the Yankee market, has been a traditional source of funds for foreign borrowers seeking long-term debt denominated in dollars. During 1964-74, when the IET was in force, this sector was effectively closed to many potential non-US issuers although it remained open to Canadian borrowers, certain international institutions, such as the World Bank, as well as to developing country borrowers. When the IET was removed, several other foreign issuers again used this market.

The Yankee bond market declined in importance relative to the overall international bond market. However, the amount of Yankee bond underwritings for borrowers previously excluded by the IET increased substantially from 1974 through to the record year 1976. Issuing activity by these borrowers remained relatively high during 1977-79, but experienced a decline in 1980 in line with a reduction in total Yankee bond volume for that year. Yankee bonds registered a recovery during 1981 but resumed their downward trend through the mid-1980s. The magnitude of this decline is particularly striking when one compares the volume of Yankee offerings with that of the total international market. In 1980, Yankee bonds accounted for 9.3% of the total market and by mid-1987 this figure dipped to 2.2%. By the 1996, Yankee issues slipped further still to account for only 0.2% of the market overall.

Despite its diminished importance to foreign issuers, the US capital market offers the attractions of one of the largest and most developed capital markets in the world, providing a wide variety of financing alternatives. Because of the important role played by institutional investors, the market is both highly liquid and flexible, making it particularly attractive to issuers with diverse financial needs.

Interest rates in the US capital market are also quite competitive (although from time to time the cost of borrowing may be lower in the Eurodollar bond market). The US capital market has achieved an advanced state of development and benefits from a continuing structured reflow of investment moneys. Issuers may also be attracted to the US because of the prestige of borrowing in New York. Further, Yankee bonds can be offered in relatively large amounts. Longer maturities than in the other dollar markets of the world for straight issues are also frequently available here.

The alternative available to certain foreign issuers since 1990 is a type of private placement under Rule 144A. This has proven a fairly painless way to access the market. The importance of the US market is apparent in its influence over its trans-Atlantic counterpart. Spread pricing (frequently in relationship to similar maturity US Treasury yields) and American syndicate practices are now becoming the accepted norm. The first convert was, understandably, the US dollar sector of the Eurobond market. However, over time, other currency sectors have followed suit.

Strong currency sectors

A. *Deutschmark*

The Deutschmark sector is one of the most important in the international bond market after the US dollar. This is largely due to the strength and availability of its currency and relatively low interest rates (fostered by a low level of inflation), together with political stability.

In the 1950s and 1960s, Germany experienced a period of rapid economic growth. Germany's export industry regained its competitiveness and this, in turn, led to an increasing percentage of foreign trade denominated in DM. The availability of the currency and its strength on foreign exchange markets, due to consistent balance of payment surpluses, increased its attraction to both international investors and borrowers. A low level of domestic inflation kept interest rates down and contributed to the rate of economic expansion. During the late 1960s and 1970s, the domestic currency experienced rapid appreciation and became a desirable reserve asset for foreign central banks and other investors wishing to diversify their holdings in response to the then weakening US dollar. In the early 1980s, the DM depreciated against the dollar as economic growth slowed and a current account deficit appeared. Interest rates were raised to attract international capital, to suppress inflationary pressures and to support the DM on foreign exchange markets. In an effort to limit capital outflows and stabilise the international DM bond market, this sector was closed at the end of 1980 and the issuing moratorium continued until February 1981, when two supranational borrowers were permitted access to the market. From 1982, through the mid-1980s, the German economy and the DM reasserted themselves. This new-found confidence underpinned the capital markets and encouraged another burst of issuing activity.

A foreign bond market has existed in Germany since 1958. On March 23, 1964, however, the government announced its intention of imposing a 25% coupon tax (in effect a withholding tax) on domestic securities acquired by non-residents. DM bonds issued by non-German borrowers were exempt from the tax. This marked the beginning of the international DM bond market. The attractions to foreign investors were obvious, but domestic investors also became active participants during those rare times when the yields on international bonds exceeded those available in the domestic market. The international DM bond market was divided into two categories: DM Eurobonds and DM foreign bonds. To investors they were essentially identical but had somewhat different issuing procedures due to the fact that DM foreign bonds were designed for placement in Germany itself while DM Eurobonds were marketed on an international basis.

The above mentioned structure of the bond market changed radically, though, with liberalisation measures which were introduced in the mid-1980s. With effect from August 1984, the German government abolished its 25% coupon tax on interest payments made to foreign investors. As a result domestic DM securities, particularly government bonds caught the attention of the international investment community.

Total sales of DM government bonds jumped in 1984 (the year of the coupon tax repeal) from DM 36.7 billion to DM 57.8 billion in 1986. The great majority of this rise was accounted for by purchases made by non-residents, causing the market to rally and increasing its trading depth. By comparison, sales of DM Eurobonds rose from DM 6.1 billion in 1984 to DM 16.7 billion in 1986. The German authorities reversed their position again by announcing in October 1987 a 10% withholding tax on interest payments by German-domiciled borrowers. DM Eurobonds were specifically exempted from this tax and can be seen as beneficiaries of this fiscal measure at the expense of purely domestic securities.

Another trend in the German market has been the progressive merger of the Euro- and foreign bond sectors. Indeed, since 1984 the foreign bond market has been largely absorbed by DM Eurobonds. Some exceptions to this trend have been issues by the World Bank and European Investment Bank which relied on the old foreign bond structure so that they could target securities specifically to domestic German retail and institutional investors. As the 10% withholding tax was only applied to German domiciled borrowers, their foreign bonds remained tax-free like DM Eurobonds.

Further steps were taken to liberalise the German capital market with the effect that all international DM bonds could have both German and foreign banks in the management group. The lead managers still had to be of German nationality but these might include German subsidiaries of non-German banks. In 1985, the Central Capital Market Committee was abolished together with its Sub-committee for Foreign Issues. These organisations had been formed to regulate, among other aspects, the access of foreign borrowers to the DM market. With their dissolution also went the quota and queuing system which scheduled new issues for the forthcoming month. Thus the procedures for all international DM securities offerings were brought into line with those of traditional Eurobonds. During to early and mid-1990s German interest rates were kept high to attract financing for the costly re-unification with East Germany. Other currencies failed to keep pace within the ERM leading to so-called Black Wednesday in September 1992. Curiously, one main beneficiary of this market disruption was the DM itself. Investors looking for a safe haven (as well as attractive high interest rates) boosted new issue sales. As may be seen from the table below, DM bond volume picked up decisively from 1992 and continued to strengthen towards the middle of the decade, especially when Japanese investors increased their appetite for securities denominated in this hard currency. So great was the demand that DM foreign bonds also enjoyed a resurgence. 1996 represented only a modest setback for this sector, with growth in foreign bond issues helping to offset the decline in Eurobond issue volumes.

Since the first DM Eurobond was issued in 1964, the international DM sector, together with Eurodollar and Yankee bonds have accounted for the majority of all international bonds, with their combined volume rising in peak periods to 80%-90% of the overall market. The significance of the DM sector is further enhanced by its role as a substitute for dollar bonds when issuing in this latter currency proved difficult. This back-up role is now shared with the Japanese yen sector which has opened up due to deregulation and which shares common advantages with DM bonds, such as strong currency value and low absolute interest rate levels. Many investors have been attracted by the potential of short-term currency appreciation offered by DM securities (and yen bonds) against the US dollar. Borrowers tend to take the longer view. They accept the fact that appreciation may occur, but judge that this will be offset over time by the lower rate of interest payable on such securities.

Exhibit 8.6
International Deutschmark bonds 1964-1996

Year	1964	1965	1966	1967	1968	1969
Eurobonds	91.3	105.0	391.3	145.0	726.3	1133.3
Foreign bonds	58.0	123.0	0.0	10.0	674.0	531.0
Total	149.3	228.0	391.3	155.0	1400.3	1664.3
Percentage of total international bond market	7.1	9.1	12.7	4.0	22.8	29.8

Year	1970	1971	1972	1973	1974	1975
Eurobonds	569.2	827.2	1167.1	902.4	213.7	1723.1
Foreign bonds	89.0	308.0	500.0	362.0	253.0	1089.0
Total	658.2	1135.2	1667.1	1264.4	466.7	2812.1
Percentage of total international bond market	14.7	18.5	18.3	17.2	6.9	14.9

Year	1976	1977	1978	1979	1980	1981
Eurobonds	2018.7	3833.4	4922.1	2597.7	3069.5	1227.4
Foreign bonds	1288.0	2181.0	3789.0	5379.0	4839.0	755.8
Total	3306.7	6014.4	8711.1	7976.7	7908.5	1983.2
Percentage of total international bond market	10.6	18.8	25.6	20.8	21.6	3.9

Year	1982	1983	1984	1985	1986	1987
Eurobonds	4498.0	5625.4	6060.4	11195.0	16686.9	15988.2
Foreign bonds	824.5	998.9	1052.6	1942.6	1958.0	58.3
Total	5322.5	6624.3	7113.0	13137.6	18644.9	16046.5
Percentage of total international bond market	6.8	8.8	6.7	7.8	8.2	8.0

Exhibit 8.6 *continued*

Year	1988	1989	1990	1991	1992	1993
Eurobonds	24270.6	17416.4	19648.6	27374.7	45927.9	75363.6
Foreign bonds	96.8	425.6	1254.8	58.8	0	0
Total	24367.4	17832.0	20903.4	27433.5	45927.9	75363.6
Percentage of total international bond market	10.7	6.7	9.2	8.9	13.8	15.4

Year	1994	1995	1996
Eurobonds	60377.2	98982.9	77301.7
Foreign bonds	8266.7	18458.8	33522.8
Total	68643.9	117441.7	110824.5
Percentage of total international bond market	13.9	23.1	16.4

Sources: Morgan Guaranty Trust Company, Datastream, Deutsche Bank, Euromoney and Capital Data.

B. *Swiss franc*

The Swiss franc is one of the four key sectors of the international bond market, together with the Eurodollar, Deutschmark and Euro-yen sectors. The Sfr sector consists exclusively of foreign bonds. However, it accommodates a very wide range of financings. Switzerland's importance as an international financial centre is further enhanced by the fact that a major portion of all Eurobonds eventually find their way into investment portfolios managed by Swiss banks. It was estimated that Switzerland accounted for 40% to 60% of the Eurobond market during its early years. More recently institutional investors have tended to dominate the market but Swiss managed funds are still significant.

Notwithstanding the important role played by Switzerland in the international capital markets, the authorities have traditionally tried to shield the country's domestic economy and capital markets from destructive external influences. Historically, a key policy objective has been a stable and low interest rate structure, particularly for the important mortgage loan rate. The authorities have also tried to limit the balance of payments surpluses of the country while minimising the role of the Sfr as an international reserve asset. These policies encouraged close control of the capital market by the Swiss National Bank (SNB, the Swiss central bank). In October 1963, the first (and only) Sfr Eurobond was brought to market in form of a Sfr 60 million 5% offering of 15 year bonds for the City of Copenhagen. This issue was organised in London and listed both there and in Luxembourg. However, the SNB was not informed, nor had any other formal permission been obtained. A protest was consequently lodged by the SNB which feared that similar financings would expose the Sfr to speculative pressures. This in turn would jeopardise the SNB's control over interest rates and the currency value of the Swiss franc. Subsequently, the SNB encouraged the development of a foreign bond market which existed entirely within Switzerland and which could be more closely monitored and regulated. Historically, the two most important forms of foreign bond issues were public bonds and private placements or notes. As a result of recent liberalisation measures nearly all of the differences between these two types of financing have disappeared.

The years 1963-67 were characterised by orderly growth, as the Sfr sector consistently maintained its position in the international bond market. Steady expansion continued through 1968-69, but these were exceptional times because of the growing popularity of the intermediate term notes or private placements. This development reflected the demand by corporate and public sector issuers for medium-term financing (in contrast to public bonds which then had maturities that extended as long as 15 years). The instrument was also intended to absorb the mounting inflow of foreign funds and to reduce domestic liquidity. Aggregate issuing volume of both forms of Sfr bonds dropped during 1980 as the US dollar appreciated against the Sfr, drawing funds out of this sector. Growth resumed again in 1981, but in that year Sfr offerings amounted to only 17.2% of the international market down from 24.7% in 1979. The growth of the overall Sfr sector during the mid-1980s reflected its low rates of interest and the strength and stability of its currency.

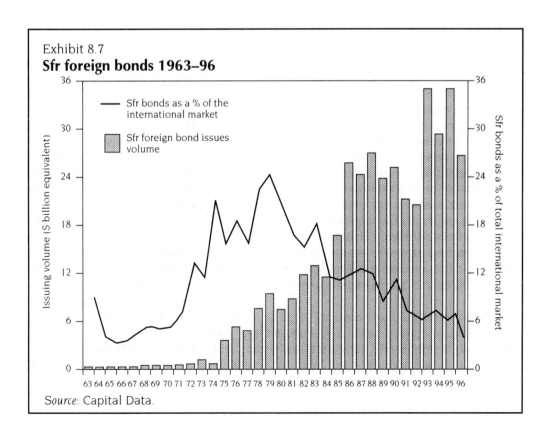

Exhibit 8.7
Sfr foreign bonds 1963–96

Source: Capital Data.

During the late 1980s the Sfr market distinguished itself with stability of issuing volumes. Activity was somewhat restrained during the recession of the early 1990s, but boomed again with the overall market expansion in the mid-1990s, slowing only somewhat during 1996. The graph below depicts the growth in issuing volume and the percentage of Sfr offerings in the total international market during the years 1963-96.

One of the interesting characteristics of the above graph is the nearly inverse relationship between Sfr issuing volume and its proportionate contribution to the international bond market overall. The real lesson here, however, is the explosive growth in international bonds which were other than Sfr-denominated securities. Sfr bonds simply have had a difficult time keeping pace. Indeed, by 1996 Sfr bonds accounted for only 3.9% of the total international market.

Sfr bonds have, though, shown an increasing trend in sophistication. During the course of market liberalisation, the Sfr sector has become increasingly open to different forms of financing. 1977 witnessed the introduction of the Sfr floating rate note, a Sfr 50 million three-year placement for AGIP (the Italian oil company). In more recent years other FRNs have been issued which have been innovative in their interest fixing formulas. Together with these FRNs, which have only been issued in modest numbers, there were also convertible notes and bonds and a growing number of warrant issues. Zero coupon bonds have likewise been brought to market. The Swiss capital market has even offered a sizeable selection of dual currency bonds which typically featured a Sfr coupon and redemption in some other currency. The reverse of this structure (coupon in foreign currency and repayment in Sfr) has also been attempted. Highly sophisticated bond swaps and option-linked bond issues are now common in this sector of the market.

C. Japanese yen

During the mid-1980s Japan's balance of trade and current account surpluses reached record levels. One consequence of this was that Japan became the world's largest exporter of capital, a role it took over from the Middle East petroleum exporting countries. It has been estimated that during 1986, Japan's net investments in foreign financings aggregated some $95 billion ($9 billion more than the current account surplus for that same year). The scale of such investments has naturally shifted the focus of world financing towards the Asia. Moves have also been made to internationalise the Tokyo market so that it might become more competitive with such other major centres as London and New York. These moves were viewed as a natural outgrowth of the country's strong domestic economy and a means of ensuring the continued prosperity of that economy. In the early 1990s the distinctions between Samurai bonds (foreign bonds denominated in yen) and Euro-yen bonds began to erode and the two instruments merged, with the Euro-yen security becoming the dominant form. This merging took place as a consequence of a decisive policy shift by the Japanese finance ministry, which wanted to encourage greater foreign access to the domestic market.

The table below charts the progress of both Euro-yen and Samurai issues. It is important to note that the first yen-denominated bond issue was actually a Samurai offering for the prestigious borrower, the Asian Development Bank, in 1970. It took another seven years before the first Euro-yen bond was launched. By the late 1980s, however, the Samurai market was all but absorbed by the Euro-yen sector.

Exhibit 8.8
Samurai and Euro-yen issues 1970-96 (US$ million equivalent)

Year	1970	1971	1972	1973	1974	1975
Samurais	15.0	92.0	311.0	271.0	0	67.0
Euro-yen	0	0	0	0	0	0
Total	15.0	92.0	311.0	271.0	0	67.0
Percentage of total international bond market	0.3	1.5	3.4	3.7	0	0.4

Year	1976	1977	1978	1979	1980	1981
Samurais	226.0	1271.0	3826.0	1833.0	1088.0	2457.0
Euro-yen	0	91.2	79.4	115.9	256.3	299.0
Total	226.0	1362.2	3905.4	1948.9	1344.3	2756.0
Percentage of total international bond market	0.7	4.3	11.5	5.1	3.7	5.4

Year	1982	1983	1984	1985	1986	1987
Samurais	3418.0	3624.0	3710.0	5791.0	4158.8	0.1
Euro-yen	420.7	298.3	1129.6	6890.6	17947.1	22345.0
Total	3838.7	3922.3	4839.6	12681.6	22105.9	22345.1
Percentage of total international bond market	4.9	5.2	4.6	7.6	9.8	11.2

Year	1988	1989	1990	1991	1992	1993
Samurais	0	0	27.9	0	0	0
Euro-yen	16826.3	18340.0	24284.5	36072.6	31218.3	41398.1
Total	16826.3	18340.0	24312.4	36072.6	31218.3	41398.1
Percentage of total international bond market	7.4	6.9	10.6	11.7	9.4	8.5

Year	1994	1995	1996
Samurais	0	95.7	228.4
Euro-yen	64492.8	73147.5	55436.7
Total	64492.8	73243.2	55665.1
Percentage of total international bond market	13.0	14.4	8.2

Source: Capital Data.

Euro-yen market
Following its policy of gradual internationalisation of the Japanese yen, the Japanese finance ministry has amended existing regulations to permit foreign borrowers to issue yen-denominated bonds in the international markets. This new currency sector, referred to as Euro-yen bonds, was formally opened with the ¥10 billion issue of 7¼% seven-year bonds offered in April 1977 by the European Investment Bank. The issue was one of the most popular in the history of the Euro-markets.

Issuance activity was restrained following the opening of this new sector, partly as a result of limitations imposed by the finance ministry on the number of borrowers allowed to issue Euro-yen securities. During the 1980s, the restrictions governing market access were relaxed. In 1980, four new issues were launched – twice the issuing activity of the preceding year – and for the next three years the volume of new offerings remained fairly constant. In December 1984, however, there were further easings of restrictions which allowed access to international borrowers rated single-A or better (the old triple-A requirements being replaced with certain net worth and ratio measures), permitted access to Japanese corporate issuers, eliminated the restriction on issue size and allowed any maturity of issue longer than five years. Issuing activity leapt during 1985 (when there were still more liberalisation moves) by over six times. From June 1985, new instruments were added to the Euro-yen bond sector. FRNs, zero coupon, deep discount, currency conversion and dual currency bonds could all be floated. Subsequently, new issues more than doubled from 1985 to 1986, rising together with Samurais to nearly 10% of the total international bond market. Still further deregulatory steps were taken in 1986 which relaxed the remaining restrictions on Japanese borrowers in the market and which dropped the earlier ratio and other eligibility standards in favour of greater reliance on the credit assessment of the established rating organisations.

During 1987, despite the global stock exchange crash, Euro-yen bonds enjoyed their best year ever. Growth has continued through the 1990s, assisted in part by the absorption of the old Samurai market. By 1995, new yen denominated issues totalled over 14% of the entire international market. In 1996, the attractiveness of the US dollar, however, diverted attention from this currency sector eroding its position to somewhat over 8% of the international market.

The Euro-yen bond market has been one of the success stories of the 1980s and mid-1990s. As mentioned, its strength derives in part from the economic power of Japan. Related factors such as an appreciating currency and stable and low interest rates, have also served to attract investors and borrowers alike.

Before finishing the discussion of yen-denominated securities, it is important to identify a type of offering which was specially structured and targeted to Japanese investors. These are nicknamed Sushi bonds. The popularity of Sushi bonds owes much to the surplus investment capital which has accumulated in Japan as a natural consequence of the country's large balance of payments surpluses. These issues further underscore the pivotal importance of Japan in world capital flows.

Other currency sectors
Over the course of the past few decades there have been bond issues in a number of other currency sectors. Some of these have opened for brief periods, only to close again in short order. Other sectors have demonstrated greater longevity and developed the institutional infra-structure to provide them with reasonable staying power.

One well-established sector is that for Euro-guilder bonds (sometimes called notes). This sector opened in 1969. It has benefited from its close currency linkage with the Deutschmark and has therefore demonstrated many of the advantages of a strong currency bond sector. Previously closely regulated by the Nederlandsche Bank, the forces of liberalisation have eased market access by simplifying procedures and reducing red tape.

Another reasonably robust sector is that for Canadian dollars. The sector has traditionally been the domain of Canadian borrowers searching for an alternative funding source other than the domestic markets. Other issuers, particularly supranational bodies like the World Bank and the European Investment Bank, have issued Canadian dollar bonds with a view to expanding their overall financing base. The dynamics of this sector are largely influenced by the absolute level of interest rates and the stability of the US$/C$ exchange rate.

The Euro-sterling sector opened in 1972 with a £10 million 8% 15 year issue for Amoco. This offering, however, did not prove to be an auspicious beginning for the new market and was, in fact, the only issue for the next five years. Since that time the sector has gone through boom/bust cycles which have gradually reduced their volatility as the market has matured. One rapid growth area is that for sterling-denominated FRN and equity-linked offerings. There is also an active bond swap market which has served to attract borrowers and broaden new issue possibilities. Foreign bond issues (called Bulldogs) have also attracted international borrowers.

To some extent the Euro-French franc sector has suffered from periods of political and economic uncertainty in common with sterling bonds. Historically, this has been a heavily regulated market. However, steps taken from the mid-1980s through the 1990s, have helped to relax controls. Nowadays, new issue procedure is very similar to that of Eurodollar bonds.

The Luxembourg franc has historically been a reasonably active sector. This reflects in part the strength of the financial community in that country. Australian and New Zealand dollar bonds have also demonstrated reasonable issuing frequency. Other Eurobonds have been brought out in Austrian shillings, Danish kroner, Norwegian kroner, Swedish kronor, Hong Kong dollars, Bahraini dinars, Kuwaiti dinars and UAE dirhams, to mention a few.

Composite currencies, especially the Ecu, have become favourite investment choices. The Ecu gained enormously in popularity after the wave of optimism about the prospect for a single European currency following the Maastricht Treaty. Later, troubles within the ERM produced a fall-out in this sector. Other one-time favourites have included the SDR, which was originally thought of as a potential international currency. One problem with such synthetic currencies is their inherent complexity and the possibility of change within the basket of currencies which comprise the individual unit. The other problem is that there already is an international currency – the US dollar.

9

EQUITY LINKED AND FRN ISSUES

Throughout the middle 1980s and early 1990s, equity-linked instruments have represented one of the most buoyant sectors of the Eurobond market. In part, this strong performance may be attributable to generally rising stock exchanges in recent years. A more permanent trend is in evidence, too. While the bond market has been operating on an international scale continuously for decades, it is only recently that common shares and equity-linked instruments have begun to be offered in great volumes as new issues on a worldwide basis. There have been waves of Euro-convertibles in the past but these have normally dried up when underlying equity prices have weakened. It has not been until fairly recently that a general acceptance of international equities has become evident. With this acceptance comes the possibility that convertibles and equity warrants will find a more permanent niche in the market.

Equity convertibles

The equity convertible has had a long history. Before its adoption by the Eurobond market, it was used primarily in the US domestic capital market. Prophetically perhaps, the first Euro-convertible issues were for Japanese borrowers who by 1985 represented the largest single category of borrower by an overwhelming margin. The performance of the Japanese Euro-convertibles owes much not only to the impressive strength of the Japanese domestic economy but also to the appreciation of the yen, in which all domestic common equity is naturally denominated. US corporations have also been major participants in the market and indeed dominated it from the mid-1960s until the early/mid-1970s. US corporate performance has been more intermittent than the Japanese but because of the importance of the US capital market, this role must still be considered an important one.

Euro-convertibles combine a debt instrument, similar to a bond, with the right of conversion into common stock, or equity, of the issuer (or owned by the issuer). In the US domestic market, it is accepted practice to set the coupon of convertible issues at a premium over the dividend yield, expressed as annual dividend paid divided by share price, of the common stock into which the bonds are convertible. This is done to induce investors to place their money in convertible bonds rather than the underlying common stock. Notwithstanding this consideration, coupons on convertibles are usually less than those on non-convertible or straight bonds, because of the additional value of the conversion feature.

Issuing activity in convertibles is traditionally at its highest when stock markets are bullish. As Exhibit 9.1 shows, a reasonable volume of new convertibles was offered in the mid-1960s, when US stock exchanges were strong. During the period 1968-73, the market share of these instruments rose from 19% to 23%, reflecting the two banner years of 1969 and 1972.

After 1973, issuing activity of US corporations paused again which depressed the sector overall. There were, however, some gains: an increase in offerings for non-US corporations. Investors were attracted to non-US corporations for two reasons (i) rising stock markets in the countries where these issuers were domiciled, and (ii) the strength of their currencies against the US dollar. This choice of currencies helped to explain the preponderance of Japanese and Swiss convertibles. The years 1978-80 witnessed a recovery of activity of US borrowers in the Euro-convertible market. The strongest sector by far, however, was that for Japanese companies. Together, these two areas accounted for over 75% of the Euro-convertibles brought to market during this period.

1981 witnessed a bumper harvest of Japanese issues. The Tokyo Dow Jones had rallied strongly from 6,950 in mid-March of that year to 7,680 by the end of April. For borrowers, there were extra incentives as the standard 15-year maturity of the Euro-convertible could not be found in the domestic market. Japanese corporate issues were soon formed in a queue and then steadily brought to the international market. The weight of new offerings, however, soon formed a glut and investor interest evaporated. By the following year new issue volume in Japanese convertibles was down by nearly 50%. Although 1982 may have been depressing for convertibles, it masked the re-opening of the equity warrant sector. This area of the market had been in existence since the early days of the Euromarkets (note: the first issuers were two Italian companies – the steel making Finsider and the property owning SGI). Its contribution, however, was not a major factor in overall issuing volumes. By the advent of the mid-1980s, though, this was destined to change.

Briefly, an equity warrant bond is a security which carries with it detachable rights to acquire shares in the issuer's (or some other company's) equity. The dynamics of warrants will be explained in further detail in a later section of this chapter.

Recovery in the convertible market occurred in 1983 with a marvellous performance by the Tokyo Dow Jones, as each month (except November) showed a rise over the preceding one throughout the year. More significantly still, the warrant bond market actually exceeded the volume of convertibles completed.

Exhibit 9.1
Eurobond convertible and warrant issues 1963-96 ($ million equivalent)

Year	1963-67	1968-73	1974-77	1978-80	1981
Convertibles	823	4,246	2,235	4,835	2,435
Warrants	90	679	151	426	–
Total	913	4,925	2,386	5,261	2,435
Percentage of total Eurobond market	19.2	23.2	6.3	11.1	9.5

Year	1982	1983	1984	1985	1986
Convertibles	1,299	1,799	4,161	4,638	6,453
Warrants	604	2,974	2,658	2,751	15,410
Total	1,903	4,773	6,819	7,389	21,863
Percentage of total Eurobond market	4.0	10.3	8.6	5.5	12.0

Year	1987	1988	1989	1990	1991
Convertibles	14,185	5,824	5,249	4,421	7,459
Warrants	23,886	28,584	67,379	19,588	27,618
Total	38,071	34,408	72,628	24,009	35,077
Percentage of total Eurobond market	23.1	17.8	30.9	12.5	12.7

Year	1992	1993	1994	1995	1996
Convertibles	5,665	17,269	18,379	9,156	22,677
Warrants	12,551	13,333	6,748	3,630	5,555
Total	18,216	30,602	25,127	12,786	28,232
Percentage of total Eurobond market	6.0	6.9	5.6	2.9	4.8

Source: Capital Data.

The recovery in the convertible market continued in 1984. During this year, the Japanese convertible sector truly eclipsed that for US corporate convertibles. Despite the relatively high $1.5 billion of US corporate issuing volume it should be noted that this amount was comprised of only four new Euro-convertibles, one of which was the jumbo $1 billion global convertible for Texaco. Importantly, 1984 marked the repeal of the US withholding tax. Previously, Euro-convertibles had been one of the most efficient ways for foreign investors to buy American equities. Euro-convertibles were typically issued through a Netherlands Antilles finance subsidiary and thus were free and clear of this tax. The removal of the withholding tax meant that investors could acquire equities without penalty, and thus, a major incentive for acquiring US corporate Euro-convertibles had disappeared. There was also the risk that the US Euro-convertibles might be absorbed into the US domestic capital market. The fact that they did not suggests the strong appeal of bearer bonds in the international market which still differentiates Eurobonds from domestic registered bonds. Furthermore, from 1982, US corporations benefited from a robust domestic equity market which proved more than capable of meeting corporate issuing needs. Many companies did the reverse, lacking suitable investment opportunities for organic growth, they acquired other companies' equity or initiated share repurchase programmes. In 1986, US corporate borrowers returned to the Euro-convertible market in substantial numbers and this level of activity accelerated through the first half of 1987. Japanese financings were comparatively restrained during this period as greater priority was given to equity warrant issues.

The warrant market remained reasonably stable through 1983-85, ranging from a low of $2.7 billion to a high of nearly $3.0 billion. What happened in the following years can only be described as an explosion. In each successive year from 1986 to 1989, there was a new volume record set in equity warrant bonds. At the 1989 peak, there were actually almost 13 times the volume of warrant issues compared with convertible offerings. Such boom times corresponded to the meteoric rise in the Tokyo Stock Exchange and, as mentioned previously, it was chiefly Japanese borrowers which availed themselves of the equity warrant possibilities. So strong was the Japanese participation in this market sector that by the end of 1988 alone there was some $18 billion of their warrant bonds outstanding. The great attraction of these securities is that they pay a reasonable coupon (albeit below levels which would be offered by a straight Eurobond) that compares favourably with the historically low dividend rate of most Japanese equities. Thus an international investor was getting the best of both worlds: a reasonable income return and a call option (which is what a warrant is) on rapidly appreciating Japanese common stocks. So long as the stock market continued to rise, so too was there ample investor demand.

By 1990, however, stock exchanges around the world began to weaken as interest rates were raised in a coordinated fashion to damp down inflationary pressures. The warrant sector was down about 71% for the year as a whole. Convertibles were also off, but their decline was less steep as they had much less further to fall. There was a recovery in warrant bonds in 1991. But, this proved to be short-lived. A decline set in from 1992 onwards and continued through to the mid-1990s. Convertible bonds were, however, somewhat more resilient and enjoyed two record years in 1993 and 1994. Following a touch of nerves, which led to a halving of the market in 1995, record stock market performances during 1996 drove the equity-linked sector to 4.8% of all Eurobonds. The most active form of offering, convertible bonds, outnumbered warrant issues by a ratio of four to one.

Convertible structure: bond value and conversion value
Convertible bonds share characteristics of both bonds and common stock. They also have values (bond value and conversion value) deriving from these shared characteristics.

Let us assume a 15-year convertible offering by ABC Brands, Inc to illustrate the mechanics of a standard convertible Eurobond. Let us also assume the issue was brought to market in May 1997 and took the form of $400 million of 7¾% convertible debentures due 2012. The convertible debentures could be exchanged for common shares in ABC Brands at the ratio of 88.1834 for each $5,000 debenture. This was the conversion ratio. A conversion price might also be calculated at $56.70 which represented the price at which 88.1834 shares would have the equivalent value of the $5,000 debenture (ie $56.70 x 88.1834 = $5,000). As usual, the conversion price would be fixed as a premium over the then prevailing stockmarket price. In the case of ABC Brands, let us say, the relevant stock market price was $44.125. The premium (called the conversion premium) would then be determined as 28.5% (|$56.70 − $44.125| divided by $44.125). This would mean that the then current ABC Brands share price would have to rise on the stockmarket by over 28.5% before the right to convert into these shares had any value to the debenture holder.

Another way of analysing this same point would be to determine the conversion value of the debenture based on the stockmarket price then currently available. If the conversion ratio of 88.1834 were multiplied by the market price of $44.125 this would produce a conversion value of $3,891.09, or expressed as a percentage of the $5,000 debenture: 77.82%. If the share price in the stock market declined then conversion value would also reduce. Say, for example, that the share price fell to $40.00, then conversion value would be $3,527.34 or 70.55% of each $5,000 debenture.

There is a limit, however, on how far a convertible's price can fall, because of the support provided by its bond value. Assuming that general interest rate levels dictated a yield to maturity of 10% for a 15-year non-convertible or straight Eurobond, the bond value of the ABC Brands convertible (based on its 7¾% coupon) would indicate a price of 82.71%, and with a conversion value of 70.55%, the convertible bond might trade in the range of 90%-91%. Investors would still place a premium value on the bonds (ie in excess of both bond value and conversion value) because of the potential for capital appreciation resulting from future share price rises of the underlying equity. The fact that the bonds retained their convertibility for the next fifteen years would mean that this potential for appreciation had significant value indeed. Assuming, in another instance, that the share price increased to $60.00 (indicating a conversion value of $5,291.00 or 105.82%) while bond value remained the same, the convertible might then trade in the range of 108%-109%. This premium would occur because investors felt that the bond characteristics of the convertible still had value as a form of insurance against future share price declines.

The trading premium of a convertible is greatest when the two values, bond and conversion, are closest together. As they move apart, they are seen by investors as providing each other with less benefit. In the last example, if conversion value indicated a price of 105%-106%, but bond value dropped to 54%-55%, the insurance provided by the bond characteristics would be less and trading would be correspondingly reduced to a very small margin over conversion value.

The premium is cut back most dramatically when a convertible is trading at a steep premium above par where the issuer has the right to force conversion into its common stock. If, for example, the ABC Brands' shares rose to $70 each, the convertible bonds would trade at or just above 123.45%, based on conversion value. Assuming the company had the right to call these securities at 105%, and announced its intention to do so, holders of the bonds would naturally prefer to convert them into common shares rather than incur the 14.95% loss, ie (123.45%-105%) divided by 123.45%. Most issuers, in fact, have every intention of forcing conversion of their convertibles after they have reached an appropriate price. In this way, equity can be raised for their companies, and this is the primary motive for doing a convertible bond issue in the first place. Investors are also well aware of these intentions and, therefore, in advance of an expected call, convertibles trade at only a very modest premium, if any at all, over conversion value.

In certain instances convertibles may even trade at a slight discount from conversion value; this reflects the loss of accrued interest and the expected transaction expenses of conversion borne by investors. If the discount were to widen beyond a particular point, this would introduce swap possibilities. For instance, one could buy the convertible and convert immediately into common shares, buying them in effect at a discount, and simultaneously sell short the same number of shares at the then current market price. An investor would receive revenues from the sale of the shares at market value while making delivery on the short sale with shares purchased at a discount. The difference would be his profit. Market price fluctuations of the bonds or the common shares would be inconsequential, as the two parts of the transaction would be handled at the same time.

Trading performance

Convertible bonds have a unique and often misunderstood trading performance. They are frequently seen as bull market instruments, and it is indeed during rising stockmarkets that the greatest issuing volume of new convertibles occurs. Their characteristics, though, suggest a visible bias towards defensive investment strategies. This may be illustrated in a graph showing a standard convertible's trading performance.

As noted earlier with the ABC Brands convertible, these securities have both a bond value and a conversion value and typically trade above one or the other of these. When the price of the common equity increases, then a convertible will trade more and more like the shares themselves. The higher conversion value rises, the less relevant bond value appears. Although the investor would obviously be happy with this performance, the capital gain achieved by the convertible would be less in percentage terms than that recorded by the underlying shares themselves. This is because convertible bonds have a higher starting point (ie the bond value line) from which to begin their climb. The common shares (as represented by conversion value) can, by contrast, begin this ascent from a much lower level, giving a greater percentage increase.

If convertibles are somewhat slower on the way up, they do provide downward protection in the event that things do not work out as planned. Should the common shares slip in price then they can lose nearly all their value. The convertible will, however, sink only to the bond value line and then stop. There would, of course, be difficulties if the company were itself approaching bankruptcy. However, even in this event, the convertible investor can take heart from the fact that common dividends will be cut before interest payments are terminated; and if liquidation occurs, then the convertible holder ranks senior to the equity investor when it comes to repayment and division of residual assets.

Notwithstanding all the above theoretical observations, practical experience shows that convertibles rise by approximately two thirds the appreciation rate of the underlying common equity and they fall only half as fast when share price declines. This relative advantage is one of the key reasons why convertibles have been perennial favourites amongst investors.

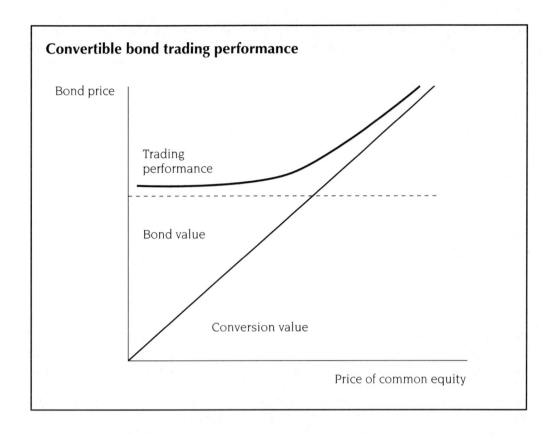

During periods when common shares are neither rising nor falling in price, then convertibles give superior returns due to their higher income. It is fair to say, though, that they do tend to underperform straight bonds during times of generally declining interest rates. This is largely because convertible securities are viewed and held chiefly because of their equity element. Consequently, they are less liable to react to interest rate movements.

Initial premium
New issues of convertible bonds typically feature a conversion premium which was noted before as 28.5% in the case of the ABC Brands issue. This would normally be considered on the high side as most conversion premia (on non-Japanese Euro-convertibles) fall into the range of 15%-20%. The amount of the initial premium is considered a vital ingredient in pricing any new issue. Justifying a high premium requires not only a healthy track record but also outstanding prospects for the future. Put another way, with a slow growth company only a low initial premium would be acceptable. This is so because investors expect that a borrower's share price should be able to reach the level where conversion can occur within a reasonable period of time.

Break-even
Another important measure in analysing a Euro-convertible is break-even. This is the number of years it takes for the higher coupon yield of the convertible bond (compared to the underlying common dividend) to recoup the conversion premium paid when acquiring the bond. There are no hard and fast rules to determine what is

acceptable but an investor would normally not wish to wait an inordinate amount of time before break-even was attained. The break-even calculation can be represented in simple form as follows:

$$\frac{CP}{BY - DY} = BE \text{ years}$$

where:

CP = Conversion premium

BY = Bond yield

DY = Dividend yield

BE = Break-even

In the case of ABC Brands, the bond yield was 7.75% (ie 7¾% coupon divided by 100% bond price) and dividend yield was approximately 4.71% ($2.08 indicated common dividend divided by $44.125 share price). As the conversion premium had already been determined as 28.5%, the break-even could be calculated as 28.5% divided by (7.75%-4.71%) or 9.37 years. Again, this would be considered at the high end of the acceptable range, and could only be justified by a convertible issuer with well above average prospects.

It is fair to say at this point that there are many measures and rules of thumb which are used in evaluating convertible bonds. Some of these include break-even analysis, conversion premium, secondary market price relationship to call price and time before first call, quality of issuer, prospects for future growth, ultimate liquidity of the securities themselves, and so forth. All of these measures, and others, have definite relevance but they are best used in combination with each other so that an analyst makes an overall assessment of a particular security. This is far more meaningful than taking one or two parameters and applying them to the exclusion of all others. Furthermore, an analyst must adapt the various measures to suit his own preferences. Convertible securities offer, for instance, an array of investment opportunities with vastly different risk/reward characteristics. It might be decided that lower risk (and lower potential return) was the preferred investment objective. If this were the case then the analytical parameters would have to be adjusted accordingly.

Features of a convertible bond may be objective as well as subjective. In the case of break-even analysis, if the dividend rate eventually exceeded the coupon on the bond then any investor would actively consider conversion, particularly if conversion value were at or above par.

Other standard convertible features

Issuers typically wish to limit their use of convertible securities, and the investor market is relatively specialised. Therefore, issue size is usually less than with straight Eurobonds. However, convertibles have been done in excess of $1 billion. With a few exceptions, US and UK/European convertibles bear annual coupons, whereas Japanese convertibles usually pay interest on a semi-annual basis.

Generally speaking, the longer the maturity of a convertible, the better, because the conversion privilege is worth more the longer it lasts. Thus, issuers can extend the maturities of their bonds out to 20 years or longer. Although some convertibles have sinking funds, mandatory amortisation is not a requirement even for 20-year maturities.

Call provisions are a sensitive subject for both investors and issuers. Usually, the call is split into two parts. The first period usually begins two or three years after the date of issue and often involves a penalty premium of 3% to 7%. The borrower is normally prohibited from making the call unless the securities have traded at prices well above par, eg at 130% to 150% for a set period of time prior to the call. The next call often begins two to three years after the first and extends in most cases through to maturity. This call usually includes penalty premia but not pre-conditions with regard to secondary market price.

During quiet periods, though, liquidity can dry up as it is often difficult to persuade professional market makers to actively trade quiescent issues, particularly when the cost of holding the necessary positions could not be fully compensated by the typically low coupon on the convertible itself.

Security provisions are similar to Eurobonds, with the exception that US convertibles are often subordinated to the other non-convertible debt of the issuer. Industry analysts tend to regard convertible debt as a type of equity capital if it is subordinated. This improves a company's debt/equity ratio and is an incentive to borrowers for giving convertibles such status.

The secondary market for convertible issues is reasonably active. This is particularly true in the first few trading days of a new offering, when the uncertainty of interest rates combined with the fluctuations of the underlying common shares produces high turnover. The trading pattern of a seasoned convertible reflects the interest of investors, which can be stimulated by, for example, rising stock prices. Investors in convertibles tend to be individuals or institutions managing discretionary accounts for individuals. A fair amount of sophistication is needed when dealing with these instruments as they are relatively volatile in the secondary market, and require an understanding of both the stock and bond markets.

For medium-size issues, the trading spread is normally 1%-2% between the bid and offered price. Clearing can be effected through either Euroclear or Cedel Bank. When making settlements, accrued interest is calculated on the basis of 12 30-day months and a 360-day year.

The initial conversion price and conversion ratio is usually adjusted to take account of stock dividends, or distribution of assets, which would reduce or dilute a shareholder's ownership in the net worth of a company. If a 5% stock dividend or scrip issues was paid, ie one extra share of common stock for every 20 shares owned, then the conversion price would be lowered by 5%.

A new offering of convertible bonds is quite similar to that of a straight Eurobond. The selling effort, however, is more intense because it is necessary to tell an issuer's story before investors become interested in the underlying common stock. It is quite common to mount a roadshow, or selling tour, through the major European financial centres. This can be costly, but publicity is essential. Additional costs include high underwriting commissions which historically have totalled up to 2½% for a standard 15-year issue and the more numerous press notices and announcements usually associated with a convertible.

For US companies issuing convertibles, the additional shares which would be created upon conversion of the bonds must be registered with the Securities and

Exchange Commission. The bonds themselves do not require registration. To avoid flowback into the United States, lock-up type procedures are followed. Legal costs, as a result of these additional procedures, are that much higher.

Japanese convertibles share many features with standard Euro-convertibles. Their unique characteristics are also important. One distinction is that the coupon levels of Japanese convertibles are typically lower than other convertible securities. This is because, as noted earlier, the dividend rate on the underlying Japanese equity is relatively low. Hence, investors require less incentive (in the form of the bond coupon) to encourage a convertible investment instead of a direct investment in the underlying equity itself. Japanese equities compensate for their low cash dividend yield by giving investors generous stock dividends or scrip issues. Adjustment is made in the conversion formula for Japanese securities to reflect such scrip issues and this ensures fair treatment for bondholders. Another curiosity with Japanese convertibles is their traditional low conversion premiums. This helps make up for the low bond coupon and also reflects the typical issuers real ambition: to raise equity.

A final attraction of Japanese convertibles is their typical fixed exchange rate. At the time of issuance, the rate of, say, US dollars to the Japanese yen is set in accordance with prevailing market levels. This does not have any influence on the bond value of the security, but the conversion value is dramatically impacted. For instance, if the underlying equity remained unchanged in price, but the yen appreciated by 10% in dollar terms, then the conversion value would also rise by 10%. This is because, of course, the underlying equity is itself denominated in yen. Hence, a Japanese convertible can be seen as having not only equity value, but currency value as well. Indeed, issuing volumes of Japanese convertibles evidence a marked pick-up when the yen is in an appreciating trend.

Although the two major types of convertibles (US corporate and Japanese) have been discussed in this chapter, there have been a host of other nationalities of issuers. To name but a few, UK borrowers have been active participants in this market, as have issuers from Australia, Canada, France and other European countries. Furthermore, there have been numerous variations on the standard Euro-convertible theme. For example, put options have been structured in convertibles to guarantee the investor a minimum level of appreciation, irrespective of the performance of the underlying equity. There have also been convertible securities which did not pay their coupon or principal in cash, but in shares of common equity instead. Such offerings were effectively equity placements and attracted investors because of the higher yield (as determined by the number of shares paid annually in lieu of interest). More recently, there has been significant innovation with convertible preference shares. These securities appeal to investors because of the high yield on the preference shares combined with the possibility of capital appreciation because of the linkage with the underlying equity. For issuers, these securities are classified as equity on their balance sheets and improve debt ratios accordingly.

Equity warrants

A warrant is nothing more than an option to purchase a fixed quantity of a certain commodity at a set price for some period of time out into the future. Warrants in the guise of options have been in active use in commerce down through the ages. Equity warrants themselves date back to the beginnings of the Eurobond market. Since these early beginnings, equity warrant issues have been done by issuers from most developed and many industrialising nations of the world.

The largest category of equity warrant issuers is formed by Japanese corporations. This is surprising in as much as the first such issue did not occur until January 1982. Subsequent offerings were programmed under a queuing arrangement which assured, among other things, a fair uniformity of terms. During the mid-1980s, for instance, most Japanese warrant issues were priced so that about 80% of their value was made up of the bond itself and the remaining 20% was the value of the warrants. The exercise price was most frequently in the range of 5%-10% above the share price at the time of issue. Nowadays, there has been greater liberalisation in the fixing of new issue terms. The next largest nationality of borrowers have been the Germans who have had a longer history of these financings but who have been less active than the Japanese in recent years. US borrowers, although visible in the market, have concentrated most of their warrant instruments on the domestic US market which is relatively sophisticated and receptive to these financings.

Structure
An equity warrant bond is similar to a convertible bond in that it combines elements of common stock with a bond investment. An offering of equity warrant bonds involves the issuance of a straight bond with warrants attached and usable typically to acquire shares in the issuer. Frequently, the warrants can be detached from the bond and sold separately. The bond in this case would then trade like a normal straight bond, although evidence suggests that they are not as liquid as standard straight bonds and suffer in the secondary market accordingly. To adjust for this, some offerings have been structured with 'usable' bonds, that is to say bonds whose principal amounts may be used to convert the warrants into equity.

What chiefly distinguishes a warrant bond from a convertible is that with a convertible the principal amount of the bond is used to acquire common shares while fresh cash (except in the case of usable bonds) must be employed to exercise equity warrants. One advantage of equity warrants for an issuer is that two financings take place essentially for the price of one. While the conversion of convertible securities necessitates the transfer of debt capital into an equal amount of equity capital, leaving the absolute amount of capital unchanged, the exercise of warrants can inject new equity capital into a corporation while allowing the bonds which once carried the warrants to remain outstanding.

The debt and equity characteristics of a warrant bond stand in particularly sharp contrast to one another. Hence, investors tend to evaluate warrant bonds somewhere in between a straight bond and a convertible. Consequently, the coupons on warrant bonds usually fall in the middle range of these two types of instruments.

Warrant bonds trading in the secondary market can be quoted on two different bases: cum-warrants, with warrants attached; and ex-warrants, without warrants. By virtue of historical precedent, the tenors of warrant issues are normally shorter than the conversion features on a convertible, lasting only about five years.

Valuation
The appreciation of Euro-warrant bonds has made significant progress. There are numerous theoretical models for assessing the value of warrants but these have limitations in everyday life as they are complex and based on assumptions which alter and are themselves based on guesswork. The valuation of warrants is mostly left up to the market to determine and this is typically done with reference to other comparable issues.

There are shorthand means of expressing warrant worth which concentrate on their intrinsic value. These will get one so far but the additional premium on top of intrinsic value is something which must be left to the market to estimate. Premium may be defined mathematically by the following formula:

$$\text{Premium} = \frac{WP - IV \times 100}{SP \times N}$$

Where:

    WP = Warrant price

    IV = Intrinsic value

    SP = Share price

    EP = Exercise price

    N = Number of shares per warrant

and where IV is determined according to the formula:

$$IV = (SP - EP) \times N$$

Assuming that N = 1, the share price is 45 while the warrant may be exercised at 40 and the warrant price is 18, then the premium on the warrant may be calculated as follows:

$$IV = (45 - 40) \times 1 = 5$$

$$\text{The premium} = \frac{18 - 5}{45 \times 1} \times 100 = \frac{13}{45} \times 100 = 28.9\%$$

The difficulty with this formula is that it assumes that the warrant price is known. Typically what an analyst wants to determine is what the right price should be. One rough rule of thumb to estimate this answer is that the price of the warrant should be approximately 40% of its exercise price. If the share price is greater than the exercise price, then the difference is halved and added to 40%. If the share price is less than the exercise price, then half this difference is deducted.

The typical trading behaviour of a warrant is portrayed graphically overleaf.

In normal market conditions, the warrant gains greater value (ie has its sharpest ascent) as it rises to its exercise price of $100. After that point, the intrinsic value of the instrument asserts itself and the premium value declines in importance. Correspondingly, the graph of ascent starts to slow above the exercise price and moves more in tandem with the rise in share price. With the loss of premium value the warrant also gives up a certain amount of its gearing or leverage characteristics as well.

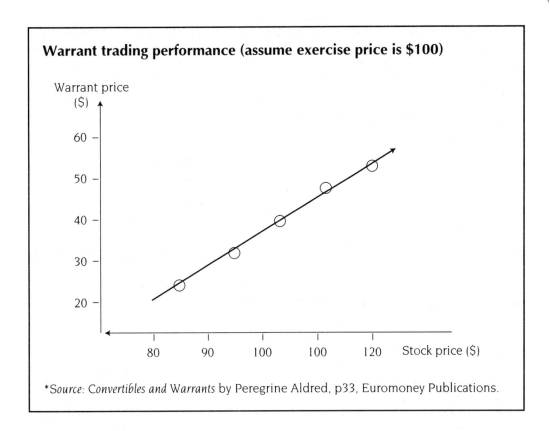

*Source: Convertibles and Warrants by Peregrine Aldred, p33, Euromoney Publications.

Floating rate notes

A major strength of the international bond market has been its ability to create new types of securities to meet the special needs of investors and borrowers. This flexibility has become a hallmark of the market and a key to its continued growth in the face of highly volatile interest rates and foreign exchange values. The market's innovative qualities can best be observed in the floating rate note and its numerous variations. Such hybrid securities show how new ideas can answer the requirements of a changing investment environment. They also illustrate certain limitations of these new instruments, chiefly their dependence on the market forces which prompted their creation in the first instance.

History

The first publicly offered floating rate note (FRN) was an issue in 1970 for the Italian electric power utility, ENEL, guaranteed by the Republic of Italy. During its first few years, this type of instrument was used chiefly by industrial borrowers. The security combined characteristics of a long-term international bond with a medium-term syndicated bank loan. At the time of the ENEL issue, there was a significant difference between the maturities available in bank loans and those in bond issues. ENEL and other industrial issuers were attracted to the FRN because it offered a longer maturity than syndicated loans, while preserving the floating interest rate feature to which they had grown accustomed through past banking relationships. Investors welcomed the new instrument, as it gave them an interest payment formula tied to short-term interest rates, thus affording protection from rapid increases in these rates.

In 1974 and 1975, there was a marked shortening of maturities on straight Eurodollar bonds. FRN issues during this period, however, particularly those for industrial borrowers, preserved many of their earlier attractions and maturities of up to 10 years were still available. The period 1976-79 represented years of major growth for this sector, with the volume of new issues increasing five times from 1975-76, over 40% in each of the years 1977 and 1978, and by over 75% in 1979.

Growth in the FRN sector continued through the early 1980s. During each of the years 1981-83 there was a gain in the volume of new issues. In 1983 the popularity of so-called jumbo FRNs contributed to a 27.3% increase in aggregate principal amount, while the number of individual issues declined. During this year the volume of new FRNs was so great as to nearly 20% of all new international bonds.

With new issue volume increasing by 2.1 times, 29.9% of all new international offerings, 1984 proved to be a banner year for FRNs. 1985 also recorded a volume increase of 74.2% and the FRN's share of the market also jumped to 32.9%. The years 1984-85 were a high watermark of the FRN sector. By 1986 a variety of factors including low short-term interest rates (to which FRN interest payments are linked) and tight offering terms, discouraged active investment. During the year, FRN new issue volume declined by 12.8% and market share slipped to 21.3%. By the first half of 1987, the crisis in the perpetual sector and the shadow it cast over ordinary FRNs, proved devastating to the sector which for the year as a whole shrank to a mere 5.7% of the total international market.

1988 witnessed a recovery in the FRN sector with issuing volume and market share both doubling from the disastrous year 1987. Over the period 1989-1990 FRNs evidenced healthy progress. Rises in short-term interest rates (intended to cool an overheated world economy) encouraged investors to seek capital preservation and high coupon rates featured by these instruments. High interest rates began to abate from 1991 and encouraged a rally amongst fixed income bonds. Attention, thus, shifted away from the FRN sector which fell to a low point of only 5.7% of the total international market. A recovery occurred in 1992 and the boom year 1993, with FRNs then accounting for some 14.8% of the market. 1994 was a disastrous year for fixed rate bonds due to the first quarter rise in dollar interest rates. Investors again sought refuge in FRNs and issuing activity jumped 41.4%. At this point the advantage of FRNs was not only their floating rate structure, but also the traditional, safety first image of this security. During 1994, there was a flight to quality and plain vanilla instruments. 1995 witnessed a continuation of this trend, although both issuing volume and market share were somewhat down. A recovery occurred in 1996, as new issue activity leapt ahead by 67.5% . During the year, FRNs' share of the market rose to 23.7%.

Issuers

With the exception of two issues, all the FRNs offered from 1970 to August 1975, were for industrial borrowers. From August 1975 onwards, the market changed radically as banking institutions active in the Eurodollar syndicated loan market became increasingly concerned about their access to the US dollar funds needed to back these loans.

The traditional source of such funds was the London interbank market for Eurodollar deposits. But in times of crisis. there was felt to be a possibility that this market could dry up. Banks without a natural source of US dollars (non-US banks) were attracted by FRNs as an alternative source of Eurodollars – as a form of dollar capital base. This provided important stability in funding as well as assistance with respect to certain capital adequacy and liquidity ratios (ie matching the maturities of liabilities and assets) applied, or in the course of being applied, by various central banks. FRNs also paid interest in much the same way as a syndicated loan. Banks were able, therefore, to match the income from their loans with the interest expense of the FRNs used to provide dollar funds. This feature gave FRNs additional popularity. Even US financial institutions such as Citicorp, Chase Manhattan and American Express with a natural source of dollars, issued FRNs.

Exhibit 9.2
FRN issues, 1981-96 ($ million equivalent)

Year	1981	1982	1983	1984
Straight FRNs	5,690	10,545	13,703	31,021
FRNs + equity warrants	–	–	400	250
FRNs + debt warrants	250	550	750	129
FRNs extendible	531	210	60	50
FRNs convertible to fixed rate	440	447	48	236
Total FRNs	6,911	11,752	14,961	31,686
Of which:				
Percentage financial issuers	68.2	62.5	44.6	61.2
Percentage other issuers	31.8	37.5	55.4	38.8
FRNs as a percentage of total international bonds	13.6	15.1	19.9	29.9

Year	1985	1986	1987	1988
Straight FRNs	54,911	47,199	11,077	22,926
FRNs + equity warrants	–	280	–	–
FRNs + debt warrants	300	477	–	–
FRNs extendible	–	–	–	–
FRNs convertible to fixed rate	–	215	230	421
Total FRNs	55,211	48,171	11,307	23,347
Of which:				
Percentage financial issuers	63.9	65.5	66.6	75.5
Percentage other issuers	36.1	34.5	33.4	24.5
FRNs as a percentage of total international bonds	32.9	21.3	5.7	10.3

Exhibit 9.2 *continued*

Year	1989	1990	1991	1992
Straight FRNs	22,476	40,143	17,416	47,863
FRNs + equity warrants	–	–	131	–
FRNs + debt warrants	337	–	–	–
FRNs extendible	–	–	–	–
FRNs convertible to fixed rate	278	106	–	179
Total FRNs	23,091	40,249	17,547	48,042
Of which:				
Percentage financial issuers	80.1	74.9	68.8	68.2
Percentage other issuers	19.9	25.1	31.2	31.8
FRNs as a percentage of total international bonds	8.7	17.6	5.7	14.5

Year	1993	1994	1995	1996
Straight FRNs	71,769	102,195	94,751	160,560
FRNs + equity warrants	–	45	50	–
FRNs + debt warrants	–	–	–	–
FRNs extendible	575	–	1,084	–
FRNs convertible to fixed rate	–	19	–	–
Total FRNs	72,344	102,259	95,885	160,560
Of which:				
Percentage financial issuers	70.0	65.1	76.6	79.9
Percentage other issuers	30.0	34.9	23.4	20.1
FRNs as a percentage of total international bonds	14.8	20.6	18.8	23.7

Note: Financial issuers include commercial banks and other financial institutions. Other issuers include governments and entities guaranteed by governments, corporations and corporations guaranteed by banks.

Source: Capital Data.

As the FRN grew in popularity, so many non-bank borrowers were attracted back into this sector. This resurgence in the non-bank sector corresponded with a general trend by borrowers to raise funds through FRNs as an alternative to syndicated loans. Such FRNs offered a yield (taking into account the high front-end commissions as well as the traditional ¼% or ⅛% spread) comparable to that of a syndicated credit, and were usually acquired by banks which could fund them in the interbank deposit market. Historically, the most active bank investors were those which did not wish to join in large syndicated loans where a minimum participation would be in the region of $5-

$10 million. Their preference was for smaller investments in a negotiable form, where a comparable yield return might be obtained. The presence of banks as investors in these instruments gave the market greater depth.

Over time this category of investor was joined by non-bank institutions, such as insurance companies and pension funds. These institutions appreciated the liquidity and high quality of the majority of these securities offerings. They were also able to participate in the market despite the persistent lowering of interest margins as a result of competitive pressures amongst bond houses. By the late 1980s and early 1990s it was common for high quality issuers to make new offerings with no interest margin or even a negative (below Libor) interest margin. Such aggressive pricing discouraged bank investors (which had their own funds costs to cover) and therefore left the institutional investors with a correspondingly greater role to play in the market.

FRNs are not unique to the Eurobond market. In July 1974, there was a 15-year FRN issue for Citicorp in the domestic US market. The offering was so successful that its principal amount was raised from $350 million to $650 million. Subsequently there were a number of floating rate issues (often with their interest return linked to the yield levels of three or six-month Treasury bills). A major portion of these also included the option to convert into fixed rate bonds, a feature which will be discussed later. The year 1977 saw the introduction of FRNs in Swiss francs with their return linked to Sfr Libor (although other formulas have been attempted). In May 1980 sterling FRNs were issued for the first time and subsequently FRNs have been permitted in the Deutschmarks, Ecu (European Currency Unit) and Japanese yen sectors as the result of the general trend towards capital market liberalisation.

Structure and interest payment mechanism

Interest on FRNs is usually payable semi-annually, as compared with the annual coupon on almost all Eurobonds. It is traditionally set as a fixed margin over the six-month London Inter-bank Offered Rate (Libor) for Eurodollar deposits. Settings over three-month or one-month Libor with quarterly (or monthly) interest payments have also been successfully attempted. The offered rate is the higher of the two quotes (bid and offered) for this rate. Sometimes the middle rate (Libmr, the mean of the bid and offered rates) or the bid rate (Libid) is used. As is the practice in the syndicated loan market, the exact deposit rate is determined on the basis of quotations made to, or by, a number of reference banks, plus some margin. For most prime issuers this margin is negligible, and, as mentioned previously, might even be a discount (that is, a margin below the deposit rate), although some issuers, particularly industrial borrowers, have historically agreed to margins over 1%. There have also been cases of margins which changed in amount over time. Whatever the exact margin, an example of the basic interest fixing formula would be:

$$7\tfrac{1}{2}\% \text{ (Libor)} + \tfrac{1}{4}\% \text{ (margin)} = 7\tfrac{3}{4}\% \text{ (FRN interest rate)}$$

Once the FRN interest rate has been set, it applies for the next one, three or six months, after which the rate is fixed again on the basis of Libor at the time of refixing, plus the old margin.

The calculation of interest assumes a year of 360 days, and payment is made on the basis of total days elapsed. This compares with the standard Eurobond formula which assumes a 360-day year, but has payment based on 12 months of 30 days each. The Eurobond formula is internally consistent but the FRN approach leads to a discrepancy in the investor's favour. The actual number of days elapsed in a year is 365, which is five days (or six days in a leap year) more than its assumed length in the FRN calculation. Thus the FRN pays an additional five days of interest, or approximately 14 basis points more yield, assuming a 10% semi-annual coupon.

An investor in FRNs historically received a minimum rate, a floor below which the interest formula could not go. If, for example, an FRN's interest formula indicated that a coupon of 6½% should be paid, but the security also had a minimum of 7%, the minimum rate would apply. The minimum protected investors against a steep decline in short-term interest rates. Some borrowers refused to have a minimum on their FRNs, or conceded only a very low one or one which lasted only for the first six months or one year.

Competitive pressures among bond houses have tended to de-emphasise minimum interest rates. Where minimums were built into interest rate setting formulae, these were often so low as to provide very little protection to investors. Instead, issuers have succeeded more recently in negotiating maximum interest rate levels beyond which the normal formula could not go. These maximums were termed 'caps'. Interest rates might rise to a level which dictated a 10½% return, but an FRN capped at 10% would only be required to pay the lower rate. This innovation had obvious benefits to issuers. They could retain the cap to insure against high interest rates or, more commonly, they could sell the cap as though it were an interest rate option and apply the proceeds against the normal interest rate, thus reducing total issue costs. A bank issuer might be prepared to sell its cap because the return generated by its loan portfolio (which adjusted automatically upwards with each increase in interest rates) would offer all the protection needed in a high interest rate environment. An industrial company, by contrast, would be less well protected and, therefore, prepared to pay a handsome price for this form of insurance. The invention of capped FRNs highlighted the flexibility of the basic floating rate note, particularly in combination with interest rate swaps. Another innovation has been the mini-maxi (or 'collared') FRN which featured both a minimum as well as a capped maximum interest rate. This innovation has grown in popularity to the extent that US agency borrowers like Fannie Mae and Freddie Mac have devised offerings of their own debt structured with both caps and floors. These in-built options (together with liberal call features) permit the agencies to offer a reasonably generous yield over Libor. Normally such agencies would fund themselves at a much lower absolute rate of interest, but the value of the in-built options is sufficiently great that they compensate for the level of Libor-based interest actually paid.

Form of offering

An FRN offering is very similar to a new Eurobond issue. The process of syndication, securities distribution and the commission structure are virtually identical. Documentation is also the same except that there is an additional agreement, the reference agency agreement, which appoints a bank to collect the Libor quotes from the reference banks and to calculate the interest coupon for each of the FRN's interest periods. The only change in time schedule is that the reference banks and a reference agent must be selected prior to the announcement of the new issue. The first interest coupon is usually determined by the reference agent two business days before closing. The issue should be scheduled so that these two days are not interrupted by a weekend or a holiday.

The costs of an FRN are somewhat higher than for a straight Eurobond. The reference agent is usually paid a fee and there are costs associated with advertising the coupon rate for each interest period, although such additional expenses may be justified as a means of disguised public relations. Fiscal agency and bond printing costs are also increased slightly because the use of semi-annual interest periods doubles the number of coupons.

Innovative FRNs

As may be seen in Exhibit 9.2, there have been a number of creative structures attempted with FRNs. Historically, FRNs have been one of the most flexible instruments in serving the needs of both issuers and investors alike.

A number of FRN issues have carried either warrants to acquire equity in the borrower or fixed rate debt instruments of the borrower. Equity warrants have been described already in this chapter. The use of debt warrants requires highly sophisticated investment strategies. Simply put, the debt warrants have value if long-term interest rates trend downwards. Should this happen, the warrantholder can exercise his option and buy a new fixed rate obligation which should have appreciated due to the lowering of interest rates. Thus, the warrantholder would stand to make a capital gain. If, however, interest rates moved up, not down, then the debt warrant would not be exercised and the investor would retain the original FRN whose own interest return would rise together with other rates. Things become more complex if short-term interest rates do not move in absolute sympathy with long-term rates. This is frequently the case.

Another variation on the traditional floating rate note was an FRN convertible into a long-term fixed rate bond. The first such issue was for Continental Illinois Bank in the US domestic bond market in April 1979. These securities had an initial maturity of eight years and paid interest on a floating rate basis during that time. The bondholders, however, had the option of converting their FRNs into fixed rate debentures any time during the first seven years. The debentures matured 25 years after issue date, irrespective of when conversion took place. If the bondholders decided not to convert, the securities remained FRNs through to their eight-year maturity.

This novel concept was so popular that the Continental Illinois issue was doubled in size. Imitators followed, although some introduced further variations to suit their specific objectives. Two weeks after the first US issue, Manufacturers Hanover introduced the first Euro-convertible FRN, which was timed to coincide with a similar offering in New York. In the Manufacturers Hanover Euro-issue, the floating rate notes were convertible into fixed rate bonds during their first seven years (like the Continental Illinois offering). However, if the bondholders decided not to convert, rather than maturing after seven years, the FRNs remained outstanding through to a 15-year maturity from issue date (the same maturity as the fixed rate bonds, if conversion was made). As can be noted in Exhibit 9.2, FRNs convertible to fixed rate bonds have been one of the more successful market innovations.

Further experimentation has been made with FRNs which allow for an extension of maturity. This allows investors to invest for an initial short or medium-term period, but then later elect to retain their FRNs for a further period if, say, interest rates appear to be on a rising trend.

One of the more sophisticated species of FRN was known as the serial FRN. This financing technique involved a mandatory amortisation of the FRN according to a fixed schedule. However, unlike a sinking fund where securities to be redeemed are normally drawn by lot or purchased randomly in the secondary market, each note was amortised individually, with principal repayment coupons clipped at the same time as the interest coupons. In the case of one of the earliest serial FRNs, the $50 million five-year offering for Gabinete da Area de Sines (the Portuguese port authority), a principal repayment of $500 was made together with accrued interest at each six-monthly interest date. The key advantage of this type of FRN is that it augmented or strengthened secondary market trading by virtue of its scheduled amortisation. Additionally, the timely re-flows of capital also created an investment pool available to be tapped by similar issuers.

10

EURO-MTNs AND EURO-CP & CDs

Euro-Medium Term Notes: Background

Perhaps one of the most dramatic changes to impact the Eurobond market was the advent of the Euro-Medium Term Note or Euro-MTN (sometimes also EMTN). Ironically, the importance of this change was lost on many market participants. This was probably because it was evolutionary at first and because nowadays the instrument (the Euro-MTN) frequently looks very much like a traditional Eurobond. In reality, the significance of the Euro-MTN is hard to over emphasise. It has greatly altered the way new issues are documented and brought to market and it has even constituted a new market sector itself.

Before examining the massive changes introduced by Euro-MTNs, it may be helpful to understand their origins and how they rose to such an important position in the markets. True MTNs began in the US capital markets in the early 1970s and were initiated by automobile finance companies which were looking for a better way of matching their assets and liabilities. This innovation was given a boost by changes in the regulations of the Securities and Exchange Commission (SEC) which allowed for the registration of multiple issues of a single borrower. These new regulations were contained in Rule 415. Prior to this change in regulations, new bonds had to be registered individually. The revised regulations permitted issuers to register a programme (or a large principal amount of securities) which could subsequently be offered in the form of different bonds. In the vernacular, the programme was kept on the 'shelf' (and indeed these securities were sometimes referred to as 'shelf issues' or 'shelf registrations') and then taken down in response to issuing opportunities in the market. American MTNs are forms of 'continuous offerings'. They have evolved in a manner similar to the US commercial paper market where the securities' prices are quoted on dealers' screens and new notes are tapped directly into the market in response to an issuer's requirements (for instance, to re-fund or 'roll over' maturing MTNs).

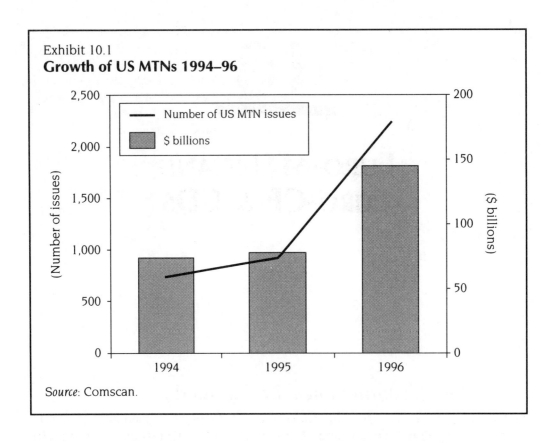

Exhibit 10.1
Growth of US MTNs 1994–96

Source: Comscan.

The MTN market transferred to the Euromarkets in 1986 in an issue for First Interstate (although there is some debate as to the identity of the initial issuer). The real popularity of the market only became evident, however, by the end of the 1980s when issuing opportunities expanded with the addition of offerings in different Eurocurrencies. There were natural impediments to Euro-MTNs. These included the varied legal and regulatory regimes which characterise the international markets. The Euromarkets are still quite fragmented when compared to the massive single capital market in the United States. Euro-MTNs, however, have either overcome obstacles or have made the necessary adjustments needed to gain greater acceptability in this market. They have consequently acquired characteristics which differentiate them from their counterparts across the Atlantic. For example, in the early years Euro-MTNs were used as a streamlined way of documenting private placements of debt. By contrast, the US market has been more homogenous and therefore public issues have long been the norm. Only in the 1990s did Euro-MTNs develop into a major sector with syndicated issues and an actively traded market. This chapter will highlight certain other differentiating characteristics and will also analyse the forces of convergence which work to unify the US with the international markets.

First, a word about definitions. What is meant by the expression Euro-Medium Term Note? The expression suggests a financial instrument with a maturity of, say, one to five years. Indeed, this is how these securities began. Currently over 40% of all new issues fall into this medium-term framework. What took a number of people by surprise was the popularity of Euro-MTNs. By the early 1990s, for instance, Euro-MTNs were used as the launch pad not just for private placements of notes by a single dealer but for everything from full-blown bond issues (a type of 'Euro-Shelf') to debt which could be viewed as a substitute for short-term Euro-commercial paper. Today, some Euro-MTN programmes state their maturities as from one month to 30 years. Other programmes do not even bother to indicate a potential maturity range. Frankly, just about anything goes. Furthermore, Euro-MTNs can be issued using a variety of different procedures. Private placements, which were used in the early days of the market, have regained their popularity both in plain vanilla offerings and a surprisingly strong growth sector called 'structured' Euro-MTNs, about which more later. Euro-MTNs can also take the form of syndicated bond issues with listings and much the same fanfare normally associated with Eurobonds. Also, sizes vary from the smaller, especially 'targeted' issues to large 'global' offerings, which frequently incorporate special marketing features which comply with national regulatory requirements. Of these, the US 'safe harbour' regulations, such as Rule 144A, are the most important. Be aware that Euro-MTNs are called by different names as well:- for instance, 'programmes for issuance of debt instruments' and 'debt issuance programmes'.

Why are the Euro-MTNs so popular?

The Eurobond market has long been known as being highly price competitive. Many bond houses have dropped out of the business simply because they could not make any money doing it. Price competition in the markets have left those surviving bond houses looking for ways to cut costs. Although Euro-MTNs did not start initially as a cost savings product line, they did evolve in that direction with most of the benefits flowing to the issuers and not the bond houses themselves.

Cost savings are achieved in Euro-MTNs because nearly all of their documentation is put in place at the start of a programme and is reusable for one issue after another. Hence, there is a significant reduction in legal expense for frequent issuers. Furthermore, listing particulars are nearly all lodged with the appropriate exchanges from the beginning and there are other associated efficiencies such as the use of temporary global notes which are photocopied from the master contained in the programme documentation. This saves printing costs and facilitates new issue settlement procedures. Finally, Euro-MTNs are not obliged to be registered with the SEC, and therefore there is no penalty attached to having a large programme volume or size.

Not only is money saved but also time. With the documentation and listing all virtually in place, there is really very little left to do but to agree the terms of a new issue and float it in the market immediately. This quick response time is critical. Opportunities in the market appear day by day (and sometimes with greater frequency). Hence it is essential to move fast or risk missing the opportunity (sometimes called the 'window' in the market). Everything comes down to money and the attraction of market windows is that they provide issuers with the chance of raising finance at the cheapest rate possible. Nearly all Euro-MTNs are swapped in some way: either (i) to allow the issuer to achieve some objective, say, to change the currency of the liability, or (ii) to create for the investor a structured product with attractive cashflows or credit profile. In the latter case, the issuer is typically 'hedged out' of these so-called structured MTNs and therefore is not exposed to the peculiarities of the instrument. Here, timing is all important because the fixing of the swap/hedge out and the issuance of the Euro-MTN have to happen simultaneously.

Another time-sensitive aspect of Euro-MTNs is an issuing procedure known colloquially as a 'reverse enquiry' deal. The easiest way to understand this is by comparison with Eurobonds. The initiative for new Eurobonds nearly always comes from the issuers. Their investment bankers may have a good idea with respect to the choice of a particular currency or swap structure. But, the process is really driven by the issuer. In the case of reverse enquiry deals, the process is driven instead by the investors. This happens because sophisticated institutions have set portfolio objectives (such as duration, currency diversification and credit profile and so forth) which need to be fulfilled. Hence, they will approach issuers (typically through their investment bankers or the issuer's dealer) in order to create one or more debt obligations which match the portfolio requirements. Euro-MTNs are ideal for this type of deal. Their documentation allows for nearly any principal amount, currency or maturity. So, the investor can 'book' a Euro-MTN asset precisely tailored to its specifications. The flexibility and speed of execution of Euro-MTNs have greatly enhanced their popularity and promoted their growth.

The table below shows the volume of new Euro-MTN programmes, and the related amount of new securities actually offered under established programmes, for the years 1992–96.

It should be noted that the table above records the number of issues (and their collective principal amount) offered each year from established Euro-MTN programmes. The programmes themselves are not shown. An effort has been made to include privately placed Euro-MTNs together with public issues. However, by their very nature, it is not feasible to obtain records for all private placements. Much the same methodology was employed in gathering data for the earlier Exhibit 10.1 which showed the growth of the US domestic market for MTNs. It is also interesting to note

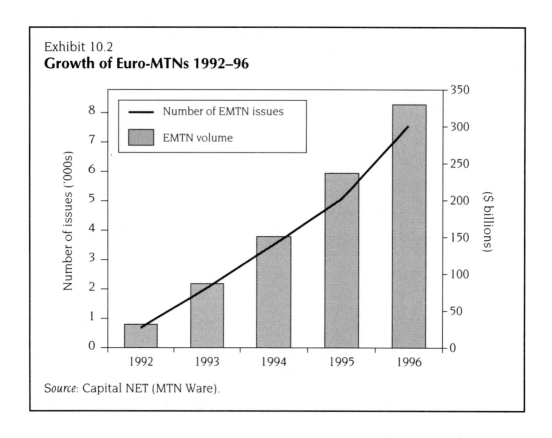

Exhibit 10.2
Growth of Euro-MTNs 1992–96

Source: Capital NET (MTN Ware).

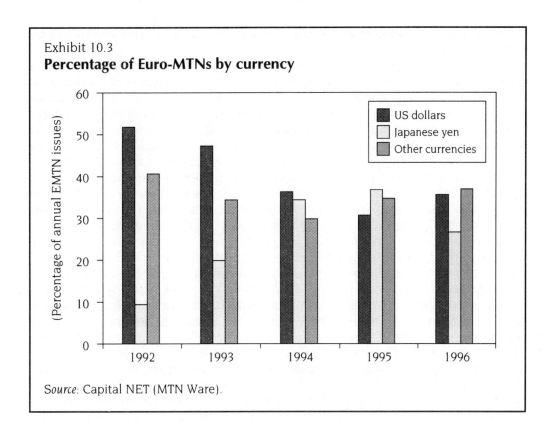

Exhibit 10.3
Percentage of Euro-MTNs by currency

Source: Capital NET (MTN Ware).

that whilst starting later than US MTNs, Euro-MTNs have now caught up and currently account for over twice the number of issues and offering volume.

Much of the growth in Euro-MTNs up to the mid-1990s was attributable to Japanese investment. Hence, yen-denominated securities are one of the two most popular currency sectors. The reason for this strong investment activity has been the high domestic savings rate in Japan relative to borrowing requirements. During periods of weakness on the Tokyo Stock Exchange, investors have turned increasingly towards debt instruments and have looked to foreign issuers particularly to achieve a pick-up in yield. As Euro-MTNs can easily be denominated in yen, Japanese investors are not exposed to foreign exchange risk.

Euro-MTNs have distinguished themselves by the number of currency sectors to which they cater. There are currently over thirty currencies in which Euro-MTNs can be issued. Alongside the yen, the other most popular currency is the US dollar. Indeed, in 1996 the dollar reasserted itself as the most frequently used currency denomination. Together with the yen, it accounted for approximately 65% of all new issues. The dollar's success lies in its abundant supply, and the fact that is easily deployed in highly structured transactions. For example, many currencies are not directly exchangeable into other currencies except via the cross exchange rate with the U.S. dollar.

The characteristics of Euro-MTNs

In many ways, Euro-MTNs are similar to Eurobonds. They are debt obligations with the same legal status as bonds. Hence, in describing Euro-MTNs, it is helpful to take

Eurobonds as the starting point and then highlight the differences which make Euro-MTNs unique.

The single largest difference (and from which other unique Euro-MTN characteristics flow) is the offering mechanism. Eurobonds are one-off transactions. So all the documentation, associated legal and accountancy opinions and regulatory and procedural steps, must be initiated and concluded during the three-week offering period up to and including the closing date. By contrast, much of the fundamental documentation of a Euro-MTN deal can be drawn up in the two to three months before the programme is formally launched. This gives ample time so that the necessary opinions and authorisations are all assembled and that the listing application has been made and granted. Sufficient time must be allowed to 'paper' a Euro-MTN deal because its related documentation is longer and more complex than that of a standard Eurobond. This is due to the fact that a variety of circumstances must be catered for in the programme. For instance, the programme may allow for a number of different forms of securities to be offered (eg fixed rate, FRN, index-linked, and registered or bearer) and may also provide for various options (puts and calls and so on) to be embedded in their structures. Additionally, if issues are going to be made in different currencies (which is the norm) then thought has to be given to two other important areas: sales restrictions in the different currency sectors and the other laws and regulations which apply to such sectors. The beauty of Euro-MTNs is that they cover almost every conceivable circumstance. This allows an issuer maximum flexibility in executing a comprehensive financing strategy incorporating all sectors of the global market. Briefly, an all-encompassing programme means that only one set of documentation need be drafted to cover a whole raft of possible financings, with pricing supplements needed only to cover individual issues.

The key Euro-MTN document is referred to as a Dealership Agreement. In substance it most resembles a Subscription Agreement in a bond issue. As noted above, however, it must be more comprehensive and drafted in more general terms to give issuers the flexibility they desire.

Another fundamental difference is that a Dealership Agreement creates an uncommitted facility. By contrast, a Eurobond Subscription Agreement is a legally enforceable contract which obliges a borrower to issue securities and the syndicate members (the managers) to pay for them, providing certain specified conditions are met. In order to make a Dealership Agreement binding, the dealers have to enter into another agreement which specifies the precise terms and conditions of the new issue being offered. This new agreement is called a Pricing Supplement. Under IPMA rules, if the new issue includes a management group then the pricing supplement must be sent out (or be available for inspection in London) not later than two full business days prior to formal agreement of terms with the issuer. Furthermore, IPMA requires that invitations to join the management group for a Euro-MTN launched issue should disclose (i) the fact that the issue is related to a Euro-MTN programme; (ii) the need (if any) of the managers to report back once they have ceased their distribution of securities and the individual at the lead manager's office to whom such confirmation should be sent; and (iii) the securities (if any) with which the new issue is to be fungible. If managers are approached and agree to join as underwriters of a new issue then their names should appear in the pricing supplement. In any event, the presence or absence of a management group should itself be disclosed in the pricing supplement.

As mentioned previously, selling restrictions are a major concern in setting up a

Euro-MTN programme. IPMA recognises this priority and recommends that potential managers take careful note of these limitations and the related regulatory formalities. US sales restrictions within Regulation S, Category 2 or Category 3, involve a restricted period which ends once distribution is completed. According to IPMA, "In such issues, when the Issuing and Paying Agent (IPA) is notified by the Lead Manager that distribution is complete, the IPA will determine when the restricted period has expired and will then inform the necessary parties of that fact". A majority of Euro-MTN syndicated issues also follow the procedures under TEFRA D, which is explained in Chapter Three. Additionally, there are those Euro-MTNs which allow for issuance in the US. Typically, these take the form of private placements under Rule 144A, although a limited number of deals have been registered with the SEC for public distribution. Such Euro-MTNs have opened the market for global MTNs. As this market expands it will assist in standardising the offering procedures and yield levels between the US and international markets.

As it happens, many Euro-MTN issues are not syndicated among different managers. Practice varies. For example, some dealership agreements specify one or a number of dealers, who are anticipated to lead most of the issues under the programme. The most common procedure is to name the dealer(s) who is initially involved in setting up the programme and then to add dealers as required to suit a specific type of offering. Such add-on dealers are often referred to as 'dealer for a day'. It often makes sense to allow for flexibility in this area as marketing or regulatory requirements may dictate that specific nationalities of dealers or co-managers be added to a new issue. If there are multiple dealers (or managers), then this commitment to acquire the issued securities will be joint and several. Sometimes a separate subscription agreement will be entered into, but the net effect is just like that of a normal bond issue. If one of the dealers (or managers) defaults then the remaining syndicate members will, in accordance with procedure, be obliged to acquire the bonds of the defaulting institutions.

Just as there may be one or more dealers (managers) in a Euro-MTN programme, so too can there be one or more issuers. Such 'multi-issuer' programmes usually revolve around a large commercial group where individual subsidiaries may wish to issue securities in their own names. In each such issue, however, the group's parent will typically act as guarantor. With some programmes there is also flexibility to add to the list of issuers (within the group). However, such additions will give rise to extra disclosure information in the related listing particulars.

Whilst on the subject of issuers, it is interesting to study the type of entity which uses the Euro-MTN market. The exhibit below shows this breakdown for 1996. Conventional wisdom is that only the most frequent borrowers utilise the Euro-MTN market. The data suggest that actually a wide range of issuers employ Euro-MTNs. Most surprising is the preponderance of issuers from the private sector: 80% compared to approximately 60% in the Euromarkets overall. Furthermore, the most active issuers are commercial banks and other private financial institutions. Sovereign state borrowing is relatively modest, with state enterprises remaining the only significant public sector issuers.

The main disclosure document in a Euro-MTN programme is the information memorandum. As with a normal Eurobond this gives all the important financial data on the issuer (and guarantor, if any) together with other background information relevant to making an informed investment decision. IPMA's rules specify if such a document (also called a prospectus) is dated more than one year earlier than the signing of a new issue, it must be updated and reprinted. IPMA also requires that a

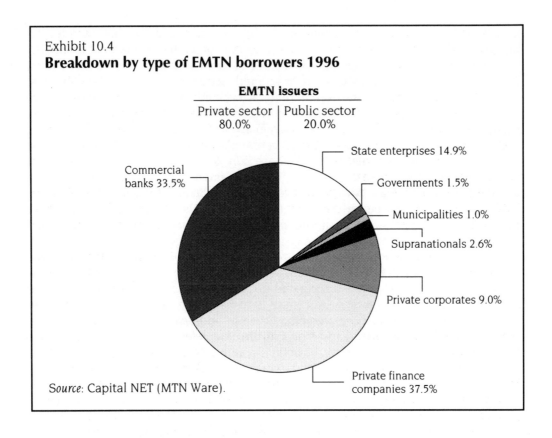

Exhibit 10.4
Breakdown by type of EMTN borrowers 1996

Source: Capital NET (MTN Ware).

certificate be obtained from a director or other equivalent senior officer of the issuer (and any guarantor) as a condition to closing. The certificate states:

> "[insert reference to prospectus and any supplements] contain all material information relating to the assets and liabilities, financial position, profits and losses of [name of Issuer and Guarantor, if there is one] and nothing has happened or is expected to happen which would require the attached documents to be supplemented or updated."

The London Stock Exchange likewise requires something which it terms an "annual technical update". Such rules and particularly the certificate mentioned above, have the marvellous quality of focusing the issuer's (and guarantor's, if any) mind on the quality of disclosure in the information memorandum.

As with a traditional Eurobond there are the other usual conditions precedent to closing. With a Euro-MTN issue, IPMA is especially precise: "The auditors' first comfort letter (if there is one) should be dated the signing date for the issue and the legal opinion(s) and auditors' second (or only) comfort letter should be dated the closing date for the issue (unless managers have been notified, before they are required to agree to become managers, that they will not be)".

Also in common with a traditional Eurobond, the issuer will give certain undertakings. Because a Euro-MTN programme is ongoing, many of the issuer's undertakings are likewise continuous. For example, the initial dealers will typically secure the issuer's promise to supply them with timely financial information and news about any re-rating of the outstanding debt. There is usually a requirement to provide annual update filings with the London Stock Exchange and other relevant regulatory bodies. Also, the issuer should undertake to continue to abide by all laws and relevant regulations pertaining to the programme. To the extent that fresh corporate or regulatory authorisations or any opinions, are required, then copies of these should be sent to the concerned dealers. Also dealers need to know what changes have occurred to the programme and the total amount and type of securities outstanding under the programme.

Usually an issuer will opt for a large Euro-MTN programme. It is commonplace to see them with total principal amounts which aggregate into the billions. Not only does this evidence 'financial muscle' but it also means that a greater volume of issues can be floated to justify the initial set-up and ongoing administration costs of the programme itself. Overhead expenses can be spread over a greater amount of financings (thus, reducing individual issue costs). Conventional wisdom is that the additional set-up costs can be amortised in only two to three deals. Euro-MTN programmes can also be increased in size but this involves compliance with a number of procedures. For instance, the named dealers typically have to agree (or at least, not object) to the increase. Also, new listing particulars must be lodged with the London Stock Exchange and the standard opinions obtained and conditions precedent satisfied. On balance, it is probably better to start off with a large programme.

Closing and payment details are somewhat simpler with a Euro-MTN programme. As noted earlier, photocopies of a master global note can be used with each new issue. This avoids the delay and possible inconvenience of asking an issuer to sign a new global note with each offering.

When it comes to paying for the newly issued securities, settlement is handled through the account of the issuing and paying agent with the clearing systems, typically Euroclear and Cedel Bank. With a normal Eurobond, settlement would be handled through the lead manager's account.

Structured Euro-MTNs

Reference has been made to structured Euro-MTNs. This has grown quickly to become the most important sub-sector of the overall Euro-MTN market. Structured issues still remain popular despite their use of derivatives and the bad press which derivatives in general have attracted following the crash of Barings. Following below is a graph showing the volume of structured Euro-MTNs over the period 1992-96.

As noted before, Euro-MTNs are ideal candidates for structured transactions because their issuing flexibility and speed of execution make them excellent hosts for swaps, options and other derivatives. Some examples of such structured Euro-MTNs are capped floaters (ie normal FRNs but with a cap above which the interest rate cannot go), collared floaters (ie like capped floaters but with the addition of a floor below which the interest rate cannot go) and inverse or reverse floaters (ie FRNs where the interest rate moves in accordance with a formula in a direction opposite to market interest rates). A relatively recent innovation is the creation of credit-linked Euro-MTNs where repayment of principal occurs as a function of, say, a particular sovereign state's repayment performance. This structure allows an investor to gain exposure to different credits with a view to diversifying risk and/or increasing yield. Other interesting formulas have linked payment terms to stock exchange indices or the projected trading levels of certain currencies and benchmark interest rates. Also, there are whole families of structured Euro-MTNs with embedded calls and puts.

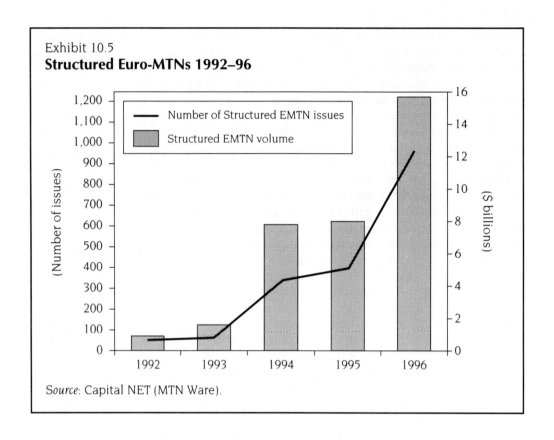

Exhibit 10.5
Structured Euro-MTNs 1992–96

Source: Capital NET (MTN Ware).

Perhaps surprisingly, the best known US government agencies have been active issuers of these instruments.

But what is the attraction to investors? Usually, it is the enhancement of return (in exchange for accepting some incremental risk). Particularly in times of low interest rates, investors become increasingly eager to find new ways of boosting yield. A capped FRN achieves just that objective because the cap itself has intrinsic value which, while potentially detrimental to the investor, compensates for this short term by providing a higher return. Such a structure has real attractions if the credit is triple-A rated (as are US government agencies) and the interest payment is Libor-based rather than utilising a US capital market index.

Structured Euro-MTNs can also be used by highly sophisticated investors who are endeavouring to achieve specific portfolio objectives such as hedging against a shift in the yield curve or a change in market volatility. Additionally, structured Euro-MTNs may be deployed in pro-active portfolio management where the objective is not to hedge but instead to take speculative positions in anticipation of forecasted events (what is called taking a 'view' of the market).

Structured Euro-MTNs are not without their drawbacks. Certain highly structured products are difficult to trade and, naturally, suffer from illiquidity. Many times, embedded swaps can be unwound (at a cost), but investors frequently wish to receive a premium return to compensate for this sort of inconvenience. Many Euro-MTNs (even the unstructured variety) are obliged to pay investors a modest premium. This is because the Euromarkets are less homogenous, say compared with the US market, as a consequence of their variety of currencies and different legal and regulatory systems. As investors have grown in sophistication and Euro-MTN programmes have increased in size, however, this premium has tended to disappear, especially for the most frequent issuers.

The use of derivatives has also met with controversy. Such products have been blamed for problems like those encountered by Orange County. Also there are examples of such products being mis-sold by market professionals. As a consequence, people are taking a fresh (and harder) look at the suitability of such instruments for different categories of investors. Additionally, greater efforts are being made to promote increased transparency in this market. As a parallel trend, new software programmes have been developed to assist in the quantification of risks under different scenarios and the monitoring of exposure on a continuous basis. In one sense, this maturing of the market was inevitable given the rekindled interest of various official regulatory bodies. On the other hand, changes needed to occur if the structured Euro-MTNs were ever to thrive in the future. The modifications in procedures and analyses have gone a long way to restoring confidence in a sector which, through its association with derivatives, has attracted its share of bad press.

Commercial paper: background

Commercial paper transactions can be traced back to the early 18th century in the then American colonies. By the middle of the 19th century an active money market grew up which was centred in New York. In those days broker-dealers intermediated between corporate issuers on one hand and end-investors (chiefly commercial banks) on the other. This distribution pattern continued virtually unchanged until 1920 when General Motors Acceptance Corporation (a modestly sized automobile finance company at that time) decided to market its commercial paper directly to investors. This process, called 'direct' issuance, has been followed by other frequent issuers, although many commercial paper programmes today are still managed through one or more dealers.

The definition of commercial paper has altered over time as the categories of issuers has broadened. It is best thought of now as short-term, negotiable debt instruments offered by entities (both public and private sector) around the world. Usually commercial paper is sold on a discount basis largely to institutional investors. In the United States, commercial paper issues are exempted from registration with the Securities and Exchange Commission (SEC).

The main driving force in the growth of commercial paper is easy access to cheap money. The main competitor to commercial paper are commercial banks and the cost (and accessibility) of their funding lines which commercial paper has to improve upon in order to have any attraction. In the US the long history of commercial paper and difficulties in the banking industry (sometimes brought about by so-called 'credit crunches') has firmly established the popularity of commercial paper. By the mid-1990s it was estimated that there was some $775 billion of commercial paper outstanding.

Euro-commercial paper

Euro-commercial paper (or Euro-CP) first emerged in the 1960s and early 1970s as an attempt to establish internationally a market for short-term corporate bearer note issues, similar in some respects to the commercial paper market in the US (which currently serves major foreign corporations and government bodies, as well as domestic corporations). At that time, although several prominent US corporations tapped the new market, it did not develop to any significant degree.

The market really began in December 1978 with a programme initiated for the New Zealand Shipping Corporation. A quiet period followed, punctuated by various efforts to re-open the market. Those issues in the early 1980s were structured to attract investment from commercial banks and were consequently offered in large denominations. The market began to grow in 1984 and by the end of that year over $26 billion of transactions were outstanding. Since then growth has come in spurts and levelled off by the mid-1990s when total outstandings were estimated at $85 billion.

One of the reasons for the recent plateau in Euro-CP outstandings is the success of the short-term Euro-MTNs which can have maturities of as little as 30 days (or less). The demand for short-term paper is actually growing in the Euromarkets. However, the Euromarkets' requirements appear to served best by Euro-MTNs whose programmes allow for the issuance of debt instruments very similar to Euro-CP. The popularity of Euro-MTNs is such that this instrument is even beginning to challenge syndicated bank loans on the basis of lower cost of money and quicker speed of execution.

Like its US counterpart, Euro-CP are short-term bearer promissory notes. Such securities are issued by both private and public sector entities, and they feature a particular niche market for bank issuers that sometimes combine a Euro-CP programme with a certificate of deposit (CD) programme. Euro-commercial paper issues are similar to tap CDs and benefit from a highly liquid market. They are sometimes issued in the form of printed securities but are also represented by global notes allowing transactions to be recorded on a book entry basis. Euro-commercial paper yields are usually quoted relative to the Libor or Libid rates. Older issues carried coupons but the newer offerings typically have zero coupons and are therefore quoted on a discount basis. Maturities range from seven to 365 days, although the greatest activity is in the 30 to 180-day tenor range. This relatively long maturity contrasts with the most actively traded maturity in the US domestic market, which is only about 30 days.

New issues are denominated in US dollars, sterling, French francs, Dutch guilders or Ecu as well as other currencies. Definitive dollar notes are generally in the amount of $500,000 although this can vary and the standard dealing size is $5 million. Some attractions of this market include the enhanced yields which are available on certain issues relative to CDs, term bank deposits and US Treasury bills. Borrowers are typically of a good credit quality and range from prime sovereign states and their agencies to corporate issuers. New offerings usually are rated by Moody's Investors Service Inc., as P1, P2 and P3, and Standard & Poor's Corporation as A1+, A1, A2, and A3: these representing the levels of investment grade paper in descending order. The availability of such credit ratings assists greatly in the making of investment decisions. From a borrower's point of view the depth of the Euro-commercial paper market represents an attractive pool of investment capital available at a moment's notice. New issues are arranged over the telephone and documentation is reduced to the actual note. Broken or odd-dated maturities are a common feature in many Euro-commercial paper programmes, which allow issuers to tailor the periods of their financings to specific funding requirements.

Euro-commercial paper has evolved over time. An early structure was the revolving underwriting facility or RUF which was used in the financing for the New Zealand Shipping Corporation. This transaction involved the issuance of three or six-month paper which was purchased and resold continuously for six years. The facility was underwritten by a syndicate of banks which in effect promised to buy any notes that third party investors had no interest in. Banks participating in the facility viewed it in a manner similar to a syndicated loan, which the RUF was designed to replace.

The next change in this instrument came with the introduction of tender panels, which allowed underwriting banks to bid for the paper at the time of issuance rather than being stuck with only the leftovers. This new modification was included in offerings called NIFs, SNIFs and others with equally exotic names.

The problem with the tender panel approach was mainly its cumbersome mechanics (requiring several days to organise) and lack of flexibility (providing only pre-set maturities and unresponsiveness to rapid movements in the market). Nowadays, the tender panel has been superseded by transactions done on an 'order basis'. This involves the issuer contacting one or more of its dealers with its day-to-day financing requirements. Typically, the issuer will set the terms of the offering, although these may be reviewed with the dealers at a later time to ensure that they continue to conform with market expectations. The specific securities are only purchased from the issuer against firm orders from investor clients. Nearly all programmes are currently set up without the support of an underwriting commitment. This obviates the need for back-up banks and tender panels. It also reduces fees to the issuers but there is no assurance that funding requirements will be satisfied if the market weakens. Issuers appear to take the view that the market has matured and deepened to the extent that such additional support is no longer necessary to guarantee access to funding in the future. In the case of highly liquid bank Euro-CP, however, dealers will frequently take a position (ie buy securities for their own portfolio) and then sell it on to fulfil market demand.

As mentioned previously, the market for Euro-commercial paper is feeling the competitive pressure from Euro-MTNs. Ironically, one of the early names for Euro-commercial paper was Euro-notes. The advantages of packaging Euro-commercial paper within a Euro-MTN programme are, however, obvious. The huge volume of Euro-MTNs makes them highly cost efficient and their sales give issuers the greatest flexibility conceivable in raising finance internationally in the most opportune circumstances.

Structured commercial paper
Like Euro-MTNs, Euro-CP can also be arranged with interest rate and currency swaps and other forms of derivatives to meet specific objectives of borrowers and investors alike. A common example is a fixed versus floating interest rate swap. This transaction works because of the margin for borrowing long-term (which is high) and commercial paper's short-term margin (which is low). The swap can be effected in the international market or in the US domestic market, where foreign borrowers have long-established commercial paper programmes. The diagram below outlines this traditional swap.

The swap above assumes (with some justification) that the international bank would have a better chance of raising fixed rate finance in the bond market than a (possibly less well known) corporate borrower. The corporation might, however, have good access to the commercial paper market where floating rate funds may be attracted cheaply. The logic of the swap is, therefore, the assumed preference of the corporation to have fixed rate finance (eg to fund the purchase of plant and equipment) while the international bank would just as soon have floating rate finance (because its loan assets are also floating rate). Because the bank is probably in a stronger bargaining position than the corporation, it will no doubt receive a discount on the commercial paper rate (itself a discount to Libor) in return for the fixed rate funding. At the end of the transaction, the corporation will have achieved its ambition of raising fixed rate finance while the bank will have been rewarded for its intervention by obtaining sub-Libor funding.

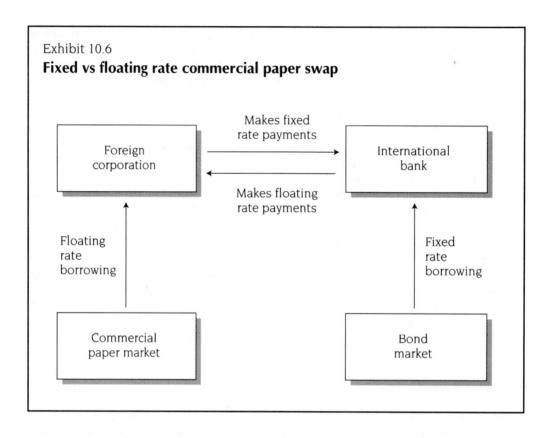

Exhibit 10.6
Fixed vs floating rate commercial paper swap

Swaps like that above, take advantage of the cheap cost of funds in the commercial paper market. They can have several variations. For example, another international bank (or investment bank) might intermediate and take the swap on its own books to satisfy other counterparties, say, investors who wish to fix a rate of return on their portfolios in return for assuming an obligation to make floating rate payments in the future. Swaps can also involve currencies, so that different nationalities of borrower can benefit from opportunities in the commercial paper market. Furthermore, swaps allow for a diversification of funding sources and sometimes permit borrowings (eg fixed rate, long term) which might not otherwise be available to certain categories of borrower.

Commercial paper transactions can also be structured so that they are asset-backed. Traditionally, commercial paper represented an unsecured claim on an acceptable corporate credit. Some companies, however, may be too weak to set up a programme. Hence, an alternative might be to fund an asset category of the borrower (such as its receivables) which might suffice to back commercial paper. Naturally, the receivables, in this case, would need to be of a high credit standing, but often the assets of a small to medium-sized company can be of a higher quality than the company itself. A generic term for using assets to back commercial paper or bonds is 'asset securitisation'. This topic is the main focus of Chapter Eleven.

Other Money Market Instruments

There are a host of securities in the international markets which fall into the broad category called 'money market instruments'. Some of these may be transplants from essentially domestic markets (eg US Treasury bills and bankers acceptances). However, with the continuing convergence of the world's markets, it must be expected that financial products will reach out to a wider audience. One particular type of instrument, called London certificates of deposit (or CDs), do however, merit special attention.

London certificates of deposit

Fixed rate CDs

Negotiable certificates of deposit (CDs) are securities issued representing funds deposited in a bank for a definite period of time and earning a specified rate of return. CDs were first issued in London in May 1986 by the local branch of First National City Bank. Their precursor was the domestic dollar CD, initially issued in 1961, also by First National City Bank. Certificates of deposit differ from normal deposits in that they may be bought and sold. Depending on market conditions, the interest offered on CDs currently varies from 0% to 0.25% (although greater differentials have existed historically) below rates offered by the same bank for time deposits with the same term. CDs benefit from a extremely liquid secondary market where substantial holdings can be transferred with relative ease and minimal expense, particularly in the maturity range of one month to one year.

Both primary and secondary markets have broadened substantially as different nationalities of banks have become issuers of these securities. A particularly important development was the permission granted in 1972 by the Japanese finance ministry for Japanese banks to enter the market. During the 1980s these institutions grew increasingly active until they reached a dominant position in the market. Indeed, the substantial growth in CD outstandings during the 1980s was nearly entirely attributable to these banks.

CDs are ideal investments at times when the future is uncertain. Thus, the CD market made strong gains in 1973-74, when the dollar sector of the Eurobond market contracted severely. The same happened in 1978, when interest rate and currency problems plagued dollar bonds. Although the December 1980 monthly turnover was down compared with December 1979, the total amount of CDs outstanding at December 1980 established a new record. Gains were recorded throughout the early 1980s, followed by a slight slump in 1984. A further fall occurred in 1985 which gave rise to predictions that this market would be absorbed by the newer Euro-commercial paper. In the event, though, CDs proved their inherent strength and 1986 recorded the highest outstandings ever. With the difficulties experienced on the world's stock exchanges in 1987, the CD again proved to be a particularly safe haven, recording a substantial boost in volume. This strong growth continued in 1988, and 1989 marked a record volume which breached US$200 billion for the first time in history. The next two years, 1990 and 1991, both slipped from this earlier peak as the global recession drained liquidity from the financial system and institutional investor confidence plummeted. There was a modest recovery in 1992 followed by a further slip in 1993 when booming bond and stockmarkets attracted funds away from alternative investments. Trouble, this time the threat of rising interest rates in the first quarter of 1994, again drove investors to concentrate their funds on short-term, floating rate investments. CDs proved an excellent option and the market rose 16% to score a new volume record in 1994 in excess of US$214 billion. This favourable level of activity continued in 1995, although at a less hectic pace than that of the preceding year.

CDs are typically issued by the foreign branches (usually in London) of major international banks, as well as by London banks themselves. Issuing activity is high during difficult market periods when banks wish to increase their liquidity. Longer-term CDs, in particular, represent a more stable liability base than Euro-deposits and are, therefore, often preferred by non-US banks – especially the Japanese – (without a natural source of dollars) when funding their portfolios. As the secondary market for CDs has expanded, these instruments have grown to be an increasingly attractive investment. They are currently purchased by institutional investors, money market funds and other similar operations, corporate treasurers and other banks.

Exhibit 10.6
The London CD market, 1966-96

	Total CDs outstanding ($ million)	% change on previous period
December 1966	225	n/a.
December 1967	597	+165.3
December 1968	1,433	+140.0
December 1969	3,699	+158.1
December 1970	3,959	+7.0
December 1971	4,800	+21.2
December 1972	8,005	+66.8
December 1973	10,010	+25.0
December 1974	12,100	+20.9
December 1975	12,947	+7.0
December 1976	16,488	+27.3
December 1977	22,999	+39.5
December 1978	27,853	+21.1
December 1979	43,414	+55.9
December 1980	49,028	+12.9
December 1981	77,856	+58.8
December 1982	91,672	+17.8
December 1983	99,350	+8.8
December 1984	96,167	−3.2
December 1985	88,596	−7.9
December 1986	105,157	+15.8

Exhibit 10.6 *continued*

	Total CDs outstanding ($ million)	% change on previous period
December 1987	146,613	+39.4
December 1988	188,070	+28.3
December 1989	206,430	+9.8
December 1990	202,310	−2.0
December 1991	192,032	−5.1
December 1992	202,891	+5.7
December 1993	185,266	−8.7
December 1994	214,487	+15.8
December 1995	217,133	+1.2
June 1996	233,520	+7.6

n/a = not available.
Source: Bank of England.

London CDs were historically offered on either a tap or (occasionally) on a tranche basis. Tap CDs, which account for nearly all CDs currently outstanding, are offered on a 'from time to time' basis: their supply can be turned on and off like a tap. Maturities usually range from one month to five years (with the majority under six months) and are issued in amounts of $1 million, although the standard dealing size is $5 million. Placement is usually made with institutional investors.

Floating rate CDs

First issued in April 1977, the floating rate CD (or FRCD) has become an important platform for structured (ie derivative-based) transactions. These securities typically pay interest at a set margin relative to three- or six-month Libor. There have been a number of variations on the standard FRCD structure and, for example, the interest margin has in certain cases fluctuated during the life of an issue or has been set over the mean of the bid and offered quotes (instead of over the offered side). FRCDs can also be offered on either a tranche or tap basis. Structured FRCDs are typically offered as individual issues and due to their linkage to one or more derivatives, lack the high degree of liquidity normally associated with CDs. Part of the popularity of the FRCD is attributable to its flexibility in meeting the unique requirements of individual issuers while attracting substantial investor support. In addition to receiving a yield improvement (compared to placing money on a six-month time deposit at or below Libid, the London Interbank Bid Rate), investors also can benefit in other ways depending on the structure employed. Like tap CDs, FRCDs are negotiable securities while term deposits are not. Although banks of several different nationalities have issued FRCDs, the preponderance of these offerings have been for Japanese institutions. FRCDs are essentially term securities, having lives in the popular short to medium-term range. Issue size varies widely with the type of placement chosen and blocks of $50 million have often been placed on offer.

Other features
Both fixed and floating rate CDs are essentially bank deposits which rank pari passu with all other deposits. This is a major advantage they have over certain floating rate notes (discussed in Chapter Nine) which, like those issued by UK banks, may be subordinated to deposits.

London CDs are governed by English law and are generally in bearer from, although CDs in registered form have also been issued.

Certificates of deposit are traded in an over-the-counter secondary market chiefly maintained by banks in London, New York, Japan and the Middle East. Much CD trading is quoted on a yield-to-maturity basis, although FRCDs are quoted on a price plus accrued interest basis.

Form of offering
Another advantage of CDs is the ease and low cost of their issue. Tap issues are made whenever a bid acceptable to the issuer appears. The whole transaction can be handled over the telephone in a matter of seconds, depending on the size of the offering. Frequently, CDs are purchased for the portfolios of institutions active in the market (often other banks) and then re-sold as market conditions dictate. CDs are about as liquid as any other security in the Euromarkets. The ability to deal in them is, in fact, comparable to the futures market. They therefore represent an attractive vehicle for taking positions in anticipation of market moves.

Floating rate CDs are also quite cheap to issue, compared to Eurodollar bonds. As a result of the simplified issuing procedures, legal and accounting expenses are negligible. Printing expenses are limited to the CD certificates or global security. There is no listing or fiscal agent or trustee. Commission amounts are modest.

Money market instrument yield calculations
Many money market instruments such as commercial paper (also Treasury bills and bankers acceptances) calculate their return (or yield) on the basis of a discount from par. This is sometimes referred to as a 'discount yield'. It should not be confused with the yield which a bond gives.

Discounts are usually calculated on a year of 360 or 365 days. This is a matter of convention as US dollars instruments assume a 360-day year while sterling securities assume 365 days, even in a leap year.

The formula used for calculating discount yield follows below:

$$P = 100 \times \left(1 - \frac{r \times f1}{100}\right)$$

Source: ISMA

P equals the percentage price and r is the percentage discount rate. f1 is the fraction of a year from settlement to redemption based on the actual days elapsed divided by the assumed (either 360 or 365) days in the year.

This form of calculation may best be explained by way of an example. If an issue of commercial paper is purchased with settlement on January 1, 1997 with redemption on June 30, 1997 (ie six months' maturity), a total of 181 days will have elapsed. Assuming, too, that the discount rate was 8%, then the calculation of discount price for a US dollar instrument would be as follows

$$P = 100 \times \left(1 - \frac{8 \times {}^{181}\!/_{360}}{100}\right)$$

$$P = 95.9778\%$$

If, on the other hand, the instrument was a sterling bill, the calculation would be adjusted as follows:

$$P = 100 \times \left(1 - \frac{8 \times {}^{181}\!/_{365}}{100}\right)$$

$$P = 96.0329\%$$

The discounted price can easily be converted back to provide a yield measure by which different money market instruments can be compared. The ISMA recommended formula is set forth below:

$$MMY = \frac{r}{p} \times 100$$

$$MMY = \frac{r}{(1 - r \times f1/100)}$$

MMY equates to the money market yield expressed as a percentage with r as the discount rate percentage. P represents the percent price solved for above and f1 is, again, the fraction of the year between settlement and redemption (maturity).

Thus, the MMY of the $ instrument would be 8/.959778

$$= 8.335\%$$

and

the MMY of the £ instrument would be 8/.960329

$$= 8.330\%$$

For US dollar floating rate CDs (FRCDs) yield is calculated in the same manner as with normal FRNs, please see Chapter Nine. For sterling FRCDs, however, interest is calculated on the basis of a 365-day year, irrespective of whether it is a leap year. All FRCDs settle like Eurobonds, with the gross price P reflecting both the trade or clean price 'CP' adjusted for accrued interest. This may be simply represented:

$$P = CP + G \times f$$

Source: ISMA

G is the coupon rate and f represents the fraction of a year from the last coupon date (or issue date) to value date.

In the case of fixed rate CDs (having more than one future coupon payment), the process of price calculation is like that for FRCDs, taking each coupon payment period in turn. Simple (not compound) interest is used including the first possible part period. For fixed rate CDs having only one coupon payment on redemption (maturity), the price percentage is calculated by a slightly modified formula:

$$P = \frac{(C + K)}{(1 + Y \times f1)}$$

Source: ISMA

P equates to the percentage price while C is the redemption value, normally 100% or par. K is the percentage coupon payment on redemption (adjusted for the fraction of the year represented by the length of the coupon payment period). Y is the quoted yield and f1 represents, again, the fraction of the year from settlement to redemption. As before, the assumed number of days in a year is determined by convention, with US dollar instruments assuming 360 days and sterling instruments assuming 365 days, even in leap years.

11

ASSET SECURITISATION

Over the past couple of decades there has been a discernible trend towards disintermediation of banks through a process called securitisation. Like so many words in finance 'securitisation' sounds exotic but in reality is quite commonplace. Even 'disintermediation' – admittedly, a mouthful – is an everyday phenomenon. A good example is the bond market itself. Bonds are simply securitised loans; a form of lending which is evidenced by certificates (ie securities). When a borrower issues a bond it raises funds from a variety of individual and institutional investors, thus bypassing or disintermediating the banking system. Banks, of course, do get involved in the bond market but for many it is more a matter of 'if you can't beat them, join them'. Other diversified, or so-called universal banks, handle investors' money and therefore find it helpful to participate in the bond market as a means of securing investment product for their customers.

A major attraction of securitisation is the access it gives borrowers to the capital markets. Cost of money is a big concern. The capital markets are open to a wide range of institutions and different groups of individual investors. Hence, securitised issues can be targeted to the most receptive investors with a view to reducing overall expense. Other objectives can also be achieved like obtaining long-term, fixed coupon debt which is a rarity in the banking system. One of the key reasons only the capital markets will provide long-term debt, for instance, is that securities are negotiable. They can be bought and sold. If investors need liquidity, their bonds may be 'monetised' by disposing of them in the secondary market. Banks may have progressed in developing a market for their own loans but there has been resistance to growth in this area and, consequently, only specialised sectors such as impaired corporate and Third World loans, have developed to any significant degree.

Because of the advantages securitisation has over normal bank finance, it is viewed by many as the wave of the future. In the US, for instance, the domestic securitisation market reached a total volume of approximately $2.5 trillion by the mid 1990s. In Europe and other parts of the world, securitisation has been slower to gain in popularity. Progress is being made, though, and the challenges faced by securitisation in different countries provide useful instruction in the dynamics of securitisation itself.

Why securitise?

As noted above, from the issuer's point of view, a securitised offering reduces the cost of money and may even provide other advantages like long-term fixed rate finance. Also securitisation may be the only way to raise money at all. For instance, a corporate credit, say, a US nursing home, may be perceived as weak by traditional bankers and, therefore, denied funding. But, look a little closer and you may find that the same nursing home has receivables (called debtors in the UK) on its books from Medicare or Medicaid. These are two US government programmes which help to meet the medical and related expenses of Americans. Receivables from these programmes are essentially US government debt (ie obligations to repay). There is no credit which is better than the US government. So, here is the dilemma. The nursing home is itself viewed as a weak credit but it has (or owns) receivables from the US government whose credit standing is unimpeachable. What is the solution? Securitise the receivables. This involves buying the receivables (usually at a discount, called factoring in the UK) and advancing the funds directly to the nursing home. The entity which acquires the receivables is typically a bankruptcy-remote special purpose vehicle (SPV). The SPV funds itself by selling securities (which represent an undivided interest in the Medicare and Medicaid receivables just acquired). The rate of return from discounting the receivables is then paid to the institutions and individuals investing in the SPV's securities.

An attraction of securitisation is that frequently everybody wins. In this case, the nursing home gets its required financing through the sales of its receivables. The investors are rewarded with a good return on an asset category (ie Medicare and

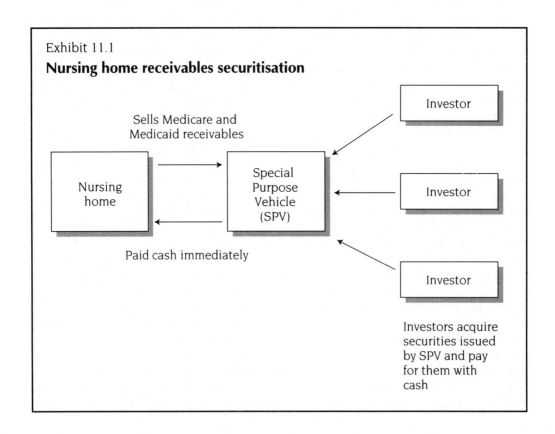

Exhibit 11.1
Nursing home receivables securitisation

Medicaid receivables) which otherwise would not have been readily available as an investment. The discounting of Medicare and Medicaid receivables is equivalent to creating US Treasury bills – only, with a higher return. Of course, as with nearly all aspects of financial engineering, there are peculiarities with this type of securitisation which require an imaginative solution. Solutions to these and other similar problems will be dealt with later in this chapter.

For borrowers, securitisation represents a way to raise finance at an acceptable cost of money. Some borrowers look to securitisation as a useful diversification of funding sources beyond traditional banks. For other borrowers, securitisation is the only way finance can be raised at all. Additional advantages can be gained if the securitisation is structured in an 'off balance sheet' manner. This means that the financing does not show up as a liability on the balance sheet of the borrower. If it did, it would add to the borrower's existing debt burden and might discourage others from extending credit (eg normal trade creditors). In the example of the nursing home above, the financing is organised to be off balance sheet. This occurs because the nursing home's receivables are purchased outright without any recourse back to the nursing home. Hence, the receivables are removed from the balance sheet and no liability is shown replacing them. Properly structured securitisations have positive tax implications as well as accounting benefits. This is especially true with international securitisations where it is sometimes possible to find tax and/or accounting advantages which are specific to individual national jurisdictions. Frequently, such opportunities are short lived as the authorities move quickly to close loopholes. It is the job of the financial engineer to spot new opportunities and to make the most of them so long as they are available.

Investors also benefit. In the nursing home example, these benefits were (i) access to a type of investment normally unavailable in the markets (ii) high credit quality collateral (due to the sovereign guarantee which backs it) and (iii) premium return. Due to the complicated structure of securitisations, investors demand (successfully) extra return to compensate them for the additional study and due diligence involved. Paradoxically, securitisations can be both high credit quality and high return at the same time This is great news for investment managers who are constantly under pressure to identify high yielding assets while maximising creditworthiness. Securitisations are also intellectually challenging; another advantage for fund managers. Not only are plain vanilla products boring but they do not justify the salary levels of highly trained and experienced financial analysts. Securitisation, then, is the answer to a maiden's prayer. Investment managers can earn their keep by analysing securitised products which enhance yield without sacrificing credit.

What assets can be securitised?

The saying goes 'if it flows then securitise it'. This means that any asset which generates a cashflow can be securitised. You need the cash flow to pay investors their return and also to repay them their capital investment. Another characteristic of a securitised asset group is that it must be homogeneous. A certain amount of difference between individual assets is acceptable, but you cannot securitise apples with oranges. It just gets too complex. Specifically, the cashflows from a diverse asset category will become so irregular as to defy the scheduled payments of interest and principal required under the securitisation. Finally, there needs to be enough of the assets to make the exercise worthwhile. Securitisation is an expensive business. Its complex characteristics represent a bonanza for lawyers and other professional advisers. Thus, there must be sufficient cost advantage to cover these expenses with a bit left over to compensate the financial engineer who conceived and structured the transaction in the first place.

So with these general rules in mind, it is easy to see that only a certain range of assets qualify for securitisation. To name a few, there are residential and commercial mortgages, trade and credit card receivables, leases (both operating and financing varieties), personal loans for automobiles, boats and trailers, and home equity and corporate loans. A new booming area is the securitisation of tax liens. This product is sourced in the US from towns and municipalities which sell off their tax claims which are past due. The vendor accelerates its cashflow, while the purchaser of the tax claim (the investor) virtually steps into the shoes of the tax collector, with a claim against real property assets senior to any bank mortgage. Frequently a tax lien can be 40 to 50 times overcollaterised, and the returns are very attractive. Experimentation is also going on in the area of securitised VAT reclaims and interesting work has been done in securitised insurance premiums.

An important sub-sector of asset securitisation is something called 'repackaging'. As the name implies, this procedure involves structuring investment vehicles which hold existing securities that for one reason or another have lost favour with the investing public. Major advances were made in the repackaging of perpetual FRNs in the late 1980s. As a result, these previously unwanted securities soon found new homes but in a securitised format more acceptable to the markets. Other forms of repackaging involve widening the market for existing securities by providing them with features designed to attract specific categories of investors. There are, for instance, US financial instruments which pay interest as a function of something called Prime Rate. These instruments can, however, be re-packaged with an interest rate swap (specifically, a Prime/Libor swap) so that Libor-based international institutions can add them to their own portfolios.

Securitisations: History and recent performance

It is difficult to identify the beginning of securitisation because as noted at the outset of this chapter, bond issues themselves are an example of securitisation. Innovative structures, however, started in the early 1970s with the first issue of mortgage-backed bonds by Government National Mortgage Association (GNMA or Ginnie Mae). By 1983, the first Collateralised Mortgage Obligation (CMO) was completed. This transaction fell into the broad category of repackaging in that the cash flows of the underlying mortgages were segregated and divided in such way that various instruments (representing the respective cashflows) could be sold to specially targeted investor groups. Different investors have different investment guidelines and preferences. For example short-term oriented commercial banks would be sold the initial (say, out to five years) of the cashflows of the CMO, while pension funds (which need to invest on a long-term basis to match their prospective commitments) would be sold the longer maturity cashflows.

It may be useful to digress a moment and examine the importance of the mortgage market and why securitisation was first spawned in the US. First and foremost, the mortgage industry is a mainstay of nearly every national financial market. The US is no exception with the annual issuance of new securitised mortgages totalling in excess of $450 billion in the mid-1990s. What makes the US different is the intervention of the US government in this market.

Not all government intervention is negative. Sometimes it can be helpful and even creative. The intervention of the US government began after the Great Crash of 1929 with the disastrous implications this had on financial institutions and asset values (including property) throughout the economy. The response of the government at that time was to explore different avenues to restore confidence. Savers were, for instance, encouraged to deposit monies in banks by insuring these sums with an effective US government guarantee up to a set deposit amount.

In order to supply the capital demands of a burgeoning housing market the US government recognised that new sources of investment needed to be tapped. Simply put, the domestic Savings and Loans (similar to UK building societies) were thought to need help from the capital markets. By mobilising the capital markets, regional differences in the supply of investable funds could be smoothed out. Hence, the pioneering works of Ginnie Mae with mortgage-backed securities offerings. Investors reacted positively to this innovation. Of course, the credit quality of the securities (which carried the explicit guarantee of the US government) was hard to fault. Additionally, a yield premium was paid above similar maturity Treasury bonds to compensate for having to understand what was then a novel instrument.

Given the importance of mortgage-backed securities, the final section of this chapter discusses them more fully. The table below also shows the volume of private label (ie non-government backed) securitised mortgage offerings in the US domestic capital market during the past five years, including other asset categories which have been securitised.

The US securitisation market has been benefited in a number of ways. Not only has the government itself been an active sponsor, but the domestic economy is so huge

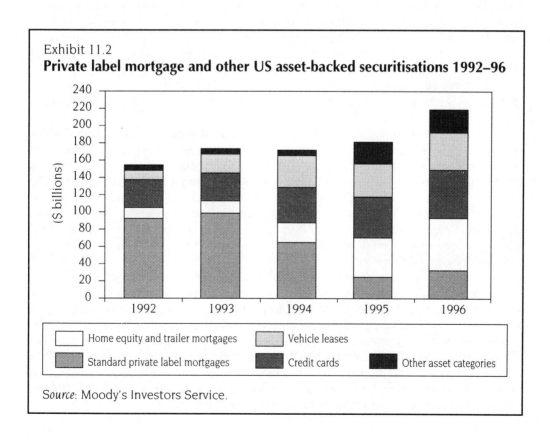

Exhibit 11.2
Private label mortgage and other US asset-backed securitisations 1992–96

Source: Moody's Investors Service.

that it easily supports the volume of assets needed to make securitisations a viable alternative. This large economy also features a wide investor base with characteristic flows of funds which can be individually targeted by CMO-type instruments. Homogeneity is also satisfied. Firstly, the greater the volume of assets, the more easy it is to identify a critical mass which will qualify for securitisation. Then, of course, the US has a single currency, legal system and set of accounting principles. These features together greatly simplify the process of securitisation. And, nothing succeeds like success. After some 20 years of robust growth, the US securitisation market has gained in maturity as well as confidence. Active primary and secondary markets encourage new investment flows which in turn prompt new, innovative structures to be brought to market. As the available product base broadens, so too are more and different types of institutions attracted to this market.

The Euromarkets have yet to enjoy this virtuous circle. This is chiefly because the international markets are still fragmented when it comes to securitisations. National laws (eg consumer credit legislation and so forth) not only vary from country to country but they can positively discourage the development of asset securitisation. What has been lacking until fairly recently is the political will to make the required changes. In the US, it was the government which took the lead. The same must be true in other countries as well.

Many of the European countries are governed by a legal system referred to as Civil Law (in France sometimes referred to as Napoleonic Law). This system has fundamental differences from the Common Law approach followed in the United Kingdom and the US. Put crudely, Common Law is more entrepreneurial allowing innovations unless specifically prohibited by law. Under Civil Law, by contrast, activities frequently need to be defined and approved by enabling legislation before they can become legitimate. This can be a time-consuming process and one whose outcome is frequently less than perfect. For example, the principle of securitisation was the subject of discussion in France for two years before formal approval was given in December 1989. More time still was required to sort out tax and accounting issues. Still, despite all this hard work, the initial rules prescribed only certain asset categories which could be securitised. This naturally restricts what is otherwise a highly innovative market concept.

Added to the legal problems are the wide range of different tax and accounting approaches from country to country. As mentioned previously, sometimes opportunities can be identified which exploit these differences. However, loopholes are inevitably closed when too many people are seen taking advantage of them. So the net effect has been to slow the growth of asset securitisations. Additionally, the individual European markets are small by comparison to the US. Therefore, the chances of finding large volumes of homogeneous assets are greatly reduced. This does not auger well for profitability because transaction costs are high and will not be supported by 'small ticket' deals.

The trend in the Euromarkets is positive but the potential of securitisations will not be realised until secondary markets deepen and a greater level of experience is achieved with this product sector. Below follows a graph of the total asset securitisations in the European market over the past five years

It is important to emphasise that total securitisations issued in Europe amounted to only some $50 billion during 1996. This was only slightly more than 8.0% of the total issuance (including government-backed mortgages) in the US domestic market during the same year. A further table below shows the breakdown of different categories of European securitisations over the 1992-96 period.

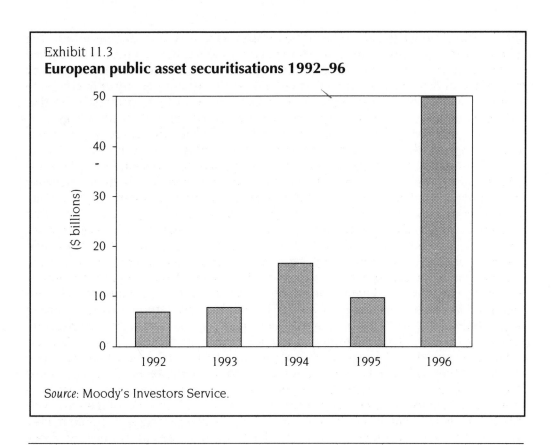

Exhibit 11.3
European public asset securitisations 1992–96

Source: Moody's Investors Service.

Exhibit 11.4
Percentage European asset type 1992–96 (as a percentage)

	1992	1993	1994	1995	1996
Mortgages	28	32	39	39	14
Credit cards	–	–	3	10	6
Vehicles	13	4	2	3	2
Aircraft	18	–	6	–	9
Bank loans	27	39	6	9	19
Consumer loans	13	18	28	30	4
Leases	–	4	1	–	1
Public sector	–	3	–	–	7
Corporate loans	–	–	–	1	12
Trains	–	–	–	–	5
Other	1	–	15	8	21
Total	100	100	100	100	100

Source: Moody's Investors Service.

303

Interestingly, mortgage-backed securities (MBS) have played a leading role in the European securitisation market, much the same as was true in the US. Asset-backed securities (ABS) also include longer-term securitisations which are collateralised by similar maturity financings such as leases and term loans on property or to corporate or government credits. Asset-backed commercial paper (ABCP), by contrast, is used to finance shorter-term consumer and credit card loans and receivables financings.

The slow growth of securitisation in Europe (despite the spurt in 1996) has reflected yet another peculiarity of this market: liquidity. Europe is overbanked, a condition exacerbated by the liberalisation of transnational banking within the EU which began in 1992. Please recall that securitisation only works if there is a need for it. In other words, there have to be imperfections in the existing system. High liquidity is good news for borrowers, but it also means that lending margins are so thin that potential savings (if any at all) from securitisation will probably be insufficient to justify the expenses related to setting up the necessary structures. The 1970s and 1980s were both characterised by easy money within the international banking system. During the earlier period, much of the liquidity took the form of petro-dollars which were recycled to oil importing nations. This period ended abruptly in 1982 with the Third World debt crisis. After a brief hiatus, liquidity returned to the markets supported in large part by the Japanese banking system and their surfeit of deposits which accumulated due to continuous balance of trade surpluses. This bubble burst with the decline of the Tokyo Stock Exchange during 1990 and the monetary tightening in most other OECD countries in response to inflation fears. Property values plummeted and many companies experienced hard times or worse. Hence, the international markets have experienced a succession of boom/bust periods with respect to their overall liquidity position. Such volatility discourages stable market growth and has consequently constrained the growth of securitisations. By 1996, liquidity had returned again to the markets, but not to a level which had previously stoked the inflationary furnace. The future of securitisations will rely in part on the skill of the central bankers to control monetary growth so that economies can expand without overheating. Additionally, there will need to be greater harmonisation of European laws, tax and accounting policies to form a coherent framework within which securitisation can thrive. Such harmonisation will assist greatly in achieving the objective of homogeneity so fundamental to securitisation structures.

Mechanics

It has been often repeated that securitisations are complex. Part of this complexity derives from the establishment of the special purpose vehicle or SPV, frequently in a tax-free part of the world. Also, one must ensure that the SPV (be it a corporation, partnership or trust) is bankruptcy remote. This means essentially that the SPV is a stand-alone entity and therefore immune from external credit risks. The cashflows within the SPV need to be structured so that the SPV can meet all its obligations to pay interest and principal to its security holders on a timely basis. Structuring must be done with great precision and an agent(s), typically a trustee, has to be appointed to administer the programme. All this needs to be documented with a web of interlocking legal agreements. Then there are the related questions of tax and accounting (and, increasingly, the issue of capital risk weighting as imposed by the relevant central banks). These matters will vary according to the jurisdiction where investors are resident. Considerable background research has to be made before a securitisation is ready for marketing.

However, even before approaching potential investors the financial engineer needs to be confident about the quality of his product. Frequently, too, the product will be rated and the relevant agency(ies) will be likewise need to be convinced of the credit standing of the deal overall.

Now, almost every securitisation deal has some quirk (frequently there are multiple quirks). Each of these impacts on the credit standing of the programme, and it is the job of the financial engineer to find solutions. Returning to the case of the nursing home, one problem with that securitisation is that the US government regularly conducts audits of healthcare providers (like nursing homes) to ensure that moneys are being well spent and invoicing and so on is done in accordance with proper procedure. If a problem is found then the US government has a claim against the nursing home. The fly in the ointment is that the government reserves the right to collect its claim by setting it off against moneys already owed (in the form of receivables) to the nursing home. It does not matter whether these receivables are the ones being queried because the right of set-off applies to all receivables (the legitimate and questionable ones alike). What happens, then, if these receivables have just been sold through a securitisation programme and are now being held in an SPV for the benefit of third party investors? You have real problems. And, the last thing an SPV's trustee wants to do is to get into an argument with the US government over the billing procedure of a nursing home located somewhere in middle America. What is the solution?

What one tries to do is to avoid the problem in the first instance. For instance, the company (called the originator) which acquires the receivables initially may be required to do due diligence on the nursing home to establish that it has a good track record with the relevant government agencies. An accounting firm might also be asked to double check this background information and have a look at the nursing home's internal procedures. Furthermore, the nursing home will routinely be asked to give representations and warranties about its compliance with government regulations. If there is a major problem then these representations and warranties may not be worth much (ie should the nursing home experience financial difficulty, there may not be much point in suing). Finally, the financial engineer, and/or the rating agency, may determine the above safeguards are insufficient to provide reasonable certainty of adequate cashflows to the SPV. An extra safety cushion may need to be added. This is called credit enhancement and it takes a variety of forms.

The purpose of credit enhancement is to absorb any reasonably predictable shortfalls in cashflows to the SPV. Naturally, one adopts a conservative approach when forecasting possible shortfalls. It is far preferable to be safe than sorry. When doing this forecasting a variety of scenarios can be examined, with each of these frequently based on industry (or an individual company's) experience with write-offs, set-offs or other credit losses. The analysis can be pushed to an extreme which is colourfully termed 'crash testing'. This means that you take the statistical possibility of a set off (or a loss) being incurred to a worst case scenario where the odds against are, say, one in a million. Then you see whether there is still enough cashflow to the SPV. If there is not, more credit enhancement will need to be added to make up the difference.

Credit enhancement can take the form of simple cash, possibly structured as subordinated debt. This is called a 'senior/sub' structure, with the third party investors holding the senior investment securities. The 'sub' portion acts as a first loss cushion because it absorbs 100% of all losses until it is entirely exhausted. In practice, the 'sub' portion typically remains intact and is returned to the provider when the programme is terminated. Cash is a scarce commodity so this may be replaced by a letter of credit or a standby guarantee, so long as the creditworthiness of these instruments is reliable. It is important to note that financial analysis of a securitisation structure frequently follows the weak link theory. The strength of the programme overall is determined to be only as strong as the weakest link in the cashflow chain and related credit support. This summary is an over-simplification. However, there is an important degree of truth in it.

Another popular form of credit enhancement is termed 'over-collateralisation'. This means that less than the full face value of collateral purchased is advanced, say, to the nursing home. If there is a difficulty, then the over-collateralised margin can be used to absorb the loss. Over-collateralisation is particularly effective if the SPV has acquired a reasonable volume of receivables from the nursing home and the right of set-off against the over-collateralised margin applies to all receivables purchased from that nursing home.

The financial engineer needs to exercise care, however, that limitations are placed on doing too much business with a single provider of receivables. This is called concentration risk. If a lot of business were done with a single nursing home which subsequently experienced financial difficulties, that could have a devastating impact on the overall cashflows to the SPV. Securitisation relies on diversification of risk. This is sometimes referred to as the Rule of Large Numbers. If you have a large enough sample of assets (or customers, like nursing homes) within a specific category, then the behaviour of the sample will mirror the behaviour of the overall asset category itself. The sample size has to be sufficiently large, for instance, to conduct the crash tests referred to above.

Seen another way, concentration risk needs to be limited. Frequently, this is achieved by capping the amount of business done with a single customer or category of customers to a set percentage of the total programme size. One nursing home may, for instance, be limited to selling the SPV up to only three per cent of all receivables then owned by the SPV. Other limitations can also be placed on purchases of receivables by the SPV to assure such objectives as geographic and industry diversification.

Financial engineers have a further arrow in their quiver. This is called excess spread. As mentioned previously, securitisations take advantage of market imperfections. They aim, for example, to provide finance in situations where alternative funding (if it is available at all) can only be attracted at an exorbitant cost. That does not necessarily mean that a securitisation always provides cheap money to the borrower (just cheaper money). Securitisation can represent a reasonably good deal for the borrower at the same time that it generates for itself (or its creators) a reasonable stream of profits. Excess spread refers to profitability within a securitisation programme. Of course, some spread is already earmarked to cover the set-up costs of the structure and the ongoing expenses, such as the trustee's fees. Typically, though, there is something left over. The financial engineer may claim all or part of this or alternatively, it may be retained in the SPV. If it is kept by the SPV it will accumulate over time and act in the same manner as the cash cushion mentioned earlier.

Finally, if all the above mentioned examples of credit enhancement have been tried and are still found wanting, or if it is decided to deploy a variety of enhancements rather than rely on one alone, the financial engineer can always buy credit insurance. Credit insurance is provided by institutions called monoline insurers. As the name implies, they focus on one thing only: the insurance cover for financial risks. The monolines themselves are virtually all rated triple-A by both Moody's and Standard & Poor's. Hence, they can upgrade virtually any financial structure to the highest credit level possible. This they do by insuring the risk (called 'wrapping') of a specific programme. Insurance wraps are like any other form of insurance. It pays to read the fine print. However, if the wrapped programme is subsequently rated by one of the established agencies, there will be a double check to ensure that the coverage provided is up to standard. It should also be remembered that all insurance costs money (called a premium). Monoline insurers are no exceptions. A financial engineer needs to be careful that the yield savings achieved by arranging an insurance wrap, justifies the cost of the wrap itself.

Conduits

No discussion of asset securitisation would be complete without a description of conduits. These curious creatures have proliferated in the US domestic capital markets and have also migrated across the Atlantic. They have a special relevance to the Euromarkets.

It is axiomatic that securitisations need to achieve a critical mass before they cover their own structure-related costs. The problem with European markets is that they are relatively small and fragmented (when compared to the US). There is a limit, therefore, to the number of European entities which can contemplate a stand-alone securitisation programme. How then does one service the several potential borrowers who are smaller but who would still benefit from securitisation? The answer is create a 'multi-originator' programme, also known as a conduit.

Conduits are ideally suited for small scale securitisation programmes. They are constructed so they will take a wide range of asset types and then fund themselves in a manner which matches these asset types. For example, short-term receivables purchased would be funded by the conduit issuing commercial paper (also short-term), while longer-term leases would be funded by the conduit's issuance of medium-term notes. Matching of assets with liabilities can also be accomplished with elaborate interest rate and currency swaps. The conduit acts like a giant hopper into which various shapes and sizes of financial assets are dumped.

What matters to third party investors is the credit quality of the conduit's own securities. These are invariably rated. Few people can be expected to understand the diverse asset categories all mixed together in the conduit without a rating. What the engineers of the conduit do is to agree guidelines with the rating agencies about the nature and amount of the different assets which can be accepted by the conduit. The ratings will remain in place so long as these guidelines are adhered to religiously.

Invariably securitised asset programmes (even small ones) require some form of credit enhancement. This is, of course, essential if the ratings are going to be maintained. Credit enhancement can be achieved in the context of a conduit in one of two ways (or by a combination of the two). The most straightforward route is to credit enhance each of the individual programmes prior to their being dumped into the conduit hopper. Alternatively, the conduit itself might be credit enhanced, say, with a cash cushion or a letter of credit. The advantage of this latter route is that it is a once for all time enhancement and, thus, allows for simple and speedy acquisitions of different asset pools. The drawback of this approach is that frequently the conduit will be 'over' credit enhanced. It would need to satisfy the rating agencies so that it can accept worse case-type assets and still retain its ratings. As mentioned previously, credit enhancement is costly; so it should be used in an economical fashion. The optimal approach is probably to bring the different securitised programmes individually up to investment grade (ie triple-B or better) and then feed them into the conduit (itself marginally enhanced) so that the prime rating objective is eventually achieved.

Experimentation with conduits and other innovative securitisation structures evidence a trend towards increasing sophistication and utility. Growth in European securitisations has been slower than in the US. However, the causes of this are easily identifiable. Consequently, the process towards international securitisations may not be as fast as would suit everyone, but its growing importance in the Euromarkets is an indisputable fact.

Mortgage-backed securities

A highly specialised but huge sector of the securitisation market is that for mortgages. They represent one of the largest category of bonds in the US and are an important feature of other national securities markets where laws and commercial considerations have permitted their securitisation. This section will concentrate on the securitisation of US mortgages as they have evidenced considerable innovation and because they are the most widely held and traded mortgage-backed securities in the international markets.

Background

The practice of owning and buying/selling property rights can be traced back to the earliest legal systems. The word 'mortgage' derives from the word 'gage', or pledge, and the Norman French word 'mort' which means dead or locked. Hence, a mortgage is a locked pledge relating to a piece of property.

As centuries passed, the concept and the use of mortgages broadened enormously. In the US, a particularly active period was the 'Roaring Twenties' when a booming real estate market fuelled parallel markets in both first and second mortgages. With the crash of 1929, the real estate market plummeted along with the stock exchange. Deflation was rampant and assets of all descriptions lost value. Mortgage lenders were, of course, hit. Soon there was little in the way of liquid funds available for new or even replacement mortgages. By 1933, the US government had little alternative but to establish an agency called the Home Owners' Loan Corporation (HOLC) which refinanced defaulted mortgages. This relieved some of the pressure felt by the mortgage lending industry nationwide. HOLC developed the first type of amortising house loan, which utilised monthly payments to reduce the principal amount outstanding as well as to pay interest. Such was the stability of this instrument that HOLC was able to extend its maturity to 30 years. This remains the norm in the US.

In most cases, long-term mortgages are also fixed rate and a level payment pattern is typically followed. This means that the monthly mortgage payments made by the home owner remain constant from the commencement of the mortgage through to its final maturity. As both interest and principal repayments are made in the one monthly payment, a large part of this payment is made up chiefly of interest in the early years and then principal in the later years.

With the twin pressures of interest rate volatility and competition in the mortgage industry, different forms of mortgages have been marketed. These include floating rate mortgages, partly floating/partly fixed mortgages and low early stage payment/later step-up mortgages. Shorter maturity mortgages have also increased in popularity.

Together with stimulating primary mortgage lending, the US government also took action to encourage liquidity by creating a secondary market in mortgages. This was accomplished by other US agencies which guaranteed the interest and principle amounts of the mortgages they packaged and sold on to the investors. Currently, the US government agencies account for the great majority of the secondary market in mortgages. The original form of securitisation was called a pass-through security. This security represented a participation in a pool of mortgages. The cashflows (interest and principal payments) of these pools are usually guaranteed by one of three US agencies. The first of these agencies is the Government National Mortgage Association (GNMA), known popularly as Ginnie Mae. This agency was created in 1968 as an amendment to the National Housing Act. Ginnie Mae is established as a government corporation within the Department of Housing and Urban Development. The mortgage pools assembled by Ginnie Mae are composed of mortgages insured by the FHA (Federal Housing Administration) or guaranteed by the VA (Veterans' Administration) or the FMHA (Farmers Home Administration). Due to its government ownership, Ginnie Mae (and its guaranteed mortgage pools) are backed by the full faith and credit of the US government as to the timely payments of principal and interest.

The second US mortgage agency is called the Federal National Mortgage Association (FNMA), known popularly as Fannie Mae. This agency was established in 1938 as a wholly-owned US government corporation. In 1968, the original entity was split in two: Ginnie Mae which remains in 100% government ownership and Fannie Mae which by 1970 became a private corporation. Although not explicitly guaranteed by the US government, the obligations of Fannie Mae are rated triple-A as they are viewed as benefiting from the moral backing of the US government.

The third US mortgage agency is The Federal Home Loan Mortgage Corporation (FHLMC), known popularly as Freddie Mac. This agency was founded in 1970 to increase the availability of mortgage credit by facilitating the development of a national secondary market in mortgages. As a government-sponsored enterprise, Freddie Mac's obligations (like those of Fannie Mae) are rated triple-A due to the implicit support of the US government.

Due to the volume of agency-backed mortgage pass-through securities, now totalling in excess of $1 trillion, efforts have been made to structure the cashflows of these securities to make them attractive to as wide a range of institutional investors as possible. One early effort in this direction was to divide or strip the interest element of these securities into a separate class of investment called an IO or interest only class. The remaining part of these securities was the PO or principal only class. Such stripping was first undertaken in 1987. Often restructurings have also been implemented through a sophisticated form of securitisation called a CMO or collateralised mortgage obligation, which is a security which evidences beneficial interest in a pool of mortgages or other pass-through mortgage-backed securities.

Collateralised mortgage obligations – CMOs

CMOs were first issued in 1983. As mentioned previously, their structuring reflects the maturity preferences of different types of institutions. Commercial banks, for example, have a clear desire for shorter to medium-term assets whilst pension funds require the certainty of long-term returns to meet their investment objectives. The solution created was to divide CMOs up into 'tranches' (frequently called 'classes') of bonds which reflected such maturity preferences.

Another concern (related to maturity preference) was the question of prepayments. All pools of mortgages have some rate of prepayment. The uncertainty is the speed at which prepayments will occur. One way to approach the prepayment question is to identify the major influences which drive prepayments. Prepayments occur when a house or other property is sold, either voluntarily or involuntarily. Simply moving house produces a prepayment. So, the habit of 'trading up' or 'trading down', say in advance of retirement, effects the pattern of prepayments. Equally, less fortunate occurrences such as divorce or insolvency can also boost prepayments. Elaborate econometric models have been devised to identify US regional shifts in prepayments behaviour in response to changing levels of growth and prosperity.

Another major cause of prepayment is the quite rational desire of the mortgage borrower to reduce his cost of funding. In the case of traditional fixed rate mortgages, there is a very strong economic incentive to save money by refinancing when interest rates move lower. The rate of refinancing soared during the early 1990s reaching previously inconceivable levels by the autumn of 1992.

Why worry about prepayments? One obvious concern is reinvestment risk. If an existing investment prepays a replacement investment must be found, hopefully one which provides an equivalent return. If prepayments are driven by falling interest rates, as they were in the autumn of 1992, then the chances of finding an acceptable replacement yield are slim indeed. Additionally, many mortgage pools (evidenced by CMOs) are acquired at a premium or a price above par. When prepayments occur they return only par, not the premium. Worse still, although the US agency credit still supports the CMOs, it covers only the par portion of the investment. Thus, when the premium is lost there is no way of recovering it. Many CMO investors have lost considerable amounts of money due to prepayments.

For some years there has been a popular prepayment model which is used as a guide to the performance of mortgage-backed securities developed by the Public Securities Association and which became known as the PSA model. The 'normal' prepayment speed is assumed to be 100% PSA. Half the speed is 50% PSA and double the speed is 200% PSA and so on. Within the PSA model itself there are assumed to be different prepayment rates over the life of a mortgage (reflecting the observable fact that prepayments in early periods are slow and only pick-up in speed as they stretch out to two to 2½ years). Within the model the prepayment rate is assumed to be 0.2% annualised rate for the first month. With each successive month, the annual rate climbs by a further 0.2% until the 2½ year point is reached and the additive prepayment rate of 6% is attained. The 6% annual rate is then assumed to carry on for all following periods.

By the autumn of 1992, the PSA rates of some CMOs rose well above 1,000% PSA. This was not the fault of the model but rather a failure of the market to anticipate the powerful incentive to refinance produced by substantially lower long-term interest rates. The PSA model, however, remains in wide use today. Indeed, CMOs are frequently quoted at different PSA rates so that investors can easily assess the impact on yield and maturity of varying rates of prepayments.

CMOs have acquired a variety of structures again to suit the preferences of selective investor groups. Mortgages may have the image of being somewhat old-fashioned or pedestrian. However, the exciting nature of the CMO market is aptly captured in colourful expressions such as the phrase 'slicing and dicing'. This refers to the structuring or carving up of mortgage cashflows. One example of slicing and dicing was the creation of floating rate CMOs (many of which took Libor as their applicable index). Such an innovation had clear appeal to international banks which fund themselves in the Libor deposit markets. It has to be remembered, though, that traditional US mortgages are fixed rate. So, the creation of a floating rate instrument by slicing and dicing also created the necessity of a mirror image instrument whose interest rate movements offset those of the normal floater. This need gave birth to a new instrument called the 'inverse floater'. If short-term interest rates rose then the normal floater's coupon would rise accordingly. The inverse floater's coupon would, however, decline, cancelling out the other's rise and producing a net result which was the original fixed rate coupon of the underlying mortgage pool.

Inverse floaters are typically highly geared instruments which results from their construction. The interest paying mechanism of an inverse floater is exemplified below:-

64 – 8 x Libor

If, say, Libor equals 7% then the inverse floater would pay 64-56% or 8%. Should Libor itself rise to 8% then the inverse floater would theoretically yield zero. However, inverse floaters typically benefit from a floor value below which its interest rate cannot drop. This also necessitates its normal floating rate counterpart to have a cap which keeps its rate from rising too high. At all times, the interest rates payable by the two different types of floaters needs to offset one another.

The gearing possibilities of the inverse floater are easy to see. If, in the above example, interest rates dropped from 7% to 6% (a mere 1% decline) then the yield of the inverse floater will rise from 8% to 16%. The volatility of this instrument makes it unsuitable for the unsophisticated or the faint of heart. Inverse floaters do, however, have their uses in sophisticated hedging strategies. Given the high gearing (8:1 in the example above), they are very helpful in protecting a large portfolio of normal floating rate securities which would otherwise suffer coupon declines during a period of falling short-term interest rates. Only one inverse floater, as in the above illustration, needs to be acquired for every eight regular floaters held in the portfolio.

Other CMO structures responded to the need to hedge against prepayment uncertainty. A new class of security called a PAC or Planned Amortisation Class, was devised. This innovation also created the need for a companion instrument (actually called a 'companion bond') which was required either to give up its entitlement to principal repayment (to meet the PAC's amortisation schedule during periods of low prepayments) or to absorb greater principal prepayments (during periods of high prepayments). Companion bonds, thus, vary in their own maturity as prepayment rates either slow down or speed up. A new type of risk was thereby created called 'extension risk'. This is of particular concern when interest rates are rising and simultaneously the floating rate CMOs interest rate cap is hit. The instrument's maturity can extend out for, say, 20-plus years (because high interest rates discourage refinancing activity) precisely at a time when the rate cap begins to hurt. As a consequence of this type of risk, companion CMOs usually have to offer a premium yield return.

There are a variety of PAC bond structures, including TACs (Targeted Amortisation Class) and SMRTs (Stabilised Mortgage Reduction Term Bonds). There is a clear advantage to understanding the composition and dynamics of each of these types of instruments. Additionally, other innovative structures exist like superfloaters, super POs and CMO residuals, merit careful evaluation.

GLOSSARY

Accrued interest
The interest earned on a bond since the latest interest payment date, but not yet paid.

Active markets
Those which are frequently traded or trading.

Agreement among managers
A legal document forming major underwriting banks into a syndicate for a new issue and giving the lead manager the authority to act on behalf of the group. The agreement also serves to define relationships between managers.

All or none
A condition that the full amount of an order to buy, or sell, securities be executed at an agreed price – a lesser amount is unacceptable.

Allotment
The amount of a new issue (ie number of bonds) given to a syndicate member by the lead manager.

Amortisation
Gradual repayment of a debt over time, for example, through the operation of a sinking or purchase fund.

Announcement
In a new bond issue, the day on which a release is sent to prospective syndicate members, describing the offering and inviting underwriters (and sometimes selling group members) to join the syndicate.

Arbitrage
General term for transactions involving moving capital from one market to another, from one security to another or from one maturity to another, in the hope of realising a higher yield or capital gain.

Asked
The price level at which sellers offer securities to buyers – see Bid.

At or better
As regards a buy order for securities, purchasing at the specified price or under; for a sell order, selling at the specified price or above.

Authorised person
An institution (or individual) which is authorised under Chapter III of Part I of the Financial Services Act 1986.

Average life
The weighted average of the maturities of all the bonds in a given issue after taking into account the amortisation provisions (ie reductions by sinking or purchase fund).

Away
An action (market, quote, trade) originating elsewhere or being offered by another dealer.

Axe (to grind)
Referring to a trading situation, eg a dealer with an axe to grind usually has a long or short position he wishes to dispose of.

Balloon maturity
The last bonds of an issue maturing in a substantially larger amount than those of earlier maturities.

Basis point
One one-hundredth of a per cent (ie 0.01%), typically used in expressing bond yield differentials (7.50% – 7.15% = 0.35% or 35 basis points).

Bear market
A period of generally falling securities prices and pessimistic attitudes.

Bearer bond
A bond for which the only evidence of ownership is possession.

Beneficial ownership
The ownership of securities or other investments through a nominee: a technique used to avoid revealing the identity of the ultimate owner.

Bid
The price level at which buyers offer to acquire securities from sellers.

Block
A larger than usual number of bonds trading as a single unit.

Bond
A negotiable certificate evidencing indebtedness-a legal contract sold by an issuer promising to pay the holder its face value plus amounts of interest at future dates.

Bond house
A firm which underwrites, distributes and deals in bonds as one of its primary activities.

Book loss/gain
The difference between a given security's cost and its market value, so far unrealised.

Book value
A given security's value as it appears in the holder's accounting records.

Bought deal
A new issue procedure whereby a lead manager acting on its own or together with co-managers commits to underwrite an entire offering of securities on previously agreed fixed terms: particularly coupon level and new issue price.

Breakpoint
The term indicating a new issue is trading in the secondary market at a discount in the amount of, or greater than, the selling concession or re-offered amount.

Broker
An individual or institution representing buyers or sellers of securities without itself owning securities. Acting as an agent as opposed to a principal in a transaction.

Bulldog bonds
Foreign bonds offered in the UK domestic market.

Bullet
A borrowing with no amortisation. Repayment of principal occurs only at maturity. Also called bullet maturity.

Bull market
A period of generally rising securities prices and optimistic attitudes.

Busted convertible
A convertible issue with a negligible conversion value due to the low market price of the underlying equity.

Buy-in
The closing of a purchase/sale contract by a buyer purchasing securities in the open market if the seller is not in compliance with the terms of the contract, for the account and liability of the initial prospective seller.

Buying ahead
Acquiring bonds in the open market for a sinking fund in advance or in excess of current requirements. Purchases pursuant to an option to double are not considered buying ahead.

Call
The optional right of an issuer to redeem bonds before their stated maturity, at a given price on a given date. Also, a contract allowing the holder to buy a given number

of securities from the issuer of such a contract at a fixed price for a given period of time.

Cedel Bank
One of the two major organisations in the Eurobond market which clears, or handles the physical exchange of, securities and stores securities. Based in Luxembourg, the company is owned by several shareholding banks and operates through a network of co-operative arrangements in various national markets. See also Euroclear.

Certificate of deposit
A negotiable, interest bearing, instrument evidencing a time deposit with a commercial bank. Also referred to as a CD.

Clean price
The price at which securities are bought and sold in the market, without adjustment for accrued interest. See dirty price.

Clear
The formal completion of a trade, brought about by proper delivery of securities by the seller and proper payment by the buyer.

Clearing system
An organisation with which securities may be deposited for safe-keeping and through which purchase/sale transactions may be handled. The two foremost systems in the Eurobond market are Euroclear and Cedel Bank.

Closing day
In a new bond issue, the day when securities are delivered against payment by syndicate members participating in the offering.

CMO
Collateralised Mortgage Obligation. A financial instrument which aggregates different cashflows from a mortgage enabling securities to be sold to a wide range of institutions with differing investment parameters.

Co-manager
A member of the management group of a securities offering other than the lead manager(s).

Commercial paper
Unsecured corporate debt with a short-term maturity used chiefly in the US capital market and sold on a discount basis.

Commissions
Fees received by co-managers and other market participants in connection with the issuing, buying or selling of securities.

Common stock
Shares, usually taking the form of certificates, which represent part-ownership in a

commercial enterprise, and which typically carry specified rights as to voting and dividend payments.

Conduit
A form of asset securitisation suitable for a variety of collateral with a principal amount too small individually to justify a stand-alone issue.

Confirmation
A formal notification from a dealer or broker to a second party giving relevant information concerning a trade made by the second party.

Contract
Unit of trading. Also, bilateral agreement between the buyer and seller of a transaction as defined by an exchange.

Conversion issue
A new issue of bonds timed to correspond with a maturing issue by the same borrower. The offering is structured in such a way that investors are given an incentive to exchange or convert the old issue into the new one.

Conversion premium or discount
The ratio, expressed as a percentage, of a convertible bond's market value to its discount conversion value (ie its value if converted into equity). A premium occurs when the conversion value of the security is lower than the market value. A discount occurs when the conversion value is higher than the market value.

Conversion price
The share price at which the principal amount of a convertible bond may be used to acquire common stock in or owned by the issuing company.

Conversion ratio
The number of shares which may be acquired upon the conversion of a convertible bond. The ratio is calculated as bond principal amount divided by conversion price.

Convertible bond
A bond convertible at the holder's option (or forced by the borrower) into other securities of, or owned by, the issuing entity, typically common stock.

Convertible FRN
A floating rate note which is convertible into a fixed rate bond, typically, at the option of the investor.

Convexity
The actual price movement of a bond as yields change compared to that movement estimated by dollar duration. A graphic representation shows the relationship to be convex. See dollar duration.

Cost of carry
Interest, storage and handling costs of owning a commodity or security until a future delivery date.

Counterparty
An institution (or client) with which another institution has agreed to effect a transaction. The term counterparty is frequently used in swap transactions.

Coupon
The stated rate of interest on a bond. One of a series of actual certificates attached to the bond, each evidencing interest owed and payable at a specific date.

Covenant
Agreement by a borrower contained in the documents of a new issue and legally binding upon the issuer over the life of the issue, unless otherwise stated, to perform certain acts such as the timely provision of financial statements or to refrain from certain acts such as incurring further indebtedness beyond an agreed level.

Cover
Buying securities to eliminate a short position.

Coverage
An indicator of the safety margin for payment of debt service. Often, the ratio of pre-tax income plus interest expense to long and short-term debt interest requirements.

Credit enhancement
The use of various techniques to improve the credit quality of certain transactions, typically asset securitisations.

Cross-default
A covenant by an issuer or a guarantor that an event of default will be deemed to have occurred in a financing if a default does occur in any of its other financings.

Cum
Means 'with', therefore the usage cum-dividend and cum-warrant.

Currency-linked bond
A bond whose payments of principal and interest are valued by reference to one currency though actually made in another.

Current coupon
A bond trading at or near par.

Current yield
A measurement of return to a bondholder, calculated as the ratio of coupon to market price and expressed as a percentage. Sometimes referred to as running yield.

Dealer
An individual or institution which buys and sells securities which it owns for its own account.

Debt ratio
The ratio of debt to equity in a commercial enterprise. A measure of the financial stability of a company and its ability to increase its level of total borrowings.

Debt service
Payments of principal and interest required on a debt over a given period.

Default
The non-performance of a stated obligation. The non-payment by the issuer of interest or principal on a bond or the non-performance of a covenant.

Delayed delivery
A provision in a new issue permitting certain individuals or institutions to acquire and take delivery of specified amounts of securities on a stated date(s) after the original offering is closed.

Derivatives
A catch-all term referring to constituent elements derived from financial instruments (such as type of interest or currency or call/put options) which can be traded and employed independently in the development of sophisticated financing strategies.

Dirty price
The traded price of a security adjusted to reflect accrued interest up to the value date.

Disclaimer
Typically a statement made by a lead manager acting as representative for an underwriting syndicate, and contained in offering documents, which asserts among other things that certain information provided in the prospectus was supplied by the borrower and therefore is not the responsibility of the managers or underwriters. A notice or statement intending to limit or avoid potential legal liability.

Discount
The computation of the present value of a given stream of future cash payments; also, the difference between the price of a bond and its face value, expressed as a percentage, for issues trading below par.

Discount basis
A means of structuring non-coupon bearing securities so that a yield return may be provided by offering the securities at less than par and later redeeming them at their full principal amount. The capital gain realised on redemption should equate with the interest return for a comparable maturity if the security had been coupon bearing.

Discount bonds
Bonds trading below par.

Dividend
Payments distributed by a corporation among its shareholders, on a pro rata basis. Preferred stock dividends are usually fixed while common stock dividends vary and their payment depends on prevailing business conditions.

Documentation
In a new bond issue, the offering circular or prospectus describing the borrower and the securities being offered; also, the underwriting contracts and other agreements, etc. Entered into during the offering.

Dollar duration
The expression of duration (see below) in dollar terms. Dollar duration estimates the dollar change in the value of a bond as a function of a change in yield.

Double taxation treaty
An agreement between two countries intended to avoid or limit the double taxation of income, under the terms of which an investor with tax liabilities in both countries can either apply for a reduction of taxes imposed by one country, or can credit taxes paid in that country against tax liabilities in the other.

Drop-lock
A hybrid form of floating rate note which converts into a fixed rate bond once interest rates drop to a predetermined level.

Due diligence
Detailed review of a borrower's overall position, conducted by representatives of the lead manager, often with the assistance of legal counsel. Due diligence is normally performed in conjunction with the preparation of the documentation for a new issue.

Duration
A sophisticated calculation of a bond's average life which takes into account interest payments as well as principal repayments. Technically, duration is the weighted average life of all cash flows arising from a bond.

Equity
See Common stock.

Eurobond
A debt instrument denominated in one of the several Eurocurrencies and sold in the international bond market.

Euroclear
One of the two major organisations in the Eurobond market which clears, or handles, the physical exchange of securities and stores securities. Based in Brussels, the company is owned by several banks and operated under contract by Morgan Guaranty Trust Company of New York. See also Cedel Bank.

Euro-commercial paper
Unsecured corporate debt with a short maturity and structured to appeal to large financial institutions active in the Eurocurrency market.

Eurocurrency
Any currency held by a non-resident of the country of that particular currency.

Eurodollar
US dollars held by a non-resident of the US, usually in the form of a deposit with a commercial bank outside the US, including deposits at foreign branches of US banks.

Ex
Means 'without', therefore the usage ex-dividend and ex-warrants.

Exchange
An established investment market where securities and derivatives are traded. Contrast with over-the-counter market.

Exercise or strike price
Price at which a person may buy or sell the underlying contract upon the exercise of an option.

Extendible
A type of Eurobond which gives an investor the option of extending its initial maturity for a given number of years. If the option is not exercised, the bond is repaid at the earlier maturity.

Face value
The amount, exclusive of interest or premium, due to a security holder at maturity and inscribed on the face of the security. Also referred to as par value.

Fail
The failure to deliver or receive payment or securities in proper form by the agreed settlement date of a trade.

Federal (Fed) Funds
Deposits, mostly by member commercial banks, at the US Federal Reserve. Payments in Fed Funds are available and good, (eg can earn interest) on the day payment is made.

Federal Funds rate
The overnight rate of interest at which US Fed Funds are traded among financial institutions; regarded as a key indicator of all US domestic interest rates.

Firm order
A buy or sell order for securities that can be completed without further confirmation during a given time period.

Fiscal agency agreement
In a new bond issue, an agreement setting out certain obligations of the issuer and appointing a fiscal agent.

Fiscal agent
In a new bond issue, a commercial bank appointed by the borrower to undertake certain duties related to the new issue, such as assisting in the payments of interest and principal, replacement of lost or damaged securities and destruction of coupons and bonds after payments have been made thereon. While performing certain clerical duties, the fiscal agent does not assume the fiduciary responsibilities of a trustee appointed under a trust deed.

Floating rate CDs
Certificates of deposit which pay interest on a floating rate basis tied to certain short-term interest rates. Also referred to as FRCDs.

Floating rate notes (FRNs)
Bonds without a fixed rate of interest, the coupon being set periodically according to a pre-determined formula typically tied to a short-term interest rate in an appropriate market.

Foreign bond
A bond issue for a foreign borrower offered in the domestic capital market of a particular country and denominated in the currency of that country.

Forward
For settlement on a mutually agreed future date.

FSA
Financial Services Act 1986, sometimes referred to as the Act. The FSA established the regulatory principles which govern the securities markets in the United Kingdom.

Fungible securities
Identical securities which are kept in a clearing system where the book-keeping is such that no specific bonds are assigned to customer accounts by their serial numbers. Only the aggregate number of identical bonds in the system and the total amount of customer holdings of such bonds are controlled.

Futures
All contracts covering the purchase and sale of financial instruments or commodities for future delivery on a commodity exchange.

Gilts
Sterling-denominated securities issued by the UK Treasury. Also referred to as gilt-edged securities.

Global bond
A temporary certificate representing the whole of a new bond issue, which remains outstanding only until definitive bonds are available and certain legal requirements allow. See Lock-up.

Good delivery
A delivery of unmutilated securities in which all legal and procedural matters are in proper order and which will be accepted by a transfer/clearing agent.

Good value
A payment for securities in cash or immediately available funds.

Grey market
The market in a new bond issue prior to formal offering.

Gross spread
The sum of the management fees and the selling concession (or re-offered amount) on a bond issue, usually expressed in percentage terms.

Gross-up
In Eurobond issues, additional payments made by a borrower to compensate for withholding tax or similar levies which reduce return to investors.

Hedging
A device used by traders and sophisticated investors to reduce loss due to market fluctuations. This is done by counter-balancing a current sale or purchase by another, usually future, purchase or sale. The desired result is that the profit or loss on the current sale or purchase will be offset by the loss or profit on the future sale or purchase.

Inside market.
The market for a specific security defined by the highest bid and the lowest offering.

In syndicate
A new issue still subject to price and trading restrictions imposed by (and on) the syndicate.

Inter-bank rates
The bid and offered rates at which international banks place deposits with each other.

Interest Equalization Tax (IET)
A tax applied on securities issues of certain foreign borrowers offered within the US, intended to discourage such offerings. First applied in 1963, finally removed in 1974.

Interest rate differential
The difference in the rate of interest offered in two currencies for investments of identical credit and maturity.

Investment bank
Term applied to a financial institution (usually US) engaged in the issue of new securities, including management and underwriting of issues as well as securities trading and distribution.

IPMA
The International Primary Market Association. IPMA has done much to standardise new issue procedures and documentation. It also acts as a spokesman for the primary or new issue managers in their relationships with the various regulatory bodies.

ISMA
The International Securities Market Association which is a Designated Investment Exchange (DIE) for the purposes of the Financial Services Act 1986. ISMA has achieved much in defining and encouraging best practice in the secondary market for Euro-securities.

Issue
Any of a company's securities, such as stocks or bonds, or the act of distributing those securities to investors.

Issue price
The gross price (before allowances or commissions) placed on a new bond issue, expressed as a percentage of principal amount and usually varying from 98% to 102%.

Issuer
Any corporation or governmental unit which borrows money through the sale of securities.

Joint and several
An undertaking by different parties (eg co-managers) to cover or fulfil an obligation (eg to underwrite a new issue). Any failure by one or more of the parties does not excuse a remaining party from fulfilling the entire commitment. A joint but not several undertaking only obligates a party to fulfil its pre-determined share of the commitment.

Kassenvereine
Depositary banks which form the securities clearing system in Germany, similar to Euroclear and Cedel Bank.

Lead manager
In a new securities issue, the managing bank responsible for initiating the transaction with the borrower and for organising (or designating another to organise) the successful syndication and placement of the issue in the primary market.

LIFFE
The London International Financial Futures and Options Exchange.

Limit order
An order to execute a securities trade at a set price or better.

Liquidate
To sell.

Liquidity
The amount of investible funds in a specific market. Also, the ease with which specific securities can be purchased and sold without materially affecting their market price.

Listed (listing)
Referring to securities, trading on one or more securities exchanges.

Lock-up
New issue Eurobond procedures lasting 40 days and designed to prohibit the flowback of securities into the US, or their sale to US persons, during the period of initial distribution. Frequently involves the use of a global bond.

London Inter-bank Offered Rate (Libor)
The rate of interest offered on deposits with prime commercial banks operating in the London Eurocurrency market.

Long
To own securities; held for investment purposes or in anticipation of future price rises, or because of temporary inability to sell. Also referred to as a long position.

Management fee
That portion of the gross spread earned by the managers of a new issue.

Manager
One of the firms participating in the management group and underwriting all or a portion of a new issue (synonymous with co-manager).

Mandate
Authorisation from a borrower to proceed with a new bond issue on terms agreed with the lead manager.

Market-maker
Any securities trading firm or bond house making prices in an issue and prepared to deal at that price.

Maturity
The date on which a given debt security becomes payable to the holder in full.

Medium Term Note
Sometimes referred to as an MTN. This is a form of financing programme which allows for multiple issues in multiple currencies for maturities which range from 30 days to 30 years.

Middle price
The arithmetic mean of the bid and asked price.

Modified duration
Similar to dollar duration; the percentage change in the price of a bond for a unit change in yield.

Money market
The market for interbank deposits and certificates of deposit. Also used to refer to the market for highly liquid securities which have an initial maturity of less than one year.

Negative pledge
Undertaking by a borrower in a new issue (which undertaking extends throughout the life of the issue and which may be worded in a variety of ways) generally not to offer improved security arrangements to other investors in bonds of a similar status to that being issued, without offering the equivalent security to the holders of the new issue.

Net annual pick-up
Income a convertible bondholder receives in comparison to the income received if the bonds were converted into common stock and received the current stock dividend.

Nominal yield
The face yield of a bond; identical to the coupon's interest rate.

Nominee
An individual or institution holding a security in its own name for the benefit of a third party, used to preserve anonymity of ultimate ownership.

Non-callable
Cannot be redeemed by the issuer for a stated period of time from date of issue.

Note
A promise to pay. A written agreement, the issuer promising to pay the holder on a given date or on demand, a certain sum of money. The difference between notes and bonds is normally that of maturity, notes typically having a shorter life.

Odd lot
Any block of securities bid for or offered which is smaller than the standard lot size for the type of security. As defined by ISMA, an amount of bonds with a principal value of less than $100,000 nominal.

Offering circular
A document giving a description of a securities issue, including a complete statement of the terms of the issue and a description of the issuer as well as its historical and latest financial statements. Also referred to as a prospectus.

One-way market
A market consisting only of a firm bid or a firm offer.

Open order
A purchase or sale order at a stated price which is good until cancelled.

Option
A contract giving the holder the right to either buy from, or sell to, an issuer of such a contract a given number of securities at a given price within a specified time period (American option). European options may be exercised only at the time of expiry.

Option to double
A sinking fund provision, allowing the issuer to double the number of securities purchased by the fund at the call price.

Overbought
A market with potential for downward movement in prices. Indicates that securities' prices have risen more than they should have.

Oversold
A market with potential for upward movement of prices. Indicates that securities prices have fallen more than they should have.

Over-the-counter
Purchases and sales of securities taking place away from the stock exchanges. The Eurobond secondary market is largely an over-the-counter market.

Par
Price of 100% of a security's face value. Principal amount at which an issuer of bonds typically agrees to redeem its bonds at maturity.

Pari passu
Generally used in the context of securities ranking pari passu, ie equally in right of payment with each other.

Participation
An invitation (together with the related documents) to underwrite a certain principal amount of a new issue. Also the size of the underwriting commitment.

Paying agent
One of a group of banks responsible for paying the interest and principal of an issue.

Perpetuals
Bonds (historically FRNs) with no fixed maturity.

Placing power
Ability of a bank to sell or place a new bond issue.

Position
The holding by a dealer of any number of securities of a given issue(s), of either the securities themselves (ie long position) or of an obligation to deliver securities not owned (ie short position).

Power of attorney
The legal authority for one party to sign for and act on behalf of another party.

Praecipium
That portion of the management fee attributable to the lead manager in respect of his services before division among the co-managers.

Premium
For issues with prices greater than par value, the amount of the difference between par and the price.

Premium over investment value
An indication of the possible downside risk an investor assumes when purchasing a particular convertible bond. Expressed as a formula, the premium over investment value or the risk factor equals the market price of the bond minus its investment value (i.e. the value of the bond without its conversion feature) divided by the investment value.

Prepayment
A payment on a bond or loan made prior to the originally appointed date.

Present value
The current value of a given future cashflow stream, discounted at a given rate.

Pricing
In a new bond issue, the day when final terms are formalised prior to offering.

Primary market
The market for new issues.

Principal
Par value or face amount of a security, exclusive of any premium or interest. The basis for interest computations.

Private placement
European: an offer of securities made to a limited number of investors or a single investor. Generally not listed.

American: a debt issue offered to a limited number of sophisticated investors and not subject to the registration requirements of the US Securities Act of 1933. See Rule 144A.

Proposal
Any communication made by a bank to a prospective borrower setting forth the issue terms on which the bank would be prepared to lead manage a new offering.

Protect (protection)
Guaranteeing a customer the execution of a securities trade at a stated price. Also guaranteeing a manager or selling-group member a specific allotment of bonds in a new issue.

Public offering
European: an offer of securities to the general public, usually through a selling group of international banks which market securities to their clients. Normally listed.

American: a public distribution of securities which are registered under the US Securities Act of 1933.

Purchase fund
An arrangement under which an issuer undertakes to buy back or arrange to have bought back a certain principal amount of bonds if they are trading below a set price, usually par, during a specified period of time.

Put
A contract allowing the holder to sell a given number of securities back to the issuer of such a contract at a fixed price for a given period of time.

Quote
The market price of a given security.

Rally/recovery
An upward movement of prices following a decline.

Rating
A letter grade signifying a security's investment quality. The chief rating agencies are Moody's Investors Service and Standard & Poor's.

Redemption
Extinguishing a debt through cash payment. The contractual right of an issuer to exercise optional redemption. Also known as a call.

Redemption price
A price at which bonds may be redeemed, or called, at the issuer's option, prior to maturity (often at a slight premium over par).

Red herring
A trade term (primarily US) for a preliminary offering circular or prospectus (so called because of the red print around its borders) giving details of an expected securities offering but subject to change, the definitive offering document being the final offering circular.

Reference agency
An agreement appointing, and setting out the duties of, a reference agent as well as the procedure for calculating the rate of interest payable on a floating rate security.

Reference agent
In the case of floating rate securities and borrowings, a bank active in the Eurocurrency deposit market appointed to determine (on the basis of deposit rates quoted to it by other appointed reference banks) and, in some cases, to publish the rate of interest payable during the next interest period.

Refinancing
Repaying existing debt and issuing new securities, typically to meet some corporate objective such as the lengthening of maturity.

Refunding
Redemption of outstanding debt by means of a new securities issue, usually to take advantage of lower borrowing costs.

Registered bond
A bond registered in the issuer's records in the owner's name. Transfer of ownership takes place only after the endorsement of the registered party and amendment to issuer's records.

Reg. S
Approved in 1990, a relaxation of sales restrictions to non-resident US persons in the course of certain Euro-securities offerings.

Repurchase agreement
Sometimes abbreviated to Repo. This arrangement involves an agreement by one institution to sell securities to another with a simultaneous agreement to buy them back again at a given price at some set time in the future.

Retail investors
Individual or institutional clients as opposed to dealers or brokers.

Retire
To repay or prepay a debt.

Retractable
A Eurobond security which gives an investor the option of early redemption a given number of years prior to the final maturity. If the option is not exercised, the securities will not be repaid until the later maturity.

Reuters Monitor
A telecommunications system providing price and other information relevant to Eurobond and other investment trading.

Round lot
A transaction which constitutes the acceptable minimum unit of trading for a particular issue or type of security. According to the ISMA definition, a holding of bonds with a total principal value of $100,000 nominal or its equivalent in other currencies.

Rule 144A
Approved in 1990, a relaxation of sales restrictions (ie exemption from registration with the SEC) on large institutional investment in privately placed securities offerings by foreign issuers.

Running the books
In a new securities issue, the function of a lead manager in preparing documentation, administering the offering (eg giving protection and making allotments), organising the syndicate and arranging for payment and delivery of the new securities.

Running yield
The ratio of coupon to market price expressed as a percentage. Also referred to as current yield.

Safe harbour
Legislation passed by the United States regulatory authorities which defines transactions which are not subject to the regulatory requirements of the SEC.

Samurai bond
Foreign bonds offered in the Japanese domestic market.

Seasoned securities
Refers to a securities issue which has been traded in the secondary market for some time; as opposed to newly offered securities. In the context of SEC regulations, securities qualify as seasoned only after they have been traded for 40 days.

Secondary market
The market for bond issues which have already been offered (ie their initial distribution has ended). Such securities may also be referred to as seasoned.

Secular trend
A long-term market movement of securities prices or interest rates, unaffected by short-term seasonal or technical influences.

Securities
A variety of financial instruments evidencing and promising the fulfilment of certain obligations. Typically, bonds and common stock.

Securities and Exchange Commission (SEC)
The US federal government agency charged with overseeing the US domestic securities industry.

Security provisions
Arrangements under the terms of a new issue which provide bondholders security in

the form of a claim (or mortgage) on certain assets in the event of default, or an undertaking by the borrower to preserve the security interests of the bondholders, eg through a negative pledge.

Selling concession
In a new issue, that part of the gross spread paid to managers and selling group members for each security actually purchased by them. Expressed as a percentage of face value.

Selling group
In a securities offering, the dealers acting only as sellers of the securities and not as underwriters. Managers also participate in the selling group to the extent that they place securities in a new offering.

Sell out
The closing of a purchase/sale contract by a seller by selling securities in the open market if a buyer is not in compliance with the terms of the contract, for the account and liability of the initial prospective buyer.

Senior securities
Securities with the first claim for payment of interest, principal, or dividends.

Serial bond
A bond issue which matures in a series of instalments. The segments are small and mature at stated regular intervals.

Settlement
The consummation of a trade involving the exchange of securities and the related payment.

SIB
The Securities and Investment Board. The senior securities regulator established by the Financial Services Act 1986.

SFA
The Securities and Futures Authority. One of the main regulatory bodies overseeing the operation of the securities houses in the United Kingdom.

Shopping
Attempting to obtain an improved price after having already received from a dealer a firm bid or offer.

Short
To sell a security not owned at the time. Usually done in anticipation of a price decline, in which case the seller can make delivery on the short sale with bonds purchased at a discount. The difference would be the seller's profit. Also referred to as a short position.

Short-term security
Generally an obligation maturing in less than one year.

Sinking fund
Repayment of debt by an issuer at stated regular intervals through purchases in the open market or drawings by lot.

Spread
In trading or the quotation of prices of securities, the difference between the bid and the asked price.

Stabilisation
The process by which a lead manager regulates the immediate secondary market performance of a new issue of securities: usually by taking short or long positions and maintaining a bid or offered price to steady the trading range of the new issue.

Stock split
When a corporation splits its stock, it divides the outstanding shares into a larger or smaller number of outstanding shares.

Stop order
An order to sell or acquire securities when a pre-stated price level is reached or exceeded.

Straight debt
A standard bond issue lacking any right to convert into the common shares of the issuer.

Strike price
The contractual price at which one security or derivative can be exchanged for another. Sometimes only the cashflows above (or below) the strike price are exchanged between the counterparties.

Subordinated debt
A claim which, in the event of the borrower's liquidation, ranks behind senior debt holders.

Subscription agreement
An agreement for the underwriting of a new issue between the issuer and the collective managers describing certain terms and conditions of the issue and the obligations of the parties to it. Sometimes referred to as an underwriting agreement in syndicates arranged by US banks.

Subscriptions
In a new bond issue, the buying orders from the lead manager, co-managers, and selling group members for the securities being offered.

Swap (switch)
The exchanging of one security for another.

Syndicate
A group of bond houses which act together in underwriting and distributing a new securities issue.

Syndicated loan
A commercial banking transaction in which two or more banks participate in making a loan to a borrower. Interest is typically paid on a floating rate basis linked to short-term interest rates in a particular currency.

Syndicate restrictions
The contractual restrictions placed on syndicate members governing prices and distribution of securities in a new offering.

Take down
Acceptance of securities allotted in a new issue.

Tap issue
A financing where only a portion of the full principal amount is initially placed on offer. The remainder is retained pending favourable market conditions or the need of the issuer for additional funds. Also referred to as a multiple tranche issue.

Terms
For a new securities issue, the characteristics of the securities on offer: coupon, amount, maturity, etc.

Through the market
As regards a new securities issue, an offering yield which is below that of comparable issues currently trading in the secondary market.

Tick
The smallest unit of change in price, either up or down.

Time decay
The loss of an option's premium value as its expiration date nears.

Tombstone
An advertisement for an offering of new securities. Typically gives the terms of the issue and lists the managers and underwriters.

Trade date
The date on which a securities transaction is executed.

Trader
An individual who buys and sells securities with the objective of making short-term gains.

Tranche
Part of a single financing which is split into different maturities or principal amounts (or sometimes different currencies). Also used to refer to block issues of MTNs, CDs or FRCDs, and sometimes to tap issues of securities where individual tranches are offered over time on terms adjusted to suit the then prevailing market conditions.

Trust deed
In a new bond issue, a contract defining the obligations of an issuer and appointing a trustee to represent the interests of bondholders. Also known as a trust indenture in the US.

Trustee
An individual or entity holding assets for another or representing the interest's of another.

Underwrite
An arrangement under which bond houses agree to each buy a certain agreed amount of securities in a new issue on a given date and at a given price, thereby assuring the issuer of the full proceeds of a financing.

Underwriter
A bank engaged in the business of underwriting securities issues.

Underwriting agreement
A legal document forming underwriting banks into a syndicate for a new issue and giving the management group (or lead manager, acting as their representative) the authority to assume certain responsibilities, such as setting the terms of the new issue and stabilising the price of the securities in the secondary market. In syndicates organised by US banks, this term is used to refer to a subscription agreement.

Value date
The closing date for a bond transaction, typically the seventh calendar day following the trade date.

Warrant
A certificate which grants the holder an option to buy a specified security(ies) at a given prices(s) for either a set period of time or into perpetuity. Commonly, warrants are exercised into the common equity of the issuer or further (usually fixed rate) debt of the issuer.

Withholding tax
A tax deducted at source and applied to investment returns such as interest and dividend payments.

Yankee bond
A bond offering by a non-US entity but registered with the SEC and therefore legally saleable as a new issue in the US domestic market.

Yield
Rate of return on a security as determined by its coupon and other characteristics, expressed as a percentage and annualised.

Yield curve
A graphic illustration of the relationship between yield and maturity for a given number of similar credit securities.

Yield to average life
The yield of a given security when its average life is substituted for its final maturity.

Yield to call
The yield of a given security when its next call date is substituted for its final maturity. Yield is also determined with reference to the next put date when the investor can require a borrower to redeem its securities.

Yield to maturity
The yield earned on a bond at a given price if held to maturity. The more sophisticated measure of yield, taking into account all expected cashflows from a bond is called redemption yield.

Zero coupon bond
A bond which carries no coupon (hence the nickname 'streaker'), but which provides a yield return by way of discount pricing.

BIBLIOGRAPHY

Aldred, Peregrine, *Convertibles and Warrants*, Euromoney Publications Limited, London, 1987.

Antl, Boris, *Swap Finance*, 2 volumes, Euromoney Publications Limited, London. 1986.

Bank for International Settlements: *Annual Reports.*

BIS – Committee on Banking Regulations and Supervisory Practices: "*The Management of Banks' Off-Balance-Sheet Exposures: A Supervisory Perspective*", BIS, 1986.

Bank of England: "Quarterly Bulletins"

Bell, G, *The Eurodollar market and the international financial system*, The Macmillan Press Ltd, London 1973.

Coninx, R. G. E, *Foreign exchange today*, Woodhead Faulkner, Cambridge 1978.

Darst, D. M., *The complete bond book: a guide to all fixed-income securities*, McGraw-Hill Inc., New York 1975.

Dattatreya, Ravi and Fabozzi, Frank, *Active Total Return Management of Fixed Income Portfolios*, Probus Publishing Company, Chicago 1989

Donnerstag, H. C., *The Eurobond market*, The Financial Times Ltd, London 1975.

Einzig, P., *The Eurobond market* (2nd edition), The Macmillan Press Ltd, London 1969.

Fabozzi, Frank, CMO *Portfolio Management*, Frank J. Fabozzi Associates, Summit, New Jersey 1994.

Fisher, F. G., *The Eurodollar bond market*, Euromoney Publications PLC, London 1979.

Fisher, F. G., *Eurobonds*, Euromoney Publications PLC, London 1988

Gooch, Anthony and Klein, Linda, *Documentation for Derivatives*, Euromoney Publications PLC, London 1993.

International Primary Market Association, *Members Recommended Standard Documentation*, London 1996.

International Securities Market Association, *Statutes, Bye-laws, Rules and Regulations*, Zurich 1995.

ISMA and Brown, Patrick, *Formulae for Yield and other Calculations*, ISMA, London 1992.

Lees, F. A., *International financial markets: development of the present system and future prospects*, Praeger Publishers, New York 1975.

McGrath, P., *Eurobond and related markets*, The Banker Research Unit, London 1978.

Morgan, E. V. and Harrington, R. L., *Capital markets in the E.E.C: the sources and uses of medium and long-term finance*, Wilton House Publications Limited, London 1977.

Morgan Guaranty Trust Company of New York: "World Financial Markets", published monthly.

Nevitt, Peter, *Project Financing*, Euromoney Publications PLC, London 1989.

Newburg, A. W. G., "Financing in the Euromarket by U.S. companies: a survey of the legal and regulatory framework", *The Business Lawyer*, Vol. 33, July 1978.

Orion Royal Bank Limited, *International capital markets: an investor's guide*, Euromoney Publications Limited, London 1979.

Parekh, Naru, *The Financial Engineer*, Euromoney Publications PLC, London 1995.

Park, Y. S., *The Eurobond market: function and structure*, Praeger Publications, New York 1974.

Prestwick, Michael, *Italian Merchants in England*, The Dawn of Modern Banking, Yale University Press, 1979.

Quinn, B. S., *The new Euromarkets: a theoretical and practical study of international financing in Eurobond, Eurocurrency and related markets*, The Macmillan Press Ltd, London 1975.

de Roover, Raymond, *The Medici Bank*, New York University Press, 1948.

Sampson, Anthony: *The Money Lenders*, Coronet. 1982

Stone, Charles and Zissu, Anne and Lederman, Jess, *Asset Securitisation: Theory and Practice*, Euromoney Publications PLC, London 1991.

Shearman & Sterling, 144A *and* Regulation S, Euromoney Publications PLC, London 1988.

Union Bank of Switzerland, *The Euromarkets: financial centers across national borders*, Zurich 1978.

US Joint Economic Committee, *Economic policies and practices, paper no. 3: a description and analysis of certain European capital markets*, US Government Printing Office, Washington D.C., 1964.

US Joint Economic Committee, Chapter IV, *"Foreign Lending and European Capital Markets"*.

Van Horne, J., *Financial management and policy*, (4th edition), Prentice/Hall International Inc, London 1977.

INDEX

Advertisements 72-73, 119-121, 222-223
Accrued interest 226-227
Agency agreement 274
Agents 283
Agreement among managers 92, 100-106
Amortisation 97, 132-135
Asset securitisations (see Securitisations)

Back office 225-232
Barings Bank 31, 222
'Big Bang' 23
'Black Monday' 25-26
'Black Wednesday' 29, 248
Bond swaps (see also Swaps) 172
Book (see Syndicate book)
Borrowers 41-59
Bought deals 17, 67-68, 84
Bretton Woods 3, 13

Call provision 97, 134, 169
Cedel Bank (see also Clearing systems) 14
Certificates of deposit (CDs) 291-296
Chicago Board of Trade (CBOT) 164-165
Chicago Mercantile Exchange (CME) 164-166
Clearing systems 232-234
Collateralised Mortgage Obligations (CMOs) 300-302, 309-311
Co-managers 66-68
Commercial paper (CP) 21, 287-290
Commissions 68
Conduits 307-308

Convertible bonds (see Equity convertibles, Currency convertibles and Japanese convertibles) 18, 98, 257-266
Convexity 144-145
Credit quality 94-95, 135
Cross-default 96-97
Currency considerations 132, 160-163
Currency swaps 173-175

Debt warrants 275
Default 96
Delivery 71-72, 229-231
Derivatives
    definition 157
    (see also Forwards, Futures, Options and Swaps)
Deutschmark sector 247-250
Documentation 68-69, 87-116
Dollar duration 143-144
Due diligence
    corporate credits 89-91
    sovereign credits 91-92
Duration (see also Dollar duration and Modified duration) 141-145

Equity warrants (see Warrants)
Equity convertible bonds 98, 257-266
Euro (The) 33-34
Eurobond/International bonds (see also Foreign bonds)
    definition xii, 239-240

origin and growth of Eurobond and
  international bond markets 10-40
Euroclear (see also Clearing systems) 14
Euro-commercial paper (see Commercial
  paper)
Eurodollar bonds 244-246
Euro-medium term notes 31, 84, 277-288
    documentation 279-280, 282
    form of offering 278-279, 281-285
    investors 280-281
    issuers 284-285
    reverse enquiry deals 280
    structured issues 285-287
European Currency Unit (Ecu) 17
European Monetary System 17-18
Exchange Rate Mechanism 28-29
Expenses 127

Financial Services Act – 1986 23, 70, 222-224
Fiscal agency agreement 69
Fiscal agent 67-68, 87
Fixed price offer/re-offer 74, 76, 82-83
Floating rate notes (FRNs) 269-276
    caps 179-180
    collars 180
    exotic issues 17, 98
    floors (see mini-maxi)
    form of offering 274-275
    interest payment mechanism 273-274
    inverse/reverse 311
    mini-maxi 180
    perpetual 24-25
    SURF 30
Force majeure 28, 93
Foreign bonds xii, 239-240
Foreign exchange operations 160-163
Forwards 160-163
FRCDs (see Certificates of deposit)
Futures 163-169

Generally accepted accounting principles
  (GAAP) 87
Global bonds 242-244
Guarantees 94
Gulf War 28

Hedging
    currency 158-163
    forwards 160-163
    futures 163-169

options 163-167, 169-172
swaps 172-184

Interest Equalization Tax (IET) 9-10, 16, 42, 65
Interest rate 131-132, 138-139
Internal Revenue Service (IRS) 22, 78-81
International Primary Market Association
  (IPMA) 14, 84-85
International Securities Market Association
  (ISMA) 14, 23-24, 225, 231-232, 236-237
International Swap Dealers Association
  (ISDA)
    1992 Master Agreement 189-219
    Master Agreement commentary 185-188
Investment criteria (see Portfolio strategy)
Investors 61-64

Japanese convertibles 266
Japanese yen sector 252-254

Launch (of new issue) 66-67
Lead managers 87-89
Liquidity 135-136
Listing 117-124
London International Financial Futures and
  Options Exchange (LIFFE) 164, 166-167
London Stock Exchange 119-125, 223
Luxembourg Stock Exchange 117-119, 122-125, 224

Maastricht Treaty 28, 33
Market-makers 129
Maturity (see also Yield to maturity) 132-135, 240-242
Modified duration 142-143
Moody's Investors Services 59, 124-127
Mortgage-backed securities 300-302, 304, 308-311
MTNs (see Euro-medium term notes)

Negative pledge 95
New issue (see Offering)

Offering 65-83
    invitations 66-67
    maturity 240-242
    size 70, 242
    timetable 72-74

342

Offering circular or memorandum (see Prospectus)
Office of Foreign Direct Investments (OFDI) 12
Options 163-167, 169-172
    call/put 97, 134, 169
    exotic 172
    trading 170-171

Participations (underwriting) 98-99
Paying agent 67-68
PORTAL 77
Portfolio strategy 64, 136-155
Praecipium 92
Pricing
    price discovery 32
    spread pricing 27, 81-82
Private placements (see also Rule144A) 79
Prospectus 75, 88-89
Prospectus Directive 88-89
Public Offers of Securities Regulations – 1995 (POS Regs) 223-224
Purchase fund (see Amortisation)

QIBs 77

Rating
    agencies 59, 124-127
    expenses 127
    procedures 95-96, 125-126
    timetable 127
Regulation S 27, 74, 76-78
Repayment (see Amortisation)
Representations and warranties 93
Risk weighting (BIS guidelines) 221, 224-225
Road show 69-70
Rule 144A 27-28, 50, 74, 76-77, 246
Rule 415 277

Samurai bonds 252-254
Secondary market 129-155, 234-236
Securities Acts (USA) 76
Securities and Exchange Commission (SEC) 76, 277
Securities and Futures Authority (SFA) 222-223
Securities switching 150-155
    average life 154
    call provision 155
    quality 151
    volatility 152-153
Securitisations 21, 28-29, 298-311
Security
    ranking of credit 94-97
Selling group 67-68
Selling group agreement 68-69, 93
Selling restrictions 79-81
Settlement 71-72, 226-231
Sinking fund (see Amortisation)
Smithsonian parities 14-15
Sovereign state
    as borrowers 41-59
    credit analysis 91-92
Special Purpose Vehicle (SPV) 298, 304-306
Standard and Poor's Corporation 59, 124-127
Subscription agreement 68-69, 93, 107-116
SUSMI 78
Swaps
    accounting and tax considerations 184
    basis 168
    circus 176
    currency 17, 173-175
    documentation (see also ISDA Master Agreement & commentary) 185-219
    exchange of borrowings 175-176
    interest rate 17, 176-179
    parallel loans 173-174
    relationship to the bond market 183
    secondary market 181-182
Swiss franc sector 250-252
Syndicate
    book 70
    stabilisation 71
    termination 93
    (see also Pricing and Fixed price offer/re-offer)
Syndicated loans 6-9

Tap issue 293-294
Taxation 79-81
TEFRA 78-79
Telexes 69
Third World Debt Crisis 20-21, 52-53
Tombstone 72-73
TRAX 227-228
Trust deed 67-68, 87

US dollar sector (see also Yankee bonds) 244-247
Underwriting
    agreement (see also Subscription agreement) 68-69
    commissions 68
    expenses 72
    techniques 98-99
    (see also Participations)

Volker package 18
Voluntary Restraint Program 12

Warrants
    issues 258-260
    structure 266-267
    trading performance 268-269
    valuation 267-269
    (see also Debt warrants)

Yankee bond sector 16, 44, 46, 50, 246-247
    borrowers 246
    investment attractions 246

Yield
    annual versus semi-annual 138-139
    current 137
    delay days 139
    improvement switch 150-155
    primary and secondary market 130-131
    to average life 139-141
    to first call 139-141
    to maturity/redemption (or equivalent life) 137-138
Yield curve 145-150
    changes in yield curve 149-150
    flat 148
    humped-back 147-148
    negatively sloped or reverse/inverse 146-147
    positive 146

Zero coupon bonds 19